S0-DOQ-271

PLEASE RETURN THIS ITEM
BY THE DUE DATE TO ANY
TULSA CITY-COUNTY LIBRARY.

FINES ARE 5¢ PER DAY; A
MAXIMUM OF $1.00 PER ITEM.

DUE DATE

DEC 01 1992		
JAN 24 1995		
FEB 09 1995		
MAR 20 1995		
201-6503		Printed in USA

Oklahoma State University Historic Old Central

CENTENNIAL HISTORIES SERIES

Centennial Histories Series

Committee

W. David Baird
LeRoy H. Fischer
B. Curtis Hamm
Harry Heath
Beulah Hirschlein
Vernon Parcher

Murl Rogers
J. L. Sanderson
Warren Shull
Milton Usry
Odell Walker
Eric I. Williams

Robert B. Kamm, Director
Ann Carlson, Editor
Carolyn Hanneman, Assistant Editor
Carol Hiner, Assistant Editor

OKLAHOMA STATE UNIVERSITY
CENTENNIAL
1890 • 1990

Oklahoma State University Historic Old Central

by LeRoy H. Fischer, Ph.D.

OKLAHOMA STATE UNIVERSITY / Stillwater

Published by Oklahoma State University
Centennial Histories Series, Stillwater, Oklahoma 74078

Library of Congress Cataloging-in-Publication Data

Fischer, LeRoy H.
   Oklahoma State University historic Old Central.

   (Centennial histories series)
   Bibliography: p.
   Includes index.
   1. Oklahoma State University—Buildings—History.
I. Title.   II. Series.
LD4297.F57 1988   378.766'34   87-35036
ISBN 0-914956-28-0

Contents

Appendices 281

Bibliography 285
Index 299

Foreword

Oklahoma State University Historic Old Central is officially volume number one in Oklahoma State University's Centennial Histories Series. Not only is it the exciting story of Old Central (the first permanent building on the campus, and the symbol of the university through the years), but it is also a mini-history of OSU's first 100 years. It is most appropriate that early in the Centennial Histories Series there be an introduction to, and an overview of, the total institution and its development through the century. Volume two, *Veterinary Medicine* (which has already been published) and subsequent volumes through the 24th volume in the series, deal with specific units and/or programs of the university. Volume 25 which will conclude the series (and which will be a coffee table model and largely pictorial) will, like *Historic Old Central,* be a mini-history, in order to provide a concluding overview and wrap-up of the series.

In the search and selection of an author for *Historic Old Central,* a writer of truly great stature emerged—Dr. LeRoy H. Fischer, Oppenheim Professor of History Emeritus at Oklahoma State University. An eminent Civil War scholar and historian, he received the $5,000 Literary Award of the War Library and Museum and the Pennsylvania Commandery of the Military Order of the Loyal Legion in 1963 for his book entitled *Lincoln's Gadfly, Adam Gurowski.*

Diligent in his research and skilled in his writing, Dr. Fischer has unusual ability to make the past come alive. Readers of *Historic Old Central* will find it hard to "put the book down," once they begin reading it.

Most American campuses have a focal point (usually its oldest building) which is a symbol of the total institution, both past and present. At the Oklahoma State University it is Old Central which fulfills this role. No other structure on the OSU campus ties past and present as closely as does Old Central. In the early decades of OSU's life it was indeed *central* in both location and college functions. In subsequent years, with substantial campus expansions and growth, it has found itself more on the edge of the campus both actually and figuratively. Yet, it has not lost a bit in stature, as the revered symbol of a great university!

Dr. Fischer tells the story of Old Central with great appreciation of what it has meant to the hundreds of thousands of students who have enrolled during the past century at Oklahoma A. and M. College, and, after the name change in 1957, at Oklahoma State University. Historic Old Central does indeed have many stories to tell about the institution it represents—and, Dr. Fischer, ably and with great sensitivity, relates a century of growth and progress of the total institution through his account of the happenings of one small but very important building.

The Centennial Histories Committee is grateful to all who have shared in the production of *Historic Old Central.* Special appreciation is expressed to Vice President Richard Poole, first coordinator of OSU's overall centennial observance, who originally conceived the idea of a Centennial Histories Project. He and President L. L. Boger have been most generous and supportive of the project. Since succeeding Dr. Poole as executive director of the Centennial Coordinating Office in the fall of 1987, Dale Ross has provided strong support. Dr. Ralph Hamilton, director of Public Information Services; Gerald Eby, head of University Publications Services; Edward Pharr, manager of University Printing Services; Heather Lloyd, reference librarian, and their respective staffs have assisted generously. Dick Gilpin's dust jacket art has added much to the series also. Judy Buchholz, first Centennial Histories editor, served ably in the initial stages of the project. Ann Carlson, as editor of this volume, and ably assisted by Carolyn Hanneman and Carol Hiner, has brought keen insight to the project and has worked devotedly to assure a high quality volume.

Robert B. Kamm, Director
Centennial Histories Project
President Emeritus
Oklahoma State University

June 1988

Preface

The histories of Old Central and the Oklahoma State University are inseparable. Indeed, the histories of Stillwater, Oklahoma, Oklahoma Territory, and the state of Oklahoma are also commingled from time to time with Old Central's past. For these reasons, as well as for human interest and breadth of insight, a broad approach is used in relating the life of the building. This method results in a panoramic view of Old Central through the years and presents a mini-history of the university from the unique perspective of the structure itself.

The book had its origins soon after Old Central underwent retirement from classroom and office use in 1969. Research materials were first accumulated on its history during preparation of the application for placing the building on the National Register of Historic Places in 1971 and then continued from time to time thereafter. Soon the need for a comprehensive study of Old Central began to emerge. Then graduate students in history at the university came to my assistance and completed much of the basic research over a period of years. They were Thomas A. Hazell, Kenny L. Brown, George N. Otey, Jeffrey B. Conner, Linda S. Holubek, and Carolyn G. Hanneman. To each of these discerning and faithful friends I owe an enduring debt of gratitude.

Meanwhile, with the organization of the Centennial Histories Project of the university in the early 1980s under the direction of President Emeritus Robert B. Kamm, I gladly accepted the task of writing the Old Central book when time became available. During this period I not only had the thoughtful and sympathetic support of Robert B. Kamm, Editor Ann Carlson, and the Centennial Histories Committee, but also the dependable and highly knowledgeable research assistance of Carolyn G. Hanneman, and to each I am deeply appreciative.

The search for source materials on the history of Old Central quickly revealed the long interest and major contributions of four people concerning the building. Alfred E. Jarrell, a member of the class of 1896, the first to graduate from the university, spent much time during his last years recalling and writing about the early history and significance of the structure and the institution. Thomas J. Hartman of the class of 1898, together with his wife, Mary, of the class of 1903, collected early photographs of Old Central and similar archival materials. They gave them to the Edmon Low Library, which is built on the land contributed by Mary's father, Alfred N. Jarrell, to help establish the university in Stillwater. Berlin B. Chapman, who first became a professor of history at the university in 1927, has collected, studied, and written about the history of Old Central throughout his professional life. It was he who encouraged Alfred E. Jarrell and the Hartmans, as well as other early alumni, to prepare and give their materials on the history of Old Central to the Edmon Low Library. Chapman has also contributed much similar material. Together these collections represent a major addition to the history of Old Central and the university. Considerable praise is due these pioneers for preserving so much of the institution's past.

Interviews proved to be unusually helpful for writing this book, and for those who gave of their time and knowledge to provide this assistance, an expression of thanks seems totally inadequate. They were Robert B. Bird, Raymond E. Bivert, Harry K. Brobst, Thomas A. Casey, W. George Chamberlain, Berlin B. Chapman, L. Whitley Cox Sr., E. Edward Davidson, Ray E. Dryden, Leo Elwell, Robert D. "Bob" Fenimore, Richard W. Giles, Peyton Glass Jr., Bill D. Halley, Hiram H. Henry, Everett E. Hudiburg, DeWitt T. Hunt, David E. Jafek, Albert E. Jones, Robert B. Kamm, Robert W. MacVicar, C. Earle Metcalf, Joseph R. Norton, James V. Parcher, Julius A. Pattillo, Bill E. Peavler, Randle Perdue, Richard W. Poole, Murl R. Rogers, J. Lewie Sanderson, James L. Showalter, Warren E. Shull, Elizabeth Oursler Taylor, Ernest Taylor, Ernest B. Tye, Al Tyson, Stephen R. Ward, and James E. Webster.

The Edmon Low Library of the university served as the center for the preparation of the book, and to those who capably staff it I owe a debt of gratitude. Especially helpful were Roscoe Rouse, Edward R. Johnson, Mary E. Greenberg, Heather M. Lloyd, Kathleen E. Bledsoe, Teresa A. Fehlig, Vickie W. Phillips, and John B. Phillips.

Carolyn G. Hanneman compiled the bibliography, and for this tedious and well-done task I extend many thanks. The bibliography contains the items in the endnotes and also several reference titles utilized in writing the book. The bibliography does not contain entries of Oklahoma State University history or state of Oklahoma history researched but not found useful in preparing the book.

When it came to placing the draft of the book manuscript on the mainframe computer of the university in preparation for editorial production, no one could top the capable services of the history department supervising secretary Jean Stiemke. Working with her on the task was the department's equally able secretary Dawn T. Carr.

Friends who critically read all or various parts of the manuscript made notable contributions to its improvement and deserve much credit for its final design. They were Al Tyson, Bill D. Halley, C. Earle Metcalf, Bob L. Blackburn, Robert B. Kamm, Murl R. Rogers, James L. Showalter, Reba N. Collins, Bill E. Peavler, James V. Parcher, Kenneth L. Davidson, Mary L. Benningfield, Douglas D. Hale, and Richard W. Giles. Three university history department colleagues, Theodore L. Agnew Jr., Berlin B. Chapman, and Norbert R. Mahnken, with whom I have been privileged to have a close and pleasing professional relationship over many years, edited the entire manuscript in detail, thus providing a priceless service.

My editors, Ann Carlson and Carolyn G. Hanneman, carefully and skillfully prepared the final draft and produced the book. Their keen attention to detail and their pleasant and steady personalities made for an excellent working situation. The editorial operation was further enhanced in the final stages of editorial production when Carol L. Hiner brought her special talents to the editorial staff.

When photographs became an important component of the book, willing assistance came from the valuable Special Collections of the Edmon Low Library of the Oklahoma State University; from the Archives of the Oklahoma Historical Society in Oklahoma City; from the Western History Collections of the University of Oklahoma in Norman; from the Archives of the Kansas State Historical Society in Topeka; and from the Oklahoma State University Public Information Services. Friends who also contributed important photographs were Harry E. Heath Jr., Elizabeth Oursler Taylor, Berlin B. Chapman, James L. Showalter, W. David Sasser, Margaret Cross, Hays Cross, Charles R. "Rick" Bellatti, and Raymond E. Bivert. Karen M. Fitch, the Oklahoma State University Public Information Services photographer, capably assisted in her area of expertise. In addition, Carol J. Bormann, Nicholas W. Bormann, and Gayle A. Hiner ably provided photographic layout assistance.

The Old Central roof and floor plans of 1894 add a necessary and important ingredient to this book. They are the capable creation of Al N. Tyson and Barry K. Collier of the Oklahoma State University Architectural Services.

Lending additional encouragement throughout the years of research and writing that went into the publication were Joan and Edgar R. Oppenheim of Oklahoma City, and Robert B. Kamm of Stillwater. Martha, my wife, aided materially throughout the preparation of the book, and for her able assistance I am most appreciative. I affectionately dedicate *Historic Old Central* to her, and to our three children, Barbara Ann, James LeRoy, and John Andrew, each of whom holds the bachelor's and master's degrees from the institution that Old Central spawned.

Despite the mountain of assistance from those I have named and from others, this study has many faults. For all errors of commission and omission, I alone am responsible.

LeRoy H. Fischer
Oppenheim Professor of History
Emeritus

June 1988

Oklahoma State University
Historic Old Central

1 Winning the College For Payne County

Old Central is a special focus on the campus of the Oklahoma State University and throughout Oklahoma. It represents the beginning of the unique land-grant college effort in Oklahoma. It symbolizes the struggles, aspirations, and consciousness of the many generations associated with the Oklahoma State University. It ties the institution to its beginning, celebrates its past, and points to its future.

In a larger sense, Old Central commemorates the entire development of higher education in Oklahoma. Refurbished and restored in the 1970s and 1980s to its original 1894 condition, it typifies the first collegiate structures in Oklahoma. Appropriately, it houses the Oklahoma Museum of Higher Education. The building itself is one of the exhibits of the history of higher education in the state.

Old Central had its origin long before the first legislative assembly of Oklahoma Territory in 1890 established the Oklahoma Agricultural and Mechanical College, renamed the Oklahoma State University in 1957. The institution and its mission basically developed from laws of the United States Congress. In 1862 President Abraham Lincoln signed the Land-Grant College Act for the creation in each territory and state of "at least one college where the leading object shall be, without excluding other scientific and classical studies and including military tactics, to teach such branches of learning as are related to agriculture and the mechanic arts . . . in order to promote the liberal and practical education of the industrial classes in the several pursuits and professions in life."[1] The climate for this legislation grew from increasing democracy, developing middle class influence, expanding industry and commerce, and enlarging awareness of the importance of technology and science. These forces created a substantial protest against a system of higher education inherited from England and aimed primarily at preparing wealthy young men for careers as ministers, lawyers, civil and military officers, and teachers.

Later legislation of Congress also shaped the founding and development of the Oklahoma A. and M. College. The Hatch Act of 1887 established agricultural experiment stations in land-grant colleges and provided for their support, while the Land-Grant College Act of 1890 authorized continuing federal appropriations for other institutional functions. Only the Smith-Lever Act of 1914, which established the Cooperative Extension Service in agriculture and home economics, would continue to shape the development of the Oklahoma A. and M. College. With this background and orientation for future growth, the Oklahoma A. and M. College would join what eventually became a chain of sixty-eight land-grant colleges nationwide to pioneer public higher education at low cost; to conduct extensive research as a legitimate function of higher education; to offer public service and continuing education; and to elevate the "useful" arts, sciences, and professions to academic respectability.[2]

Meantime, while Congress passed laws establishing land-grant colleges and broadening their base of operations, conditions in Indian Territory moved toward the establishment of the Oklahoma A. and M. College and the construction of Old Central. Land-hungry homeseekers, urged on by corporate interests such as the railroads, began casting cov-

Homesteader wagons wait to cross the Salt Fork of the Arkansas River in the Cherokee Outlet just before the Run of 1889. Because of flooding conditions, the crossing was made on the bridge (shown in the distance on the far right) of the Atchison, Topeka, and Santa Fe Railroad. The bridge was floored with heavy planks over the cross ties to make wagon passage possible. Many of these settlers soon located in Stillwater and vicinity.

etous glances at the sparsely settled areas of central and western Indian Territory during the 1880s. By 1889 the pressure was irresistible, and in that year Congress opened the Oklahoma District for homesteading. Popularly known as the Unassigned Lands, the area of nearly two million acres had not been assigned for Indian settlement. By the evening of April 22, the day of the land run, nearly every homestead claim and town lot in the settlement zone had been staked. Major townsites included Guthrie, Oklahoma City, Kingfisher, Norman, El Reno, Stillwater, and Edmond. The population of Stillwater appeared to be about five hundred at the close of the day of the run.[3]

Just over a year later, May 2, 1890, Congress established a territorial government. The Oklahoma Organic Act provided for a territorial governor and a supreme court of three judges, who also would function as district court judges. These officials were to be appointed by the President of the United States. The voters would elect a delegate to the United States Congress and a bicameral legislature consisting of a house of representatives of twenty-six members and a council of thirteen. An important provision of the Organic Act provided for the growth of Oklahoma Territory by specifying that all reservations in western Indian Territory, when opened to settlement, would be automatically annexed to Oklahoma Territory. The Organic Act established the counties soon to be known as Canadian, Cleveland, Kingfisher, Logan, Oklahoma, and Payne in the Unassigned Lands area, and Beaver in the Panhandle. Beaver County was later divided into Cimarron, Beaver, and Texas counties. In addition, the Organic Act located the territorial capital at Guthrie.[4]

Oklahoma voters went to the polls on August 5, 1890, to select members for the legislative assembly. Fourteen Republicans, eight Democrats, and four People's Party Alliance (Populists) members were elected to the house of representatives. The council had six Republicans, five Democrats, and two People's Party Alliance members. At the opening of the first legislative assembly on August 28, 1890, the Republican majority split along townsite lines and was not able to organize leadership; while in the council, the nearly equal representation made organization impossible. As a result the People's Party Alliance members, who were unusually capable and assertive, dominated both houses, even though a minority. People's Party Alliance member George W. Gardenhire of Stillwater became president of the council, and his fellow party member, Arthur N. Daniels of rural Canadian County, won election as speaker of the house of representatives. The second election in Oklahoma Territory, held on November 4, 1890, selected David A. Harvey of Oklahoma City as Oklahoma's first territorial delegate to Congress.[5]

The first legislative assembly faced much basic work in activating the government established by the Oklahoma Organic Act. Nevertheless, the assembly wrangled over locating the capital, for Oklahoma Territory already had a group of vigorous, enterprising, and aggressive towns. According to the federal census of 1890, the largest was Guthrie with a population of 5,333, followed by Oklahoma City with 4,151; Kingfisher, 1,134; Norman, 787; El Reno, 537; Stillwater, 480; and Edmond, 294. Guthrie, Oklahoma City, and Kingfisher soon emerged as the leading contestants for the capital. First a bill passed establishing the capital at Oklahoma City, then another locating it at Kingfisher, but Governor George W. Steele vetoed both proposals, and by default the capital remained at Guthrie.[6]

Stillwater, soon to be the support community for the Oklahoma A. and M. College and the construction of Old Central, had a fragile existence for nearly two years following its settlement on the opening day of the Unassigned Lands. Most of its rival rural villages soon disappeared. The requirements for survival at the time included a productive surrounding agricultural area for tillable crops, railroad transportation, and a tenaciously progressive citizenry. The land in the Stillwater locale appeared of questionable fertility; the area was known as cow country, suitable only for grazing. The nearest railroad, the Atchison, Topeka, and Santa Fe, was about twenty miles to the west with stations at the tiny villages of Orlando and Mulhall and another station further north at Perry. It took hours to travel the distance by horseback, wagon, or stage. Stillwater would have died except for the vitality and ingenuity of its people.[7]

The crisis for the survival of Stillwater began the day of settlement. Someone had to have the courage to open a store before a town could be located with any hope of permanence. Wagons of merchandise arrived the second day, but the owners would not unload until there was assurance that the town had a probable future. Robert A. Lowry, an attorney of Angus, Iowa, reached Stillwater on the opening day. At once he persuaded his friend, William A. Swiler, a grocer of Angus, to come to the new town and open a store. But the store needed to be established immediately, so Lowry joined with his friend, John H. Barnes, also of Angus, and hastily put up a small tent to sell groceries and hardware to keep the town functional. The day after Swiler arrived, his friends erected a wooden store building that would give the town a look of permanence. Almost immediately other commercial buildings appeared, and construction forged ahead of rival towns.[8]

At once competition shaped up for the seat of Payne County, soon to be organized as part of Oklahoma Territory in 1890. Payne Center, located three miles south of Stillwater, even built a courthouse; and Perkins, situated eleven miles south of Stillwater, campaigned to become the county town. Payne County residents voted informally to make Stillwater the upcoming county seat, but this did not stop the opposition.

Payne Center residents tried to remove a small collection of county records from Stillwater by force. Fortunately, cool heads on both sides avoided bloodshed. Payne Center, unlike Stillwater, was unable to get a post office, and its newspaper, the *Oklahoma Hawk,* moved to Stillwater, lured by its progress and the concrete offer of money for advertising.

Perkins was not as easily curbed, because it retained its population and secured a post office. One summer evening a large armed group of its citizens came to Stillwater to get the county records. An armed party from Stillwater met them on the bank of Stillwater Creek. William A. Knipe of Perkins and Robert A. Lowry of Stillwater debated across the creek while both groups waited with their readied weapons. Lowry emphasized that bloodshed would not settle the dispute and would bring federal troops. Such action, he said, would stunt growth and development for years. Fortunately, armed conflict did not erupt. Stillwater citizens in due time erected a court house for Payne County from contributions of its citizens, and the Oklahoma Organic Act of May 2, 1890, designated Stillwater as the county seat. By its first anniversary, Stillwater had about 50 business buildings and more than 150 homes.[9]

Stillwater's struggle for survival continued unabated throughout 1890. Disaster struck in the spring. The year before, the homesteaders had arrived too late in the growing season to do much about planting crops. Slowly the pioneers broke the unworked sod, but they knew little about the climate, rainfall, and suitable crops for the locale. Some small fields were planted. Many who had no farm implements dug holes in the soil every few feet and dropped seeds in them. Not enough production resulted to support even the farmers themselves, let alone the town dependent on them.

Stillwater turned out for a downtown celebration of its first anniversary on April 22, 1890. This photograph of the event was taken looking north between Ninth and Tenth streets.

Those who did not go back to their old homes dug wells, improved their tents, sod houses, or log cabins, and in other ways prepared for the cold months and the year to come. Some managed to plant small fields of winter wheat, although they were not sure it would grow so far south. Fortunately, the first winter was moist and mild. March and April of 1890 brought ample rain, buoying hope. Gardens thrived and the oats, corn, and wheat looked good. These homesteaders did not know the fate that awaited them.

In June 1890, the gardens and crops withered and perished when drought took over. Only the energetic and resourceful homesteaders survived the persistent semi-arid conditions. The winter wheat, with a yield of about four and one-half bushels to the acre, had stalks so short they could barely be bound. After stacking and curing the wheat, horses stamped the grain from the heads of the stalks. Wind, as nature produced it, was used to separate the chaff from the grain. Wagons then took the wheat to market in Arkansas City, Kansas, about sixty miles due north, and exchanged it for flour. Hunting with rifles produced ample meat from deer and turkeys found in the countryside. Huge buffalo fish seined in Stillwater Creek found a cash market at the town grocery of Orlando M. Eyler, who also extended credit to the farmers. Not all homesteaders were as ingenious, and many gave up, abandoned their land claims, and left Oklahoma Territory.

When starvation struck, the town also suffered. Some businesses failed, and a number of residents moved. After more than a year in Stillwater, most had reached the point of no return to their former homes; they had to tough it out. In August ample rain came and continued into the fall. Turnips, a late summer and fall crop, appeared to be the answer for man and beast. Immediately Stillwater's lots were plowed or dug by hand for the planting of turnip seed, as was much land in the surrounding rural area and throughout the newly organized Oklahoma Territory. A luxuriant crop resulted, including some oversized specimens a foot in diameter.

Housewives introduced variety to eating turnips by serving them fried, boiled, stewed, baked, raw, and as pie. Hogs and cattle thrived on them, although fried bacon had their smell and taste, and milk had their flavor. Horses turned away from them at first, but soon developed a ravenous taste for them. Robert A. Lowry received a gift-wrapped turnip under his Christmas tree in 1890.[10]

While the Stillwater community struggled with nature for its economic and physical survival, a leadership group emerged, strong from the first day of settlement. These were the better educated people. Edward F. Clark, John R. Clark, Frank A. Hutto, and Charles W. McGraw, for example, had taught public school. Frank J. Wikoff, a lawyer and banker, Robert A. Lowry, an attorney, and William A. Knipe, a Perkins businessman, attended land-grant colleges before moving to Oklahoma Territory. Many of the territory's oversupply of lawyers, including John R. Clark, Sterling P. King, Robert A. Lowry, Van Martin, Alexander T. Neill, Thomas J. Richardson, Jerome Workman, and Frank J. Wikoff, settled in Stillwater and some had attended college before commencing their legal careers. A few of the ten clergymen in the town had schooling enough to qualify for local educational work. This ample supply of able community leaders enthusiastically recommended and vigorously supported the effort to capture the land-grant college for the town. Youthful, experienced, and hardened, they entered the struggle for this ultimate achievement.[11]

As soon as Oklahoma Territory organized during the summer of 1890, the town of Stillwater entered the competition for one of the public service institutions with unabated enthusiasm. A month before the election of members of the territorial assembly, a mass meeting gathered at Swope Hall on the corner of Ninth and Main streets in July, to consider the possibility of obtaining the territorial capital or prison, either of which would bring status and income. At this point, little or no mention was made of securing the land-grant college. The Stillwater Board of Trade wanted the penitentiary. No consensus was reached, but the meeting stimulated an informal group of town council members, called the "Sanhedrin," to consider the matter diligently, including the land-grant college.

The August election sent George W. Gardenhire of Stillwater to the territorial council; James L. Mathews of Stillwater, Samuel W. Clark, also of Stillwater, and Ira N. Terrill of rural Payne County won seats

George W. Gardenhire of Stillwater won election to the first council, the upper chamber of the legislative assembly of Oklahoma Territory. He was soon made president of the council and in this role played a significant part in winning the college for Payne County.

in the territorial house of representatives. These four men made up the Payne County legislative delegation. Another caucus of townspeople, including Robert A. Lowry, James B. Murphy, William A. Swiler, Charles W. McGraw, and Frank J. Wikoff, met in the local post office and decided to pursue the land-grant college upon the strong recommendation of Councilor Gardenhire. Later Gardenhire, Mathews, Lowry, and Wikoff met in Wikoff's law office on East Ninth Street to plan the legislation and chart the politics to win the college. Significantly, Lowry had attended Iowa State College, and Wikoff had been a student at the University of Illinois, both land-grant institutions. Each man was acutely aware of the status and steady federal money the land-grant college would bring to Stillwater.[12]

At some point before Governor Steele drafted his opening message to the first legislative assembly, he renewed contact with James C. Neal, an Indiana boyhood friend, in Washington, D.C. Then serving on the staff of the Agricultural Experiment Station of the Florida State Agricultural College, Neal brought to Governor Steele's attention the mission of the land-grant colleges and emphasized the significance of the recent Hatch Act.[13] "Still, few know what a bonanza it was," Neal related later, "and in my correspondence with the first governor, in 1890, his ideas were so very hazy as to its value and importance that I gave him line upon line, letter after letter, even to the extent of an outline of a law, embracing the results of some years of experience of one of the oldest, and best conducted, and stable colleges in the United States."[14]

Governor Steele included in his first message to the territorial legislative assembly the recommendation that a land-grant college and agricultural experiment station be established, and three weeks later he sent to the same body a certified copy of the Land-Grant College Act of 1890, pointing out that additional federal funds would be available. He also suggested that the legislators petition Congress for consent to use the first grant money available to construct a college building, because the Land-Grant College Act of 1890 limited expenditures to paying teachers' salaries and purchasing laboratory and classroom teaching equipment. Steele thought this request might be granted due to the newness of the territory and the dire condition of the agricultural economy resulting from drought, and also because homestead farms would not be taxed until the first settlers proved-up on their land four years later.[15]

The legislative assembly, led by Councilor Gardenhire of Stillwater, responded by moving ahead with plans to establish the land-grant college. The assembly also forwarded to the federal government the request that the first land-grant college funds of the territory be used for the erection of an educational building. Gardenhire's efforts increased the interest of his constituents in bringing the institution to Stillwater.[16]

The first legislative assembly of Oklahoma Territory met in 1890 in Guthrie. This body placed the college in Payne County at a location to be selected near a town.

Yet the legislative assembly did not designate where the land-grant college would be located. Governor Steele wanted the legislation drawn up in such a way as to bring about competition between possible sites for territorial institutions. He noted: "I would earnestly impress upon you the importance of so legislating as to invite competition for locating them, according to the benefits the people of the several counties may place upon them."[17] Gardenhire decided to attempt a mutually satisfactory arrangement. According to tradition, he met with a group of legislators in a smoke-filled upstairs hotel room in Guthrie and promised to support the Democratic bid for removal of the capital from Guthrie to Oklahoma City if they would vote to place the agricultural and mechanical college in Payne County. An agreement appeared to have been struck. At this point, Gardenhire recommended the proposition to the other members of the Payne County legislative delegation and then made the thirty-four mile trip to Stillwater to consult with his constituents.[18]

The aspirations of the residents of Stillwater had increased since Gardenhire's last return home. At still another town strategy meeting, those attending instructed him to put in for nothing less than the capital itself. Gardenhire returned at once to Guthrie with every intention of following his latest instructions. But Hays Hamilton, a grocer who had attended the meeting, could not sleep that night because he concluded that the town meeting had asked for more than it could reasonably hope for. Stillwater, he observed, did not even have a railroad. He rose early and at dawn headed for the business district to persuade influential friends to rethink the decision made the night before. Hamilton prevailed, and he sent a message to Gardenhire that the "voice of the people clamored for the College."[19] From that point forward, Stillwater residents, without wavering, enthusiastically sought the land-grant

Hays Hamilton, a grocer and community promoter in Stillwater, convinced the leadership of the town to attempt to win the college, rather than the territorial capital, in the first legislative assembly of Oklahoma Territory. He reasoned that an effort to capture the capital would be doomed because Stillwater did not have a railroad.

college. A steering committee from Stillwater composed of John R. Clark, grocer; Amon W. Swope, banker; Robert A. Lowry, the postmaster; and Frank J. Wikoff, attorney, lobbied in Guthrie for the college through most of the remaining legislative session.[20]

Stillwater citizens soon found that they were far from winning the land-grant college. Councilor Gardenhire discovered that his trading program failed to materialize. In order to spearhead the campaign for the land-grant college, four separate bills to establish it were introduced in the territorial legislative assembly: one by Gardenhire in the council, one by James L. Mathews of Stillwater in the house of representatives, and two by Ira N. Terrill of rural Payne County in the house of representatives. When one of the bills passed both houses of the legislative assembly, Governor Steele returned it without his signature, explaining with little basis that it was likely unconstitutional because Oklahoma Territory did not appear to qualify for land-grant college funds. He said he could not sign the bill until Washington officials clarified his concern. The people of Stillwater and Payne County had again met temporary defeat, this time because of the governor's political manipulations.[21]

Undaunted, and fearful of losing momentum for the land-grant college plan of his Stillwater constituents, Gardenhire introduced a similar bill in the council in less than two weeks, as did Representative Darius Farnsworth of Kingfisher. Both bills were permanently sidetracked in sub-committee. Then Mathews of Stillwater introduced yet another bill in the house of representatives, but it lay dormant for nearly a month. Finally, as the legislative session approached its end, Mathew's bill was brought out of committee and passed the house of representatives by a vote of 14 to 2 on December 20, 1890. Two days later Gardenhire moved it through the council by another huge majority. Governor Steele considered the bill for several days, and without doubting its constitutionality, signed it into law on Christmas Eve, the last working day of the legislative assembly session. Mathews was credited by his fellow legislators as being chiefly responsible for locating the college in Payne County. First he moved the college bill through the legislative assembly by forming a combine to change the territorial capital from Guthrie to Oklahoma City, and then he convinced Governor Steele to sign the bill placing the college in Payne County. The other members of the Payne County legislative delegation also supported the combine.[22]

Some legislators, disappointed in the choice of location for the college, charged bribery and corruption on the part of the Payne County delegation. This criticism probably caused the college to be handicapped in its future legislative assembly support in Guthrie. Even the law itself appeared strange to James C. Neal, the adviser of Governor Steele on the land-grant college. Neal termed the law a strange combination of "bad English, uncertain phrase and indirectness that makes it one of the curiosities of legislation." On a positive note, he emphasized that the "members of the stormy first session of the territorial legislature, especially those from Payne County, builded much wiser than they knew

James L. Mathews of Stillwater served in the house of representatives of the first legislative assembly of Oklahoma Territory. He was credited by his fellow legislators as being chiefly responsible for locating the college in Payne County.

when they asked for the Agricultural college, and 'through thick and thin' worked, schemed, intrigued, and nobody knows what else they did to get it.''[23]

Winning the land-grant college for Payne County was basically the work of Stillwater and its legislative delegation. Rural Payne County did not possess an organized method of voicing its opinion. In addition, the tiny villages and vast countryside of the area confronted the most fundamental problems of frontier survival due to the severe drought of 1890. The concerns of securing a college, even the land-grant institution, did not excite their interest or capture their imagination.

Although Stillwater faced severe hardships resulting from the drought of 1890, the town emerged from the first phases of settlement survival and turned its attention to economic growth and cultural development. The leadership of Stillwater saw the land-grant college emerge as an obtainable and unique economic and educational possibility. Led by those who respected, understood, or had experienced collegiate education, there quickly emerged the ability, unbeatable determination, and unabated enthusiasm to pursue the goal at all costs. The Stillwater legislative delegation cooperated to perfection, and they won the land-grant college for Payne County. The ultimate quest of locating the college in Stillwater remained.

Endnotes

1. United States Congress, *The Statutes at Large, Treaties and Proclamations of the United States of America From December 5, 1859, to March 3, 1863,* edited by George P. Sanger, vol. 12 (Boston, MA: Little, Brown and Company, 1863), p. 504.

2. United States Congress, *The Statutes at Large of the United States of America From December, 1885, to March, 1887, and Recent Treaties, Postal Conventions and Executive Proclamations,* vol. 24 (Washington, DC: Government Printing Office, 1887), pp. 440-442; United States Congress, *Statutes of the United States of America Passed at the First Session of the Fifty-first Congress, 1889-1890 and Recent Treaties and Executive Proclamations,* [vol. 26, part 1] (Washington, DC: Government Printing Office, 1890), pp. 417-419; United States Congress, *The Statutes at Large of the United States of America From March, 1913, to March, 1915, Concurrent Resolutions of the Two Houses of Congress and Recent Treaties, Conventions and Executive Proclamations,* vol. 38, part 1 (Washington, DC: Government Printing Office, 1915), pp. 372-374.

3. Arrell Morgan Gibson, *Oklahoma: A History of Five Centuries,* 2nd edition (Norman: University of Oklahoma Press, 1981), pp. 172-177; Berlin B. Chapman, *The Founding of Stillwater: A Case Study in Oklahoma History* (Oklahoma City, OK: Times Journal Publishing Company, 1948), p. 40.

4. United States Congress, *Statutes of the United States of America,* [vol. 26, part 1], pp. 81-100.

5. Gibson, pp. 178-179.

6. Gibson, p. 179; United States Department of the Interior, Census Office, *Report on the Population of the United States at the Eleventh Census: 1890,* [vol. 1], part 1 (Washington, DC: Government Printing Office, 1895), p. 283.

7. Robert E. Cunningham, *Stillwater: Where Oklahoma Began* (Stillwater, OK: Arts and Humanities Council of Stillwater, Oklahoma, 1969), p. 37.

8. Cunningham, pp. 4-8, 15-17; Chapman, p. 175.

9. Chapman, pp. 109-110; Cunningham, pp. 23-25; United States Congress, *Statutes of the United States of America,* [vol. 26, part 1], p. 83.

10. Cunningham, pp. 35-37.

11. Philip Reed Rulon, *Oklahoma State University—Since 1890* (Stillwater: Oklahoma State University Press, 1975), p. 3; *Stillwater Daily Press,* 15 June 1939, pp. 1, 5; Eldon L. Clemence, "A History of the Democratic Party in Oklahoma Territory" (Master of Arts thesis, Oklahoma State University, 1966), pp. 15-16; Record Book Committee, compiler, "Selections from the Record Book of the Oklahoma Agricultural and Mechanical College, 1891-1941. Compiled on the Occasion of the Fiftieth Anniversary of the Founding of the College," vol. 1, copy 2, p. 98, Special Collections, Edmon Low Library, Oklahoma State University, Stillwater, Oklahoma; *Portrait and Biographical Record of Oklahoma* (Chicago, IL: Chapman Publishing Company, 1901), pp. 758-759, 844-847, 868, 889, 1053, 1210-1211.

12. James K. Hastings, "Oklahoma Agricultural and Mechanical College and Old Central," *Chronicles of Oklahoma,* vol. 28, no. 1 (Spring 1950), p. 81; Payne County, Oklahoma Territory, Manuscript Census of 1890, Oklahoma Historical Society, Oklahoma City, Oklahoma; E. Bee Guthrey, "Early Days in Payne County," *Chronicles of Oklahoma,* vol. 3, no. 1 (April 1925), p. 76; Rulon, p. 4; *Oklahoma A. and M. College Mirror,* 15 May 1895, pp. 1-2; Gerald Forbes, *Guthrie: Oklahoma's First Capital* (Norman: University of Oklahoma Press, 1938), pp. 11-12; Kay Nettleton, "The First Ten Years: An Abundance of Better Minds and Better Hearts," *Oklahoma State University Outreach,* vol. 53, no. 1 (Fall 1981), p. 16; Alfred E. Jarrell to Berlin B. Chapman, 10 July 1958, Alfred E. Jarrell File, Berlin B. Chapman Collection, Special Collections, Edmon Low Library.

13. Rulon, p. 4.

14. *Oklahoma A. and M. College Mirror,* 15 May 1895, p. 1.

15. Oklahoma Territorial Assembly, *Journal of the First Session of the Legislative Assembly of Oklahoma Territory Beginning August 27, 1890* (Guthrie, OK: Oklahoma News Publishing Company, 1890), pp. 19, 127.

16. Oklahoma Territorial Assembly, pp. 133, 151-152; Rulon, p. 5.

17. Oklahoma Territorial Assembly, p. 127.

18. Oklahoma Territorial Assembly, pp. 127-128, 133, 151-152; Otis Wile, "Sixth Founders' Day is Best Yet," *Oklahoma A. and M. College Magazine,* vol. 5, no. 4 (January 1934), p. 3; *Stillwater NewsPress,* 3 December 1986, p. 1B.

19. Houston Overby, "The Story of Aggieland" in *Oklahoma Agricultural and Mechanical College Yesterday & Today* (Guthrie, OK: Cooperative Publishing Company, [1927]), unpaged. This article was reprinted in the *1927 Redskin,* pp. 167-168, Oklahoma A. and M. College Yearbook, and this citation is from p. 168.

20. Freeman E. Miller, *The Founding of Oklahoma Agricultural and Mechanical College* (Stillwater, OK: Hinkel and Sons, 1928), p. 2; *1921 Redskin,* p. 252; Overby, unpaged; *1927 Redskin,* pp. 167-168.

21. Oklahoma Territorial Assembly, pp. 118-124, 130, 169-171, 221-222, 301; Rulon, pp. 6-7.

22. Oklahoma Territorial Assembly, pp. 380, 590, 593, 663, 411-412, 564-565, 850, 920-921, 992-995, 1000-1001, 1013-1015, 1084, 1087, 1093, 1104, 1112-1113, 1121; Robert Martin, compiler, *Statutes of Oklahoma, 1890* (Guthrie, OK: State Capital Printing Company, 1891), pp. 81-85; *Stillwater NewsPress,* 7 December 1977, p. 22; *Stillwater Gazette,* 7 February 1901, p. 1; Stillwater *Daily Democrat,* 18 February 1905, p. 1.

23. Oklahoma Territorial Assembly, p. 1015; *Oklahoma A. and M. College Mirror,* 15 May 1895, p. 1.

2 Winning the College For Stillwater

Locating the Oklahoma A. and M. College in Payne County but not in Stillwater was undoubtedly political punishment for the Stillwater delegation in the Oklahoma Legislative Assembly. With Republicans and Democrats almost evenly divided in the council and the house of representatives, members of the People's Party Alliance held the balance of power. The Payne County legislative delegation belonged to the People's Party Alliance, and three of the four Payne County members were from Stillwater. Thus the Payne County delegation was in the forefront of political maneuvering, making substantial numbers of firm friends and staunch enemies in the Democratic and Republican ranks.

A member of the house of representatives reflected on these factors subtly in casting his vote on the bill locating the college in Payne County: "This Legislature has been charged with bribery and corruption, and rumors in this regard have pointed to no delegation, as it has to that of Payne County. Under such circumstances to see the best institution in the Territory, go to that county is the reason why one should hesitate and I therefore vote 'No.'"[1] Nevertheless, the bill passed with one substantial amendment calling only for the college's location near an unspecified municipality in Payne County.

With this action the struggle for Stillwater to win the college began anew. The bill required Governor George W. Steele to name three commissioners to determine the best location, thus encouraging competition on the local level as desired by the governor. Stillwater, the largest of the towns in Payne County, had possible rivals in Clayton, Ingalls, Perkins, and Windom.[2]

The bill also required that either Payne County or the town selected for the college give no less than eighty acres of suitable land for the college itself as well as the Agricultural Experiment Station. In addition, either Payne County or the town nearest the college would be required to issue bonds in the amount of $10,000; the money from the sale of the bonds, could be used only for the erection of "the building for such institution." The secretary of Oklahoma Territory, the bill stated, would sell the bonds "at no less than their par value, the proceeds thereof . . . to be placed to the credit of such institution."[3] The bonds would run for twenty years, pay 5 percent interest, and be payable semi-annually, They would be issued in denominations of $1,000 each, have interest coupons attached, with both interest and principal payable to the bearer. The bond issue needed to be approved by a majority of qualified voters in Payne County or the municipality involved. Finally, if the county or town should fail to issue the bonds or provide the land required, the college could be located elsewhere in the territory.[4]

The University of Oklahoma and the Oklahoma Normal School (presently the Central State University), also established by the legislative assembly in 1890, had fewer handicaps. The bill founding the University of Oklahoma located it at Norman in Cleveland County. The land requirement consisted of forty acres within one-half mile of Norman. Cleveland County had six months for authorizing $10,000 for the buildings and equipment of the institution "by the sale of bonds or otherwise." If voted by the public and issued, the bonds would run for twenty years, bear 5 percent interest, and would not be sold for less than par value. If Cleveland County did not comply with the University of Oklahoma act within a year, the legislation would be void.[5]

George W. Steele, the first governor of Oklahoma Territory, encouraged municipal competition in locating the institutions of territorial government. He realized this desire when the college was located only in Payne County, unlike the towns designated for the Oklahoma Normal School and the University of Oklahoma.

ARCHIVES, OKLAHOMA HISTORICAL SOCIETY

18

The act of the legislative assembly establishing the Oklahoma Normal School located it within one mile of the village of Edmond. Forty acres of land needed to be furnished by Edmond, ten of which were to be used as a building site of the institution. The remaining thirty acres were to be laid out in town lots and blocks, and then sold for cash for the use of the school. In addition, if authorized by a vote of the people of Oklahoma County, the county commissioners were directed to issue bonds for the school buildings in the amount of $5,000, payable in twenty years. Bearing 7 percent interest, the bonds could not be sold at less than ninety-five cents on the dollar. No provision was made in the act for removing the normal school from Edmond in case of failure to qualify under terms of the law. Nor was a deadline written into the legislation.[6]

The citizens of Cleveland County readily consented at the polls to issue bonds in the amount of $10,000 to construct a building for the University of Oklahoma. The bonds sold for only $7,200, but the people of Norman, a thriving city of 1,218 inhabitants when incorporated in 1891, and on the Atchison, Topeka, and Santa Fe Railroad, made up the deficit of $2,800. They also raised money to purchase the forty-acre campus. Norman qualified for the university just five days before the deadline of one year expired.[7]

Further north, at Edmond, also on the Atchison, Topeka, and Santa Fe Railroad, preparation intensified to qualify for the Oklahoma Normal School. Anton H. Classen, then a resident of Edmond and later a major real estate developer in Oklahoma City, led the effort. Oklahoma County passed the required $5,000 bond issue, and Edmond, a village of 294 people in 1890, responded with a $2,000 bond issue. Of the three offers of land for the institution, a forty-acre tract given by Classen on high ground immediately east of Edmond seemed most desirable. As required by law, thirty acres were sold as village lots to help finance the school building. This raised about $3,500. Thus, armed with a total of $10,500, a contract could be let for the permanent building of the Oklahoma Normal School.[8]

Although the legislative assembly designated municipal locations for the University of Oklahoma and the Oklahoma Normal School, it did not do so for the Oklahoma A. and M. College. This likely resulted from the political balance-of-power struggle in the legislative assembly resulting from the People's Party Alliance membership of the Payne County legislative delegation. From the center of this legislative cauldron in which the Payne County delegation operated came the probably penalty of locating the Oklahoma A. and M. College in Payne County but not in Stillwater. Governor Steele's desire to bring about competition between various sites for territorial institutions possibly influenced the situation also. He realized this hope when competition developed in

Payne County for the location of the Oklahoma A. and M. College.

While the leadership of Norman and Edmond developed plans to acquire land and to construct permanent buildings for their collegiate institutions, the struggle to determine the site of the Oklahoma A. and M. College in Payne County continued. In addition to Stillwater, the four other villages and towns in Payne County that had a post office and enough population to capture the college could have competed for the college, but only Perkins chose to do so. Plans in Stillwater, with a final population count of 569 in 1890, were handled mostly by an informal executive committee of the town's board of trustees. The Stillwater Board of Trade, the commercial club of the town, also assisted. Membership of the two groups largely overlapped. The planning group, seeking to bring the college to Stillwater, worked early in 1891 to pass a Payne County bond issue for $10,000 to construct the permanent building of the college at an undetermined location in the county at an election on February 3. The bonds failed by a vote of 776 to 375.

The Payne County defeat of the bonds resulted in part from a recent favorable vote on a county-wide railroad subsidy. Also, the college building bond vote did not carry because the election had been held hurriedly

This quality early home of weatherboard siding in Stillwater was constructed by Henry B. Bullen, the first lumberman in the town. Located at the corner of Lewis and Tenth streets, it was first occupied on April 5, 1890.

and without adequate campaigning to give the county time to qualify for federal money during the current fiscal year. The lingering impact of the severe drought of the previous year must also have been a factor in the defeat. If Stillwater still desired to have the college, it would be necessary to secure the needed land and to raise $10,000 through a bond issue to construct the college building.[9]

The people of Stillwater continued their efforts with renewed enthusiasm and determination to win the Oklahoma A. and M. College. The failure of the Payne County election for the college building meant that Stillwater needed to incorporate before it could vote on a bond issue for the building. On March 23, 1891, the town trustees petitioned the Payne County Board of Commissioners for permission to hold an election to designate three temporary town officials to supervise the incorporation procedure. This election was held on April 7, and then on April 20 the newly created offices were filled permanently.

With incorporation accomplished, Stillwater officials designated May 4 as the day for voting on the building bond issue. The *Stillwater Gazette* and the *Oklahoma Hawk* newspapers staunchly supported and publicized the effort. This time the bonds gained unanimous approval with a vote of 132 to 0. The *Wichita Eagle* contracted to print the bonds for $85, and Councilor George W. Gardenhire personally delivered them to Secretary of State Robert Martin, who served only as custodian of the bonds, although by law he should have sold them. Stillwater needed to find a buyer, but no one would initially purchase them at face value, as the law establishing the college required, because of depressed economic conditions.[10]

With substantial progress made toward raising the money for the college building, the Stillwater college planning committee consisting of John R. Clark, George W. Gardenhire, James L. Mathews, and Frank J. Wikoff directed its attention to locating a suitable tract of land for the college. Although the Oklahoma A. and M. College Act called for a donation of eighty acres, the committee desired a two hundred acre plot immediately adjacent to the northwest Stillwater boundary. Alfred N. Jarrell, Charles A. Vreeland, Oscar M. Morse, and Frank E. Duck, all farmers, had homesteaded the property.[11]

Duck's land, because it joined the town boundary, likely had the most value; and Duck, together with Jarrell, promised to donate forty acres each. Jarrell reportedly said to Duck: "If you will give your northwest forty, I will give my northeast forty . . . and we will locate the Oklahoma A. and M. College and Experiment Station, so none of the politicians can ever move it, and we will build a school where we can give our children all the education they are capable of holding."[12]

The land needed for the use of the college had not been homesteaded long enough to be owned. Thus it became necessary to purchase it at

$1.25 an acre before it could be deeded to the town of Stillwater, which in turn would transfer it to the board of regents of the college. Stillwater citizens raised the money needed for this purpose. Duck converted his homestead claim to a cash payment plan on June 13, 1891; Jarrell and Vreeland did the same on November 3; and Morse followed this pattern on November 5. Duck and Vreeland probably gave their forty acres each without receiving any money in return. Jarrell, however, received enough money to pay the filing fee on his gift. Morse, who offered twice the amount of land for the college as the others, received $15.00 per acre. The gifts and sacrifices of these homesteaders and the people of Stillwater merit considerable praise and appreciation.[13]

Real estate speculators, much in evidence in the early development of Oklahoma Territory, entered the scene at this point. Duck alleged that he was visited by the Stillwater college planning committee consisting of Gardenhire, Clark, Wikoff, and Mathews at the time Duck planned to give the northwest forty acres of his land. On this land the college building would be constructed. The committee later contacted Duck and told him he would need to sell his south eighty acres so the college could be located on his northwest forty acres. The committee also told Duck that the town of Stillwater would purchase the eighty acre tract and deed it to Joseph W. McNeal, president of the Guthrie National Bank (currently the Guthrie First National Bank), as a condition that the Stillwater location be chosen for the college. McNeal purchased the eighty acres from the town for $2,500, and at once McNeal employed Wikoff to subdivide the property and sell the lots. Duck himself received only $800 for the eighty acre tract, although the deed for the property called for $2,500. The area became known as the College Addition to Stillwater.[14]

Meantime, Governor Steele gave the towns and villages of Payne County ample time to prepare for the contest to win the college. Not until May 31, 1891, five months after he was authorized by law to do so, did he name the three commissioners to select the site for the college. Steele chose William H. Campbell, William H. Merten, and James M. Stovall. They appeared to be well qualified to carry out their task. They had grown up on farms, had been soldiers during the Civil War, had been associated with education in various ways before reaching Oklahoma, had come to Oklahoma in 1889, and had served in the first legislative assembly of the territory. Governor Steele, also a veteran of the Civil War, placed implicit trust in former military men to carry out the duties of government efficiently and honestly.[15]

The governor's three site-location commissioners and visiting Congressman Jonathan P. Dolliver of Iowa reached Stillwater on the evening of June 24, 1891. The delegation stayed at the City Hotel. Councilor Gardenhire, leaving nothing to chance, took a room for the night next to the visitors. Under escort the next morning, the commissioners

Governor George W. Steele named three Civil War veterans, William H. Campbell (*upper left*), William H. Merten (*lower left*), and James M. Stovall (*lower right*), as commissioners to select the location for the college in Payne County.

reviewed the records of the town bond election to raise the $10,000 required for the college building and determined to their satisfaction the legality of the procedure. They then were taken on an inspection tour of the two hundred acre site offered by Stillwater for the college and agricultural experiment station. The commissioners were impressed by the size of the acreage and the wide variety of upland and lowland soil it contained, typical, it was pointed out, of the many types of soil found throughout Oklahoma.[16]

After finishing their duties in Stillwater, the site location commissioners rode unescorted about noon to Perkins, almost ten miles to the south. The night before a delegation from Perkins had come to Stillwater to invite them to visit the village of about 250 people, not generally considered a serious contender for the college. The commissioners were met at the village limits by a delegation and escorted to the only meeting hall, a small room over the drug store. After the commissioners outlined their purpose, William A. Knipe, the founder of Perkins and its leading citizen, took them for a tour of the rich Cimarron River valley land just north of the village. Always a vigorous competitor, Knipe had grown up in Manhattan, Kansas, home of the land-grant Kansas State Agricultural College, which he attended.

Knipe compared the fertile sandy loam soil topped with six foot high bluestem grass and the big white oak trees of the Perkins area with the rolling prairie at Stillwater covered with little bunch grass, scrub trees, and hard pan clay. He related how the Cimarron River valley land at Perkins compared favorably with the Kansas State Agricultural College location in the Blue River valley at Manhattan. Then Frank Rankin, the village boomer and advertising man, spoke at length on the commercial value of Perkins, citing its proximity to the territorial capital at Guthrie and the forthcoming railroad connecting the valley towns, all advantages not offered by the inland town of Stillwater. The commissioners seemed favorably impressed, enjoyed themselves, and stayed into

COURTESY OF W. DAVID SASSER

William A. Knipe, the founder of Perkins, located eleven miles south of Stillwater, took the commissioners selecting the location for the college on a tour of the rich Cimarron Valley land just north of the village. Always a vigorous competitor, he realized the value of a land-grant college, for he had attended the Kansas State Agricultural College.

the late afternoon when they asked for an option on the land shown them. The entire Perkins population then turned out for a street welcome and celebration.[17]

The Stillwater college location committee grew restless late in the afternoon and sent a delegation to Perkins consisting of Robert A. Lowry, Hays Hamilton, Charles Donart, and Frank A. Hutto to retrieve the commissioners. The Stillwater group arrived in the middle of the street celebration and was cordially greeted by Warren Chantry, well known to the visitors. Lowry quipped: ''We didn't come to take any part in your jubilee. We just came to arrange for your funeral.'' While the commissioners and the visitors returned to Stillwater for the night, a mass meeting in Perkins outlined a program for the college and arranged to obtain the option for the college site by noon of the next day.

About noon a rider arrived with a message from Hays Hamilton inviting the Perkins leaders to Stillwater for a conference in the evening. Knipe took the invitation to mean that Stillwater had given up its effort to win the college. He thought it wanted a political trade such as an option to purchase the best building sites and other real estate in Perkins before the college located there. When Knipe and his committee reached Stillwater early in the evening, they found the college locating

The Methodist Church of Perkins was erected in 1892. The building suggests a high degree of social and economic development for the town of about 250 people when it was competing for the college location.

commissioners and the town leaders at a banquet table, their faces "red and glowing" from drinking champagne, celebrating what appeared to be the selection of Stillwater for the college site.

Looking completely dejected, Knipe turned to Chantry and exclaimed: "We are sunk. These Stillwater fellows are just a damned shrewd bunch of horse traders." Knipe and his delegation joined in the revelry by drinking champagne and eating wild turkey and prairie chicken. They also promised solid support for the Oklahoma A. and M. College.[18] The official report to Governor Steele about two weeks later revealed that the commissioners had "selected a body of land containing 200 acres, that contained the various qualities of soil as we thought would be most suitable . . . and asked the citizens . . . of Stillwater . . . to make a formal tender of deeds."[19] The property was transferred to the Oklahoma A. and M. College Board of Regents on November 25, 1891.[20]

On the surface, it appeared that Stillwater had won the college beyond question, just as it had earlier captured the county seat of Payne County. The town had not only voted unanimously to issue the $10,000 in bonds required for the college building, but it had also authorized taxes to provide interest payments on the bonds and create a sinking fund to pay off the bond principal when due. Governor Steele named the regents for the college as soon as the Stillwater site was selected. The regents decided, with the full support of the Stillwater leadership, to commence instruction with forty-five students on December 14, 1891, in the local Congregational Church, believing this would make it more difficult for the legislature to relocate the institution. Meanwhile, on November 29, the Stillwater Board of Trade held a reception and banquet for the regents in the newly completed courthouse. Then the Agricultural Experiment Station broke its first sod on the college land in early December. On December 10 the regents authorized construction contracts, with money from the limited federal funds available, for the residence of the director of the Agricultural Experiment Station, a station laboratory, and a horticultural barn, the first temporary buildings on the college property. Other provisional structures to come would be a small residence for the college farm superintendent, built in 1892, and an engine and seed house, constructed in 1893.[21]

But Stillwater had time to reflect only momentarily on the glory of winning its two coveted institutions, the county seat and the land-grant college. Almost immediately a crisis developed because the bonds for the permanent building of the college had not been sold. Weeks turned into months while the business and college leadership of Stillwater could not locate a buyer for the bonds, due largely to depressed economic conditions. Finally, on March 3, 1892, the Stillwater Board of Trustees asked Robert J. Barker, the president of the college, to meet with them. Charles

Taken in January 1892, this photograph shows the college property near Stillwater. The prairie sod was turned for the first time in December 1891 for the use of the Agricultural Experiment Station. Old Central would not be completed until June 1894.

W. McGraw, the president of the trustees, explained to the group that he was gathering records concerning the financial condition of the town, including the valuation of real estate within the town limits. These materials, McGraw said, were being assembled for a man named Vandergraff who indicated that his company might buy the bonds.[22]

A message soon came to the town board of trustees from Vandergraff's firm indicating that a federal statute had been found stating that a territorial municipality could not indebt itself beyond 4 percent of the value of its taxable property. Charles Donart, the Stillwater Township assessor, validated the accuracy of the communication for the board and also related that the town had only $110,000 of taxable property, which fell $140,000 short of the amount needed to support the $10,000 bond issue for the college building. Donart likewise pointed out that the latest census figures indicated that the town had inadequate population to incorporate.[23]

Courageously, the town board of trustees took action at once to correct both problems. First, the trustees authorized Hays Hamilton to restudy the census count. He soon came up with enough additional names to reincorporate the town. A friend years later said Hamilton even counted names on the tombstones in the town cemetery. Second, the trustees named Van Martin a special town assessor. He quickly came up with a town property valuation of $263,000, a startling growth in value more than sufficient to call for a vote on new college building bonds. The town trustees then scheduled an election on July 26, 1892, to authorize a new bond issue of $10,000 for the college building, including interest and a sinking fund to pay off the bond principal. The voters passed the proposition by a margin of 167 to 6.[24]

The leadership of Stillwater renewed efforts to sell the bonds, and before long the rumor circulated that they had been marketed and that construction would soon begin on the college building. Although the rumors were premature, the town board of trustees, however, had a plan of action. Eli Reed, the treasurer of Payne County, had worked for several months to sell $25,400 worth of county bonds to the St. Joseph, Missouri, Loan and Trust Company through George Theiss, its agent. Treasurer Reed, a strong supporter of Stillwater and the college effort, agreed to work out a sales program combining the county and college bonds. When word of this plan leaked out, some citizens feared that this might imperil the county issue and even threatened a court injunction to prohibit the proposed combined bond issue. At this point the announcement came that the St. Joseph firm was sending Theiss, its representative, to Stillwater. Then immediately the county treasurer mysteriously disappeared, and rumors spread that he had been kidnapped, an explanation that seemed plausible because many infamous outlaws operated in Oklahoma Territory. The county treasurer had actually gone to Wichita, Kansas, where he secluded himself with the county bonds. He returned just after Theiss agreed to purchase both sets of bonds. Thus the college building bonds, considered undesirable at the time by the financial community, appeared to be sold. Then, on November 2, 1892, the Stillwater Board of Trustees authorized the submission of the new college bond issue to the territorial secretary in Guthrie.[25]

The St. Joseph firm represented by Theiss did not at first offer a definite amount of money for the college bonds because informed people knew they would bring less than face value on the market due to the depressed economy and the possible removal of the college from Stillwater. At this point the Payne County Board of Commissioners voted not to accept the offer of the St. Joseph firm to market their bonds at ninety-one cents on the dollar, perhaps not desiring to associate Payne County with the effort to sell the college building bonds of the town of Stillwater. Theiss soon thereafter informed the Stillwater officials that his firm would offer seventy-eight cents on the dollar for the college bonds if his company received a bonus of $381. At what appeared to be the last opportunity to market the bonds, the Stillwater Board of Trustees accepted the offer, recalled the first set of bonds from the territorial secretary on August 6, 1892, and burned them in a meeting of the trustees on January 19, 1893. When a messenger from the Stillwater officials took the new bonds to the territorial secretary in Guthrie, an excited group of Stillwater citizens, led by a college faculty member, rode toward Orlando to meet the courier on the stagecoach returning to Stillwater from the train. He told them that the last problem hindering the construction of the college building had been resolved.[26]

The officials of Stillwater soon faced disappointment again. The St. Joseph Loan and Trust Company withdrew its offer, likely because it had heard of the unusual circumstances associated with the last town population count and property evaluation. This situation created the possibility that the legislature would move the college to a wealthier urban area such as Guthrie or Oklahoma City. The territorial legislative assembly, then in session, resolved the problem with an act on March 14, 1893, declaring the college building bonds of Stillwater legal and authorizing their sale. The legislative assembly also gave the town power to borrow money by issuing warrants to make up the deficiency if the bonds sold below their face value of $10,000.[27]

Then Charles W. McGraw, Stillwater trustee president, worked out a substitute plan to sell the college building bonds to Joseph W. McNeal, the Guthrie banker and real estate dealer who had purchased Frank E. Duck's south eighty acres next to the college tract. No one in Stillwater, including the banks, had enough available money to purchase even one

Joseph W. McNeal (*left*), the president of the Guthrie National Bank and leading Republican, purchased the ten $1,000 bonds issued by the municipal government of Stillwater for the construction of Old Central at the discounted price of $7,825. He soon sold one-half of the bonds to his Republican Party friend, Governor Abraham J. Seay (*right*) of Oklahoma Territory.

of the ten $1,000 bonds. McNeal paid $7,825 for the bonds, slightly more than the previous offer. McGraw delivered the bonds to McNeal personally in Guthrie and received a bank deposit slip for the money paid by McNeal to buy the bonds. This would prove to the town trustees that the bonds had been sold. McGraw lost no time in returning to Stillwater, and that night, about a mile from town, William A. Swiler, W. E. Hodges, Frank J. Wikoff, J. Harry Swope, and Hays Hamilton met McGraw's stagecoach. They demanded proof that the bonds had been sold. When McGraw offered them the deposit slip, they lit a match, read the slip, and rushed back to town. They got out the town band and began a celebration that lasted far into the night. Soon McNeal sold one-half of the college building bonds to his Republican Party friend, Governor Abraham J. Seay of Oklahoma Territory.[28]

Only one more hurdle remained to raise the full $10,000 required by the territorial legislature for the college building. Because the bonds sold for $2,175 below face value, this amount needed to be raised quickly and sent to the territorial treasurer in Guthrie. Fifty-five Stillwater citizens, including several members of the college faculty, purchased short-term town government warrants issued in the amount of $33 each. Purchasers could not be found for an amount approximately equal to eleven shares. This deficiency was met with a loan from the Stillwater Farmers and Merchants Bank in the amount of $532. Alexander Campbell, an officer of the bank, refused to loan the town government that amount, but gave it to Charles W. McGraw and Charles J. Knoblock on their joint personal note. When McGraw called the town trustees together to tell them of this arrangement, William A. Swiler and Curtis D. Shaffer shouted, "I'll sign it with you." Saloon license income redeemed the principal money of the town warrants, but in the meantime interest payments on them were paid from special town warrants and money borrowed from the town road and bridge account. Thus all money loaned for the college building was secured for both interest and principal.[29] These events, said Frank J. Wikoff, a Stillwater attorney at the time, seemed like "life and death to us. We practically fought, bled and died for the college."[30]

Partisan politics in Stillwater, however, criticized the effort to raise the $10,000 for the college building. The *Oklahoma Hawk*, a Democratic Party newspaper in Stillwater, hit hard in April 1893 at the Republicans who had negotiated to obtain funding for the college building. The reporter listed the expenses of the town trustees in attempting to sell the bonds during the unsuccessful transaction with the St. Joseph Loan and Trust Company. It was alleged that a total of $530 had been paid to F. C. Hunt, John J. Shaffer, Charles W. McGraw, Charles J. Knoblock, and to the brokerage firm itself. In addition, the reporter charged that a bid for the bonds from Martin L. Turner, a Guthrie banker and a lead-

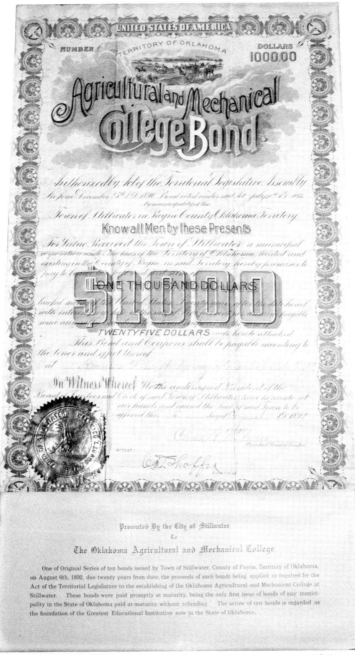

This is one of the ten $1,000 bonds issued by the municipal government of Stillwater to construct Old Central. It was presented to the college at a banquet by the city commissioners when the bonds were paid off at maturity in 1913.

ing Democrat, had been ignored even after he purchased an option on the bonds for $2,500. The evaluation concluded that politics predominated in determining who purchased the bonds and at what price. The criticism was largely ignored by the *Stillwater Gazette*, a Republican newspaper, as well as by the people of the town. This attitude prevailed because the bonds for the college building had been marketed about three months earlier and the deficit on them successfully financed. Also, more than a month before the attack of the *Oklahoma Hawk,* the Oklahoma Legislative Assembly on March 13, 1893, had appropriated $15,000 to provide adequate funds to complete the construction of the college building and to equip it. Stillwater had not only won the college, but by this appropriation that fact had been reaffirmed by the legislative assembly.[31]

The $10,000 in bonds issued to construct the first permanent building of the Oklahoma A. and M. College were promptly paid off at maturity in 1913 by the municipal government of Stillwater. These proved to be the first issue of bonds by any municipality in Oklahoma paid at maturity without refinancing. The city of Stillwater took the bonds returned by the purchasers at the time of redemption in 1913 and presented them as gifts of appreciation at a banquet commemorating the occasion. They were given to leading original settlers still living in the community and to prominent civic leaders at the time of the banquet. The Stillwater municipal government had carried through to perfection the will of its citizens to win the land-grant college.[32]

Thus Stillwater had succeeded in the additional task of winning the Oklahoma A. and M. College after the legislative assembly located it in Payne County. Stillwater leadership surmounted the problem by obtaining the college location through careful planning, initiative, vigilance, and determination. When the electorate of Payne County overwhelmingly refused to vote bonds in the amount of $10,000 for the college building at a site yet undetermined in the county, Stillwater voters unanimously approved the bonds on the first vote, and on the second vote, after the first bond issue was found to be illegal, only six persons objected at the polls. Hence virtually all Stillwater voters stood solidly behind the leadership of the town in desiring the college. Careful planning, initiative, vigilance, and determination increased among the leadership of Stillwater as adversity set in at various stages in completing and marketing the bond issue. Even a generous population count and property evaluation, later legalized by the legislative assembly, became a part of the effort. The leadership of the town and its people steadfastly refused to accept defeat because the stakes were too high not to succeed.

Endnotes

1. Oklahoma Territorial Assembly, *Journal of the First Session of the Legislative Assembly of Oklahoma Territory Beginning August 27, 1890* (Guthrie, OK: Oklahoma News Publishing Company, 1890), p. 1015.

2. Robert Martin, compiler, *Statutes of Oklahoma, 1890* (Guthrie, OK: State Capital Printing Company, 1891), p. 82; George H. Shirk, *Oklahoma Place Names,* 2nd edition (Norman: University of Oklahoma Press, 1974), pp. 53, 123, 188, 190, 258; Philip Reed Rulon, *Oklahoma State University—Since 1890* (Stillwater: Oklahoma State University Press, 1975), p. 8.

3. Martin, compiler, *Statutes of Oklahoma, 1890,* p. 82.

4. Martin, compiler, *Statutes of Oklahoma, 1890,* pp. 82-83.

5. Martin, compiler, *Statutes of Oklahoma, 1890,* pp. 1195, 1199-1200.

6. Martin, compiler, *Statutes of Oklahoma, 1890,* pp. 718-721.

7. Roy Gittinger, *The University of Oklahoma, 1892- 1942* (Norman: University of Oklahoma Press, 1942), pp. 5-6.

8. Stan Hoig and Reba Collins, *In the Shadow of Old North Tower* (Edmond, OK: Central State University, 1972), pp. 2, 5.

9. Rulon, pp. 8-9; *Annual Catalog, Oklahoma A. and M. College, 1894-1895,* pp. 8-9; John Alley, *City Beginnings in Oklahoma Territory* (Norman: University of Oklahoma Press, 1939), pp. 93-94; Berlin B. Chapman, "Founding of the College," *Oklahoma A. and M. College Magazine,* vol. 1, no. 4 (December 1929), p. 7; Dora Ann Stewart, *Government and Development of Oklahoma Territory* (Oklahoma City, OK; Harlow Publishing Company, 1933), p. 187.

10. Freeman E. Miller, *The Founding of Oklahoma Agricultural and Mechanical College* (Stillwater OK: Hinkel and Sons, 1928), pp. 8-9; Rulon, p. 9; *Annual Catalog, Oklahoma A. and M. College, 1894-1895,* p. 9; Stewart, p. 187; "Record of the Minutes of the Board of Trustees of the Town of Stillwater, April 7, 1891 to June 30, 1901," Stillwater City Clerk's Office, Stillwater Municipal Building, Stillwater, Oklahoma, pp. 32-40, 47, 52.

11. Berlin B. Chapman, *The Founding of Stillwater: A Case Study in Oklahoma History* (Oklahoma City, OK: Times Journal Publishing Company, 1948), pp. 145-146.

12. Alfred E. Jarrell to Berlin B. Chapman, 25 June 1956, Alfred E. Jarrell File, Berlin B. Chapman Collection, Special Collections, Edmon Low Library, Oklahoma State University, Stillwater, Oklahoma.

13. Record Book Committee, compiler, "Selections from the Record Book of the Oklahoma Agricultural and Mechanical College, 1891-1941. Compiled on the Occasion of the Fiftieth Anniversary of the Founding of the College," vol. 2, copy 2, pp. 319-320, Special Collections, Edmon Low Library; Chapman, *The Founding of Stillwater,* pp. 146-148.

14. Chapman, *The Founding of Stillwater,* pp. 145-146, 183; "Record of the Minutes of the Board of Trustees of the Town of Stillwater," p. 59; Frank E. Duck to Berlin B. Chapman, 3 March 1946, original in Archives Division, Oklahoma Historical Society, Oklahoma City, Oklahoma, copy in Old Central Centennial History Collection, Special Collections, Edmon Low Library; *Stillwater NewsPress,* 3 December 1986, pp. 1B-2B; Houston Overby, "The Story of Aggieland" in *Oklahoma Agricultural and Mechanical College Yesterday and Today* (Guthrie, OK: Cooperative Publishing Company, [1927]), unpaged. This article was reprinted in the *1927 Redskin,* pp. 167-168, Oklahoma A. and M. College Yearbook.

15. *Portrait and Biographical Record of Oklahoma* (Chicago, IL: Chapman Publishing Company, 1901), pp. 202, 205, 890-891, 398-400; Berlin B. Chapman, "The Men Who Selected Stillwater as the College Site for A. and M.," *Oklahoma A. and M. College Magazine,* vol. 2, no. 4 (December 1930), pp. 108-109; Oklahoma A. and M. College *Daily O'Collegian,* 20 March 1942, pp. 1, 4; Chapman, *The Founding of Stillwater,* p. 145; *Annual Catalog, Oklahoma A. and M. College, 1894-1895,* pp. 8-9; Miller, p. 7; *Stillwater NewsPress,* 3 December 1986, p. 1B.

16. *Biographical Directory of the American Congress, 1774-1971* (Washington, DC: Government Printing Office, 1971), p. 870; "Register of the Stillwater City Hotel," Payne County Historical Society, Stillwater, Oklahoma, unpaged; Rulon, p. 10; *Stillwater Daily Press,* 14 December 1938, p. 1.

17. *Stillwater Daily Press,* 14 December 1938, p. 1; *Portrait and Biographical Record of Oklahoma,* p. 1053.

18. *Stillwater Daily Press,* 14 December 1938, p. 1.

19. *Oklahoma Agricultural Experiment Station, Bulletin No. 1: General Information, Organization, and History, Stillwater, Oklahoma, December, 1891* (Guthrie, OK: Daily News Print, 1891,), p. 7.

20. Chapman, *The Founding of Stillwater,* p. 147.

21. "Record of the Minutes of the Board of Trustees of the Town of Stillwater," pp. 36-37, 39; *Stillwater Gazette,* 22 January 1892, p. 2; *Annual Catalog, Oklahoma A. and M. College, 1894-1895,* pp. 10, 13; Miller, pp. 12-14; Amos A. Ewing, "The First Board of Regents," *Oklahoma A. and M. College Magazine,* vol. 1, no. 4 (December 1929), p. 4; [Freeman E. Miller], "The Oklahoma Agricultural and Mechanical College," *Oklahoma Magazine,* vol. 3, no. 5 (May 1895), pp. 295, 297; "The Founding and Struggle for Survival," *Oklahoma State Alumnus Magazine,* vol. 10, no. 5 (May 1969), pp. 14-15; *Report of the President of the Oklahoma Agricultural and Mechanical College to the Secretary of the Interior and the Secretary of Agriculture for the Year Ending June 30, 1894, and the Biennial Report to the Governor of Oklahoma, December 31, 1894* (Guthrie, OK: Representative Print, 1895), p. 7; Amie Neal Jamison to Berlin B. Chapman, 22 April 1961, James Clinton Neal Collection, Special Collections, Edmon Low Library.

22. "Record of the Minutes of the Board of Trustees of the Town of Stillwater," p. 64; "The Founding and the Struggle for Survival," p. 15; Miller, pp. 17-18; Rulon, pp. 11-12.

23. "Record of the Minutes of the Board of Trustees of the Town of Stillwater," pp. 64, 80; *Stillwater Daily Press,* 1 January 1939, p. 1; United States Congress, *Supplement to the Revised Statutes of the United States, 1874-1891,* 2nd edition, revised and continued, vol. 1 (Washington, DC: Government Printing Office, 1891), p. 504; *Stillwater Gazette,* 29 July 1892, p. 1; Miller, pp. 18-19.

24. *Stillwater Gazette,* 29 July 1892, p. 1, 26 August 1892, p. 4; "Record of the Minutes of the Board of Trustees of the Town of Stillwater," pp. 83-89; Chapman, *The Founding of Stillwater,* pp. 141-143; Miller, pp. 19-20.

25. *Stillwater Gazette,* 23 September 1892, p. 5; Hays Cross, "Memories to Be Revived," *Oklahoma A. and M. College Magazine,* vol. 11, no. 3 (December 1939), p. 4; "'We Get the College!'" *Oklahoma A. and M. College Magazine,* vol. 1, no. 4 (December 1929), p. 31; *Daily O'Collegian,* 14 December 1938, p. 1; "Record of the Minutes of the Board of Trustees of the Town of Stillwater," pp. 89, 98; Miller, pp. 20-21.

26. "Record of the Minutes of the Board of Trustees of the Town of Stillwater," pp. 89, 98; "'We Get the College!'" pp. 6, 31.

27. Rulon, p. 13; *Stillwater Gazette,* 28 March 1913, p. 4; Robert Martin, compiler, *The Statutes of Oklahoma, 1893, Being a Compilation of All Laws in Force in the Territory of Oklahoma* (Guthrie, OK: State Capital Printing Company, 1893), pp. 135-136.

28. Stillwater *Oklahoma Hawk,* 27 April 1893, p. 1; *Stillwater Daily Press,* 1 January 1939, p. 1; *Stillwater Gazette,* 14 March 1913, p. 1, 28 March 1913, p. 4; Stillwater *Payne County News,* 18 December 1936, p. 6; Chapman, *The Founding of Stillwater,* pp. 143-145.

29. *Stillwater Gazette,* 14 March 1913, p. 1; *Payne County News,* 18 December 1936, p. 6; *Stillwater Daily Press,* 1 January 1939, p. 1; "Record of the Minutes of the Board of Trustees of the Town of Stillwater," pp. 206, 252, 314; Miller, pp. 20-21.

30. Frank J. Wikoff to Thomas J. Hartman, 30 November 1940, History File, Berlin B. Chapman Collection.

31. *Oklahoma Hawk,* 27 April 1893, p. 1; Martin, compiler, *The Statutes of Oklahoma, 1893,* pp. 130-132; Rulon, p. 14; Miller, p. 22.

32. One thousand dollar bond presented to Charles F. Babcock, Museum, Sheerar Cultural and Heritage Center, Stillwater, Oklahoma; One thousand dollar bond presented to Hays Hamilton, Special Collections, Edmon Low Library. The redeemed bond gifts, under glass and neatly framed with a presentation statement, usually caused the descendants of the leading original settlers who received them to believe their forebearers actually purchased one of the bonds, which none of them did. These settlers did not have enough available money to do so. Those who received the redeemed bonds were President J. H. Connell of Oklahoma A. and M. College, Robert A. Lowry, William A. Swiler, Orlando M. Eyler, Mayor Frederick M. Stallard, Commissioner J. L. Moore, Commissioner M. W. J. Holt, Henry B. Bullen, Charles F. Babcock, and Hays Hamilton. *Stillwater Gazette,* 14 March 1913, p. 1.

3 Constructing the College Building

Although the municipal government of Stillwater finally raised the $10,000 necessary to win the college, a basic problem remained. The money proved insufficient to finance even a permanent building already admittedly inadequate in its planning stages. Action had to be taken immediately to remedy the funding situation. Fortunately, the same need had developed for the first permanent buildings under construction at the University of Oklahoma and the Oklahoma Normal School. In response to this condition, the Oklahoma Legislative Assembly on March 16, 1893, authorized territorial bonds for the use of the three collegiate institutions in completing the construction of their first permanent buildings. Of the $48,000 appropriated, the University of Oklahoma received $18,000, with $15,000 each for the Oklahoma Normal School and the Oklahoma A. and M. College.[1]

With $25,000 now available for construction of the first permanent building, the board of regents of the Oklahoma A. and M. College planned to let a contract for the structure. The regents appeared satisfied with the preliminary architectural plans and specifications for the small building and evidenced little or no concern for its adequacy. While the plans and specifications were being finalized, the regents busied themselves with selecting a site for the building before letting a construction contract.

Meanwhile, the people of Stillwater also concerned themselves with the selection of a site for the college building. Information came to the residents of the town that some of the regents desired to have the college building and the temporary structures of the Agricultural Experiment Station located on the high ground in the northwest area of the two hundred acre college location. This would have placed the college building and the entire campus at the furthest point from the town limits of Stillwater, a distance of more than three-quarters of a mile. Many townspeople opposed this positioning of the college building for several reasons. The proposed location, they said, would "work an injustice to the people who have sacrificed most to secure the college." Moreover, students from the town, who would always attend the college in large numbers and board at home, would for all practical purposes be denied a college education. Thirdly, the appeal continued, the distance would be too extensive "for students to walk every day and the cost would be too great to ride."[2] The entire college faculty, it was claimed, wanted the permanent building constructed on the southeast corner of the college land near the temporary structures of the Agricultural Experiment Station. This would make the location immediately north and west of the town limits. Finally, the reasoning concluded, the people of the town "without a dissenting voice" favored locating the building adjacent to the corporate limits.[3]

Sentiment for the site of the college building polarized dramatically as the weeks passed. With the time nearing to open the bids of contractors for the structure, the board of regents took steps to resolve the issue. The body assembled on June 1, 1893, in James C. Neal's house on the Agricultural Experiment Station grounds to hold a public hearing on the two sites and make a decision. The meeting aroused unusual interest, and signed petitions from those supporting each of the two sites were considered. Attorneys Frank A. Hutto and C. H. Stewart represented those who desired the far northwest location on high ground, explaining that it afforded a commanding view, beautiful surroundings, and ample room for growth. The petition had many names of country residents, but only five from the town.

Attorney Freeman E. Miller, a speaker of extraordinary ability, presented the petition from those desiring the site location as near the corporate limits as possible. He spoke of the convenience for the students attending the college, easy access to the Agricultural Experiment Station structures already erected, the abundance of room for present and future needs, and an elevation high enough to appear attractive. No effort was made to obtain signatures from the nearby countryside, but 166 citizens of the town had signed the petition.

Next the board of regents visually examined the two proposed locations for the college building. They then decided on the location nearer the town. The site was designated as being about 120 feet north of present University Avenue, opposite the College Addition to the town. Residents seemed pleased, and a report circulated that construction of the college building would begin about July 1, 1893. The structure reportedly would cost approximately $20,000, and "be a fine structure of brick and stone." This cost would leave $5,000 "to be used in providing furniture and fixtures for the building."[4]

Meantime, the board of regents had employed Herman M. Hadley of Topeka, Kansas, as the architect for the college building. He had studied for five years at Cornell University, Ithaca, New York, and graduated first in his class in 1876 with the bachelor of architecture degree. He had practiced architecture for fifteen years. In addition to designing many elaborate private residences, he had planned churches, hotels, railroad depots, college buildings, city halls, and business buildings, and assisted with designing the Kansas State Capitol. He also served as a founder and initial officer of the Kansas State Association of Architects. At the time of his death in 1904, he was credited with designing some of the best buildings in Kansas.[5]

The next task of the board of regents was to let a contract for the construction of the college building. On June 20, 1893, the board accepted the bid of $14,948 of Henderson Ryan, a contractor and builder from Fort Smith, Arkansas. The bid did not include the heating or furnishing equipment for the building. Little is known of Ryan or the structures he built except that he had the contract in Edmond for the

Construction on Old Central began in June 1893. This photograph of the basement stonework underway, taken from the northwest, shows workmen standing on or near the south wall overlooking the chemistry laboratory room. In the background is the roof of the contractor's temporary office and storage building.

Oklahoma Normal School building, already under construction.[6] Optimism prevailed. The *Stillwater Gazette* editorialized: "It is expected that enough of the new building will be completed in time for the opening exercise of the college next fall where work can be accomplished much better than under present environments."[7] The *Oklahoma State Capital* of Guthrie also predicted that "there will be no hindrances to the building being finished in time to move the school into it for winter quarters."[8]

Cash Cade of Kingfisher was made superintendent of construction on the college building, and work moved rapidly ahead. Skilled labor, including qualified Stillwater tradesmen, such as stone masons, brick layers, and experienced carpenters, made up the full-time work force. Quite a few students of the college, including members of the first graduating class of 1896, also assisted with the construction of the building. Their rate of pay was ten cents an hour. Thomas J. Hartman of the class of 1898, while working on the building, proposed an improvement for carrying bricks and mortar. Instead of lifting these materials up ladders, he introduced ramps (inclined planes) as a substitute, and this device was used effectively in completing the construction. People, including Josiah Rogers and his three sons, who operated wagons to transport rock, came to Stillwater to haul material for the building. Each wagon and driver earned two dollars a day. Nearly fifty men were employed in the construction of the building.[9]

Materials came from several directions. The pressed and kiln-fired face brick used for the exterior wall surface originated in Kansas and were sent to Orlando or Perry on the Atchison, Topeka, and Santa Fe Railroad. Then they traveled by wagon nearly twenty-five miles over rough unimproved roads to Stillwater. The common or back-up brick used in the building came from the Stillwater kiln of Louis J. Jardot. The red hammered-cut exterior sandstone used to face the foundation walls six feet above ground level and also utilized for the exterior wall surface and trim around the windows and doors came from the Cross farm south of Stillwater. The limestone steps of the entrances likely originated in a Ponca City quarry. The lumber and other materials in the framing and finish work on the interior of the building came primarily from trade centers in Kansas. The cedar shingles used on the gables and belfry, as well as the tin shingles applied to the roof, probably came from Kansas also. Other materials channeled through Kansas included the prefabricated fireplace mantel in the president's office, the door and window hardware, the gas piping for light fixtures, and the gaslight fixtures themselves. Other items coming from Kansas were the ceramic tile, the wall and floor grills, the slate blackboards, the plaster, the paint, the venetian blinds, the carbide processing machine used in making gas for the lights and the chemistry laboratories, the central steam boiler

Louis J. Jardot owned and operated a brickyard on his claim west of Stillwater that provided the back-up brick used on the inside of the exterior and interior walls of Old Central. An immigrant from France, Jardot reached Stillwater at the time of the Run of 1889.

located in the basement, and the steam radiator heating units throughout the building.[10]

Although the original architect's plans and specifications known to have been used for the building no longer exist, the basic features of the original building can be determined from the structure itself. The building is 67 feet 9 inches (east-west) by 67 feet 2 inches (north-south) in size. Overall, it consists of two floors over a full basement. The main entrance on the first floor level is on the south, and on the northwest corner of the building a spacious stairway leads also to the first floor level. A secondary outside below-ground level stairway under the main south entrance serves the basement, as did an entrance, no longer existing, located in the north center wall under the interior stairway. In addition, the basement could be reached from the northwest corner through a door, long since removed, leading to the steam boiler room. The basement, once lighted by tall windows with exterior window wells, was constructed four feet below ground level. Distinctive features of the building exterior are the gabled roof, topped by a belfry and bell, a ventilation tower, and two chimneys. One chimney served the boiler and the other the fireplace in the president's office. Built-in gutters and downspouts drain the roof.[11]

The building contains sixteen rooms, including the assembly hall. The basement originally housed the chemistry laboratory; the chemistry lecture and demonstration classroom; the boiler room housing the steam generating equipment, the water pumps, and the storage tanks; and two classrooms. The basement originally had ceilings of about 10 feet although they presently measure but 8 feet 9 inches. The first floor had two classrooms, the college library room, a reception room, and the president's office. The first floor rooms have ceilings of 14 feet. The second floor contained two classrooms, one storeroom, the assembly hall, a combination office and recitation room, and the night watchman's room located under the bell tower. The second floor rooms have ceilings of 13 feet 4 inches. The assembly hall measures 40 by 55 feet, with a ceiling of 16 feet 4 inches. The south interior stairway serves the first and second floors, the attic, and the belfry, while the north interior stairway provides access to the basement and to the first and second floors. Wide hallways run north and south through the basement and first floor, but the second floor does not have a hallway because of the assembly hall. Of the six rooms on the second floor, four open into the two stair wells and four have doorways into the other rooms. Although two of the rooms have doorways opening on the assembly hall, these doors need not be used when the assembly hall has activities underway.[12]

In addition to overall design, some construction details are of interest. According to Contractor Ryan, the foundation extends one foot below the basement floor, "thus affording a perfectly solid bed to support the heavy building."[13] Other structural techniques, considered the best at the time, called for the use of uncut sandstone, held together by soft mortar, in the foundation and the walls. The exterior walls were sheathed with hammered and machine-cut sandstone and kiln-fired pressed brick bonded by soft mortar. The machine-cut sandstone cap one foot wide, girding the building between six and seven feet above ground level, has a chiseled border groove and a punch mark design laid out geometrically. The exterior walls in the basement are twenty-four inches thick, on the first floor eighteen inches thick, and on the second floor twelve inches thick. The interior load-bearing masonry walls of sandstone and brick start and stay a half-foot thinner, their progression from the basement to the second floor being eighteen, twelve, and seven inches. Non-load bearing interior walls were constructed of wood framing. All interior wall surfaces consisted of plaster, wood wainscoting, and slate blackboards.[14]

The building has an interior of wood in addition to the inside masonry walls. The structural wood consists of rough-cut beams and planks, but all exposed wood used for interior finishing is machine planed. Ample quantities of structural wood were used throughout the building. Wood finishes dominate the interior of the building, a typical pattern of the time. All rooms and hallways have wood wainscoting, and the wood stairways are another feature of the hallways. The floors were tongue-and-groove yellow pine approximately four inches in width. The original floor in the basement was of smooth finished plaster-like material installed over a crushed stone sub-base. With few exceptions, yellow pine is the wood used throughout the building, both structurally and for finishing. This is fortunate, for yellow pine is both strong and durable.[15]

Most of the heat in Old Central came from steam radiators boxed in and suspended from the ceilings of the rooms and hall of the basement. Air ducts ran from the floor to the radiators to pick up cold air. This photograph of heating units was taken in the restored chemistry laboratory room.

Another interesting aspect of the building is the heating, cooling, and ventilating system, thoroughly modern for its time. About three months after letting the contract on the building, the board of regents advertised for bids on the construction of a "boiler room" and a steam heating and ventilating system for the structure. A. C. Prescott and Company of Topeka, Kansas, received the contract to install the heating and ventilating system for $3,490, an amount later increased due to the installation of additional equipment.[16]

The northwest corner of the basement provided the space for the steam boiler, gas generators, and other equipment. Wood likely fueled the boiler, for, unlike coal, it could be had nearby. A limited supply could be stored in the boiler room, and some was stacked outside near the boiler room door. The majority of the heat in the building came from steam radiators boxed in and suspended from the ceiling of the rooms and hall of the basement. Air duct enclosures ran from the floor to the radiators to pick up cold air. Half of the radiators with open vents warmed the rooms and hall of the basement, while the other half vented up through open floor grills in the first and second story floors to heat those areas. The heat rose passively but effectively through both the grills and the stairwells. The basement had about ten radiators, the first floor one, and the second floor between three and six, making a total radiator count of fourteen to seventeen for the building. Whatever the winter temperature outside, the heating system generally proved satisfactory at that time. But the sound transmitted through the heat vents between the floors, combined with the echo effect of sound in the rooms, must have been deafening during class periods.[17]

The designer of the building carefully planned the cooling and ventilating systems. The windows provided direct cooling and ventilating throughout, except for the attic. Most windows were double hung permitting high and low ventilation, and, in addition, those on the first floor featured operable transoms at the top which could be opened to provide cross ventilation of warm air at the ceiling line. The hallway doors at all room entries were also constructed with operable transoms permitting ventilation of both rooms and interior corridors. Each room was also vented through a series of wall grills connected to compartmentalized vent shafts in the exterior walls. These shafts were then vented through round metal ducts in the attic to a cupola, an elevated wood box-type enclosure constructed below the roof-mounted vent hood. Wall shafts not used for other air discharge purposes vented the fume hoods installed in the basement chemistry laboratory and chemistry lecture and demonstration classroom to prevent chemical odors from spilling over into rooms above. Wind-blown air, assisted by artificial heat in the winter, provided adequate circulation to draw stale air from the building.[18]

True to the late Victorian tastes of the period, the exterior wood paint colors of the structure generally set greens against the red brick and rock. The tin shingles of the roof likely carried a green paint similar to the hue of the exterior wood. The total paint scheme of the outside consisted of three shades of green, intended to accent quietly the woodwork detail. Additional Victorian taste is suggested by the venetian blinds used on the windows. Manufactured by the Burlington Venetian Blind Company of Burlington, Vermont, they were made of wood slats held together by cotton tape and designed to slide up and down on a rod at each end of the slats. The rods eliminated most slat motion and rattle caused by air moving through open windows.[19]

Both students and faculty, as well as Stillwater and Oklahoma Territory, anxiously awaited the completion of the building. Space needs continued critical as Contractor Ryan and his large labor force worked rapidly, hoping to meet the January 1894 completion deadline.[20] The June 1893 commencement, held in the Stillwater Methodist Episcopal Church South, had seating for only 250 persons. "To say that it was all occupied would be expressing it too mild," related the *Stillwater*

42

Gazette. "The seats were full, little ones being held on laps, the standing room was full, the vestibule was full, and every window had its full quota of people looking in and enjoying themselves as best they could under the circumstances."[21] Some believed that the new building would soon be completed, and the *Blackwell Rock-Record* predicted that it would be ready for occupancy about December 1, 1893.[22]

Then a major problem arose over the financing of the building. A delay occurred in the sale of the $48,000 in territorial bonds authorized on March 16, 1893, by the Oklahoma Legislature for buildings at the University of Oklahoma, the Oklahoma Normal School, and the Oklahoma A. and M. College. The Stillwater institution was to receive $15,000 from this fund to complete its first permanent building. Months passed without the bonds being sold, and Contractor Ryan ran out of funds to continue work on the Stillwater building before it had a roof. The Norman structure had reached completion in August 1893, and a portion of the Edmond building had opened in January 1893. Thus money needed to place the Stillwater structure in use had reached critical proportions.[23]

The problem had its origins in the election in 1892 of Grover Cleveland as President of the United States. A Democrat, Cleveland took action to remove Abraham J. Seay, a Republican, as governor of Oklahoma Territory, and appoint William C. Renfrow, a Democrat, to the post. Governor Renfrow attempted to remove a number of Republican appointees from office, including the five regents of the Oklahoma A. and M. College, but they refused to resign. Renfrow appointed his own Democratic board of regents for the college, and the problem continued for months. Meanwhile, Renfrow and the broker for the college bonds, Martin L. Turner, a Guthrie banker and also an ardent Democrat, held up the bond issue. While the newspapers debated the controversy, work ceased on the college building in Stillwater.[24]

Newspapers in Stillwater and elsewhere in the territory took up the regents' issue in August 1893, continuing to emphasize its impact on the college building. Turner finally sold the bonds in March 1894. The Republican *Stillwater Gazette* had reported on August 18, 1893, that the building "is progressing right along as nicely as can be, and if the Democratic papers of Guthrie will hold their peace a while they will see it completed on time."[25] With the Republican board making monthly payments to Contractor Ryan, the $10,000 raised by the town of Stillwater for the construction of the college building would soon run out. According to Republicans, Governor Renfrow and Turner deliberately delayed the marketing of the bonds to embarrass the Republican board of regents and bring about their resignation. The Republican *Oklahoma State Capital* of Guthrie, as quoted in the *Stillwater Gazette*, quipped that if the students at Stillwater did not have their new building by the

Three Democrats, President Grover Cleveland (*lower left*), Governor William C. Renfrow (*lower right*), and Martin L. Turner (*upper right*), a Guthrie banker, were instrumental in holding up the completion of Old Central for months.

scheduled completion date in January 1894, it would "be because the governors pet, the scrip broker, has not been able to resell the bond[s] and fails to comply with his contract for which Governor Renfrow and not the board is responsible."[26]

When the $10,000 raised by the town of Stillwater for the construction of the college building ran out in the late fall of 1893, work on the structure ceased. Republicans openly blamed Renfrow for the situation, claiming that he did not wish Treasurer Amos A. Ewing of the Republican board of regents to administer the construction money, thereby pressuring that board of regents to resign to make room for the governor's Democratic board of regents.[27] The Republican *Stillwater Gazette* blamed the governor for "his manifest desire to run the college on a political basis, regardless of the good of the institution."[28]

In the meantime, Ewing wrote the college faculty explaining the need for a petition from the citizens of Stillwater to Governor Renfrow urging continued work on the building. The faculty agreed with Ewing and also appointed its own committee of three to visit Governor Renfrow and other territorial officials to request that funds be made available at once to complete the building. Alexander C. Magruder, professor of agriculture and horticulture; George L. Holter, professor of chemistry and physics; and Edward F. Clark, professor of mathematics and literature, made up the committee. Magruder served as chairman.[29]

On December 1, 1893, President Robert J. Barker of the Oklahoma A. and M. College informed the Republican board of regents that Governor Renfrow assured him that the bonds were printed and on his desk waiting for his signature as provided by law. Early in 1894 Treasurer Ewing of the Republican board of regents complained that the college building, still without a roof, had "its walls and materials . . . exposed to the wintry storms" because of "the governor's individual grievances."[30] Finally, on January 25, 1894, Governor Renfrow signed all bonds in the $48,000 territorial issue authorized by the Oklahoma Legislative Assembly on March 16, 1893, for building uses at the University of Oklahoma, the Oklahoma Normal School, and the Oklahoma A. and M. College.[31]

Meantime, Treasurer Ewing of the Republican board of regents filed for a writ of mandamus from the Oklahoma Supreme Court to require Martin L. Turner, recently appointed territorial treasurer by Governor Renfrow, to make available $19,000 in federal funds sent to the territorial treasurer for the use of the Oklahoma A. and M. College. The court refused to issue the mandamus, although the funds, according to Republican sources, would lapse at the end of June 1894. The Republican *Eagle-Gazette* of Stillwater deplored this situation and complained that "the college building stands in an unfinished condition, exposed to the storms of winter, the contractor being unable to carry the work on without funds. Our merchants, who have been cashing the contractor's checks, with the understanding that the money would soon be forthcoming are getting just a little impatient and out of sorts waiting for the show to close and the performers to get down to business." The *Eagle-Gazette* con-

In a view of Old Central taken from the southeast during the last phase of construction, an Agricultural Experiment Station crop is shown growing in front of the building, and a privy stands to the left. Sanitary facilities were not installed in Old Central until 1903.

cluded by emphasizing that Stillwater and the college ''have been injured to no inconsiderable extent by the unbusinesslike proceedings of Governor Renfrow, who is indirectly to blame by reason of being mentally incapacitated to properly perform the function of his high office, and the effect is being severely felt by our citizens and business men.''[32]

Although Governor Renfrow had signed the collegiate building bonds on January 25, 1894, weeks passed before money from their sale became available at the three territorial collegiate institutions. Optimism and pessimism went hand in hand concerning the situation at the Oklahoma A. and M. College. The Stillwater *Payne County Populist* reported on February 23, 1894: ''Work on the college building will be resumed as soon as material can be had. It is hoped to have the building ready for occupancy April 1.''[33] Yet the *Perkins Bee* of February 23, 1894, voiced considerable frustration: ''The report has been brought to us frequently that the $15,000 appropriated by the last legislature is ready to be turned over to the proper authorities to be used for the completion of the college building. Yet, notwithstanding these seemingly available funds, the college doors may be closed.''[34]

But by March 16, 1894, optimism prevailed in both the *Stillwater Conder* and *Eagle-Gazette:* ''The people of Stillwater have watched with

Robert J. Barker, the first president of the college, served from 1891 to 1894. He worked with the Stillwater municipal government and Governor William C. Renfrow to obtain bond funding for the construction of Old Central.

interest the progress of the endeavors of the governor and the courts to settle the controversies existing over the board of regents who have the management of the Oklahoma Agricultural and Mechanical college, located here. They rejoice that light seems to be breaking."[35] Treasurer Ewing of the Republican board of regents and Governor Renfrow cooperated long enough to make adequate money available from the $15,000 territorial bond issue fund to complete the construction of the college building. By April 1894, the Democratic regents appointed by Renfrow gained firm control of the college, for the members of the Republican regents, including Treasurer Ewing, had resigned one by one.[36] With construction money finally in hand, the Stillwater *Oklahoma State Sentinel* on April 26, 1894, commented favorably: "The work on the college building is rapidly nearing completion, and it will be ready for use by the end of the present school year."[37]

Two weeks later the *Oklahoma State Sentinel* reassured its readers: "The new college building is nearing completion and when finished will be a credit to our young territory. Although it is not as large as some buildings of the kind in older states, it is well constructed."[38] A week later the editor of the *Stillwater Conder* toured the unfinished college building "from its bottom floor to the top, even up into the belfry," accompanied by James C. Neal, the director of the Agricultural Experiment Station.[39]

With commencement weekend scheduled less than a month away on June 15-17, 1894, Contractor Ryan pushed for completion of the college building while administration and faculty planned the final details for its dedication. This ceremony would take place in the assembly hall of the building on Friday evening, June 15. A committee consisting of faculty and students was appointed to decorate the assembly hall for the occasion.[40]

The public invitation to the dedication ceremony of the college building expressed much enthusiasm: "Stillwater's Pride . . . will be thrown open to the citizens of the territory . . . . The college faculty will spare no labor in making this one of the brightest episodes in the history of Stillwater. The college building will be brilliantly lighted from basement to dome, and the spacious assembly room will be gorgeously decorated by Oklahoma's fairest flowers . . . . The faculty will receive the public and spare no pains in making them feel at home."[41]

When the opening hour for the dedication ceremony drew near, the assembly hall of the college building filled to capacity with students of the college, townspeople, visitors from the territory, and honored guests. The Stillwater *Eagle-Gazette* exclaimed: "Whose heart was so dead to pride as to refuse to respond with thrills of pleasure at the sight of our beautiful, new and imposing college building, brilliantly lighted

In this photograph of Old Central taken from the northwest during the last phase of construction, the basement steam boiler room outside entrance is being built. Rock for the entrance is stacked near the building.

This dedication photograph of Old Central was taken in June 1894. The end of a construction table is evident in the lower right. Only the prime coat of red paint covered the wood surfaces on the exterior. Green paint of three shades would soon be applied to garnish the exterior wood.

from basement to dome—for the first time—reflecting bright gleams of radiance . . . . But the beauty of its outside appearance was almost forgotten when the magnificent assembly room . . . was entered. The stage was very fittingly and appropriately decorated with wheat, corn, oats and flowers artistically arranged."[42] The *Oklahoma State Capital* of Guthrie explained that the college building represented the realization of the faith of the people "so long held in abeyance."[43]

President Robert J. Barker presided at the dedication ceremony. After a selection by the Stillwater Orchestra, he introduced the Reverend Richard B. Foster, who delivered the address. Foster served as pastor of the Congregational Church of Stillwater and had also worked as the first superintendent of schools in Payne County. He was well educated, a clear thinker, an able speaker, and an attractive personality. He opened his talk by saying that he planned to interpret the meaning of the land-grant college as he viewed it. In the past, he said, societies had been divided into privileged classes and the masses. The privileged classes were expected to receive considerable formal education and do little manual labor, while the masses engaged in endless manual toil and received only a bare minimum of formal education. The land-grant college, Foster explained, was intended to break down these barriers, and the Oklahoma A. and M. College possessed this democratic power intended for those it served.[44] In conclusion, he advised the laboring men in the audience to "put religion in your hearts, education in your heads, and money in your pockets, and take your place—the world cannot keep you from it. When that is generally done, there will cease to be privileged classes." Foster deeply impressed his audience in the forty minutes he spoke, and applause continued at great length.[45]

Then President Barker introduced Governor Renfrow, who made a few appropriate remarks. Next, Frank Caruthers, the treasurer of the Democratic board of regents, made a brief talk and accepted the college building on behalf of the regents. Finally, James C. Neal, the director of the Agricultural Experiment Station, commented on the work accomplished in his experimental and administrative activities. Also at the dedication the announcement came that the college building would be opened for student use when the next term began on September 15, 1894.[46]

Two secondary tasks remained to complete work on the college building. First, the bell that had been ordered for installation in the belfry finally arrived by mid-November 1894 and soon was set in place by raising it with a block and tackle. Second, a water system, designed to serve the building's heating boiler, the gas generating equipment, the chemistry laboratory, and the chemistry lecture and demonstration classroom, was constructed during the spring and summer of 1894 for use when the college opened in the fall. A well was dug and a windmill erected west of present Theta Pond to pump water with a stationary steam engine into a nearby water tower. Students dug the well and a trench sheltering the pipe carrying water to the building. Student labor cost eight to ten cents an hour to construct the water system. Soon a well was dug immediately north of Old Central to provide drinking water.[47]

The college building nestled in a newly designed campus laid out in walks and driveways, and a large number of shade trees and shrubs were planted. The building itself, equipped with "all modern appliances," cost nearly $20,000. "Enough remained of the building funds," the faculty reported, "after settling all contracts, to fully furnish the college building, and this has been well done under the direction of the board of regents." The details followed: "The seats, desks, cabinets, cases, and fixtures which have been procured are plain but well finished, suited to the building and their respective uses, and durable of their kind. No public institution in the territory is now more thoroughly or better furnished."[48]

When the college opened its fourth academic year in September 1894,

This windmill and water tower, located immediately west of present Theta Pond, provided well water for Old Central's steam heating boiler, the gas generating equipment, the chemistry laboratory, and the chemistry lecture and demonstration classroom. Students dug the well and a trench for the pipe that carried water to the building.

it fully occupied the new building, and 8 faculty and 144 students settled down to work. Only the senior year remained to be offered by the college for it to have a complete undergraduate program. The faculty was somewhat fatigued by moving the teaching equipment from the Methodist Episcopal Church South to the new building and by the work needed to ready the classrooms and the laboratories for the students. In addition, some of the faculty helped to landscape the eight-acre campus, as did students who worked on the project. With the landscaping program underway, the college building completed, and the structures of the Agricultural Experiment Station nearby, the campus began to look like an institution of higher education.

It is likely that the instructional staff furnished the office of Henry E. Alvord, the new president of the college, in advance of his arrival. Two faculty members, James C. Neal and Alexander C. Magruder, must have known Alvord both personally and by reputation, for he was a well-known and respected leader of the land-grant college movement. Neal and Magruder could not have missed making his acquaintance at meetings of the Association of American Agricultural Colleges and Experiment Stations, which they had all attended. Other faculty members were undoubtedly pleased also to obtain a person of Alvord's stature to head the college. As a result, there must have been a special effort to make him feel welcome.[49]

With the completion of the structure, it became known as the College Building, or simply the College. At the same time, it also went by the name of Central Building and Main College Building because of temporary agriculture-related structures nearby. It next became known for a brief period as the Assembly Building since it housed the only auditorium on the campus until the completion of two major permanent structures in 1902. Then its name changed again to Central Building with the completion of a new auditorium in the original Library Building. The administrative officers of the college continued to call it Central Building until 1923, when the name changed to Old Central Building, two years following its condemnation for classroom use. Then in 1929 it became Old Central at the time President Henry G. Bennett took steps to refurbish it. In general usage, the name Old Central can be found as early as 1908, and it continued in sporadic application along with Central Building and Old Central Building until 1929, when the title Old Central came into exclusive use.[50]

Considering the low budget restraints involved in the construction of Old Central, unusual and desirable features still resulted, such as the heating, cooling, and ventilating systems, all relatively efficient and modern for the time. The acetylene gas lighting layout, with electrical illumination not yet available in Stillwater, could not be surpassed. Even the venetian blinds specified for the structure employed a device to reduce slat rattle caused by air flow through open windows. Outside paint colors utilized three shades of green to accent the red brick and stone, true to Victorian tastes of the era. Less successful design features, however, were the sandstone foundation, basement drainage, and the basement window wells. These early on proved inadequate, although at the time of construction they were generally considered suitable and wholly acceptable.

Endnotes

1. Robert Martin, compiler, *The Statutes of Oklahoma, 1893, Being a Compilation of All Laws in Force in the Territory of Oklahoma* (Guthrie, OK: State Capital Printing Company, 1893), pp. 128-132.

2. *Stillwater Gazette,* 31 March 1893, p. 4.

3. *Stillwater Gazette,* 31 March 1893, p. 4.

4. Stillwater *Payne County Republican,* 8 June 1893, p . 1.

5. A. T. Andreas, *History of the State of Kansas* (Chicago, IL: A. T. Andreas, 1883), pp. 564-565; *Kansas State Gazetteer, 1888-89* (St. Louis, MO: R. L. Polk and Company, 1889), p. 10; *Topeka Capital-Commonwealth,* 1 January 1889, pp. 11-12; John M. Peterson, *John G. Haskell: Pioneer Kansas Architect* (Lawrence, KS: Douglas County Historical Society, 1984), pp. 180-181; *Topeka State Journal,* 11 October 1904, p. 4; *Topeka Daily Capital,* 12 October 1904, p. 4; Freeman E. Miller, *The Founding of Oklahoma Agricultural and Mechanical College* (Stillwater, OK: Hinkel and Sons, 1928), p. 22.

6. *Annual Catalog, Oklahoma A. and M. College, 1894-1895,* p. 14; Guthrie *Daily Oklahoma State Capital,* 22 June 1893, p. 1; Miller, *The Founding of Oklahoma Agricultural and Mechanical College,* p. 22; *Stillwater Gazette,* 23 June 1893, p. 5, 18 August 1893, p. 4; *Arkansas State Gazetteer and Business Directory, 1892-3,* vol. 3 (Detroit, MI: R. L. Polk and Company, 1892), p. 200; *Ft. Smith 1894-95 City Directory* (No place: Maloney Directory Company, no date), pp. 134, 167; Stan Hoig and Reba Collins, *In the Shadow of Old North Tower* (Edmond, OK: Central State University, 1972), p. 6.

7. *Stillwater Gazette,* 23 June 1893, p. 1.

8. *Daily Oklahoma State Capital,* 22 June 1893, p. 1.

9. *Daily Oklahoma State Capital,* 22 June 1893, p. 1; Alfred E. Jarrell, "My Class," *Oklahoma A. and M. College Magazine,* vol. 27, no. 11 (July 1956), p. 13; Oklahoma A. and M. College *Daily O'Collegian,* 15 December 1935, p. 2; Berlin B. Chapman to LeRoy H. Fischer, 4 June 1985, and Josiah Rogers to Zachariah Rogers, 3 August 1893, in Old Central Centennial History Collection, Special Collections, Edmon Low Library, Oklahoma State University, Stillwater, Oklahoma; *Stillwater Gazette,* 25 August 1893, p. 4.

10. *Stillwater Gazette,* 25 August 1893, p. 4; *Report of the President of the Oklahoma Agricultural and Mechanical College to the Secretary of the Interior and the Secretary of Agriculture for the Year Ending June 30, 1894, and the Biennial Report to the Governor of Oklahoma, December 31, 1894* (Guthrie. OK: Representative Print, 1895), p. 6; Ida A. Merwin interview with J. D. E. Owen, 19 August 1937, Indian-Pioneer Papers, vol. 137, p. 312, Archives Division, Oklahoma Historical Society, Oklahoma City, Oklahoma; James L. Showalter, "A Structural History of Old Central," unpublished typed manuscript, pp. 5-6, 15, Old Central Centennial History Collection; Alfred E. Jarrell to John W. Hamilton, 10 November 1954, and Alfred E. Jarrell to Berlin B. Chapman, 2 June 1958, in Alfred E. Jarrell File, Berlin B. Chapman Collection, Special Collections, Edmon Low Library; *Daily O'Collegian,* 6 December 1941, pp. 1, 4, 26 March 1957, p. 1; Oklahoma City *Daily Oklahoman,* 20 February 1959, p. 40.

11. Showalter, pp. 13-15; Nomination Form, National Register of Historic Places, Old Central Centennial History Collection.

12. Nomination Form, National Register of Historic Places, and Floor Plan of Old Central, Old Central Centennial History Collection; Showalter, p. 22.

13. *Stillwater Gazette,* 25 August 1893, p. 4.

14. Showalter, pp. 3-4, 6-7.

15. Showalter, pp. 9-11, 20-21.

16. *Stillwater Gazette,* 15 September 1893, p. 8, 13 October 1893, p. 8; Miller, *The Founding of Oklahoma Agricultural and Mechanical College,* p. 22; Oklahoma Territorial Council, *Journal of the Council Proceedings of the Third Legislative Assembly of the Territory of Oklahoma, Beginning January 8, 1895, Ending March 8, 1895* (Guthrie, OK: Daily Leader Press, 1895), p. 72.

17. Showalter, pp. 23-24; Author interview with Al Tyson, 24 October 1985, Old Central Centennial History Collection.

18. Tyson interview; Showalter, pp. 13, 16-17; Author interview with Ray E. Dryden, 5 November 1985, Old Central Centennial History Collection; Harvey M. Trimble, "Fifty Years of Chemistry at Oklahoma Agricultural and Mechanical College," unpublished typed manuscript, 1942, p. 3, Special Collections, Edmon Low Library.

19. Showalter, pp. 18-20, 27.

20. *Stillwater Gazette,* 18 August 1893, p. 4.

21. *Stillwater Gazette,* 23 June 1893, p. 1.

22. *Blackwell Rock-Record,* 2 November 1893, p. 2.

23. Roy Gittinger, *The University of Oklahoma, 1892-1942* (Norman: University of Oklahoma Press, 1942), p. 15; Hoig and Collins, p. 5.

24. James F. Morgan, "William Cary Renfrow: Governor of Oklahoma Territory, 1893-1897," in LeRoy H. Fischer, editor, *Oklahoma's Governors, 1890-1907: Territorial Years* (Oklahoma City, OK: Oklahoma Historical Society, 1975), pp. 52-53; John H. N. Tindall, editor, *Makers of Oklahoma* (Guthrie, OK: State Capital Company, 1905), p. 84.

25. *Stillwater Gazette,* 18 August 1893, p. 4.

26. *Stillwater Gazette,* 18 August 1893, p. 4.

27. *Stillwater Gazette,* 1 December 1893, p. 4.

28. *Stillwater Gazette,* 8 December 1893, p. 4.

29. Oklahoma Agricultural and Mechanical College Faculty, "Minutes of the First Faculty, March 17, 1892, to June 2, 1899," unpublished typed manuscript in two volumes, vol. 1, 6 November 1893, p. 151, Special Collections, Edmon Low Library.

30. Stillwater *Eagle-Gazette,* 26 January 1894, p. 4.

31. *Eagle-Gazette,* 26 January 1894, p. 4.

32. *Eagle-Gazette,* 9 February 1894, p. 4.

33. *Payne County Populist,* 23 February 1894, p. 4.

34. *Perkins Bee,* 23 February 1894, p. 2.

35. *Stillwater Conder,* 16 March 1894, p. 1; *Eagle-Gazette,* 16 March 1894, p. 1.

36. Philip Reed Rulon, *Oklahoma State University—Since 1890* (Stillwater: Oklahoma State University Press, 1975), pp. 46, 48.

37. Stillwater *Oklahoma State Sentinel,* 26 April 1894, p. 5.

38. *Oklahoma State Sentinel,* 10 May 1894, p. 1.

39. *Stillwater Conder,* 18 May 1894, p. 1.

40. Oklahoma Agricultural and Mechanical College Faculty, "Minutes of the First Faculty," vol. 1, 7 June 1894, p. 174.

41. *Oklahoma State Sentinel,* 7 June 1894, p. 1; *Payne County Populist,* 8 June 1894, p. 4.

42. *Eagle-Gazette,* 21 June 1894, p. 1.

43. *Daily Oklahoma State Capital,* 18 June 1894, p. 1.

44. *Eagle-Gazette,* 21 June 1894, p. 1; Freeman E. Miller, "Exit the Bandit—Enter the College!," *Oklahoma A. and M. College Magazine,* vol. 1, no. 5 (January 1930), pp. 4, 24-25.

45. Miller, "Exit the Bandit—Enter the College!," p. 25; *Oklahoma State Sentinel,* 28 June 1894, p. 5; *Stillwater NewsPress,* 29 April 1987, pp. 1B, 6B.

46. *Eagle-Gazette,* 21 June 1894, p. 1; *Edmond Sun-Democrat,* 22 June 1894, p. 2; *Daily Oklahoma State Capital,* 18 June 1894, p. 1.

47. *Stillwater Messenger,* 16 November 1894, p. 3; *Payne County Populist,* 30 November 1894, p. 4; Comments on the First Water System, Thomas J. Hartman File, Alfred E. Jarrell to Berlin B. Chapman, 10 January 1958, and Campus Notes, Alfred E. Jarrell File, in Berlin B. Chapman Collection.

48. Oklahoma Territorial Council, pp. 72, 76.

49. Rulon, pp. 52-53; Fall Semester Enrollments, Registrar's Office, Oklahoma State University.

50. *Annual Catalog, Oklahoma A. and M. College, 1898-1899,* p. 8; *Annual Catalog, Oklahoma A. and M. College, 1899-1900,* p. 8; *Annual Catalog, Oklahoma A. and M. College, 1902-1903,* p. 9; *Annual Catalog, Oklahoma A. and M. College, 1923-1924,* p. 27; *Annual Catalog, Oklahoma A. and M. College, 1929-1930,* p. 12; *Oklahoma State Capital,* 2 April 1892, p. 2; Oklahoma A. and M. *College Paper,* 1 February 1902, p. 109; Oklahoma A. and M. College *Orange and Black,* September 1908, pp. 4, 5, 18 September 1912, p. 4, 19 September 1914, p. 1, 4 October 1915, p. 2, 10 January 1916, p. 2, 8 September 1916, p. 1, 16 September 1916, p. 1; *Stillwater Gazette,* 24 July 1914, p. 1; *1916 Redskin,* p. 220, Oklahoma A. and M. College Yearbook.

4 Turbulent Politics

Old Central began its life of service in a frenzied sea of political activity. The building was barely occupied before the raging torrent struck. When the college opened the school year of 1894-1895, the administration, faculty, and students crowded into it, and no one seemed to have enough room. Immediately the structure became the nerve center of the institution. All administrative activity centered in it, and all departments of study, with the exception of some agricultural teaching and laboratory work, offered their courses there. Students, without exception, had nearly all of their collegiate studies within its walls, as did the preparatory school pupils. Professors did not have space enough for private offices in the building, so they occupied desks in the classrooms where they did most of their teaching.

The basement of Old Central housed the chemistry lecture and demonstration classroom in the northeast room and the chemistry laboratory in the southeast room. The two remaining rooms in the basement, south of the steam boiler room, served general classroom purposes. On the first floor, the southwest room containing a functional fireplace housed the college president. A room immediately to the north accommodated the college secretary and served as a reception and conference area for the president. North of this, a large room sheltered horticultural classes. Across the hall, the northeast room was used for mathematics and surveying classes. On the same side of the hall, the large southeast room held the library in its west end and English studies and their teacher in its east end. On the second floor, the small room on the south under the bell tower had only enough space to house the student serving as janitor and night watchman of the building. The assembly hall on the second floor contained about 225 chairs and was used daily for chapel meetings required of all students. Large classes met in it also. The preparatory department, organized to prepare grade school and high school level students for college entry, occupied the large room and the small adjacent room used for an office and recitations. This department regularly used the assembly hall as well. The Agricultural Experiment Station headquartered in the southwest room.[1]

The inauguration of President Grover Cleveland, a Democrat, in March 1893 severely impacted the first administrative and faculty occupants of Old Central. The President controlled appointments in the territories, including Oklahoma. He appointed a new governor, William C. Renfrow, a Democrat, who took office in May 1893 and replaced the Republican board of regents of the college with Democrats. President Robert J. Barker, a Republican, had resigned under pressure for that reason, as had W. W. Hutto, professor of English literature and military tactics. Hutto's brother, Frank A. Hutto, was a Stillwater lawyer and leader in the Republican Party. The Republican *Eagle-Gazette* of Stillwater opposed his firing and emphasized that Hutto had won the "love and esteem of the students and the respect and confidence of its patrons." His replacement, Freeman E. Miller, a Stillwater lawyer and Democrat, received bachelor's and master's degrees from DePauw University in Greencastle, Indiana, where he graduated as valedictorian of his class. Although his academic qualifications seemed adequate, the *Eagle-Gazette* still maintained that his appointment resulted from his political affiliation rather than from his credentials.[2]

Henry E. Alvord served as president of the college for four months in 1894. He was the first executive to be housed in Old Central, a building he considered inadequate for the needs of a land-grant college.

When the newly-appointed president of the college, Henry E. Alvord, reached Stillwater in September 1894, he immediately found himself in the center of political pressures and urgent catch-up duties. He came to his post highly recommended by officials of the United States Department of Agriculture in Washington, D.C., where he worked as a deputy assistant to the Secretary of Agriculture. In addition, he had served in various capacities with the land-grant college movement since 1869 and had become one of its disciples. The regents of the college would likely not have relented to the pressure from Washington to appoint him had they known of his recent resignation from the presidency of the Maryland Agricultural College because of a clash with his superiors.[3]

Alvord began work in the well-furnished president's office in Old Central by revising and completing the institution's annual report for the board of regents begun by President Barker. This tedious task afforded Alvord the opportunity to evaluate the current conditions of the college and make recommendations for change. In his sharp and often harsh military-type approach, he did not hesitate to reveal weak spots as he viewed them. First of all, varying enrollments from term to term captured his attention. "The students," he complained, "do not seem to appreciate the necessity for persistent application to their work, their own needs and the opportunities now offered them. And parents are too prone to permit, or even encourage, absences for every insufficient reason. The full strength of the college and its teaching force is exerted to overcome these evils and to impress upon the minds of students themselves, as well as upon parents, the importance of punctual and regular attendance and the advantages of continued and well sustained effort in study."[4]

SPECIAL COLLECTIONS, OSU LIBRARY

In October 1894, Old Central was called the "College." The other structures are (*left to right*) the Agricultural Experiment Station barn, laboratory, and director's residence.

Alvord turned next to the preparatory department where more students were enrolled than on the college level. He hoped to consolidate the two years of sub-collegiate work into one in the near future. "The federal government," he cautioned, "sends the generous annuity to this territory for . . . the college grade and not for providing any substitute for grammar schools or high schools."[5]

Instructional-related matters needed immediate attention, Alvord explained. The professor of chemistry and physics had so many college duties that he had no time for the Agricultural Experiment Station work. The new president recommended that additional professors and teaching assistants be employed in order to free more faculty for research and extension work. "The salaries of the professors," the executive said, "are not equitably arranged, either in regard to one another or to the proper relations existing between the college and its experiment station department."[6] Botany and horticulture, Alvord pointed out, should be combined under one department because both concerned the plant kingdom. The report to the regents also urgently recommended that a woman be added to the faculty "to give proper advice as to study, health and conduct to girls and young women who are for the first time removed from home influences, and at a critical age."[7]

Then President Alvord took up the need for additional buildings. He reminded the regents that Oklahoma Territory made an agreement with the federal government to provide the land, buildings, and furniture for the Oklahoma A. and M. College as long as the money for instruction and equipment came from the federal treasury. The accommodations in Old Central, he said, were inadequate, for there was but space to present a single course of general study strong in agriculture and horticulture. To shape the college properly and meet public demands, he continued, engineering and home economics departments should be organized at once. He reasoned that because females composed nearly half of the student body, a home economics department should be established first. It would be hopeless, said the president, to establish any new department under present circumstances, since no space could be found.[8]

Alvord concluded his report to the regents by calling for a building to provide adequate housing for the horticulture department, and another to accommodate the chemistry and physics department. "As was expected," he complained, "the chemical laboratory in the basement of the college building is giving trouble. The odors, fumes and gases cannot be fully controlled, and reach every part of the building at times. Occasionally classes in upper rooms have to be dismissed. This trouble will increase as the hours of laboratory practice are increased. Experience has demonstrated that chemical laboratories should be in buildings to themselves, or, at all events, with no other work in rooms above."[9] If

The college library in 1894 was located in the west end of the southeast room of the first floor of Old Central. The other end of the room housed the English office and classroom.

chemistry and physics could be located in a separate building, Alvord explained, then a home economics program could be commenced in Old Central, and the English department would have a room of its own, thus providing space for library expansion. He also called for $500 to purchase reference books for the library, $100 to construct a plank walk connecting Old Central with the western town limits of Stillwater, and an adequate water supply not only for Old Central but for distribution elsewhere on the campus.[10]

Overall, President Alvord did not like Old Central and related this sentiment to the Secretary of the Interior and the Secretary of Agriculture: "It was evidently designed by one experienced in building, but who unfortunately had no conception of the requirements of an institution of this kind. The building committee of regents was equally unqualified and apparently took no pains to inform itself, even by consulting the experienced professors already in the service of the college. Several of the rooms are small and the structure is not at all adapted to laboratory work of any sort." At the same time, Alvord confided that the wooden frame buildings of the Agricultural Experiment Station had been planned "with judgment and economy" by those who knew what was needed.[11]

Simultaneously, Alvord recommended that the useless positions of farm superintendent and college secretary be eliminated. The president labeled the secretary as "illiterate and unfit for keeping ordinary records. During the first six months of his employment he was present for duty less than thirty days, going and coming at will and declaring himself independent of any superior."[12] In March 1893 the Oklahoma Legislative Assembly had prohibited the college board of regents from receiving compensation other than per diem and mileage payment for their services. Although Alvord heartily approved this action, he scolded that the regents have "since adopted an equally pernicious practice of putting friends and adherents into college vacancies or creating offices for them."[13]

Less than a month after he had settled down in his office in Old Central, President Alvord found himself in trouble with the board of regents. They disliked his procedures and recommendations, and he returned the disapproval. After only four months, on December 21, 1894, Alvord submitted his resignation to the regents in a well-thought-out statement: "The government of the United States and the public generally consider me in a large measure responsible for the conduct of the affairs of this institution. I cannot afford to maintain relations by which I may appear to be . . . a consenting party to the payment of large salaries to positions at this College and Station, which are unnecessary and where the

ANNUAL CATALOG, OKLAHOMA A. AND M. COLLEGE, 1894-1895

When Henry E. Alvord occupied the president's office on the first floor of Old Central in 1894, this functional wood-burning fireplace occupied a corner of the office. The prefabricated mantel, along with other materials for the building, came from trade centers in Kansas.

duties performed do not justify the expenditure. The result is nothing less than the diversion of public funds from the objects for which they are specifically provided." He concluded: "As your Board has seen fit to decline action notwithstanding my presentation and protest on this subject, I hereby tender my resignation."[14]

Local and territorial reaction came at once. The *Stillwater Messenger* set the tone by calling for an investigation of the board of regents by the Oklahoma Legislative Assembly in 1895.[15] James C. Neal, the director of the Agricultural Experiment Station, told Representative Robert A. Lowry of Stillwater of two plans in the legislative assembly to relocate the college and the Agricultural Experiment Station. One of the plans proposed moving both institutions to another location in Oklahoma, and the other called for transferring the Agricultural Experiment Station alone to an area that had better quality soil and a more desirable location. "No matter what the arguments as to unsuitability of location, poor soil, out of the wayness and that Payne County got it by 'finesse and trading,'" Neal confided, "the facts are that Payne County has worked for it for all she was worth, and sacrificed both time and money to hold it, and here it should stay. Some of these times a Railroad will make this place as accessible as Guthrie or Oklahoma City, and all the other objections can be overcome."[16]

Meanwhile, a joint resolution of the legislative assembly made the members of the agricultural committees of the house and council a special group to investigate the college, including its financial management, personnel appointments and dismissals, and other complaints made by Alvord. The investigating committee, after taking a wide range of detailed testimony, reached these conclusions: first, the site for the college had not been well selected because of poor soil and inadequate water; second, the positions of farm superintendent and college secretary should be abolished; third, the officers of the institution should keep better and exact financial records; and fourth, administrators should expand the geographic area from which students came, thus serving the entire territory. The committee noted that 90 percent of the students in attendance were from Payne County, and that those from Stillwater and Payne County received special consideration. Perhaps, the report said, this condition could be attributed in part to the comparatively inaccessible location of the college.[17]

In closing, the investigating committee explained that it "found little to commend and a great deal to condemn" in the financial management of the college. "Where public officers," the report observed, "admit that they have charged for services rendered for every day in the month, including Sundays, and then in addition collect pay from the territory for the same time that they have charged the institution for service as an agent in another capacity, it is time such officials, in charge of educa-

The chemistry laboratory, as it appeared in 1894 in the southeast room of the basement of Old Central, served both the students of the college and the staff of the Agricultural Experiment Station. Odors from the laboratory often caused classes in the building to be dismissed.

tional institutions, should be taught to observe a law which is older than colleges, states or nations."[18] Amazingly, the report implied nothing more than moral laxity and suggested that the laws of Oklahoma Territory had not been broken. The report did not recommend court action against the Democratic board of regents. The investigation, however, resulted in much ill feeling between the Republican and Democratic parties and activated the latent desire to move the entire college from Stillwater.

Neal urged Representative Lowry of Stillwater to sponsor a bill in the 1895 legislative assembly to increase the size of the board of regents to protect the remaining Republicans on the faculty from being removed and to keep the financial abuses from continuing. Neal even submitted to him a draft of the proposed bill. Almost immediately Councilor John H. Pitzer of El Reno introduced a bill in the legislative assembly to remove the college to El Reno, located on the Rock Island Railroad. Simultaneously, Representative William A. Knipe of Perkins introduced a plan in the legislative assembly to extend the southern boundary of Payne County nine miles into Lincoln County and move the Payne

County seat of government to Perkins. The fire that had destroyed the courthouse in Stillwater in December 1894 undoubtedly encouraged this effort.[19]

The people of Stillwater united and dropped local political differences long enough to work together to keep both of their prized establishments. "When you tackle Stillwater and her institutions," the Stillwater *Oklahoma State Sentinel* admonished, "you will be facing Spartans and not the chicken hearted."[20] Charles W. McGraw led the caucus of Stillwater leaders determined to save the county seat, and they sent a special lobbyist to the territorial capital at Guthrie for this purpose. "If you get the common gabber started an assertion is soon made a positive fact," he advised Representative Lowry, "and continues to get larger. Kill Knipes Bill in Committee. We will send money to do so."[21] The record does not reveal if Lowry resorted to bribes, but the county seat remained in Stillwater at the request of Lowry without a public political fight.

Following the destruction of the all-wood courthouse by fire in December 1894, the people of Stillwater by popular subscription provided all construction materials for a new courthouse and the county commissioners appropriated $595 for the labor to build it. The new all-wood structure, also located in the middle of the present courthouse square, had two stories and a fire-proof vault of ample size to protect all vital records.[22] When reflecting that earlier Stillwater had built the first courthouse in Oklahoma Territory, the *Oklahoma State Sentinel* jubilantly concluded: "Our push and enterprise is legion, and it is one of the impossibilities to keep us down."[23]

Representative Lowry also deserves considerable credit for keeping the Payne County seat of government and the Oklahoma A. and M. College in Stillwater. Considered the favorite for speaker of the house of representatives in the 1895 legislative assembly, Lowry would then have been in line for the next presidential appointment as governor of Oklahoma Territory. Cassius M. Barnes, however, opposed Lowry for the speakership, but when Barnes promised Lowry political favors in time of need, Lowry decided to support him for the position. As expected, Barnes became speaker of the house of representatives in 1895. That same year Lowry called on Barnes to keep the Oklahoma A. and M. College and Agricultural Experiment Station from being moved to El Reno without a public political fight. When this was accomplished quietly by Barnes, Old Central continued to serve its purpose. No other serious political efforts took place to move the college in the future. Later, in 1897 President William McKinley, a Republican, appointed Barnes governor of Oklahoma Territory. Thus Representative Lowry had indeed likely forfeited the governorship to save the Payne County seat of government and the Oklahoma A. and M. College for Stillwater in the crisis

Robert A. Lowry (*left*) of Stillwater, a favorite in the house of representatives of Oklahoma Territory, probably forfeited his chance to become governor of the territory in 1897 because he had earlier supported Cassius M. Barnes (*right*) for speaker of the house. This action by Lowry, however, saved both the college and the Payne County seat of government for Stillwater during the crisis of 1894 and 1895. Barnes became territorial governor in 1897.

of 1894 and 1895. When the legislative assembly came to a close in March 1895, the Stillwater Board of Trade arranged a public reception, followed by a banquet, in appreciation of the successful efforts of Representative Lowry to keep the Payne County seat of government and the college in Stillwater.[24]

The turbulent political situation in Stillwater and at the Oklahoma A. and M. College also impacted the alteration, furnishing, and equipping of Old Central, and even threatened to cause its sale because of a lien on the property. This would not have happened if adequate contract procedures and financial records had been maintained. Two highly skilled Stillwater carpenters and contractors, Charles F. Willis and William R. Bradford, doing business as the firm of Willis and Bradford, sued the board of regents of the college on August 27, 1895, in the district court of Payne County. They maintained that they had not been paid for their labor and materials for cabinet-type work in Old Central between February 25 and June 10, 1895. By terms of the alleged contract, Willis and Bradford were to receive twenty-five cents an hour for their labor and furnish the materials at cost. The cost of the labor and materials came to $574.34, plus $75.00 for attorney fees and interest at 7 percent from June 10, 1895, the amount for which Willis and Bradford sued.[25]

Since the establishment of the college in Stillwater in 1891, Willis and Bradford had done all of the interior finishing work for the Agricultural Experiment Station. Known for their high-quality woodwork and lumber business, they had already done much finish work under a written contract on the interior of Old Central, including permanent cases, benches, and similar fixtures required in the chemistry lecture and demonstration classroom, chemistry laboratory, and other rooms of the building. Willis and Bradford did this work, for which they received payment, under the immediate supervision of the professors concerned and under the oversight of President Alvord. Willis and Bradford claimed that the additional work they did in Old Central in 1895, for which they had not been paid, had been authorized in writing by Alvord. Alvord's office, they said, had the only copy of the alleged contract. They submitted to the district court, however, when filing their petition, a five-page ledger book list of the daily hours worked and materials used, including itemized costs.[26]

George L. Holter, professor of chemistry and physics, stands behind the demonstration desk in the chemistry lecture and demonstration classroom in Old Central in 1894. The location was in the northeast room of the basement.

C. A. Galbraith, the attorney general for Oklahoma Territory, served as the attorney for the college. He had the records of Alvord's office searched for the alleged contract, but it could not be found. A contract statement for the work and materials of Willis and Bradford in Old Central in 1894 did turn up, and this amounted to a claim of $1,683.01 paid earlier. As a result, Galbraith reasoned that all work done in Old Central by Willis and Bradford under a valid contract had been paid in full.[27]

Before the case came to trial in Stillwater in the district court of Payne County, the college board of regents obtained additional legal counsel to assist Attorney General Galbraith from John D. DuBois of Guthrie, an assistant territorial attorney general, and Robert A. Lowry of Stillwater. Attorneys Sterling P. King and Frank A. Hutto of Stillwater represented Willis and Bradford in their court case. Frank Dale, the trial judge in the Payne County District Court, also served as chief justice of the supreme court of Oklahoma Territory. Dale denied a request by the attorney general for a delay of the trial. He impaneled a jury, but it never deliberated on the evidence presented because he decided the case on a procedural maneuver in favor of Willis and Bradford. He awarded them $610.25, plus fees for court costs, and provided sixty days for payment by the board of regents of the college. Meantime, the regents would need to sell Old Central to pay Willis and Bradford or raise the money elsewhere.[28]

At once the college filed a motion in the district court of Payne County for a new trial based on nine reasons why the college had not been treated fairly by the trial court and why Judge Dale's decision was

C. A. Galbraith, the attorney general of Oklahoma Territory, served as the legal counsel for the college in the Charles F. Willis and William R. Bradford lawsuit of 1895 involving Old Central. The case, decided by the supreme court of Oklahoma Territory, is considered a legal landmark in Oklahoma history. It established the important principle that the territory and later state of Oklahoma could not be sued except by its consent.

not based on adequate evidence. No action came from the district court, so the college appealed the case to the Oklahoma Supreme Court. When the supreme court finally decided the case on February 18, 1898, Dale, now an associate justice, did not participate in the proceedings because of his earlier involvement in the case. All other justices of the supreme court agreed, however, that the district court decision needed to be reversed. Uniquely, the issue of adequate evidence did not decide the case, but rather a finding of no jurisdiction. This rarely happens.[29]

The Oklahoma Supreme Court, although claiming no jurisdiction in the case, took the occasion to establish the general legal principle that public educational institutions, such as the Oklahoma A. and M. College, cannot be sued unless authorized by law. In reasoning the case, the justices explained the difference between private corporations and public or quasi corporations, such as the Oklahoma A. and M. College, based on relative powers, purposes, and the length of their corporate lives. In essence, the court felt that because there was no statute either in Oklahoma Territory or nationwide authorizing a lawsuit against a public corporation like the Oklahoma A. and M. College, a court of law could not hear a case against it.[30]

In concluding the Willis and Bradford case, the supreme court thought that "to hold that these [higher education] institutions can be sued and the property, held by them for the most important of all public purposes, seized under execution, attachment and other such process, would be to greatly impede their progress and usefulness, while it has ever been the policy of our people, through their legislative assemblies, to foster and encourage them in every proper way."[31]

The supreme court told Willis and Bradford to look to Oklahoma Territory for payment when "there is no fund appropriated for the payment of their claims." If a fund exists for the payment "of any just claims" against the Oklahoma A. and M. College and its board of regents refuses to consider and pass on it, a writ of mandamus should be used to command the board to do so. If the claim should be allowed, and the college had no money to pay for it, Willis and Bradford should "look to the legislative power of the Territory for payment."[32] Willis and Bradford apparently did not further pursue their claims against the Oklahoma A. and M. College. There is no known record of payment.

The Willis and Bradford case is considered a legal landmark in Oklahoma political history. The fundamental principles decided in this case are recognized to be permanent standards for governing the public higher education institutions of Oklahoma in three areas: first, how services and sales claims are to be processed; second, the role of the legislature in providing funds for the payment of claims for services and sales; and third, jurisdictional limitations on the state judicial power over claims for services and sales against public higher education institutions. The same principles were reaffirmed by the Oklahoma Supreme Court in 1909 shortly after statehood. The court at that time ruled that all of the Oklahoma A. and M. College's territorial legal powers and protections became a part of the institution's governance at statehood and thus constitutional in their permanence. In 1981 the state supreme court once again sustained this legal interpretation. No supreme court decision over the years has in any way diminished the responsibilities, legal powers, and immunities of the Oklahoma A. and M. College as defined in the landmark Willis and Bradford case concerning Old Central.[33]

Thus Old Central continued in a crisis pattern during the school year of 1894-1895. The building, due to inadequate planning and funding for the special needs of the college, proved unsatisfactory from the beginning. The turbulent political situation in Oklahoma Territory, caused in part by a change in political parties in the White House, severely impacted the board of regents of the college. In addition, the board had engaged in questionable financial and personnel manipulation. This likely arose from inadequate restraints in the law establishing the college, brash dishonesty, and perhaps frontier permissiveness.

During the 1894-1895 crisis, President Henry E. Alvord served notably for the four months he held office. His thoroughly informed and disciplined approach to administrative problems provided a basis for slow but certain change in the college and its board of regents. His work hastened the development of the college into a well-rounded land-grant institution. He also provided administrators in the territorial capital at Guthrie and the national capital at Washington with reliable information concerning the college and Old Central, the institution's primary building. In four months Alvord completed a reorganization of the college that would probably have taken a less experienced and knowledgeable administrator years to finish. Yet the problems of the college were not permanently resolved.

Endnotes

1. Floor Plan of Old Central, Mary Nielsen Taylor to Berlin B. Chapman, 5 October 1971, and Old Central Visitor Brochure, *The Oklahoma Historical Society Presents Old Central*, in Old Central Centennial History Collection, Special Collections, Edmon Low Library, Oklahoma State University, Stillwater, Oklahoma; Emma G. Dent to Berlin B. Chapman, 7 June 1961, Berlin B. Chapman Collection, Special Collections, Edmon Low Library; *Annual Catalog, Oklahoma A. and M. College, 1894-1895*, pp. 43-114; *Stillwater NewsPress*, 13 December 1967, p. 3, 7 September 1980, p. 7B.

2. Stillwater *Eagle-Gazette*, 28 June 1894, p. 1.

3. Philip Reed Rulon, *Oklahoma State University—Since 1890* (Stillwater: Oklahoma State University Press, 1975), pp. 49-52.

4. Oklahoma Territorial Council, *Journal of the Council Proceedings of the Third Legislative Assembly of the Territory of Oklahoma, Beginning January 8, 1895, Ending March 8, 1895* (Guthrie, OK: Daily Leader Press, 1895), p. 78.

5. Oklahoma Territorial Council, p. 78.

6. Oklahoma Territorial Council, p. 79.

7. Oklahoma Territorial Council, p. 80.

8. Oklahoma Territorial Council, pp. 80-81.

9. Oklahoma Territorial Council, p. 81.

10. Oklahoma Territorial Council, p. 82.

11. *Report of the President of the Oklahoma Agricultural and Mechanical College to the Secretary of the Interior and the Secretary of Agriculture, for the Year Ending June 30, 1894, and the Biennial Report to the Governor of Oklahoma, December 31, 1894* (Guthrie, OK: Representative Print, 1895), pp. 6-7.

12. *Report of the President of the Oklahoma Agricultural and Mechanical College,* pp. 20-21.

13. *Report of the President of the Oklahoma Agricultural and Mechanical College,* p. 20.

14. *Report of the President of the Oklahoma Agricultural and Mechanical College,* Appendix, p. 1. See also Alvord's open letter to the people of Stillwater, dated 11 January 1895, Stillwater *Oklahoma State Sentinel,* 17 January 1895, p. 1.

15. *Stillwater Messenger,* 18 January 1895, p. 2.

16. James C. Neal to Robert A. Lowry, 12 January 1895, Robert E. Cunningham OSU History Material Collection, Special Collections, Edmon Low Library; *Stillwater NewsPress,* 10 February 1988, p. 12B.

17. Oklahoma Territorial Legislature, *Session Laws of 1895 Passed at the Third Regular Session of the Legislative Assembly of the Territory of Oklahoma* (No place: no publisher, 1895), pp. 271-272; Oklahoma Territorial Council, pp. 662-665.

18. Oklahoma Territorial Council, p. 665.

19. James C. Neal to Robert A. Lowry, 16 January 1895, 31 January 1895, 11 February 1895, 15 February 1895, Robert E. Cunningham OSU History Material Collection; *Oklahoma State Sentinel,* 14 February 1895, p. 1; Perkins *Payne County Democrat,* 15 February 1895, p. 1; *Stillwater Messenger,* 15 February 1895, p. 2; *Perkins Journal,* 14 March 1895, p. 1; Oklahoma Territorial Council, p. 431; Stillwater *Daily Democrat,* 27 August 1904, p. 1; Oklahoma Territorial House of Representatives, *Journal of the House Proceedings of the Third Legislative Assembly of the Territory of Oklahoma, Beginning January 8, 1895, Ending March 8, 1895* (Guthrie, OK: Daily Leader Press, 1895), pp. 638-639, 644.

20. *Oklahoma State Sentinel,* 14 February 1895, p. 1.

21. Charles W. McGraw to Robert A. Lowry, 24 February 1895, Robert E. Cunningham OSU History Material Collection.

22. *Eagle-Gazette,* 10 January 1895, p. 1; *Stillwater Gazette,* 7 March 1895, p. 2, 11 April 1895, p. 1.

23. *Oklahoma State Sentinel,* 11 April 1895, p. 1.

24. *Stillwater NewsPress,* 18 March 1963, p. 3; Oklahoma Territorial House of Representatives, p. iv; Nudie E. Williams, "Cassius McDonald Barnes, Governor of Oklahoma Territory, 1897-1901," in LeRoy H. Fischer, editor, *Oklahoma's Governors, 1890-1907: Territorial Years* (Oklahoma City, OK: Oklahoma Historical Society, 1975), pp. 66, 71; Rulon, p. 64; F. C. Hunt to Robert A. Lowry, 6 March 1895, Robert E. Cunningham OSU History Material Collection.

25. Petition, 27 August 1895, *Willis and Bradford versus Oklahoma Agricultural and Mechanical College,* Case Number 489, Payne County Court Clerk's Office, Payne County Courthouse, Stillwater, Oklahoma.

26. Petition, 27 August 1895, Motion for a Continuance, 3 December 1895, *Willis and Bradford versus Oklahoma Agricultural and Mechanical College.*

27. Motion for a Continuance, 3 December 1895, *Willis and Bradford versus Oklahoma Agricultural and Mechanical College.*

28. Robert A. Lowry Affidavit, 30 April 1896, Journal Entry, 30 April 1896, *Willis and Bradford versus Oklahoma Agricultural and Mechanical College*; Berlin B. Chapman, "Old Central of Oklahoma State University," *Chronicles of Oklahoma,* vol. 42, no. 3 (Autumn 1964), p. 277; "A Trip Down Memory Lane," *Oklahoma A. and M. College Magazine,* vol. 24, no. 4 (December 1952), p. 21.

29. Motion for New Trial, undated, *Willis and Bradford versus Oklahoma Agricultural and Mechanical College*; John H. Burford, compiler, *Reports of the Cases Argued and Determined in the Supreme Court of the Territory of Oklahoma,* vol. 6 (Muskogee, OK: Muskogee Printing Company, 1898), pp. 593, 602; Kenneth L. Davidson to LeRoy H. Fischer, 8 February 1986, Old Central Centennial History Collection.

30. Burford, compiler, pp. 593-602; Kenneth L. Davidson to LeRoy H. Fischer, 8 February 1986, Old Central Centennial History Collection; Stillwater *Oklahoma State,* 23 February 1898, p. 4.

31. Burford, compiler, pp. 600-601.

32. Burford, compiler, p. 601.

33. Kenneth L. Davidson to LeRoy H. Fischer, 8 February 1986, Old Central Centennial History Collection; Howard Parker, compiler, *Oklahoma Reports: Cases Determined in the Supreme Court of the State of Oklahoma, May 13-November 9, 1909,* vol. 24 (Guthrie, OK: State Capital Printing Company, 1910), pp. 850-862; *Oklahoma Decisions: Cases Decided in the Supreme Court, Court of Criminal Appeals, and Court on the Judiciary,* vol. 638 (St. Paul, MN: West Publishing Company, 1982), pp. 464-469.

5 Growth Pressures

Following the crisis of 1894-1895, Old Central continued to play a primary role in the development of the Oklahoma A. and M. College. The building still housed the president's office but soon witnessed the removal of most of its first departmental occupants to new permanent structures nearby. The vacant space then became the birthplace or developmental location of still other primary collegiate units until they also moved to buildings designed for their needs. While some instructional functions continued in Old Central without change for years, the usual usage patterns of the early period was removal to new buildings during this era of dynamic growth.

Edmond D. Murdaugh, the new president who came to office in Old Central in January 1895, lacked interest in agriculture and had little experience in higher education. A Virginia aristocrat by ancestry, he had served for eighteen years as the superintendent of a vocational school in Eaton, Maryland. Like the regents of the Oklahoma A. and M. College, he was a President Grover Cleveland Democrat. Strikingly handsome and articulate, President Murdaugh won wide acceptance at first, but six months later he lost his job because of alleged immoral conduct. Rumors concerning Murdaugh were soon accepted as fact. Two months before his dismissal, John Clark, the president of the Democratic board of regents, had invited him on a camping trip. The group took a large supply of liquor to their overnight location on Stillwater Creek. After some of the campers became intoxicated, someone sheared Murdaugh's hair in an irregular pattern, leaving much evidence that no barber had done it. Another allegation had Murdaugh intoxicated in a neighboring city and at a later date in Stillwater sending out for liquor from his residence. In addition, on the evening of his discharge from the presidency, he appeared drunk on the streets of Stillwater, in saloons, and at his residence.[1]

Murdaugh had some redemptive qualities, however. His administration established a college press bureau in Old Central under the direction of Freeman E. Miller, professor of English. Miller wrote both press releases and magazine articles. Murdaugh likely created this office to counteract the adverse college publicity resulting from the legislative investigation of 1895. The press bureau became a permanent feature of the college.[2]

In addition, Murdaugh went on to a somewhat distinguished administrative career in higher education. He immediately became president of the Oklahoma Normal School in Edmond, which boasted the largest collegiate enrollment in the territory. He later organized the Northwestern Oklahoma Normal School at Alva and then served as its president. Next, Murdaugh returned to Maryland to organize the Frostburg Normal School and served as its president. He apparently liked Oklahoma. He returned to accept the presidency of the Southwestern Oklahoma State College at Weatherford and then concluded his academic career by working as a professor of psychology at the Central Oklahoma State College in Edmond. Thus Murdaugh played an important role in shaping the character of the regional territorial and state teachers' colleges of Oklahoma. He has even been described as the father of this system.[3]

Murdaugh must have realized that his vocational education interests did not comply with the agricultural emphasis at the Oklahoma A. and

Edmond D. Murdaugh lasted nearly six months as president of the college in 1895. He lacked interest in agriculture and had little experience in higher education. He lost his job, however, because of alleged drunkenness.

M. College, so he did not protest his release from the presidency. At that point the board of regents authorized its next president, S. H. Kelsey, a Republican, to locate a new executive for the institution. He found a firm apostle for the agricultural mission of the college in George E. Morrow of the land-grant University of Illinois. At nearly fifty-five years of age, Morrow had served agriculture with considerable worthiness in several capacities. Although he graduated from the University of Michigan in 1865 with a law degree, he had but limited formal education in agriculture. He decided, nevertheless, to work as an agricultural journalist with the intention of popularizing agriculture. He became one of the nation's leading authorities on agriculture as a writer with the *Western Rural* and as co-publisher of the *Western Farmer*, both newspapers.[4]

When the *Western Farmer* failed during the economic depression years of the 1870s, Morrow accepted a teaching appointment with the land-grant Iowa State Agricultural College at Ames in 1876. Although warmly welcomed, he stayed less than a year and took a position with the University of Illinois. There he served for eighteen years and developed an international reputation in agriculture. His engaging personality, broad knowledge, literary fluency, research, and writing brought rapid professional promotion and several administrative posts. Disappointment set in as students became more interested in engineering than in agricultural education. He traveled across the state to recruit students for his agricultural classes when enrollment dipped dangerously low. Despite his efforts, he could not turn back the trend toward urbanization and industrialization in Illinois. When the offer for the presidency at the Oklahoma A. and M. College reached him, he accepted at once. He had high hopes that in Stillwater he could develop an outstanding program in agriculture during the formative years of Oklahoma.[5]

President Morrow evangelized for the preservation of rural life. Morrow, as also had President Alvord, served as the president of the Association of American Agricultural Colleges and Experiment Stations. Morrow believed agriculture was the basic industry of the world and that land-grant colleges should make agriculture more popular and profitable, thereby slowing the urbanization trend. As Morrow settled down in his office in Old Central, he expanded on this theme. He emphasized that Morrill institutions should take on only limited tasks and not serve the purposes of general education. All collegiate education, he said, could be divided into three groups: general, professional, and industrial. As a result, the Oklahoma A. and M. College needed to be classified as an industrial institution concerned primarily with the science of food production.[6] The college, he emphasized, must "join the trained mind and the trained hand together for the conquering of the world, for the subjugation of the hostile forces of nature. This special purpose . . . may well be termed the highest."[7]

The new president, as had his predecessors, worked closely with the Agricultural Experiment Station. He thought the station could make the college different by providing the information and skills for classroom instruction. The station, he said, should also promote research as well as serve as a model farm and a technical institute. In the final analysis, research would set the college apart from classical collegiate institutions.[8]

President Morrow spent most of his first year at the Oklahoma A. and M. College publicizing the institution throughout the territory. He desired to counteract the undesirable publicity given the college during the Alvord administration, the legislative investigation, and the release of Murdaugh. During his travels in Oklahoma he visited prospective students and delivered speeches to farmers. The extent of these activities becomes evident when reviewing his schedule for a month soon after he occupied the president's office in Old Central. He lectured in Oklahoma City, spoke at the college, and talked at public school teachers' meetings in El Reno, Oklahoma City, Perry, and Pond Creek. In addition, he attended horticultural and agricultural assemblies in Oklahoma City and Guthrie.[9]

Meanwhile, President Morrow brought his wife and two daughters to Stillwater, built a house, and continued to identify himself with the people of the territory, unlike any president who preceded him. He told the citizens of Stillwater that he would enhance the usefulness of the college to the community and promised a warm welcome when visitors attended programs on the campus. With his wife, he soon attended farmers' meetings at Guthrie, Oklahoma City, and El Reno. During his four years as president, he accepted most invitations to speak or visit with the public, often in the company of his wife. In addition, he encouraged his faculty to travel throughout the territory to serve its people. Soon these informal talks and lectures led to programmed extension courses held in makeshift instructional locations around the territory, such as in nearby Shawnee, Perkins, Hennessey, and Perry. With this procedure, Morrow initiated extension work at the Oklahoma A. and M. College.[10]

President Morrow decided to expand the services of the college even more, and to accomplish this the faculty needed to be enlarged. Fortunately, during his entire administration he had chairmen of the board of regents from Stillwater. They were Robert A. Lowry and Frank J. Wikoff, and both were familiar with his notable work at other land-grant institutions. The two worked closely and sympathetically with Morrow to improve the college. Lowry, a lawyer, knew the president when he taught at the Iowa State Agricultural College. Then in 1898, Wikoff, a lawyer turned banker, succeeded Lowry, who went off to the Spanish-American War. Wikoff had become acquainted with Morrow at the

George E. Morrow (*left*) served as president of the college for a four-year period from 1895 to 1899 and emerged as a firm and effective apostle of the agricultural mission of the college. Frank J. Wikoff (*right*), a Stillwater banker, became chairman of the board of regents of the college and worked vigorously with Morrow to fund the construction of the first permanent buildings to supplement Old Central.

University of Illinois. Both of these Stillwater leaders respected the president highly and worked closely with him to secure able young scholars who believed in the teaching, research, and extension mission of the Oklahoma land-grant college. New professors came mainly from other land-grant college campuses, such as Ohio State University, Pennsylvania State College, Iowa State Agricultural College, and Cornell University. Most of these faculty members remained for some years, and Lowery L. Lewis, a much loved and respected professor of veterinary medicine, stayed until his death in the 1920s.[11]

During the period when Morrow occupied the president's office in Old Central, he squarely faced the troublesome problem of increasing territorial funding on a dependable basis for general operations, but especially for building construction. Most all federal money by law went to the Agricultural Experiment Station, and much of it could not be utilized because of inadequate territorial money for buildings and general purposes. Because of this situation, the administration began an intensive effort to increase territorial appropriations.[12]

Other assistance came from the national government. Congress in 1893 had authorized the executive branch of the federal government to reserve for leasing sections thirteen and thirty-three, known as school land, in each township of the Oklahoma Panhandle. The proceeds were to go to the Oklahoma Legislative Assembly for the improvement of the general welfare, including higher education. In 1897 the fund had provided $5,500 for the Oklahoma A. and M. College, but by 1899 only $900 had come from this undependable and inadequate source. Simultaneously Morrow and the board of regents brought vigorous pressure on territorial officials for building funds.[13]

President Henry E. Alvord had asked the legislative assembly for increased funding for building purposes and general uses, but it had not been forthcoming. President Morrow and the board of regents in their reports to territorial officials in 1896 and 1897 made requests for additional funding, again without success. Finally, in May 1898, the regents let a contract to erect an engineering building backed by $3,500 in Oklahoma Panhandle school land lease funds. The structure, 80 by 86 feet, was made of native sandstone and had two stories, with a one story annex for a boiler and engine room. At the same time, the regents equipped it with a boiler and engine as well as complete iron and woodworking machinery of the most advanced design at a cost of about $7,000. By this procedure, short of legislative funding, the board of regents complied with the basic law establishing the institution and added a new department to the college.[14]

Morrow and Wikoff continued to press for building funds in the

Students about 1896 promenade in front of Old Central on the boardwalk connecting the building with the western town limits of Stillwater. Student pranksters sometimes removed sections of the boardwalk.

report of the college submitted to Governor Cassius M. Barnes for 1897 and 1898. They explained first of all how federal legislation for land-grant colleges required the territories and states to provide funds for the construction of buildings to house this type of institution. "It is thus clear," they pointed out, "that the erection of buildings for the proper utilization of the moneys appropriated by Congress for instruction and investigation devolves upon the Territory." Their reasoning continued: "The opinion that this institution is well provided with [building] funds rests on a false assumption." This could be proven, they said, by drawing comparisons with the incomes for buildings of agricultural colleges in the states and territories west of the Mississippi River. The Oklahoma A. and M. College had the lowest totals, with its buildings valued at only $20,000, as compared with the average of $72,500. Even New Mexico Territory had land-grant collegiate buildings worth $32,500. "Oklahoma, the prosperous, home of the generous leads at the wrong end, the little end," the plea continued, "a position to which this great Territory is not accustomed."[15]

Morrow and Wikoff also pointed out that the "character of instruction" envisioned in the federal law establishing land-grant colleges "demands space and facilities unheard of in the days of classical education." Providing this instruction, they said "requires . . . expensive apparatus; alert and active instructors; strong, energetic students—*and room in which to work.* The college now possesses the first three—the last is wanting and the Territory must provide it." Finally, they used statistics of the United States Department of Agriculture to prove that attendance at the Oklahoma A. and M. College was "larger in proportion to money invested in buildings, than that at any similar institution in the west, twice as large as in Kansas, six times as large as in Texas."[16]

Morrow and Wikoff then turned to specific building needs by explaining that the work of the college "is carried on at present principally in one brick building [Old Central] that is overcrowded and unsuited for much of the work which must be done in it. The Chemical Laboratory, where a large amount of practical work involving the production of noxious fumes is done, is located in the basement. Great inconvenience to other departments is caused by this, and the risk of fire and cost of insurance is increased by the presence of explosive and inflammable chemicals in the College building." In addition, the college library of nearly 5,000 volumes "is located in a room directly over the laboratory and the reading room in connection therewith is small and continually crowded and is unfitted for the convenience of those who must use it." Finally the assembly hall in Old Central "does not . . . comfortably seat the students at present in attendance and on occasions when a special program is presented, the space is totally inadequate to the numbers who wish to attend."[17]

Specific requests for construction money followed. First, a building designed to house chemical laboratories for the college and the Agricultural Experiment Station was needed at a cost of $10,000. Second, a multi-purpose structure planned to house the library and reading room should be built. Also in it would be an assembly hall adequate to "comfortably seat the increasing number of students"; two laboratories and lecture rooms for veterinary science, zoology, botany, and entomology; space for a domestic science program to be instituted as soon as accommodations became available; and room for the commercial course already underway, at a total cost of $35,000 for the building. Third, a central heating plant intended to serve all buildings on the campus should be constructed, "thus economizing greatly in the item of fuel which is at present one of our most troublesome questions." This structure had a listed estimate of $5,000. "These are the needs," Morrow and Wikoff emphasized in their appeal for space, "that are at present imperative. Unless we are provided with a sufficient appropriation to enable us to obtain this room, growth of the institution must stop. It is earnestly hoped that the Legislature will in some way provide the funds necessary for the construction of these buildings."[18]

In response to the urgent and impelling plea of Morrow and Wikoff for $50,000 in construction funds, the 1899 Oklahoma Legislative Assembly appropriated only $20,000 for the purpose. This proved to be enough funding, when added to available miscellaneous monies, to construct two substantial structures. The Chemistry Building, designed by Carlos C. Cooke, an architect and contractor from Shawnee, cost $10,009. When completed in early 1900, it contained separate laboratories for the college and Agricultural Experiment Station as well as lecture rooms and the offices of the Agricultural Experiment Station. The Library Building, designed by Joseph P. Foucart of Guthrie, cost $19,910 and reached completion near the close of 1900. Foucart had planned many unusual and attractive structures in Guthrie and elsewhere in Oklahoma Territory. The Library Building, in addition to books and periodicals, contained a reading room, lecture rooms, and biological science laboratories and museums. When the college library moved from Old Central to its new quarters, it had 6,000 volumes; with the increased space, 4,000 additional titles were ordered at once. In 1899 Morrow and Wikoff also convinced the legislative assembly to provide annual tax money for the first time in the amount of one-tenth of a mill with a dollar amount unspecified for the general operating budget expenses of the college, such as the University of Oklahoma and the Oklahoma Normal School regularly received.[19]

The plea of Morrow and Wikoff for an assembly hall of adequate size in the Library Building and a central heating plant for the college probably went unheeded by the 1899 legislative assembly because of an event

Before President George E. Morrow resigned in 1899, his administration funded three major structures near Old Central. They were (*left to right*) the Chemistry Building, the Engineering Building and Annex located northwest of Old Central, and the Library Building.

in 1897. For the first time in the history of higher education in Oklahoma Territory, the legislative assembly faced the question of racial segregation for blacks and whites. By 1895 blacks had already begun applying for admission to Oklahoma colleges, as noted by the campus newspaper in Stillwater: "The colored people have demanded entrance to the Normal school at Edmond, and special facilities will be prepared for them under the control and instruction of their own teachers. This disturbing question has not yet arisen here, but it is coming up for solution soon."[20]

This situation demanded President Morrow's close attention as soon as he occupied his office in Old Central. One or more blacks had already sought admission to the Oklahoma A. and M. College, but had been rejected. The answer came not only for the college but for all the territorial supported institutions of higher education in Oklahoma when the 1897 legislative assembly established the Colored Oklahoma Agricultural and Normal University, later the Langston University. The school was located at Langston, an all-black settlement in Logan County only twenty-two miles southwest of Stillwater. Like the Oklahoma A. and M. College, it was a land-grant institution. The founding law provided merely $5,000 for the erection of one wing of a building for the Langston school, but in 1899 the legislative assembly took $15,000 of federal money from the Oklahoma A. and M. College and appropriated it for the Colored Oklahoma Agricultural and Normal University. In addition, the 1899 assembly appropriated one-tenth of all future federal operating money coming to the Oklahoma A. and M. College for the Langston institution and also allocated $10,000 for building purposes.[21]

The Second Morrill Act of 1890 had authorized states and territories to establish "separate but equal" colleges for blacks. This procedure permitted the Oklahoma Legislative Assembly to appease blacks, to preserve white supremacy, and to establish a new university by using a fractional amount of the federal funds of another land-grant institution within its political jurisdiction. The division of the Washington endowment money, however, hurt both land-grant schools.

President Morrow requested that the legislative assembly fairly distribute federal funds between the two land-grant colleges on the "relative proportion of white and colored school population" in the territory, but his plea did not alleviate the situation. The available federal funds simply could not meet the needs of both schools. Of the sixty-four Morrill institutions in the United States in 1898, fourteen served only blacks. President Morrow's dismay must have increased when he read at the time in statistical tables and charts that the Oklahoma A. and M. College ranked at or near the bottom in all measured categories, even below many of the all-black colleges in the South. He did not live to see the Oklahoma A. and M. College recover from the blow, and the Langston institution remained underfinanced and unaccredited until the 1950s.[22]

Two major course additions occurred during President Morrow's tenure. When the board of regents met in April 1898, they authorized planning for a mechanical engineering department. Morrow also arranged to include work in civil and electrical engineering. The building erected in 1898 to house the department contained space enough to begin basic

During the administration of President George E. Morrow, the students of the college turned out to be photographed on the northwest side of Old Central.

course instruction and shop work in the three areas. The regents also authorized a commercial department offering courses in stenography, typewriting, and bookkeeping at its meeting in April 1898. The commercial department was housed in a small basement room on the west side of Old Central. Its only equipment in the beginning consisted of one typewriter for the use of the eight students enrolled. Instruction in both engineering and commercial courses began in September 1898.[23]

President Morrow's health broke under the pressures of office, and four years after he reached Stillwater he resigned his position and introduced his successor to the student body in the assembly hall of Old Central in June 1899. During his tenure the enrollment moved from 155 to 366, an increase of 136 percent. He retired at Paxton, Illinois, near the University of Illinois, where he had served for nearly two decades. Less than a year later he died.[24]

Morrow fortunately experienced administrative harmony from the White House down through his own governing board of regents during his four years as president of the college. The Republican Party had complete administrative control at all levels. In this favorable environment, he constructed the first building for engineering and organized its curriculum, the beginning of the College of Engineering. In addition, he instituted a commercial course of study in Old Central, a development that led to the College of Business Administration. During his administration he established the pattern of specific legislative appropriations for building purposes at periodic intervals and launched the institution's extensive building program. He also led the effort to convince the legislature to make annual operating appropriations for the college.

Morrow's work as president brought stability and respect to the Oklahoma A. and M. College. He firmly planted the institution in the lives of innumerable Oklahomans, and won their admiration as he worked with them. He inaugurated a new breadth of purpose at the college by developing training in engineering, business, and extension. His outreach to students, farmers, and others in his home community and throughout the territory gave new vigor to the college and opened the way for dynamic development in the years ahead.

Endnotes

1. *Stillwater Gazette*, 18 July 1895, p. 1; Frank J. Wikoff to Thomas J. Hartman, 30 November 1940, History File, Berlin B. Chapman Collection, Special Collections, Edmon Low Library, Oklahoma State University, Stillwater, Oklahoma; Harry E. Thompson, "The Territorial Presidents of Oklahoma A. and M. College," *Chronicles of Oklahoma*, vol. 32, no. 4 (Winter 1954-1955), pp. 365-366; *Stillwater NewsPress*, 15 April 1963, p. 3.

2. Oklahoma Agricultural and Mechanical College Faculty, "Minutes of the First Faculty, March 17, 1892, to June 2, 1899," unpublished typed manuscript in two volumes, vol. 1, 11 March 1895, p. 202, Special Collections, Edmon Low Library; [Freeman E.] Miller, "Stillwater and Payne County," *Oklahoma Magazine,* vol. 3, no. 5 (May 1895), pp. 307-308; [Freeman E. Miller], "The Oklahoma Agricultural and Mechanical College," *Oklahoma Magazine,* vol. 3, no. 5 (May 1895), pp. 292-306.

3. Philip Reed Rulon, *Oklahoma State University—Since 1890* (Stillwater: Oklahoma State University Press, 1975), pp. 67, 71.

4. Rulon, pp. 71-72.

5. Rulon, pp. 72-73.

6. Rulon, pp. 73-74; *Oklahoma A. and M. College Mirror,* 16 September 1895, pp. 6-7.

7. *Oklahoma A. and M. College Mirror,* 16 September 1895, p. 7.

8. Rulon, p. 74.

9. *Stillwater Gazette,* 22 August 1895, p. 3, 26 September 1895, p. 2; *Oklahoma A. and M. College Mirror,* 16 September 1895, p. 12.

10. *Stillwater Gazette,* 17 October 1895, p. 3, 12 December 1895, p. 3, 15 July 1897, p. 3, 24 November 1898, p. 1; Thompson, p. 366.

11. Frank J. Wikoff to Thomas J. Hartman, 30 November 1940, History File, Berlin B. Chapman Collection; *Oklahoma A. and M. College Mirror,* 16 March 1896, p. 5, 15 June 1896, p. 7; *Stillwater Democrat,* 2 September 1898, pp. 1, 5, 8; Oklahoma A. and M. *College Paper,* 1 October 1899, pp. 53-55; *Stillwater Gazette,* 9 June 1898, pp. 2-3.

12. Rulon, p. 76.

13. Rulon, pp. 76-77.

14. Oklahoma Territorial Council, *Journal of the Council Proceedings of the Fourth Legislative Assembly of the Territory of Oklahoma, Beginning January 12, 1897, Ending March 12, 1897* (Guthrie, OK: Daily Leader Press, 1897), pp. 206-207; *Oklahoma Educational Institutions: Biennial Reports of the Board of Regents, Clerk and Treasurer of the Territorial Agricultural and Mechanical College, 1897-1898* (Guthrie, OK: State Capital Printing Company, 1899), p. 42.

15. *Oklahoma Educational Institutions,* pp. 38-40.

16. *Oklahoma Educational Institutions,* pp. 40-41.

17. *Oklahoma Educational Institutions,* pp. 41-42.

18. *Oklahoma Educational Institutions,* p. 42.

19. Oklahoma Territorial Legislature, *Session Laws of 1899 Passed at the Fifth Regular Session of the Legislative Assembly of the Territory of Oklahoma* (Guthrie, OK: State Capital Printing Company, 1899), pp. 67, 221; Oklahoma City *Daily Oklahoman,* 15 April 1899, p. 2, 9 June 1899, p. 1; *College Paper,* 1 May 1900, p. 20; *Annual Catalog, Oklahoma A. and M. College, 1899-1900,* pp. 8-9.

20. *Oklahoma A. and M. College Mirror,* 15 May 1895, p. 4.

21. *Stillwater NewsPress,* 21 April 1978, p. 15, 18 September 1985, p. 1B; Oklahoma Territorial Legislature, *Session Laws of 1897 Passed at the Fourth Regular Session of the Legislative Assembly of the Territory of Oklahoma* (Guthrie, OK: Leader Company, 1897), pp. 37-41; Oklahoma Territorial Legislature, *Session Laws of 1899,* pp. 67-68.

22. *Oklahoma Educational Institutions,* p. 43; United States Department of Agriculture, Office of Experiment Stations, *Bulletin No. 51: Statistics of the Land-Grant Colleges and Agricultural Experiment Stations in the United States for the Year Ending June 30, 1897* (Washington, DC: Government Printing Office, 1898), pp. 10-27.

23. Stillwater *Daily Oklahoma State,* 15 April 1898, p. 1, 21 April 1898, p. 8; Oklahoma A. and M. College *New Education,* 15 June 1910, p. 1; Oklahoma A. and M. College *Orange and Black,* 17 May 1919, p. 4; Oklahoma A. and M. College *Daily O'Collegian,* 24 March 1938, p. 4; *1910 Redskin,* p. 61, Oklahoma A. and M. College Yearbook.

24. *College Paper,* 15 June 1899, p. 40, 1 April 1900, pp. 2-3; Fall Semester Enrollments, Registrar's Office, Oklahoma State University.

6 Breakout Procedures

Angelo C. Scott, a man of unique and extraordinary ability, followed George E. Morrow as president of the Oklahoma A. and M. College. A year and a half earlier, in January 1898, Scott had taken charge of English language and literature at the college, succeeding Freeman E. Miller, a Democrat. Only a week before his appointment, Scott had delivered a well-received lecture in the assembly hall of Old Central, and this probably had some influence on his appointment. In addition to being highly qualified for the position, he had the same Republican Party affiliation as Governor Cassius M. Barnes and President William McKinley, who controlled political appointments in Oklahoma Territory.[1]

With Morrow's declining health, and Scott's political persuasion, the suggestion was made that he would be in line for the presidency of the college "at a later day." Scott explained: "I had been very active in Republican party affairs up to the time of my appointment to the faculty. I had spoken extensively in every local and congressional campaign. I had been a member of the Territorial senate. At the time of my entering the faculty I was President of the Territorial Republican Club, but I immediately resigned that position and from that time on completely ignored politics in the College and out of it."[2]

The son of a physician, Scott grew up in Kansas and completed the bachelor of arts and the master of arts degrees at the University of Kansas. After teaching in public high schools for three years, he completed two law degrees at the George Washington University in Washington, D.C. He then practiced law in Iola, Kansas. With the opening of the Unassigned Lands of Oklahoma in 1889, he settled in Oklahoma City, established a law office, built and operated a hotel named the Angelo, and

Angelo C. Scott served as
president of the college from
1899 to 1908. In addition to
being well qualified for the
position, as a leading Republican
he had the political support of
the territorial governors of Oklahoma and the presidents of the
United States, also all
Republicans, during his entire
administration. Scott was the last
president of the college to be
housed in Old Central.

with his brother, Winfield W. Scott, founded Oklahoma City's first newspaper, the *Oklahoma Journal*. As a civic and cultural leader, he was chosen to preside as chairman of the initial town meeting and served on
the townsite board. He helped found the Oklahoma City Chamber of
Commerce and the Oklahoma City Young Men's Christian Association.
In 1892 he barely missed being appointed governor of the territory by
President Benjamin Harrison. In 1893 he organized the Oklahoma exhibit
at the World's Columbian Exposition in Chicago.[3]

Unlike many of his administrative counterparts in land-grant colleges, Scott was not an agriculturalist. Although he believed in the special agricultural and mechanical emphasis of the Oklahoma A. and M.
College, he planned to broaden its scope and shape all education for
the practical welfare of the general public. Scott, like Morrow, found
it difficult to persuade students to enroll in agricultural courses, and
often parents desired their children to follow other pursuits. The older
agricultural generations considered farming hard work and at times
unprofitable. Scott thought the liberal arts as well as the sciences would
widen the reach of the college and increase its opportunity to serve
through an enlarged student body and broader public support. Scott
desired to see the name of the institution changed to the Oklahoma State
College, thus extending its appeal and widening its acceptance. He
dreamed of developing a multipurpose and comprehensive state university, and he diligently worked to bring about popular support for the

institution. He also labored to develop a campus and territorial environ-ment where cultural and intellectual activity would flourish.[4]

In addition to the talents, training, and experience Scott brought to his office in Old Central, he had the support of his brother and his father. His brother, Charles F. Scott, a Republican and a Kansas newspaper pub-lisher, served as a member of the United States House of Representa-tives from 1901 to 1911. His father, Dr. John W. Scott, also a Republican, held a seat in the Oklahoma House of Representatives, where he worked for the interest of the land-grant college in Stillwater. President Scott also had the political support of the territorial governors of Oklahoma and the presidents of the United States, all Republicans, during his administration.

Scott's board of regents, likewise Republicans, provided conscien-tious support during his years as president. The chairman of the board, Frank J. Wikoff of Stillwater, served throughout his administration. Wikoff had attended the University of Illinois, a land-grant institution, and then completed a law degree at the University of Cincinnati. He con-tributed sympathetic continuity, practical fiscal knowledge, and astute political guidance. John Fields, the new director of the Agricultural Experiment Station, had graduated from the Pennsylvania State College

President Angelo C. Scott had the active political support of his brother and his father. Charles F. Scott (*left*), a Kansas Republican newspaper publisher, worked for the interests of the col-lege as a member of the United States House of Representatives from 1901 to 1911. His father, Dr. John W. Scott (*right*), also a Republican, held a seat in the Oklahoma House of Representa-tives, where he also promoted the concerns of the college.

and was well known as the co-discoverer of tuberculosis in cattle. Scott, Fields, and Wikoff worked as a team, "a sort of sub-board of regents," said Scott, taking charge of the college between meetings of the regents.[5]

The three men cooperated to expand and strengthen the faculty with young scholars, and the board of regents agreed. Walter R. Shaw came from Stanford University, and Edwin M. Wilcox hailed from Harvard University. Both held doctorates from these institutions. Other new faculty moved from graduate degrees at Johns Hopkins University, University of Maryland, University of Wisconsin, and University of Chicago. These teachers, when added to the professors employed earlier by President George E. Morrow, made up a faculty unexcelled by any land-grant college in the surrounding territories and states. New standards of academic achievement promptly resulted.[6]

Soon after Scott took over the president's office in Old Central, a railroad finally came to Stillwater. Since its founding in 1889, the town had been isolated, a fact causing Stillwater to be described as an "inland" community. Most merchandise, building material, and people had to be transported from the Atchison, Topeka, and Santa Fe Railroad at Mulhall, or from Orlando or Perry, each located about twenty or more miles distant. Although Stillwater had precariously retained the college for a decade, determined leaders of the community and the college had worked valiantly, however, for rail transportation. Finally the dream came true when the Eastern Oklahoma Railroad, a subsidiary of the Atchison, Topeka, and Santa Fe Railroad, agreed to bend a proposed track from Ripley to Esau Junction, near Pawnee, to connect Stillwater. This was a 40.4 mile length of track, begun in 1899.[7]

When work began on the bridge of the new railroad across the Cimarron River at Ripley in March of 1900, the *Payne County Populist* predicted: "In thirty days . . . we may expect to see the iron horse of the Santa Fe make its first appearance in Stillwater."[8] Three weeks later the same newspaper reported: "The construction train is now within five miles of the city, and . . . in ten or twelve days the road will be completed into Stillwater."[9] In a week this article followed: "Last Saturday night the track layers reached Boomer creek and early Sunday morning the pile driver began driving piles for the bridge. Early as the hour was, 300 or more men, women and children were there to watch the proceedings. As the day progressed everybody in the city walked or drove out to watch the work." The excitement continued: "By Monday morning the bridge was built and track laying was in progress towards the city. At 1:30 P.M. the track was laid to Tenth Avenue and by 6 o'clock P.M. the track was laid through the corporate limits of the city headed towards Pawnee."[10]

As soon as the railroad began operating through Stillwater, college officials arranged for a special train to take students and townspeople on May 4, 1900, to the territorial oratorical contest and intercollegiate athletic meeting at Guthrie. The railroad agreed to sell a round trip ticket for a one-way fare provided two hundred people subscribed.[11] The excursion train, with five coaches and three hundred persons, left Stillwater at 8:30 A.M. on the day of the meet and reached Guthrie at 11:00 A.M. "The ride down the beautiful Stillwater valley was most enjoyable," wrote a student, "and many for the first time realized the beauties of the country in which we live." Upon arriving, the Stillwater delegation and its band marched up Oklahoma Avenue in a column of four to the Royal Hotel, where the band played several selections and the students cheered. Following the competitions and festivities of the day, the excursion train left for Stillwater at 1:00 A.M. the next morning and reached there at 4:00 A.M. A student later called the travelers "a sleepy, tired, good-natured, happy crowd that got a part of what it went after and had no kick coming at all, at all."[12]

With the coming of the railroad, Stillwater and its college changed drastically. The school's first football team went on the road, and the Agricultural Experiment Station began to send its specialists and demonstration equipment to farmers throughout the territory. More than ever, with modern transportation available, the college established itself as a fundamental educational institution of the territory, quieting complaints that the school was local in its impact and therefore a waste of money. Much less was said thereafter in the legislature about moving

WESTERN HISTORY COLLECTIONS, OU LIBRARY

These men connected Stillwater with the rest of the nation in 1900 soon after Angelo C. Scott became president of the college. The coming of the railroad ended the delay in providing modern transportation that hindered the growth of the isolated college and town for a decade.

the college to a more accessible location. Enrollment at the college increased dramatically during the Scott administration, moving from 366 to 856, a growth of 134 percent. With an increasing population, the town took on an entirely new image. Adequate transportation combined with increasing numbers of people made it financially feasible for Louis J. Jardot to build and operate an opera house on East Ninth Avenue to provide quality entertainment for the town and the college. Major theatrical productions were lured to Stillwater, making it no longer necessary to travel to Oklahoma City or Kansas City, Missouri, for current stage entertainment.[13]

President Scott faced increasing pressure for additional buildings at the college because of the enlarging enrollment, more faculty members, new curriculum developments, and greater service throughout the territory. The space problem had long prevailed due to the widely held misconception that the institution had federal funding to meet all of its needs, including buildings, although in reality the money from Washington, D.C., could be used almost without exception only for salaries and teaching aids. Scott called for augmented territorial funding from the legislative assembly.

In the 1901 meeting of the legislative assembly, the Payne County delegation consisted of Councilor Freeman E. Miller and Representative James L. Mathews, both of Stillwater. They led the effort to obtain funding for an expansive building program at the college. On January 16, 1901, Miller introduced in the council a bill authorizing the allocation of $46,000 for the construction of buildings and other improvements at the college, to be financed by a special tax levy in 1901 and 1902. Mathews introduced the same bill in the house of representatives on the same day. At this time President Scott and the business leadership of Stillwater arranged for the members of the legislative assembly to visit the campus and the town.[14]

On Friday, February 1, 1901, a day the legislative assembly was not in session, twenty-six of its thirty-nine members visited Stillwater by train from Guthrie. In addition, a number of wives and legislative support personnel accompanied the group. When the train arrived at 3:45 P.M., a large crowd at the station welcomed the visitors as mill whistles blew and church bells rang. Carriages supplied by the townspeople took the delegation to the various parts of Stillwater and then to the college. Under the guidance of President Scott and Director Fields of the Agricultural Experiment Station, the group toured the buildings, including Old Central, and all academic departments. Professors briefly explained the work and teaching aids in each department. Next a tour of the Agricultural Experiment Station took place, including an explanation of the vegetation experiments and the premium-quality livestock. The education committees of the legislative assembly then returned to

The student body of the college assembled in front of Old Central in 1900. President Angelo C. Scott, holding an object in his hands, stands in the front row to the immediate right of Old Central's main entrance. The intricate Victorian ornamentation above and below the roofline of the portico over the basement entrance shows in detail.

the new domestic science department quarters in the basement of Old Central. There the supper meal in the small dining room, prepared and served by students of the department, illustrated in a practical way one aspect of student training at the college. The other legislative guests were treated to supper by the business community at the Youst Hotel downtown.[15]

At 7:30 P.M. the supper guests at the Youst Hotel were driven back to the campus to join the education committees of the legislature in the assembly hall of Old Central. Councilor Miller of Stillwater served as chairman of the program for the evening. Following a reception with the faculty and students, President Scott ably addressed the visiting legislators for forty minutes. He carefully explained the financial affairs of the college, pointed out the use limitations of the various federal funds for buildings, related the unique type of instruction in this and other land-grant colleges, and emphasized the building needs of the institution. He specifically called for a new mechanical engineering building, plus an addition to the Library Building containing an auditorium and space for the botany and entomology department. Like President Morrow, he tellingly used statistics concerning money appropriated for buildings at land-grant colleges located in other states and territories west of the Mississippi River to demonstrate the total inadequacy of similar allocations in Oklahoma Territory. He also emphasized space needs brought about by the doubling of student enrollment in a two-year period.[16]

Scott spoke convincingly about the inadequate assembly hall in Old Central as he appealed for an enlarged facility: "The citizens of Stillwater would have been delighted to be at this meeting tonight in force. But I was obliged to say to the Commercial Club last night that we simply had not the room to take care of them. And I was obliged to say to our students at the chapel exercises today that while I should have been glad to allow them to invite their friends here tonight, I could not do it." His plea continued: "At the last Commencement scores of people told me they could not get a seat. Will you not agree with me, gentlemen, that we should have a commodious, attractive audience room, one that will hold our students and their friends at the same time, one that is not rendered gloomy by a line of blackboards used for recitation purposes?"[17]

Director Fields of the Agricultural Experiment Station then spoke briefly but convincingly of the special needs of agricultural investigation and teaching, with emphasis on space requirements, including new housing for livestock and agricultural equipment. He said in conclusion: "Gentlemen, we ask you to raise the limit, and I am certain that your hurried inspection has shown the need of it. But, if there be any here who doubt, I ask that you remain with us tomorrow, spend the day in the classrooms and in the shops and laboratories, talk with students from the districts which you represent, and determine by personal inquiry the exact situation. I have no fear as to the result."[18] Favorable comments by five members of the legislative assembly followed, including the speaker pro tempore of the house of representatives. After an enthusiastic response by the students, a male quartet sang the college song, and the meeting concluded by the audience singing "America."[19]

The members of the legislative assembly and their wives were then driven to the Youst Hotel, where the women were escorted to their rooms for the night. The men attended a smoker at 10:00 P.M. given by the Commercial Club of the town. The complimentary hors d'oeuvre menu consisted of twenty-three items, including cigars. With Senator Miller of Stillwater again presiding, the storytelling began and continued until 2:00 A.M., when everyone present had been called on to comment at length. No one left the smoke-filled room uninformed about the bright future of the college, Stillwater, and Oklahoma.[20]

On February 19, 1901, the bill to provide $46,000 in construction funds for the Oklahoma A. and M. College passed the council with but one negative vote, and on February 26 it won unanimous approval in the house of representatives.[21] The *Stillwater Gazette* considered the approval by the legislative assembly "a vote of confidence in the college as well as a grant of material aid. The visit of a large portion of the legislature to Stillwater no doubt had much to do with the result, . . . and at the banquet given by the Commercial Club they could not but have been impressed by the unbounded enthusiasm shown for the institution by the business men of Stillwater.''[22] On February 28 both the president of the council and the speaker of the house of representatives signed the bill. Only the signature on the bill of Governor Cassius M. Barnes remained to be obtained, and that seemed a certainty.[23]

Then lightning struck on March 4, 1901, when the council voted 9 to 2 to recall the bill from the governor. Councilor J. F. Todd of Chandler, who originally opposed the bill, explained his viewpoint: ''I think the appropriations carried in this bill excessive and beyond our ability to pay without increasing our rate of taxation to an exorbitant and unnecessary extent . . . I oppose a gigantic treasury raid whenever opportunity affords, and no matter by whom proposed.''[24] Councilor Miller immediately gained the floor and denounced the recall of the bill in an eloquent three and one-half hour speech. He vigorously criticized the members of the council for attempting to punish him and his constituents by recalling the bill from the governor. On March 8, the last day the legislature met, the governor returned the bill with his veto message. He pointed out that within the three previous years over $40,000 had been expended for buildings at the college, and that the bill would add to an already increased tax rate for 1901 and 1902. Moreover, the enrollment of something over three hundred, he said, did not justify additional space. He suggested, however, that the general appropria-

In 1901 John H. Burford, the chief justice of Oklahoma Territory, authorized a writ of mandamus at Councilor Freeman E. Miller's request, resulting in a bonanza of $54,000 for building purposes at the college. Burford agreed with Miller's contention that the five-day limit for Governor Cassius M. Barnes to veto the bill had expired.

tions bill should include an item of $5,000 for a barn to house the blooded livestock at the college.[25]

Fortunately, both Councilor Miller and Representative Mathews served on the general conference committee meeting during the last hours of the 1901 legislative assembly. They followed through on the recommendation of Governor Barnes to place a provision in the comprehensive appropriations bill of the territory for construction money at the college. Instead of the $5,000 Barnes recommended, they asked for $15,000, only to have the amount trimmed down to $8,000 by Republican opposition.[26]

After several days passed, Councilor Miller questioned the legality of the governor's veto of the $46,000 building appropriation bill of the college. He maintained that more than the legally allowable limit of five days had elapsed after the governor received the bill before he vetoed it. Thus the bill, Miller reasoned, had become law without action by the governor. In a friendly lawsuit filed in the district court of Logan County at Guthrie, Miller asked Judge John H. Burford, also serving as chief justice of Oklahoma Territory, for a writ of mandamus. Judge Burford authorized this court order which required William M. Jenkins, the secretary of Oklahoma Territory, to print the $46,000 building appropriation bill as a valid law in the forthcoming volume of Session Laws of 1901 of Oklahoma Territory.[27] This court action was taken with the approval of Oklahoma Attorney General J. C. Strang, and also of Governor Barnes, who telegraphed from Washington, D.C.: "Give the Stillwater college people every possible facility to enable them to test in the courts the question as to whether the bill making their appropriation become a law notwithstanding the veto."[28] When Judge Burford authorized the writ of mandamus, he agreed with Miller's contention that the five-day limit for vetoing the bill had expired, and thus the bill had become law before the governor returned it without his signature. Although political fallout continued to impact the college over the use of this court procedure, the Burford decision remained legally undisputed.[29]

With the $8,000 item in the general appropriations law of 1901, the college received a total bonanza of $54,000 for building purposes. According to the $46,000 appropriation law for the college, 50 percent of the money would be expended for an addition to the Library Building to house an assembly hall and botany and entomology department; 30 percent would be used to construct an engineering building; 10 percent would be utilized to build a smokestack and steam boiler facility to centralize the college heating system; and 10 percent would go to erect a barn for the Agricultural Experiment Station. Any remaining money could be used for repair of existing buildings of the college and for the construction of fences for the Agricultural Experiment Station. The money provided for the construction of the buildings could also be used to purchase and install the needed heating, lighting, and furniture equipment.[30]

Architect Joseph P. Foucart of Guthrie planned the addition to the Library Building. It contained not only an auditorium (later known as the Prairie Playhouse) designed to seat 1,000 people and quarters for the botany and entomology department, but also ample space on the first floor for the domestic science department then located in the basement of Old Central. The brick and sandstone addition cost $17,508. Foucart likewise supplied the plans for the new Engineering Building consisting of two stories and a basement. Built of brick and sandstone, the structure contained testing laboratories, a wash room, a lecture room, office space, a drawing room, and a reading room. The cost of the building came to $10,850. Carlos C. Cooke of Shawnee drew the plans for the barn built of brick with frame gables. It contained a livestock judging room, cattle and horse stalls, a farm office, tool rooms, and ample storage space in the second story. A driveway extended through the barn on the second floor. The cost of this structure with approaches amounted to $5,600. The price of installing heating, lighting, and furniture equipment in the buildings would be extra.[31]

Ample money still remained from the $54,000 appropriated in 1901 by the legislative assembly to carry out additional construction. While the territorial tax levy money drifted in, a smokestack of eighty feet to accommodate five steam boilers went up, as well as a structure to house the boilers, which included a coal bin. This made possible the centralized heating system for the campus, including Old Central, that went into operation in November 1902. A year earlier the college connected with the newly established municipal water plant of the town. This assured ample water for campus use except for the heating plant, plentifully supplied by nearby Willow Lake, a reservoir located immediately west of the present Student Union. At the same time, a septic tank sanitary sewer system went into operation on the campus, although the city did not operate a similar sewer arrangement until 1909. The campus sewer system made it possible to install toilet facilities in the permanent buildings, including Old Central. Other improvements and repairs were also made to existing buildings, such as Old Central. Early in 1903 work commenced on a brick walk system connecting all permanent buildings on the campus with walks leading to the business district of Stillwater. With a residue of the 1901 construction appropriation remaining, and the use of allowable federal funds, the first Dairy Building went up in 1904. It replaced the ''cramped and unsanitary'' quarters in a corner of the College Barn.[32]

Even before the building funds appropriated for the college by the 1901 legislative assembly were fully utilized, pressure mounted on the

The sophomore class of 1900-1901 turned out for this photograph on the northwest steps of Old Central in the spring of 1901. When entering as freshmen, the class consisted of about ninety students, by far the largest up to that time.

campus for a major agricultural building. In 1902, when the domestic science department moved out of the basement of Old Central, the agriculture department moved in and also occupied one room on the first floor. The quarters were cramped and inadequate, President Scott emphasized. He then said that instructional work of the horticulture department still took place in a very small and unsuitable wooden building, a legacy of the emergency arrangements of the early days of the college. The Chemistry Building no longer had room to house the chemical laboratory and office of the Agricultural Experiment Station. Moreover, the growing agricultural short courses, as well as increasing full-time agricultural enrollment, needed special housing. For these circumstances, Scott reasoned, the answer lay in an agricultural building large enough to provide for the agriculture and horticulture departments, the Agricultural Experiment Station work in agriculture, horticulture, and chemistry, and the general administrative offices of the college, including new quarters for the president.[33]

Nothing came of the effort for an agricultural building in the 1903 legislative assembly. This defeat was not due to the lingering resentment in the assembly resulting from the procedure used to obtain a favorable court decision in 1901. Rather, the defeat was directly due to the fact that in 1902 Dennis T. Flynn, the delegate of Oklahoma Territory to Congress, had succeeded in attaching a rider to an appropriations bill of that legislative body prohibiting the erection of additional

In 1902 Dennis T. Flynn, the delegate of Oklahoma Territory to Congress, attached a rider to an appropriations bill which prohibited the erection of additional public buildings in Oklahoma until statehood. This delayed an appropriation for the construction of Morrill Hall at the college. Thus Old Central remained overcrowded.

public buildings in Oklahoma until statehood. The Republicans had promoted this legislation to hold the capital at Guthrie.[34] Undaunted, the *Stillwater Gazette* accurately forecast the future of President Scott's plan for a major agricultural building: "It is intended to ask the next legislature to appropriate one hundred thousand dollars for an agricultural, horticultural and administration building. When this is secured the school will be fully equipped so far as buildings are concerned to accommodate and properly instruct a thousand students."[35]

A notable development for the college, however, occurred in the 1903 legislative assembly when the original appropriation in 1899 for annual general operating budget purposes experienced an increase to $12,000 annually for the years 1903 and 1904. This provided much-needed money for faculty salary purposes in the liberal arts not available from the federal land-grant college endowment funds. This legislative action commenced a pattern of periodic increases in annual general operating budget funds for the college.[36]

Soon after the 1903 legislative assembly opened, the *Stillwater Democrat* in a scathing editorial charged that no Democrats served on the board of regents; the regents dismissed Democratic professors and filled their positions with Republicans; President Scott had campaigned for Republican candidates for local and territorial offices; Republican faculty members had also campaigned for Republican candidates; and Democratic staff employees who dared to announce their party affiliation had been dismissed. The *Stillwater Democrat* demanded that "this debasement . . . should forever cease," and called for a legislative investigation of the college.[37] The *Stillwater Gazette*, of Republican persuasion, said that Freeman E. Miller, a Democrat, had precipitated the attack, and considered it "the most dastardly blow ever struck at the largest institution of our town."[38] Miller had been defeated in his bid for reelection to the territorial council in 1902. Although President Scott vigorously refuted each of the charges, some political damage had been done, even though no legislative investigation of the college resulted.[39]

By 1905 the political situation in Oklahoma Territory appeared less menacing for the construction of a major agricultural building at the college than it had two years before when the legislative assembly last met. Although greater numbers of people in the territory were becoming Democrats, the Republicans steadfastly retained administrative control of the territory's institutions through President Theodore Roosevelt in the White House. Miraculously, the Republicans also controlled both houses of the territorial legislative assembly. Even if the assembly desired to vote the necessary funding to construct the new agricultural building to be called Morrill Hall, it could not have done so because of the 1902 law of Congress still in effect prohibiting the construction of additional public buildings in Oklahoma Territory until statehood.[40]

While operating from his office in Old Central, President Scott conceived the idea of taking action to modify the federal law of 1902 to permit the Oklahoma Legislative Assembly to vote money to construct Morrill Hall. Both Scott and John Fields, the Agricultural Experiment Station director, made a trip to Washington, D.C., in early January 1905, to attend the annual meeting of the Association of American Agricultural Colleges and Experiment Stations. Scott stayed on for nearly five weeks to reshape the laws of Congress to make possible the construction of Morrill Hall and other campus buildings before statehood. He also worked to obtain a larger portion of the Cherokee Outlet leased land revenues for the college and to procure a section of public school land adjacent to the college campus for the use of the institution.[41]

Resolutely, Scott believed he could accomplish these objectives. He had studied law in Washington and had familiarized himself with procedures of Congress. In addition, his brother, Charles F. Scott, served in the United States House of Representatives, and he could depend on him for advice and introductions to key legislative personnel. Of the three measures President Scott planned to shepherd through Congress, the Morrill Hall bill was the most difficult. Scott drafted the bill and then testified before the senate and house of representatives committees to which it was referred. He explained that the students of the college were literally "hanging out of the windows" and that the territorial legislature would still need to make the appropriation for the buildings if Congress passed the bill. Congressman Edward L. Hamilton of Michigan steered the bill through the house of representatives, and Senator Albert J. Beveridge of Indiana moved the bill in the senate. With the approval of President Theodore Roosevelt on February 16, 1905, the new law permitted the Oklahoma Legislative Assembly "to make such appropriations as seem to it proper for the erection of buildings for the Agricultural and Mechanical College at Stillwater."[42] The two other bills proposed by Scott benefitting the college were also passed by Congress at its "unanimous consent" hour.[43]

Meanwhile, back in Oklahoma, John Fields went to Guthrie to request that the legislative assembly appropriate funds for the erection of Morrill Hall as well as a building to provide additional shops and recitation rooms for the civil, electrical, and mechanical engineering departments. The asking also included money for a gymnasium and for the purchase of furniture, machinery, and appliances to equip the new structures. He succeeded in having the bill introduced in the Oklahoma House of Representatives on February 14, 1905, two days before President Roosevelt signed the bill of Congress legalizing its content.[44]

Fields then turned his attention to obtaining the support of the Oklahoma Territorial Board of Agriculture for the proposed building improvements at the college. The board, organized in 1902, not only supported the building fund request in a resolution, but also called for $30,000 for obtaining, improving, stocking, and equipping the section of land granted by Congress to the college at the request of President Scott. In addition, the board desired an amendment to the law for the free distribution of cattle vaccine. "With more than three-fifths of the people of Oklahoma engaged in Agricultural pursuits," the board of agriculture

This view of the campus skyline from the southwest across Washington Street was taken during President Angelo C. Scott's administration from 1899 to 1908. From left to right are the Chemistry Building, the 1902 Engineering Building, Old Central, and the Library Building with the auditorium addition. Other structures, not shown, completed during Scott's tenure included the College Barn, Morrill Hall, the Dairy Building, and the Gymnasium Building

concluded, "expenditures for higher education along these lines in the Territory should, in some measure, bear a similar proportion to the total expenditure for higher education." This resolution had but limited effect, for the board of agriculture had not yet acquired the political power it attained in later years.[45]

Scott and Fields decided to leave nothing to chance concerning the legislative funding of Morrill Hall and the other proposed buildings at the college. They planned a special visit to the campus on Friday, February 17, 1905, for members of the legislature and other friends of the college to review the expansion needs. A citizens reception committee of Stillwater business and professional men cooperated with college officials to arrange and stage the event. The Atchison, Topeka, and Santa Fe Railroad also helped by furnishing free round-trip excursion train transportation from Guthrie to Stillwater. When 450 people in Guthrie boarded the train, scheduled to leave for Stillwater at about 9:00 A.M., an additional coach was located and pressed into service.

The delay caused by the unexpected crowd resulted in the train reaching Stillwater over an hour later than planned, at a little after twelve noon. The Stillwater Concert Band and the Stillwater Ladies Band serenaded the guests at the depot while they were greeted by the citizens reception committee. A large number of buggies and other vehicles supplied by the people of Stillwater took the visitors to the college auditorium, located in the Library Building. There a delegation of women from the town and campus greeted the guests, and President Scott extended a few words of welcome.

A complimentary luncheon for all visitors came next. The twenty legislators present were taken to the dining room of the domestic science department and served food prepared by the students and their faculty. The other guests remained in the college auditorium, where they also ate food prepared by the domestic science students.

Following the luncheon, President Scott called the meeting to order in the college auditorium at 2:00 P.M. Then the College Glee Club sang a number humorously titled "The Bill of Fare," which received hearty applause interspersed with laughter. After a choral encore, Scott spoke ably for the greater part of an hour. He emphasized the need for adequate money to keep the college growing in proportion to the development of the territory. He pointed out that the request for $100,000 for new buildings and for $30,000 for developing the section of federal school land recently transferred to the college by Congress were conservative figures. Scott largely patterned his speech after the presentation he made in 1901 when a similar legislative delegation visited the college. Following Scott, seven of the visiting legislators spoke briefly, pledging their support for additional funding.

After a walking tour of Old Central and the other campus buildings, they boarded carriages for a thorough round of the Agricultural Experiment Station facilities, including all field tests, and finally for a view of the recently acquired section of federal school land adjoining the college property on the west. The visitors returned to the train station by 5:30 P.M. for the return trip to Guthrie.[46] A newswriter spoke of the "liberality" of the railroad company in transporting the guests to Stillwater at no cost and quipped that if "they had been compelled to pay their fares, not over 25 would have come."[47]

Overall, the thorough preparation of Scott and Fields for the visit of the legislature and other friends of the college paid off. They did not win in all respects, for the $30,000 requested to possess and improve the newly acquired section of school land adjacent to the campus had been reported on unfavorably by a committee of the legislative assembly even before the Stillwater meeting. The pleading of Scott with the visiting legislators resulted in $8,000 to pay the lessees on the new section of school land and to improve, stock, equip, and develop it for the use of the college and the Agricultural Experiment Station. Most of the $100,000 requested for the construction of Morrill Hall and the other new buildings came from an additional territorial tax levy for the years 1905, 1906, 1907, and 1908, which provided $92,500 for the purpose. In the council, ten voted for the bill and one voted against it; in the house, nineteen voted for it and six voted against it. Three house members voted against it because they considered it extravagant, and one who voted for it pointed out that Governor Thompson B. Ferguson had the ability and honesty to see that there would be no graft in the use of the money. Also in 1905 the legislative assembly increased the annual general operating budget of the college from $12,000 to $17,500. Scott commented that the assembly cooperated to his complete satisfaction.[48]

With money available for additional construction, party politics again played a major role. When the board of regents of the Oklahoma A. and M. College let the contract to the A. O. Campbell Company to construct Morrill Hall, another construction firm, the Sherman and Kruger Company, immediately contested its legality. Sherman and Kruger protested to Governor Ferguson that they had submitted the lowest offer, and that other construction companies attempted to bribe them not to bid. Sherman and Kruger also maintained that the Campbell firm had been permitted to submit a lower second offer. Both the governor and the regents made investigations. These revealed that the allegations of the Sherman and Kruger Company were true and that their bid had been lower than the one originally submitted by the Campbell Company.[49]

Then Governor Ferguson called a meeting of all groups concerned about the Morrill Hall bidding process. At first the board of regents desired to correct the problem, but Dennis T. Flynn, the territorial delegate to Congress and a Republican, allegedly insisted that the contract

Morrill Hall reached completion in 1906. Agriculture, located since 1902 in the basement and first floor of Old Central, moved into it, as did the president's office and the general administrative services of the college, housed in Old Central since its opening in 1894.

stand with the Campbell Company for $63,800. The contract went unaltered, but Democrats rumored that $20,000 of the $63,800 contract went into the pockets of the regents. The installation of heating, plumbing, and other fixtures brought the total cost of the building to $78,000. Some Democrats had even threatened to report the incident to President Theodore Roosevelt, but did not do so.[50] The *Daily Oklahoman* editorialized that "there is a packing house scent about the transaction that will not down, however, and some men in high places have fallen from the pedestal of popular esteem as a result of the affair."[51]

Morrill Hall, planned as the centerpiece of the first campus quadrangle, went up about four hundred feet north of Old Central. Solomon A. Layton, a capable young architect of El Reno, designed the structure. Considered of first-class construction and as fireproof as practicable, the new commodious building consisted of three stories of steel, concrete, brick, and limestone. Built on classical lines, it faced south with an elaborate outside staircase leading to the second floor. The cornerstone ceremony took place in January 1906, and the structure went into operation the following October. Agriculture, located since 1902 in the basement and first floor of Old Central, moved into it, as did the president's office and the general administrative services of the college, housed in Old Central since its opening in 1894. Agricultural units in the new building included the offices of the Agricultural Experiment Station, and suitable offices, lecture rooms, and laboratories for the animal husbandry, agronomy, horticulture, and agricultural chemistry departments. In addition, the chemistry laboratories of the Agricultural Experiment Station were also in the building. Only the field work of the agricultural department and the Agricultural Experiment Station did not center in Morrill Hall, the first major agricultural building on the campus.[52]

Following the removal of agriculture and administration from Old Central in 1906, the printing office of the college moved into the basement. The preparatory department continued to be housed on the second floor, while the assembly hall served, as before, both the preparatory department and large college-level classes. English, mathematics, and business courses were taught without interruption in classrooms throughout the building well past the territorial years. The preparatory department and the printing office also remained in the building for many years.[53]

By the time President Scott's tenure moved to a close and Oklahoma became a state, administrative planning in Old Central had resulted in seven permanent first generation buildings of brick and stone construction. They were, in addition to Old Central, the Chemistry Building, the Library Building, the Engineering Buildings (a complex), the College Barn, Morrill Hall, the Dairy Building, and the Gymnasium Building. Of these permanent structures, only Old Central and Morrill Hall remain. The others were demolished to make way for more modern edifices. With construction of the Library Building, the 1902 Engineering Building, and Morrill Hall, the original campus quadrangle had its inception. It reached completion with the construction of a new Engineering Building (the present Gundersen Hall), the Auditorium Building (the present Seretean Center for the Performing Arts), the Gymnasium Building, and the Women's Building (the present Bartlett Center for the Studio Arts). In this pattern and environment, Old Central shaped its position.[54]

Although the controversy surrounding the construction of Morrill Hall must have caused President Scott considerable embarrassment, his effective work continued. In 1906, while still officed in Old Central, he returned to Washington, D.C., to make sure that when Oklahoma became a state the Stillwater college would get the endowment land it was entitled to under the Morrill Act of 1862. Upon reaching Washington, Scott discovered that President David R. Boyd and Henry Asp of the University of Oklahoma were there, using an 1850 law providing land-grants to newly-formed states for public improvements. Under this law the college could receive 250,000 acres of land, while under the Morrill Act of 1862 it could obtain only 210,000 acres. Upon the advice of Senator Chester I. Long of Kansas, who introduced the bill, Scott successfully obtained 250,000 acres for the college, as did Boyd and Asp for the university. Not only did Scott secure 40,000 additional acres for the college, but in addition some of the land would not need to be allocated to the Colored Oklahoma Agricultural and Normal University at Langston, as required by the Morrill Act of 1890. Overall, the Langston institution also fared much better under the 1850 land-grant law.[55]

Following the removal of the president's office from Old Central to Morrill Hall in the autumn of 1906, Scott continued to work for increased funding for the college from the first Oklahoma State Legislature. Soon after statehood, this body convened at Guthrie in December 1907. The appropriation patterns Scott established while in Old Central continued and even improved. First, the legislature substantially increased the annual general operating budget appropriation of the college from $17,500 to $41,000. Second, the legislature appropriated $62,000 for the construction of the Women's Building. Third, the legislature allocated $25,000 for the Boys' Dormitory, later known as Crutchfield Hall. Beyond question, Scott had overcome the reluctance of the legislature to provide enough building and general operating budget money to fund the college.[56]

The November 1907 elections in Oklahoma resulted in a full slate of Democratic state officials. Scott immediately received word from the office of the state superintendent of public instruction that all Republican presidents of state higher education institutions would be dropped. Meantime, the effective working relationship that Scott had developed with the Republican board of regents of the college collapsed when the Oklahoma State Board of Agriculture, all Democratic, assumed jurisdiction of the Oklahoma A. and M. College and the new chain of six state agricultural and mechanical secondary schools. Scott also heard he would likely be dismissed early in 1908. He decided to chance "a small

Late in the Scott administration, this formal entrance to the campus from Knoblock Street consisted of an ornamental fence, a semicircular road, and brick walk in front of the Library Building and Old Central connecting with Hester Street one block west. The campus brick walk system, constructed in 1903, connected all permanent buildings on the campus with walks leading to the business district of Stillwater.

coup d'etat," as he phrased it. He resigned at once, effective July 1, 1908, and much to his surprise the state board of agriculture accepted his terms.[57]

Meanwhile, Scott coached the board's new choice for president, J. H. Connell of Dallas, previously editor of the *Farm and Ranch Magazine*. Connell worked with the legislature and other public officials while Scott guided campus affairs. Scott invited Connell to deliver the approaching commencement address and introduced him at the event.[58] Following Connell's remarks, Scott spoke directly to the assembled students, and concluded by commenting that the "choicest memory I take with me in leaving the A. and M. college is that of the friendship and affectionate loyalty of its students . . . .I shall never see your brave orange and black without claiming it also as mine, or hear your multitudinous yell without feeling moved to join in it."[59]

After leaving Stillwater, Scott served twice as a professor at the University of Oklahoma and also twice as a professor at Oklahoma City University. Throughout his life of ninety-two years, he lectured widely and wrote books as well as many pamphlets, brochures, and magazine articles. Wherever he served, he generally created a more sophisticated cultural level, thus making Oklahoma a better place to live.[60]

During the nine years that Scott served as president of the Oklahoma A. and M. College, he worked in a favorable political climate. As a leading Republican before he became president of the college, he readily won the support of the Republicans in the White House and in the executive office of Oklahoma Territory. In addition, members of the board of regents during his tenure were all Republicans, and the chairman, Frank J. Wikoff, conveniently lived in Stillwater.

Although Scott capably promoted the special agricultural, engineering, and domestic science emphasis of the college, he planned to broaden its scope and also shape all education for the practical welfare of the general public. Emphasis on the liberal arts as well as on the sciences would widen the reach of the college, thought Scott, and increase the opportunity to serve an enlarged student body and broaden public support. Under his competent administrative leadership, he made the college sensitive to the needs of the masses. He dreamed of developing a multipurpose and comprehensive state university, a plan that became dormant until revived by Henry G. Bennett, who became president of the institution in 1928.

Endnotes

1. Angelo C. Scott, *The Story of an Administration of the Oklahoma Agricultural and Mechanical College* ([Stillwater: Oklahoma Agricultural and Mechanical College, 1942]), p. 3.
2. Scott, pp. 6-7.

3. *National Cyclopaedia of American Biography,* vol. 37 (New York, NY: James T. White and Company, 1951), pp. 337-338; Harry E. Henslick, "Abraham Jefferson Seay: Governor of Oklahoma Territory, 1892-1893," in LeRoy H. Fischer, editor, *Oklahoma's Governors 1890-1907: Territorial Years* (Oklahoma City, OK: Oklahoma Historical Society, 1975), p. 31.

4. Philip Reed Rulon, *Oklahoma State University—Since 1890* (Stillwater: Oklahoma State University Press, 1975), pp. 113-114; Mrs. Angelo C. Scott, "Biographical Notebook of Angelo C. Scott," pp. 13-14, Angelo C. Scott Collection, Special Collections, Edmon Low Library, Oklahoma State University, Stillwater, Oklahoma.

5. *Biographical Directory of the American Congress, 1774-1971* (Washington, DC: Government Printing Office, 1971), p. 1667; Scott, p. 10; Rulon, pp. 118-119.

6. Oklahoma A. and M. *College Paper,* 25 July 1900, pp . 48-49, 1 November 1901, p. 108, 15 October 1903, pp. 82-83.

7. Robert E. Cunningham, *Stillwater: Where Oklahoma Began* (Stillwater, OK: Arts and Humanities Council of Stillwater, Oklahoma, 1969), p. 69.

8. Stillwater *Payne County Populist,* 1 March 1900, p. 1.

9. *Payne County Populist,* 22 March 1900, p. 10.

10. *Payne County Populist,* 29 March 1900, p. 1.

11. *College Paper,* 1 April 1900, p. 12; *Stillwater Gazette,* 5 April 1900, p. 5; *Payne County Populist,* 26 April 1900, p. 1.

12. *College Paper,* 1 May 1900, p. 18.

13. Fall Semester Enrollments, Registrar's Office, Oklahoma State University; Cunningham, p. 70.

14. Oklahoma Territorial Council, *Journal of the Council Proceedings of the Sixth Legislative Assembly of the Territory of Oklahoma, Beginning January 8, 1901, Ending March 8, 1901* (Guthrie, OK: State Capital Printing Company, 1901), p. 44; Oklahoma Territorial House of Representatives, *Journal of the House Proceedings of the Sixth Legislative Assembly of the Territory of Oklahoma, Beginning January 8, 1901, Ending March 8, 1901* (Guthrie, OK: State Capital Printing Company, 1901), p. 79; Oklahoma Territorial Legislature, *Session Laws of 1901, Passed at the Sixth Regular Session of the Legislative Assembly of the Territory of Oklahoma* (Guthrie, OK: State Capital Printing Company, 1901), pp. 227-230; *Stillwater Democrat,* 7 February 1901, p. 1; *Stillwater Gazette,* 7 February 1901, pp. 1, 8; Rulon. p. 119.

15. *Stillwater Democrat,* 7 February 1901, p. 1; *Stillwater Gazette,* 7 February 1901, pp. 1, 8.

16. *Stillwater Democrat,* 7 February 1901, p. 1; *Stillwater Gazette,* 7 February 1901, pp. 1, 8.

17. *Stillwater Democrat,* 7 February 1901, p. 1.

18. *Stillwater Gazette,* 7 February 1901, p. 1.

19. *Stillwater Democrat,* 7 February 1901, p. 1; *Stillwater Gazette,* 7 February 1901, p. 1.

20. *Stillwater Democrat,* 7 February 1901, p. 1; *Stillwater Gazette,* 7 February 1901, pp. 1, 8.

21. Oklahoma Territorial Council, *Journal, 1901,* p. 217; Oklahoma Territorial House of Representatives, *Journal, 1901,* p. 303.

22. *Stillwater Gazette,* 28 February 1901, p. 1.

23. Oklahoma Territorial Council, *Journal, 1901,* p. 282; Oklahoma Territorial House of Representatives, *Journal, 1901,* p. 321.

24. Oklahoma Territorial Council, *Journal, 1901,* pp. 309-310.

25. Oklahoma Territorial Council, *Journal, 1901,* pp. 310, 369; *Stillwater Democrat,* 7 March 1901, p. 1.

26. Oklahoma Territorial Legislature, *Session Laws of 1901,* p. 59; *Stillwater Democrat,* 14 March 1901, p. 1.

27. *Stillwater Democrat,* 4 April 1901, pp. 1, 5, 11 April 1901, p. 6; *Stillwater Advance,* 4 April 1901, p. 1.

28. *Stillwater Gazette,* 4 April 1901, p. 2.

29. *Stillwater Democrat,* 4 April 1901, pp. 1, 5; Oklahoma Territorial Legislature, *Session Laws of 1901,* pp. 227-230.

30. Oklahoma Territorial Legislature, *Session Laws of 1901,* p. 228.

31. *Stillwater Democrat,* 5 September 1901, p. 1; Oklahoma City *Daily Oklahoman,* 7 September 1901, p. 1; *Stillwater Gazette,* 6 June 1901, p. 1, 12 September 1901, p. 8.

32. *Stillwater Gazette,* 12 September 1901, p. 8; *College Paper,* 1 November 1901, p. 109, October 1902, pp. 70-71, November 1902, p. 109; Stillwater *Peoples Press,* 26 August 1909, p. 1, 9 September 1909, p. 1; Stillwater *Advance-Democrat,* 9 September 1909, p. 1; Cunningham, pp. 85-87; *College Paper,* 28 January 1903, pp. 197-198, January 1904, p. 174, February 1904, p. 203, November 1904, p. 41.

33. *College Paper,* October 1902, p. 71; *Report of Oklahoma Educational Institutions, 1902* (Guthrie, OK: State Capital Company, [1902]), pp. 19-20; *Report of the President of the Board of Regents, Oklahoma Agricultural and Mechanical College of the Territory of Oklahoma, 1901-1902* (Guthrie, OK: State Capital Company [1902]), pp. 5-6; *Stillwater Gazette,* 29 January 1903, p. 1.

34. Oklahoma Territorial Legislature, *Session Laws of 1903 Passed at the Seventh Regular Session of the Legislative Assembly of the Territory of Oklahoma* (Guthrie, OK: State Capital Company, 1903), throughout; United States Congress, *The Statutes at Large of the United States of America, from December, 1901, to March, 1903, Concurrent Resolutions of the Two Houses of Congress, and Recent Treaties, Conventions, and Executive Proclamations,* vol. 32, part 1 (Washington, DC: Government Printing Office, 1903), p. 148.

35. *Stillwater Gazette,* 26 March 1903, p. 1.

36. Oklahoma Territorial Legislature, *Session Laws of 1899 Passed at the Fifth Regular Session of the Legislative Assembly of the Territory of Oklahoma* (Guthrie, OK: State Capital Printing Company, 1899), pp. 220-221; Oklahoma Territorial Legislature, *Session Laws of 1903,* pp. 231-233.

37. *Stillwater Democrat,* 22 January 1903, p. 3.

38. *Stillwater Gazette,* 22 January 1903, p. 1.

39. *Stillwater Gazette,* 22 January 1903, p. 1, 29 January 1903, p. 1.

40. United States Congress, *The Statutes at Large of the United States of America,* vol. 32, part 1, p. 148; Arrell Morgan Gibson, *Oklahoma: A History of Five Centuries,* 2nd edition (Norman: University of Oklahoma Press, 1981), p. 186.

41. Scott, p. 13; Rulon, p. 120.

42. United States Congress, *The Statutes at Large of the United States of America, from November, 1903, to March, 1905, Concurrent Resolutions of the Two Houses of Congress, and Recent Treaties, Conventions, and Executive Proclamations,* vol. 33, part 1 (Washington, DC: Government Printing Office, 1905), p. 717.

43. Scott, pp. 14-16.

44. Oklahoma Territorial Legislature, *Session Laws of 1905 Passed at the Eighth Regular Session of the Legislative Assembly of the Territory of Oklahoma* (Guthrie, OK: State Capital Company, 1905), p. 49; Oklahoma Territorial House of Representatives, *Journal of the Proceedings of the House of Representatives of the Eighth Legislative Assembly of the Territory of Oklahoma, Beginning January 10, 1905, Ending March 10, 1905* (Guthrie, OK: State Capital Company, 1905), pp. 233, 235.

45. Minutes, Oklahoma State Board of Agriculture, 16 February 1905, pp. 24-25, Oklahoma Archives and Records Division, Oklahoma Department of Libraries, Oklahoma City, Oklahoma.

46. *Stillwater Gazette,* 17 February 1905, p. 1; *College Paper,* February 1905, pp. 77-78; *Stillwater Advance,* 23 February 1905, p. 1; Stillwater *Daily Democrat,* 18 February 1905, p. 1.

47. *Daily Democrat,* 18 February 1905, p. 1.

48. *Stillwater Advance,* 23 February 1905, p. 1; Oklahoma Territorial Legislature, *Session Laws of 1905,* pp. 49-51,61, 67; Oklahoma Territorial Council, *Journal of the Council Proceedings of the Eighth Legislative Assembly of the Territory of Oklahoma, Beginning January 10, 1905, Ending March 10, 1905* (Guthrie, OK: State Capital Company, 1905), p. 183; Oklahoma Territorial House of Representatives, *Journal, 1905,* pp. 315-316; Scott, p. 16.

49. *Daily Democrat,* 10 November 1905, p. 1; *College Paper,* November 1905, p. 31; *Advance-Democrat,* 28 September 1905, p. 1, 9 November 1905, p. 1, 16 November 1905, p. 4.

50. *Advance-Democrat,* 9 November 1905, p. 1, 16 November 1905, pp. 1, 4; *Daily Democrat,* 18 October 1906, p. 1; Stillwater *People's Progress,* 26 September 1907, p. 1; *College Paper,* November 1905, p. 31; Scott, p. 16.

51. *Daily Oklahoman,* 2 November 1905, p. 7.

52. *College Paper,* March 1905, p. 98, February 1906, pp. 63-64, October 1906, p. 14; *Annual Catalog, Oklahoma A. and M. College, 1906-1907,* p. 11; Harvey M. Trimble, "Fifty Years of Chemistry at Oklahoma Agricultural and Mechanical College," unpublished typed manuscript, 1942, pp. 3-4, Special Collections, Edmon Low Library.

53. *College Paper,* October 1906, p. 14; *Annual Catalog, Oklahoma A. and M. College, 1906-1907,* p. 12; *Annual Catalog, Oklahoma A. and M. College, 1911-1912,* p. 10; Oklahoma A. and M. College *Orange and Black,* 8 September 1916, p. 1.

54. *Annual Catalog, Oklahoma A. and M. College, 1906-1907,* photographic frontispiece; *Orange and Black,* 8 September 1916, p. 1.

55. Scott, pp. 17-18.

56. Oklahoma State Legislature, *Session Laws of 1907-1908 Passed at the First Session of the Legislative Assembly of the State of Oklahoma, Convened December 2, 1907, [Adjourned May 26, 1908]* (Guthrie, OK: Oklahoma Printing Company, 1908), pp. 106, 93-95.

57. Scott, pp. 18-19.

58. Scott. p. 19.

59. Angelo C. Scott's Address to Graduating Class, June 3, 1908 (Farewell Address), pp. 6-7, Angelo C. Scott Collection.

60. *National Cyclopaedia of American Biography,* vol. 37, pp. 337-338.

7 Students at Work

Throughout the history of Old Central, student life moved in unusual and interesting patterns in the building and its immediate environment. The procedures and conditions of living and learning in the earlier frontier situation contrast sharply with the styles of life in the institution of later years. Yet there is an evident cultural, social, and intellectual blending of the old and new ways. The first students and faculty of Old Central left a proud heritage, including a firm academic beginning for the college.

After being housed in several churches and other structures in Stillwater for the greater part of three years, the students of the college were elated when they moved into their new building in September 1894. Students had even helped with its construction. In addition to earning ten cents per hour, they desired to speed up construction to have separate classrooms for each instructor in a building specifically designed for college classes. The students could then move out of their makeshift classrooms and in addition have an assembly hall large enough to seat the entire student body.[1] "Most of us were so anxious to move into Old Central classrooms," explained Alfred E. Jarrell of the class of 1896, "that I think most of us would have worked for free, to rush the building."[2] George L. Holter, professor of chemistry and physics, also spoke for the student body when he said: "No wonder we were actually 'chesty' when we got in our new . . . building."[3] Perhaps James H. Adams of the class of 1896 said it best of all: "And what a home! Was ever a College more finely housed, or more splendidly equipped? We had separate classrooms for different classes and different subjects, an Auditorium of mammoth proportions . . . , Library and reading room, laboratories with

The class of 1896, the first to graduate from the college, appeared in 1895 at the main entrance to Old Central. Left to right are Ervin G. Lewis, Arthur W. Adams, Kate Neal, Alfred E. Jarrell, Emma Smith, James H. Adams, Oscar M. Morris, and Frank E. Duck. The two women did not graduate. These eight students were the survivors of the class of sixty-four who had enrolled in the preparatory program in 1891-1892.

running water and artificial gaslights, and all needed equipment and teaching apparatus. What more could anyone ask?''[4]

When Old Central first housed the college in September 1894, graduation classes had been formed through the junior year, scheduling the first class to complete its academic work in 1896. The college administration and faculty attempted faithfully to carry out the purposes of the institution, but would take years to inaugurate the broad curriculum called for in the founding law of the college passed by the Oklahoma Legislative Assembly in 1890 and in federal legislation applying to land-grant educational institutions. The *1894-1895 Catalog* emphasized that the basic purpose of the institution was not to offer a university-type education, but to prepare students for the industries of life. Laboratory and field work, called practicum, supplementary to classroom study, was required in many courses. ''A further advantage arises through this system of instruction in that the daily employment of the student at manual tasks keeps him from growing into a distaste for manual labor which too often accompanies the too exclusively intellectual training of colleges and universities . . . which . . . unfits the student for duties beyond the College,'' the catalog advice stated.[5]

The nine month academic year had three equal quarters to accommodate students who needed to return home to help on the farm at planting and harvest time. The preparatory department, where most students finished their pre-college-level studies, accepted applicants fourteen to thirty years of age. This procedure was necessary because most towns in Oklahoma Territory, including Stillwater, did not offer high school training. Students sometimes entered the preparatory department with no more than five years of grade school, but acceptance depended on passing an examination in spelling, reading, writing, English grammar, and geography. Preparatory students followed the same rules and regulations and had the same advantages as college students. Their attendance was required only for recitations and college functions such as military drill and chapel. Preparation for recitations took place elsewhere.

Harry E. Thompson served as principal of the preparatory department when Old Central reached completion, and a year later Ella E. Hunter began working as an assistant in the preparatory department. The prescribed study consisted of a sequence of thirteen courses in arithmetic, reading, writing, English grammar, geography, United States history, agriculture, and physiology. After a year or two of intensive training in the preparatory department, some students had advanced enough to be admitted to the next college freshman class. For years enrollment in the preparatory department exceeded enrollment in the college, due to the slow development of high schools in Oklahoma Territory.[6]

The administration and faculty required students "to be ladies and gentlemen in the highest sense. It is not expected that students enter upon a course of study merely for the purpose of passing a few years in pleasantry, but . . . it is presumed that the attainment of useful knowledge and skills is the dominant motive, which prompts young men and young women to enter the institution." The college promised meticulous care in guiding and directing students, but should a student be unable or unwilling to follow successfully the prescribed course of study, "he will quietly be informed of such fact and kindly requested to put forth more energy or withdraw from the institution."[7]

Expenses for students, the college advertised, "are as low as can be found in any town in the Territory." There were no incidental expenses, fees, or tuition charges. Room and board were not available on the campus. Board and a private room off campus cost from $2.50 to $3.50 a week, while a furnished room could be obtained at $1.50 a month. Table board in a private residence ranged from $2.00 to $2.50 a week, but these costs could be reduced in boarding clubs to rates between $1.50 and $2.00 a week. Books cost between $6.00 and $10.00 a year although prices could be cut by purchasing secondhand copies. The faculty and administration hoped in the near future to supply all students with free

Harry E. Thompson, the principal of the preparatory department of the college, sits at his desk in Old Central in 1895. For several years the preparatory department had more students than the college itself because of the slow development of high schools in Oklahoma Territory.

textbooks.[8] Many students, college authorities emphasized, paid a large portion of their expenses by working on the Agricultural Experiment Station farm, where wage rates increased from eight to ten cents an hour soon after Old Central reached completion. Other work on the campus, in addition to opportunities in Stillwater, helped many students work their way through the institution.[9]

Faculty and students worked together to establish and maintain academic standards in college-level courses. Instructors used a grade scale of 100 points and needed to record at least one grade in each course per month. To pass a course, students were required to maintain an overall average of 70 percent and achieve at least 50 percent on the final examination. Separate records were kept for practicum grades. Seniors, in addition, had to prepare a 3,000 to 5,000 word thesis and orate on it at commencement.[10] The student body successfully petitioned the faculty to adopt an examination honor system in 1895. After an instructor distributed an examination, he did not stay in the room to supervise it. When the class period came to a close, the student would write at the end of the paper: "I hereby certify on honor that I have neither received nor given assistance on this examination." Both students and faculty liked the honor system, and students violating it were promptly dismissed from the college.[11]

A variety of rules, considered unusual in later years, governed the lives of the first students in Old Central. Upon entering the college, students signed a pledge to "deliver to the President . . . all arms and deadly weapons of any description" and promised not to join any "secret club, society, fraternity, or other organization, composed in whole or in part of students of the College, or attend the meetings of or wear the badge of any such secret organization.'' Students also promised ''not [to] engage in 'hazing' or any other maltreatment of a student lately admitted to the Institution.'' Any student violating this pledge would be dismissed from the college.[12]

In addition, students were prohibited from using intoxicating liquors and from visiting ''any saloon or place of dissipation.'' The entire student body had to attend the morning chapel meetings, at which all official announcements were made, in the Old Central assembly hall. At the end of terms, professors gave the class standing of each student on the college bulletin board. Altogether, twenty-five rules regulated the academic, social, and personal lives of students. Perhaps the most unusual rule of all provided that students could not be found on the streets of Stillwater, or be absent from their residence, any evening except Friday, Saturday, and Sunday without the written permission of the president of the college. In the military tradition, the faculty approved a demerit system for rule violations. One hundred demerits during the college year or forty during a single term resulted in suspension from the institution. All demerits became a permanent part of the student's academic record. Although some of the rules were relaxed eventually, a disciplined approach to regulating the lives of students continued, and the use of demerits persisted well into the twentieth century.[13]

Literary societies for students reached their zenith on the campus in the early years of Old Central and also flourished on other campuses nationwide. They filled instructional gaps, stimulated intellectual growth, provided debate and public speaking practice, and promoted social contacts. Membership in a literary society was thought to be prestigious and an indication that its members had leadership potential. The Webster Debating Society and the Sigma Literary Society had functioned nearly a year when Old Central went into service in 1894. Both groups had faculty and administrative approval and encouragement. The Websters, which admitted men only, and the Sigmas, composed of both men and women, met regularly in Old Central, usually in the assembly hall. The groups operated under the direct control of their student membership, subject to supervision by a faculty committee. Each society held weekly programs, with the public invited. The members arranged regular meetings although special events required the approval of the faculty committee in charge.[14]

Each of the literary societies had a constitution approved by the faculty and administration. The meeting agenda of the Websters provided for a roll call, the reading of the previous minutes, the initiation of new members, a business session, a debate, the report of the debate critic, and planning for the next meeting. A typical program of

A Sigma, Clarence R. Donart (*left*) explains a situation to Arthur B. McReynolds, a Webster. The Sigma Literary Society and the Webster Debating Society filled instructional gaps and promoted social contacts in the early days of Old Central.

the Sigmas included opening music, a roll call, a declamation, a dramatic reading, additional music, a debate, a session of extemporaneous speaking, parliamentary procedure training, the reading of the previous minutes, the report of the critic, comments from the audience, and planning for the next meeting. The wide variety of subjects taken up by literary societies dealt with education, history, philosophy, politics, and society.[15]

Perhaps rivalry was inevitable between the two literary societies because of competition for new members and hope for community approval. By 1896 serious trouble developed. When the Sigmas met in the Old Central assembly hall for a Thanksgiving Day program that year, the Websters refused to attend the meeting. Just as Norris T. Gilbert took the platform to announce the debate subject, the bell system used regularly for class changes commenced ringing constantly. The Sigma men and some others present rushed to the control clock on the first floor of Old Central and quickly corrected the faulty wiring that had caused the problem. Although the program continued without further interruption, the Sigmas blamed the Websters for the incident. Then the faculty requested that the two literary societies meet jointly. That occurred on Friday evening, December 4, but before the meeting began in the assembly hall, a fight erupted over the election of a chairman. Both nominees,

Louis C. Miller and John T. Clark, claimed victory and commenced scuffling. Thomas J. Hartman ran to the stage to separate them, but a cane struck him above his right ear, he recalled. He "bled like a stuck pig."[16]

The college administration and faculty investigated the incident and finally ordered both societies disbanded in early 1897. Despite the severity of the decision, later the same year the faculty and administration acted favorably on a request of students to organize a new literary society and authorized it to meet in the Old Central assembly hall. This new group became the Omega Literary Society, and it flourished with a large membership well into the twentieth century. Soon other literary-type societies followed: the College Legislature Club, the Alpha Society, the A. and M. Literary Society, the Young Ladies' Society, the Philomathian Society, the Oratorical Association, and the Social Club. But the peak period for literary societies at the college passed with the demise of the Sigma and Webster organizations. The future belonged to academic discipline clubs such as the Agricultural Society, the Chemistry Association, and the Biological Science Club, all formed by the early 1900s.[17]

The Old Central assembly hall continued to be the favorite meeting location of early student organizations. Together the groups provided students with much of their social and cultural life. Amazingly, the oratorical contests of the first students in Old Central produced as much excitement as athletic events and were often held in connection with them. Oratorical meets sometimes had college yells, featuring the names of the participants. The young orators performed between music entertainment in the jammed assembly hall. Then came a period of suspense while the judges pondered the verdict, and finally the anxiety grew even more intense when the third and second place winners were announced. With the naming of the first place winner, supporters yelled, applauded, stormed the stage, and affectionately crowded around their hero. Literary societies meeting in Old Central had truly brought the fine art of debate and oratory to its summit on the Oklahoma A. and M. College campus as similar organizations did throughout the nation.[18]

When instruction began for the first time in Old Central in September 1894, most of the original faculty of the college continued in charge. With a special building for collegiate needs, the faculty made a concerted effort to increase and improve instructional aids and raise its standard of teaching to levels not possible in temporary housing. Old Central, even with the inadequate and unsuitable space it provided, made possible standards of instruction comparable to those maintained by other land-grant colleges west of the Mississippi River.

Old Central's first students had a thoroughly competent and highly qualified faculty for the time. James C. Neal, the first director of the Agricultural Experiment Station, was the oldest and most experienced member of the faculty. He received two degrees from the University of Michigan, including that of doctor of medicine. He worked first for the Smithsonian Institution in Washington, D.C., and then as an official of the Agricultural Experiment Station at the Florida State Agricultural College before coming to Stillwater. Colleagues and students characterized him as a dedicated and tireless worker. He firmly believed that the Agricultural Experiment Station should first provide farmers with practical information needed at the time concerning soils, temperatures, rainfall, and crop varieties instead of emphasizing theoretical investigations. He also thought that the experiment station staff should combine instruction and research for their mutual advantages.[19]

The faculty and administration of the college gather in 1895 soon after the completion of Old Central. Left to right are Frank A. Waugh, horticulture; Freeman E. Miller, English and literature; Harry E. Thompson, preparatory department principal; Ella E. Hunter, preparatory department instructor; James C. Neal, natural sciences and Agricultural Experiment Station director; Tazwell M. Upshaw, college secretary; Alexander C. Magruder, agriculture; Edmond D. Murdaugh, president; Edward F. Clark, mathematics; and George L. Holter, chemistry and physics.

Neal made it possible for three other men to give direction to the college and its Agricultural Experiment Station. Perhaps the leader of the three was George L. Holter, professor of chemistry and physics. His contemporaries considered him the best trained person on the faculty. He came to the Stillwater institution after graduating from the Pennsylvania State College and studying in two German universities. He held the master of science degree. Possibly more than any other member of the faculty, he attempted to evolve an appreciation of scholarship in his students. He also assisted them in developing self-discipline through his intellectual demands and taught them to realize the significance of a college education.[20]

Alexander C. Magruder served as professor of agriculture. He graduated from the Mississippi Agricultural and Mechanical College, did postgraduate work in Germany, received the master of science degree, and obtained practical experience at the West Virginia Agricultural Experiment Station. At Stillwater, Magruder created respect for scientific agriculture and academic excellence by presenting a gold medal to the student writing and delivering the best oration on some agricultural or scientific subject. In 1893 and 1894 the award went to freshmen and in 1895 to a junior. The orations of 1894 and 1895 took place in the Old Central assembly hall, but in 1895 they ceased due to the dismissal of Magruder from the faculty. In addition, Magruder established an agricultural experimental plot, which ranks next to the University of Illinois Morrow Plot for continuous agricultural research. Magruder joined Holter in searching by mail for procedures in the United States and Europe for increasing research productivity. With a well-developed concept of the land-grant college mission, Magruder generally fathered the excellence of scholarship long a part of agricultural research and teaching on the campus.[21]

The third member of the Neal trio, Frank A. Waugh, completed the master of science degree at the Kansas State Agricultural College. He served as professor of horticulture at the Oklahoma A. and M. College, where he pioneered the idea that science classes should be taught as technical and liberal arts courses instead of being confined to vocational areas. Science, he reasoned, including horticulture, should help in the total intellectual and aesthetic development of people. Waugh's approach to instruction and his interest in scientific horticultural research did not set well with several members of the board of regents. When removed from his position, he went to Germany for further study. He later had a long and distinguished academic career at the University of Massachusetts.[22]

Another early faculty member in Old Central was Freeman E. Miller. A lawyer by profession, he had earned the bachelor of arts and the master of arts degrees at the DePauw University. He served as professor of

English literature, performed well, and published widely. He also became the first librarian of the college, prepared the first magazine articles and press releases for the school, and orated ably for the institution.[23] As a reader and interpreter of literature, Miller displayed incomparable talent. "He could make the characters come out of the musty pages and speak to you, as if they were alive! What I would give to be able to read a page . . . like Miller!" explained a student.[24]

Edward F. Clark served as professor of mathematics for a six-year period but died at a young age of cancer. He graduated from an unidentified teacher training school in mathematics, but did not receive a bachelor's degree. His Stillwater public school class of almost fifty students became the central unit of the first freshman class at the college, and in that capacity he served as the first principal of the college preparatory department. His classical educational background and excellent personality made him popular with students. When Harry E. Thompson became principal of the preparatory department in 1893, Clark stayed on at the college to teach the four-year sequence in mathematics, his field of specialization. He believed that the subject should be taught to demonstrate practical applications and lead students to think accurately and precisely. He early won acclaim as a capable instructor.[25]

Harry E. Thompson proved to be an able headmaster of the preparatory department. He received a bachelor of science degree from the Southern Normal School, presently the Western Kentucky State University. Before reaching Stillwater, he had taught in public schools in Kentucky and Texas and had served as a high school principal. He was tall, lanky, and affable, but a tough disciplinarian and an unsympathetic recitation grader. Even with more than half of the total enrollment of the college in the preparatory department, Thompson, like Clark, proved equal to the educational task. Both believed in the value of higher education for the masses and skillfully trained many a student to the level of passing the college entrance examinations in English grammar, United States history, arithmetic, physiology, and general and physical geography. Thompson's success continued for the eight years he served as principal of the preparatory department.[26]

Not only were the first students in Old Central treated to a high standard of preparatory and collegiate academic training, but in addition, the equipment and teaching aids used in the classrooms and laboratory were plentiful and of the highest quality due to ample amounts of federal land-grant money for that purpose. The college library housed in the building grew rapidly and soon became unusually well supplied with periodical publications. The chemistry laboratory, well arranged and equipped, had a large collection of apparatus for teaching chemistry and physics. Other instructional aids included an unusually valuable mineralogical accumulation and increasing quantities of botanical and entomological specimens. Students also had available a large and valuable assemblage of models for the study of agriculture, botany, horticulture, physiology, veterinary science, and zoology. Other teaching aids included ample numbers of new microscopes, maps, and charts.[27]

Other equipment in Old Central for the use of its first students included factory-built classroom and library chairs with arms for taking notes and chemistry laboratory work tables equipped with Bunsen gas burners and abundant shelf space for chemicals. An acetylene gas generator used to supply the laboratory and lighting needs for the building stood under the basement stairway, operated by a heavy weight, similar to a grandfather clock. Reflector-backed kerosene lamps supplemented gas lighting throughout Old Central when the building was first used. The inadequate steam heating system in the structure sometimes caused students to desert the library room for their homes.[28] "Where possible," one student explained, "we would sign for the book, take it home, put our feet in the oven of the old wood burning cook stove, and make our notes in comfort!"[29]

When Old Central opened, the curriculum provided students with only a major in agriculture, although specialization in engineering and domestic science was in the planning stages. Meantime, unexpected student pressure created a demand for the elements of teacher education to meet the pressing need for public school teachers. President George E. Morrow emphasized the effort to meet this new necessity when he advertised the spring term of 1896: "While the College makes no attempts to do the work of the Normal School, the work of the term will be especially useful to teachers."[30] The following summer the first teachers' institute offered by the college was held in Old Central, and these became annual summer events thereafter. With this beginning, the teacher education curriculum at the institution developed, and the College of Education had its origin.[31]

The four-year agricultural major completed by the first graduates of the college constituted a general science program and certified students for the bachelor of science degree. It called for classroom lectures and laboratory experimentation in Old Central and work on the college farm. Graduates had to complete 330 quarter term credits. The required freshman schedule consisted of courses in agriculture (including dairying), algebra, etymology, physical geography, English composition, English structure, botany, bookkeeping, arithmetic, drawing, and military science and tactics. In the sophomore year, a student studied physics, chemistry, geometry, English literature, drawing, agriculture, entomology, geometrical drawing, and military science and tactics. During the junior year, students took classes in horticulture, agricultural chemistry, rhetoric, trigonometry, orthographic projection, zoology, logic, drawing, comparative anatomy, general history, surveying, and mili

The first class of the college graduated on June 10, 1896, in the Old Central assembly hall. Standing left to right are James H. Adams, Arthur W. Adams, Ervin G. Lewis, and Oscar M. Morris. Seated left to right are Alfred E. Jarrell and Frank E. Duck. Arthur W. Adams received his bachelor's degree first, thereby becoming the initial graduate of the college.

tary science and tactics. In addition to courses in agriculture and military science and tactics, seniors enrolled in courses in analytical geometry, civics, botany, surveying, history of English literature, structural botany, political economy, mineralogy, meteorology, geology, mental and moral science, lectures in common law, and lectures in applied science. Only men took military science and tactics courses, although a misinterpretation by the college administration in 1892 caused women to participate briefly in military drill. Beginning in 1899 students were no longer required to take courses in agriculture.[32]

By the time the first class graduated in the Old Central assembly hall on June 10, 1896, four commencements had already been held by the college. These observances occurred in Stillwater churches in June of 1892 and 1893 and after Old Central reached completion, in its assembly hall in 1894 and 1895. Although no students graduated, the occasions established commencement tradition and renewed hope for the future of the college. The annual ceremonies also gave the students, faculty, and administration the opportunity to demonstrate their personal intellectual and cultural abilities and promote the achievements of the college. Program participants included political dignitaries, such as the governor of the territory, and large audiences always filled the Old Central assembly hall to overflowing. Commencement activities involved a three- or four-day program designed to advertise the college. During this period participants heard a baccalaureate sermon and a variety of recitations, dialogues, vocal solos, medleys, duets, octets, orchestral music, student orations, addresses, and finally, beginning in 1896, the presentation of diplomas.[33]

The six young men who graduated at the 1896 commencement were all Stillwater residents who lived within a radius of a mile of the col-

Jessie O. Thatcher (Bost), center, became the first woman graduate of the college in 1897 in the smallest class ever to receive bachelors' degrees. Behind her left to right are George W. Bowers and Andrew N. Caudell. Their graduation occurred in the Old Central assembly hall.

lege campus. The graduates, Arthur W. Adams, James H. Adams, Frank E. Duck, Alfred E. Jarrell, Ervin G. Lewis, and Oscar M. Morris, were among those who had been selected for the freshman class in September 1892. The commencement program in 1896 opened with music and a prayer. Governor William C. Renfrow of Oklahoma Territory made an address, followed by a speech by Horace Speed, the United States district attorney for Oklahoma Territory. Then, as required by a college rule, each graduate made an oration. Their topics ranged widely with little suggestion of their agricultural major. They spoke on "The Esthetics of Emotion"; "The Study of Nature"; "Sir Humphrey Davy"; "Abraham Lincoln"; "Man, the Master"; and "Pictures in the Fire." These subjects suggest a well-rounded academic program within the limits of a land-grant college. Then President George E. Morrow conferred the degrees. Arthur W. Adams received his diploma first and so became the initial graduate of the college.[34] When President Morrow handed each graduate his diploma, he gently slapped him on the back and quietly said: "We have done our very best by you! —from here on out, you are on your very own!"[35]

At the 1897 commencement in the Old Central assembly hall, only three students graduated, half as many as in 1896. They majored in science and literature, not agriculture, as did the class of 1896. The 1897 class won distinction because Jessie O. Thatcher became the first woman graduate of the college.[36] She orated on the "Dawning of the Twentieth Century." As she reviewed the advancements of the nineteenth century, she noted: "Perhaps the greatest improvement has been in education, especially for the women . . . in almost every civilized country of the world." Overall, she said: "Education is the one all-important thing, paramount to everything else." She explained: "The future race will, perhaps, be one of specialists. This will be necessary, on account of the vast amount of knowledge involved, but, in all probability, the whole volume of human knowledge will be gradually rewritten and condensed." All this would be accomplished in the twentieth century, she concluded, "in the reign of liberty."[37]

Orations at commencements by all graduating seniors continued to be required as long as the Old Central assembly hall hosted the annual ceremony. A total of thirty-five students gave their senior orations and received their bachelor of science degrees in the assembly hall. In 1902 a new and larger auditorium went into service in the Library Building, and this facility housed commencement for the first time. In that year the graduating class numbered eighteen, too many to require orations. Two graduating seniors, however, represented the class with orations. Soon the senior class oration custom faded completely.[38]

With the construction of Old Central in 1894, academic life for students took on traditional land-grant college patterns. The administrative and faculty desire to develop practical education caused laboratory and field work to be emphasized, and aimed at dignifying manual labor to keep students receptive to it following graduation. Even the nine month academic year with three equal quarters had the purpose of making students available for agricultural labor at planting and harvest time. In a compatible manner, most of the first students in Old Central worked their way through the college, at least in part, because their parents could not afford to support them. The minimal cost of room and board in Stillwater ideally met this need, while employment on the campus and in town made it possible to graduate with little or no monetary support from home.

Due to James C. Neal, the first director of the Agricultural Experiment Station, the early faculty in Old Central functioned at a competent academic level because they were carefully selected, usually from a land-grant college background, either in training or experience. They were not generally political appointees, although politics sometimes removed them. The overall abilities of the faculty remained at a high level during the territorial years and provided students a standard of training equal to that provided by the leading land-grant colleges west of the Mississippi River. The maintenance of high academic achievement came first at the Stillwater institution.

Endnotes

1. Alfred E. Jarrell to Berlin B. Chapman, undated, Alfred E. Jarrell File, Berlin B. Chapman Collection, Special Collections, Edmon Low Library, Oklahoma State University, Stillwater, Oklahoma.

2. Alfred E. Jarrell to Berlin B. Chapman, 2 June 1958, Alfred E. Jarrell File, Berlin B. Chapman Collection.

3. Oklahoma A. and M. College *Orange and Black,* September 1908, p. 5.

4. James Homer Adams, "Some Lines From History," *Oklahoma A. and M. College Magazine,* vol. 1, no. 4 (December 1929), p. 12.

5. *Annual Catalog, Oklahoma A. and M. College, 1894-1895,* pp. 31-32.

6. *Annual Catalog, Oklahoma A. and M. College, 1894-1895,* pp. 32, 37, 98-102; Stillwater *Daily Oklahoma State,* 15 April 1898, p. 1.

7. *Annual Catalog, Oklahoma A. and M. College, 1894-1895,* p. 33.

8. *Annual Catalog, Oklahoma A. and M. College, 1894-1895,* pp. 33-34.

9. Oklahoma A. and M. *College Paper,* 1 October 1901, p. 92.

10. Oklahoma Agricultural and Mechanical College Faculty, "Minutes of the First Faculty, March 17, 1892, to June 2, 1899," unpublished typed manuscript in two volumes, vol. 1, 30 September 1895, p. 218, 7 October 1895, p. 219, 21 October 1895, pp. 220-221, Special Collections, Edmon Low Library.

11. *Annual Catalog, Oklahoma A. and M. College, 1906-1907,* pp. 75-76.

12. Oklahoma Agricultural and Mechanical College Faculty, "Minutes of the First Faculty," vol. 1, 17 March 1892, pp. 101-102; Oklahoma A. and M. College *Daily O'Collegian,* 2 December 1941, p. 1.

13. Oklahoma Agricultural and Mechanical College Faculty, "Minutes of the First Faculty," vol. 1, 17 March 1892, pp. 102-104, 1 April 1892, p. 106, 28 November 1892, p. 120; *Daily O'Collegian,* 2 December 1941, pp. 1-2, 31 January 1942, pp. 1, 3.

14. Philip Reed Rulon, *Oklahoma State University—Since 1890* (Stillwater: Oklahoma State University Press, 1975), pp. 100-103; *Annual Catalog, Oklahoma A. and M. College, 1894-1895,* pp. 114-115; "Sigma Literary Society Minutes—February 8, 1895, to November 28, 1896," manuscript book, throughout, Special Collections, Edmon Low Library; "Webster Literary Society Minutes—October 16, 1893, to October 3, 1896," manuscript book, throughout, Special Collections, Edmon Low Library; *Oklahoma A. and M. College Mirror,* 16 September 1895, p. 13.

15. Rulon, pp. 101-103.

16. Willa Adams Dusch, *The Sigma Literary Society, 1893-1897: A Chapter in the History of the Oklahoma A. and M. College,* edited by Berlin B. Chapman (Stillwater: Oklahoma A. and M. College, 1951), pp. 24-25.

17. Oklahoma Agricultural and Mechanical College Faculty, "Minutes of the First Faculty," vol. 2, 7 December 1896, p. 269, 14 December 1896, p. 270, 16 December 1896, p. 271, 25 January 1897, p. 276, 11 November 1897, pp. 302-303; *Annual Catalog, Oklahoma A. and M. College, 1898-1899,* p. 34; *Oklahoma State,* 9 March 1898, p. 4; *College Paper,* 1 April 1900, p. 9, 1 October 1901, p. 92, 1 March 1902, p. 205, February 1904, pp. 198-199, March 1904, p. 226, January 1905, p. 68, March 1905, pp. 95-96, February 1906, p. 61, March 1906, p. 86; *Orange and Black,* November 1908, p. 29; *Stillwater Gazette,* 5 November 1903, p. 5; William A. Worley to Willa Adams Dusch, 20 February 1951, Old Central Centennial History Collection, Special Collections, Edmon Low Library.

18. Angelo C. Scott, *The Story of an Administration of the Oklahoma Agricultural and Mechanical College* ([Stillwater: Oklahoma Agricultural and Mechanical College, 1942]), pp. 11-12.

19. Rulon, pp. 25-27; *Stillwater Daily NewsPress,* 13 May 1951, p. 15; Berlin B. Chapman, "The Neal Family and the Founding of the Oklahoma Agricultural and Mechanical College," unpublished manuscript, Old Central Centennial History Collection.

20. Rulon, pp. 27-28; Alfred E. Jarrell to Berlin B. Chapman, 30 August 1951, Alfred E. Jarrell File, Berlin B. Chapman Collection; *Stillwater Daily NewsPress,* 13 May 1951, p. 15.

21. Rulon, pp. 28-29; *Annual Catalog, Oklahoma A. and M. College, 1894-1895,* p. 34; *Stillwater Daily NewsPress,* 13 May 1951, p. 15; Alfred E. Jarrell to John W. Hamilton, 3 February 1953, Alfred E. Jarrell File, Berlin B. Chapman Collection; Magruder Medal Collection, Special Collections, Edmon Low Library; *Stillwater NewsPress,* 16 November 1983, p. 12B.

22. Rulon, pp. 29-30; *Stillwater Daily NewsPress*, 13 May 1951, p. 15.

23. Rulon, pp. 49, 93.

24. Alfred E. Jarrell to Berlin B. Chapman, 30 August 1951, Alfred E. Jarrell File, Berlin B. Chapman Collection.

25. Rulon, pp. 30-31, 88-89.

26. Rulon, pp. 31-32; Harry E. Thompson, "The Territorial Presidents of Oklahoma A. and M. College," *Chronicles of Oklahoma*, vol. 32, no. 4 (Winter 1954-1955), p. 364; *Annual Catalog, Oklahoma A. and M. College, 1894-1895*, p. 32.

27. *Report of the Secretary of the Interior Being Part of the Message and Documents Communicated to the Two Houses of Congress at the Beginning of the First Session of the Fifty-fourth Congress in 5 Volumes*, vol. 3 (Washington, DC: Government Printing Office, 1895), p. 519; *Annual Announcement, Oklahoma A. and M. College, 1896-1897*, p. 4; Stillwater *Oklahoma State Sentinel*, 2 May 1895, p. 4.

28. Alfred E. Jarrell to John W. Hamilton, 10 November 1954, Alfred E. Jarrell to Berlin B. Chapman, 1 September 1958, and Alfred E. Jarrell, "Oklahoma A. and M. College, Then and Now," 1953, manuscript, p. 6, Alfred E. Jarrell File, in Berlin B. Chapman Collection; Author interview with Elizabeth Oursler Taylor, 2 November 1985, Old Central Centennial History Collection.

29. Alfred E. Jarrell to John W. Hamilton, 10 November 1954, Alfred E. Jarrell File, Berlin B. Chapman Collection.

30. *Cushing Herald*, 3 April 1896, p. 2.

31. James K. Hastings, "Oklahoma Agricultural and Mechanical College and Old Central," *Chronicles of Oklahoma*, vol. 28, no. 1 (Spring 1950), p. 84; *Oklahoma State Sentinel*, 29 July 1897, p. 1; Faculty of the Summer Normal School and Teachers' Institute at the Oklahoma A. and M. College, 1908, Announcement, Old Central Centennial History Collection; *Stillwater Daily NewsPress*, 24 August 1952, p. 12, section 2.

32. *Annual Catalog, Oklahoma A. and M. College, 1894-1895*, pp. 37-40, 93-97; Oklahoma Territorial Board of Agriculture, *First Biennial Report of the Oklahoma Territorial Board of Agriculture, 1903-1904* (Guthrie, OK: State Capital Company, 1905), pp. 188-189.

33. Oklahoma A. and M. College Commencement Programs, 1892, 1897, 1899, 1901-1903, 1906, Oklahoma Agricultural and Mechanical College Commencement and Baccalaureate Programs File, Special Collections, Edmon Low Library; Oklahoma A. and M. College Commencement Programs, 1895-1896, 1898, 1904, Commencement Program File, Berlin B. Chapman Collection; *Stillwater Gazette*, 23 June 1893, p. 1; Guthrie *Daily Oklahoma State Capital*, 18 June 1894, p. 1; Stillwater *Eagle-Gazette*, 21 June 1894, p. 1; *Oklahoma A. and M. College Mirror*, 15 June 1895, p. 9.

34. Alfred E. Jarrell Radio Speech, 27 May 1951, typescript, Alfred E. Jarrell File, and Oklahoma A. and M. College Commencement Program, 1896, Commencement Program File, in Berlin B. Chapman Collection; *Stillwater NewsPress*, 2 May 1979, p. 8, 18 March 1981, p. 19, 23 April 1986, p. 1B.

35. Alfred E. Jarrell to Berlin B. Chapman, undated, Alfred E. Jarrell File, Berlin B. Chapman Collection.

36. Oklahoma A. and M. Commencement Program, 1897, Oklahoma Agricultural and Mechanical College Commencement and Baccalaureate Programs File, Special Collections, Edmon Low Library; James L. Showalter, "Oklahoma A. and M. College Territorial Student Survey," typescript, Old Central Centennial History Collection.

37. Berlin B. Chapman, editor, *Old Central in the Crisis of 1955* ([Orlando, FL: Golden Rule Publishing Company, 1964]), pp. 96-102; *Stillwater NewsPress*, 1 July 1987, pp. 1-2B, 22 July 1987, pp. 1B, 6B.

38. *Stillwater Gazette,* 8 June 1899, p. 3, 6 June 1901, p. 1, 5 June 1902, p. 1; *College Paper,* 15 June 1899, p. 1, July 1902, p. 64; Stillwater *Payne County Populist,* 14 June 1900, p. 1; *Stillwater Democrat,* 6 June 1901, p. 1, 22 May 1902, p. 1, 5 June 1902, p. 1; Oklahoma A. and M. College Commencement Program, 1902, Oklahoma Agricultural and Mechanical College Commencement and Baccalaureate Programs File, Special Collections, Edmon Low Library; Showalter, "Oklahoma A. and M. Territorial Student Survey," Old Central Centennial History Collection. R. Morton House, in "The Class of 1903 at Oklahoma A. and M. College," *Chronicles of Oklahoma,* vol. 44, no. 4 (Winter 1966-1967), p. 408, credits the class of 1903 as being the first to graduate in the Library Building auditorium, but this is incorrect. Mary Nielsen Taylor, also a member of the class of 1903, held this same opinion as noted in the letter of Mary Nielsen Taylor to Berlin B. Chapman, 31 July 1966, in Old Central Centennial History Collection. House and Taylor believed this to be so, in all probability, because the auditorium was undergoing alteration when the class of 1903 graduated in it.

8 Students at Play

During the early years of Old Central, the discipline of learning did not wholly dominate student life. Time could be found for adventurous activity, and much of this liveliness centered in and around Old Central. The lure of the building for future student generations continued with but little loss of interest. The amusing and mischievous incidents usually became high points in the memory of those who experienced them and frequently revolved around class rivalry and loyalty. The future, however, would erode the spirit of class loyalty as well as the glee of pranksterism. This condition likely developed, at least in part, from the growth of the institution, the increasing professionalism of education, and the competition of other forms of entertainment.

Student pranks at Old Central began the Halloween after the building opened in 1894. The next morning the south entrance to the structure contained old carts, harness, boards with Halloween painted on them, and a collection of many other things.[1] The *Eagle-Gazette* of Stillwater did not approve: "The college boys are getting a little too funny of late and unless they learn something from their past week's experience that will be a benefit to them they a[re] liable to get into more serious trouble. The judicious use of a small amount of good horse sense is a good thing even among college students."[2]

Several months later an amusing prank occurred in the chapel meeting in Old Central. The new assembly hall had enough space to accommodate all students of the college, and daily chapel meetings were held like those at most smaller colleges of the day throughout the nation. The students met in the hall for the first class period after the Old Central bell called them to the campus. The faculty, numbering six at the time, took their seats at the rear of the platform while one of them checked the attendance by noting the vacant assigned seat numbers. With roll taking completed, another faculty member stepped forward to the speaker's stand on which a large Bible rested, read a few verses of scripture, and concluded with a short prayer. Then he would make announcements and call on the president to end the meeting with any appropriate comments he might care to give.[3]

After an unusually dignified member of the faculty had read from Genesis each morning in chapel for about a week, a student decided to manipulate two pages of the scripture by neatly gluing them together. Once accomplished, the name of Noah's wife appeared at the bottom of one page and the dimensions of Noah's Ark at the top of the next. This made Noah's wife the size of the ark. The professor turned the page, continued reading, and paused while the students laughed. Not believing what he thought he had read, he turned back the page, and then a strange look came across his face when he realized what he had done. Next he slowly reread the verses amidst the student uproar, paused briefly, and said: "Thus reads the record—let us Pray!"[4] Even the professor caught the humor of the occasion.

Another unusual student incident in Old Central shaped up at a meeting of the Chemistry Association. Following the scheduled program, held on a snowy winter night, the group decided to prepare a banquet in the chemistry laboratory. Had George L. Holter, the faculty sponsor of the association, been present, the party would not have occurred. Fortunately for the party, the chemistry laboratory student assistant and the Old Central student janitor attended the meeting and enthusiastically helped. The party got underway when the women used the sugar, acetic acid, porcelain bowls, glass stirring rods, and the gas Bunsen burners of the laboratory to make taffy candy for dessert.

The men helped the women pull the taffy, except for George W. Stiles of the class of 1900. He volunteered to locate a refreshment and the ingredients for preparing chicken stew. After being away about an hour, he returned with a container filled with milk to drink and a white rooster for the stew. Someone volunteered to wring the chicken's neck and prepare it for the stew, cooked over the flame of a Bunsen burner. No one ever found out or seriously questioned whose cow was milked or who lost the rooster. The faculty and administration apparently ignored the incident.[5]

Student pranks also occurred in classes in Old Central. On one occasion when John H. Bone, a teaching assistant in agriculture, stood before a class in the first-floor mathematics room above George L. Holter's chemistry lecture and demonstration classroom, two students disappeared undetected by the instructor. There were not enough chairs to seat the entire class, so the two students stood up until roll call concluded and then sat on the floor. This gave them the advantage of not being called on to recite, but after a couple of weeks they tired of sitting on the floor. One dared the other to skip class by jumping out of an open window. He accepted the dare, and the next day when Bone turned his back to explain a point on the blackboard, the student went out of the window. "I had to jump far out on account of the basement windows [window wells]," the student explained, "and as a result I landed all in a heap. As I picked myself up I saw Professor Holter standing at one of the basement windows, his hands in his pockets, and a good sized grin on his face. I don't know whether he knew what I was doing or not." The student ran to the northwest door of the building, making for the library room. "Just as I was passing the door of the class room I had so lately left," the explanation continued, "my heart jumped to my throat, for the door . . . opened and out came . . . Bone. He looked hard at me, but said never a word. He hadn't seen me often enough to know I belonged to his class."[6]

Another classroom incident in Old Central shaped up when Harry E. Thompson, the principal of the preparatory department, found him-

In the early years of Old Central, a student jumped, undetected by the teacher, to the ground from a window of the first-floor mathematics classroom, barely missing a basement window well. Edward F. Clark, the professor of mathematics and surveying, studies at his desk.

self detained at a special faculty meeting long past the time of his next class. A noisy group of freshmen awaited him for a drawing period in the basement classroom. The students soon became restless, locked the stairway door to the basement, and bolted the windows of their room. They decided that they would not draw that afternoon. Thompson, a well-experienced hand at besting unruly students, soon found his way into the basement and had the students draw for the rest of the period. The freshmen, concluded a newspaper reporter, went away "uncertain whether or not they really gained anything."[7]

Student romance abounded in and around Old Central in the early years. Andrew N. Caudell, class of 1897, and Penelope Cundiff, a former student, were married on April 12, 1900. The ceremony took place by telegraph, with the groom in Kansas City, Missouri, and the bride in her hometown of Mulhall, Oklahoma Territory. Caudell had planned to come to Mulhall in June for the wedding from his home in Washington, D.C., where the United States Department of Agriculture employed him as an entomologist, but he came to Kansas City in April because of the death of a relative. Since his leave did not permit him to come to Oklahoma, the idea occurred to him of being married by telegraph to save the inconvenience and expense of the trip in June. He also could meet his bride in Kansas City to make the return trip to Washington together. The unique marriage ceremony attracted nationwide attention, and one newspaper reporter thought that the bride and groom "could easily build an interesting scrap book of the many pretty comments on the affair."[8]

Another Old Central romance would soon blossom with unusual aspects. In 1902 Thomas J. Hartman, class of 1898, became a member of the board of regents of the Oklahoma A. and M. College and its treasurer, a position he held by appointment of Governor Thompson B. Ferguson until 1906. Hartman was the first graduate of the college to serve on its governing board. While working as cashier of the Bank of Deer Creek, Oklahoma Territory, he married Mary A. Jarrell of the class of 1903. As a regent, he signed her diploma. She was the sister of Alfred E. Jarrell, a graduate of the first class in 1896. Both were the children of Alfred N. Jarrell, who contributed forty acres of land in the present central campus to bring the college to Stillwater.[9]

The south portico of Old Central and the flight of steps leading to it became a favorite social and academic gathering point for early students of the college. A semi-circular road in front of the south entrance of Old Central conveniently led from Knoblock Street to Hester Street, thus making the building the focal point of the original campus quadrangle. The south steps and portico served the early campus as the principal location for the exchange of academic information and the making and breaking of social engagements. In some respects, it filled the need of the modern Student Union.[10] The south steps and portico of Old Central meant much more to Vingie E. Roe, a student at the college, who wrote a poem in 1902 titled "On the College Steps". It reads in part:

"Tall, black, and shadowy, the College stands.
And sitting here upon the steps which make
A dim, white bulk amid the darker gloom.
A dream, born of the twilight, fills my heart—
A dream of all the faces which have passed
In at these portals, and come forth again
In armor strong, invincible, to meet
The world."[11]

Soon after the construction of Old Central, a small canopy-type roof was built over the south basement entrance to drain away rainwater. One morning when President Angelo C. Scott went to his office in the building he noticed a donkey, hitched to a cart, peacefully munching a bale of hay atop the basement entrance canopy. This distressed Scott, but he found a cow tied to the south door of the first floor blocking his way, and this upset him even more. After gaining entrance to the building through the northwest door, he hurried to the assembly hall for the chapel program about to begin. Much to his consternation, he found the college skeleton standing in his place, with his own song book in the skeleton's hands opened to his favorite German song, "The Watch on the Rhine."[12]

A few months later, in the spring of 1900, the main social event of the class of 1903 occurred. This was the freshman class party held in the large Alfred N. Jarrell house south of the campus. His daughter, Mary, a member of the freshman class, hosted the party. In the middle of the event a group of sophomore boys rushed in and scattered liquid ammonia about the room, splashing it on several girls' faces, arms, and dresses. A group of freshman boys chased the sophomores from the room and gave immediate pursuit.

The freshmen found sophomores George M. Janeway hiding under the hay in the loft of his father's barn, Marion M. Woodson under the bed in the farthest corner of his upstairs room, and Arthur W. Flower cowering on the front steps of Old Central. The pursuing freshmen punished only Flower. They took him to the well on the north side of the building, pumped water in his face, and almost drowned him.[13] "It would have been awful if we had," said R. Morton House of the class of 1903. "All of us learned much that evening. Arthur took his punishment like a man. All of us were good friends as long as we were together in college."[14]

Class identity, spirit, and rivalry continued strong for some years. Out of that an incident developed in the Old Central assembly hall during the preparatory training year of the class of 1912. At some point dur-

This view of Old Central taken during the administration of President George E. Morrow, 1895-1899, shows the canopy over the south basement entrance, the flagpole on the roof, and smoke coming from the steam boiler in the basement. Because of class rivalry, the flagpole became inoperative in 1902 when a student climbed to the roof to cut the flagpole rope and remove the class of 1903 colors.

ing the report on an emblem for the class, those in attendance noticed an owl perched high on a bust in the room. A freshman had likely placed it there. This "large, living specimen of the proverbial bird of wisdom," wrote a class representative, carried much meaning. "By exerting considerable effort, signifying that it, wisdom, was not to be attained without a struggle, the bird was captured." The owl, the class decided, should be its emblem. "After adjourning, the class gathered south of 'Old Central' where the Owl, which now carried the Green and White, our class colors, in its talons, was liberated. It flew beyond our range of vision—a symbol of the five years of the unknown before us."[15] Finally, the business majors of the class of 1912 returned to Old Central long enough on a dark night to daub their class colors on the outside of the building. The administration required the class to remove the colors or be expelled from the college.[16]

The same class identity and rivalry also centered around the Old Central flagpoles. After a year passed following the opening of Old Central, newly-arrived President George E. Morrow had a flagpole placed on the high east end of the Old Central roof. The rope for raising and lowering flags by means of a pulley at the top of the flagstaff was anchored to a second-story window frame below. One bright moonlight night in 1902 members of the class of 1903 hoisted their class colors by means of the rope to the top of the flagpole. R. Morton House of the class of 1903 had assisted with this stunt. Soon after returning to his lodging for the night, he heard that the class of 1904 was out in force on the campus. He returned to Old Central in time to see a young man come out of the building's belfry, crawl to the apex of the roof, and slide east to the flagpole. The student cut the rope, anchored below, to lower the class of 1903 colors and in so doing pulled the rope from the pole, making it unusable.[17] "I cringed," said House, "for he was in a high, steep, and dangerous place, where a fall would have meant crippling or death, but he slipped back safely to the belfry and to the ground."[18]

With the flagpole inoperable, it was soon removed by college officials, and a flagstaff installed at ground level in front of Old Central. In the years ahead, students seemed little concerned about hoisting their class colors on the flagpole, but they turned their attention to class fights in the large cottonwood tree immediately west of Old Central. The tree provided a new and exciting challenge for group class participation and an unusual way to demonstrate class loyalty at a time when classes were small enough to retain their identity.

Organized freshman class fights in and around the Old Central cottonwood tree reached their peak at the time of World War I. The 1913 fight took four and one-half hours on a hot Friday afternoon in September.[19] The temperature reached 104 degrees in the shade and soared to 120 degrees in the sun. The freshmen at 1:00 P.M. placed a large orange flag in the top of the tree, daubed grease on their faces for recognition, and waited for an attack by preparatory department students and sophomores. About one hundred people gathered to watch the fracas. The first round began at 2:15 P.M., continued for twenty minutes, and concluded with a freshman win. Following a long rest, the second round began. By this time more sophomores had arrived, and in this phase of the encounter, wrestling took place in a large rose bed near the cottonwood tree. "It is needless to say the thorns did their work," commented a student following the fifteen minute round. By this time the afternoon laboratory work had concluded, and then many more students assembled at the cottonwood tree. Some even sat in the open windows of Old Central to view the fight.

Although the second round of the fight ended indecisively, in the third round the sophomores captured the tree. To get through the five freshmen in the top of the tree proved to be another problem. The sophomores finally put one man in the tree, but the freshmen isolated him so he could not reach the class flag. Other attempts by the sophomores failed to place another man in the tree. Then the preparatory department students and the sophomores withdrew. Soon the fourth and last round began. The preparatory department students and the sophomores quickly recaptured the base of the tree, but even after repeated efforts they could not get a man into the tree. Finally at 5:30 P.M., the attackers tossed a box of matches to a man in the tree, whereupon the freshmen burned their own class colors, thus winning the encounter. According to a student reporter, "the fight was one of the hardest and cleanest seen on the campus in a good many years."[20]

The freshman class fight in 1914 took on similar patterns at the opening of the fall term in September. Yet there was a certain newness about the event. A wedge of sophomore men charged the tree in which the freshmen had planted their class colors of crimson and gold. The dust flew while clothing was torn to shreds. Spectators, present in greater numbers than before, gathered in a wide ring around the tree and cheered the contestants. Even the open windows of Old Central were again filled with students viewing the fight, and others rushed here and there taking snapshots with Kodak box cameras. A group of freshman women attracted considerable attention by their antics. "They wrung their hands, they wept, yet always eagerly cheered their class men," reported a Redskin writer. "The tears ran in little rivulets down their dusty cheeks and their faces were pictures of agony. Every move on the part of either class was a signal for a fresh outburst of enthusiasm—poor little dears."[21]

After withdrawing briefly, the sophomore men collected into a mass and forced their way through a freshman defense to the base of the tree. While the crowd cheered wildly, the strongest boys were quickly lifted onto the shoulders of other men. Reaching up for sturdy tree limbs, they swung themselves into the branches. Then the struggle began in earnest, as more and more sophomores made their way into the tree. The freshmen climbed higher and higher while the sophomores moved upward. With one final effort the sophomores reached the top, only to see the defending freshmen throw their class colors to the ground. The sophomores tore them to shreds, and thus won the fight. There remained, with broken tree limbs and innumerable parts of clothing, the Redskin writer observed, "the memory of a good old fight."[22]

Although much stayed the same in the cottonwood tree fights at Old Central, each September usually brought innovations. In 1915 the defending freshmen splotched their faces with red ink for identification. When the attacking sophomores found that their inadequate numbers made it impossible for them to win the fight, they turned a fire hose on the freshmen in the tree, only to have freshmen on the ground promptly cut the hose to pieces. "That's how and why the sophs lost the fight," the Orange and Black quipped, "it's also why the freshies

A student struggles to reach the top of the cottonwood tree immediately west of Old Central to remove the freshman class colors. The tree fights were annual events at Old Central from 1913 to 1919, except for the World War I year of 1918.

will have to pay for a new hose."[23] The Old Central bell rang in 1916 to call freshmen and sophomores to the annual tree fight for a contest lasting nearly four hours. After a while, the sophomores attempted to carry away and lock up "the most husky" freshmen until the fight concluded. The sophomores again tried to use a college fire hose on the defending freshmen, but to no avail.[24]

With the beginning of the new college year in September 1917, another tree fight at Old Central shaped up. The sophomores had added a new dimension when earlier in the afternoon they tackled and captured freshman men, tied their hands and feet, placed them in waiting automobiles, and under guard took them several miles out in the country, leaving them there. The sophomore women entered the effort by guarding the prisoners awaiting transportation to the country, while the freshmen women, who outnumbered the sophomore women, struggled to free the prisoners. The freshmen again won the fight, but not until many of the men on both sides had lost all of their clothing above the waistline. No one came out of the fight seriously hurt, although many had bruises and scratches. Likely the most amusing incident of the fray occurred when five prisoners in an automobile won their freedom, bound their captors, and returned to town triumphantly. Many of the freshmen came back to the campus in "tin-lizzie" Model T Fords driven out by their classmates.[25]

For the first time, the annual Old Central cottonwood tree fight became publicly controversial when in 1917 someone on the *Orange and Black* staff dared to speak against it. Perhaps World War I, which the United States entered on April 6, 1917, helped to bring out the sentiment. "Many are hoping now, as many have hoped in the past, that the College will substitute some other form of sport for this annual scrap . . . .If we wait until a bad accident occurs it will be too late . . . .Why not a pushball contest, or some other contest to take the place of this ancient, primeval custom?''[26]

When September of 1918 came around, the students of the college did not organize the usual fight at Old Central. World War I had left a severe scar on the student body, but the armistice agreement in Europe ending the war on November 11, 1918, settled the student body well enough for another tree fight in September 1919. Again new combat techniques emerged, some reminiscent of World War I battlefields. After the freshmen placed their red and white class colors in the top of the cottonwood tree, the sophomore men preparing for the attack posed for a photograph. At the command of "forward," the sophomores silently marched toward the tree in a massed column, and ten yards before they reached the freshman defenders they went into a low crouching run. Immediately tear gas shot from spraying apparatus and soot from bags filled the air while the sides wavered but did not give way.

After a while, the sophomores withdrew and decided to change tactics. Again they advanced, but in sets of three or four; each group had the assignment of returning with a defending freshman. The captured freshmen were bound and taken away in a truck. Meantime, when freshman women tried to free the freshman men, they were tied up by sophomore men. Then a freshman woman located a knife and cut the ropes on the other freshman women. At this point the sophomore women started scuffling with the freshman women.

Meanwhile, junior and senior men joined the sophomore men to form what they called the Triple Alliance of the World War I era. This group lined up in single file, with athletes at the head of the column. The first man would charge and throw himself as far as possible over the heads of the defending freshmen, and then others would follow until steps had

1920 REDSKIN

In September 1919 a large group of spectators crowded around the cottonwood tree west of Old Central for the annual tree fight. Viewers even used the windows and roof of Old Central.

been formed of struggling bodies reaching to a point where a firm grasp could be had of a sturdy limb on the tree. Although used again and again, this style of attack did not succeed because four freshmen standing on upper tree limbs freely stepped on the hands of anyone gaining a secure grasp of a lower limb. Once again the freshmen won the fight.[27]

As usual, the *Orange and Black* reported no angry words or blows and complimented the classes on a clean fight. "The class spirit derived from such scrapping cannot be excelled . . . And long will they remember the friendliness displayed by the antagonists . . . .Previous enemies were again friends, laughing and jesting and going off with arms about each other." Even President James W. Cantwell approved after witnessing the class fight: "There is nothing the student body could do to promote and fix the solidarity of the freshman class like this annual hand to hand, class against class fight."[28]

Even with this enthusiasm for the annual Old Central tree fight, there would never be another. The resolute cottonwood tree could not tolerate the abuse, for it died and was removed. The next year, in 1920, the annual class fight continued, however, on the college athletic field when the freshmen nailed their class colors to the top of a fifteen foot pole. For two hours the struggle persisted, and again the freshmen won. When the whistle blew at 5:00 P.M., the only injuries were skinned shins, lame backs, sprained limbs, and a broken bone. In 1921 another rousing class fight took place at a pole on the college athletic field. The sophomores won for the first time since 1914.[29]

Pole fights were not as exciting as tree fights, and by the time President Bradford Knapp came to the campus in 1923, they no longer existed. Freshman-sophomore interests in an annual class contest lagged even more when Knapp, in line with the suggestion made in 1917, substituted a pushball contest between the two classes each year held as a special feature of the interscholastic high school meet. Athletic department officials refereed the events. Although Knapp contended that the pushball contests gave more sport to the participants, the students did not agree. Soon the annual class fight tradition, established at Old Central, dwindled and died.[30]

Meantime, students had developed a special and enduring fascination for the Old Central belfry, bell, and bell clapper. From the opening of the building in 1894, indeed even before the bell arrived, a major student escapade involved Old Central's belfry at Halloween. In the dead of night, several students liberated a young prize bull from the horse and cattle pens of the Agricultural Experiment Station and took it to Old Central. While two or more students held the bull on the ground below the belfry, other students entered the building carrying a block and tackle pulley assembly and climbed the precarious stairway leading to the belfry. They tied the pulley device to the belfry, dropped it to the ground,

The original cradle for the Old Central bell was constructed of iron and wood in a lower carriage, which rested on the floor of the belfry, and had a wheeled drive. The bell itself, made in West Troy, New York, in 1894, is presently cracked in at least three places.

and then the students below hoisted the bull into the belfry. They tied the bull to the inside of the belfry, raised the entire pulley assembly into the belfry, and descended by the inside stairway. Then they carefully nailed shut the doorway leading to the belfry and made their escape undetected.[31]

The next day college officials used the set of pulleys in the belfry to lower the bull to the ground. No newspaper publicity resulted from the incident, but a faculty committee investigated it at length to no avail, for the culprits were never located. "Had they found them," said Alfred E. Jarrell of the class of 1896, "the faculty would have given them one of the *greatest cleaning jobs ever recorded* and probably expelled them besides."[32]

Within a week or two after the Old Central bull in the belfry incident, the bell, clapper, and bell cradle arrived from the foundry of Meneely and Company of West Troy, New York. The bell is twenty-two inches in height and has a diameter of thirty and one-half inches and, according to the inscription on the bell, was made in 1894. It is made of cast iron, although it may contain some copper and is presently cracked in at least three places. Two major cracks run from the rim to near the top, but they have been filled and leveled. The third and smallest crack runs from the rim and is about three inches long. The various parts composing the clapper were made by drop-forged and cast methods. The original cradle for the bell utilized iron and wood in a lower carriage, resting on the floor of the belfry, and had a wheeled drive. When the bell assembly reached the campus, people wondered how it would be placed in the belfry. A block and tackle pulley likely assisted. The bell soon called students to the campus each morning of the week at 7:40 A.M. for chapel in the Old Central assembly hall at 8:00 A.M. During the daily class hours, an electric battery-operated bell system in Old Central controlled by a master time clock took over.[33]

To welcome Old Central's bell, an unknown student immediately feted it in a poem:

"At three o'clock the work was done,
    And over the tower the new bell hung;
Then the boys, just for fun,
    Clim[b]ed the stairs and the bell was rung.
The chimes rang loud and clear
    And was heard for miles by many an ear.
The thought of fire made many fear,
    But the students greeted it with cheer after
        cheer."[34]

Access to the belfry became so popular that the second floor doorway to it remained locked at all times. By various methods students managed to undo the door lock or remove the battered door itself for the perilous climb to the belfry. Sometimes students were caught in the belfry, and many more nearly were.

On one Saturday evening three men students reached Old Central early to attend a meeting of the Sigma Literary Society in the assembly hall. They decided to let themselves into the belfry with a pass key one of them had obtained, but they failed to lock the door behind them. Soon the student janitor appeared, and when he tried the belfry door, he found it unlocked, thus suspecting that someone was upstairs. Gleefully, the janitor locked the door and left his key in the lock. When the students came down from the belfry and tried to unlock the door, they found that their key would not go in the lock. They tried to crawl through the transom, only to find they could not open it far enough. Meanwhile, each answered the roll call of the Sigma Literary Society through the transom. Then, with assistance from their pocket knives, they unscrewed the hinges of the transom, and one crawled through to unlock the door for the other two. They must have been greeted with smiles and smirks when they joined the literary meeting in the assembly hall. (The belfry door does not presently have a transom.)[35]

At another time a little later, several men students busily amused themselves in Old Central when they found about a hundred feet of coiled rope in the belfry. They took it down to the vacant assembly hall

The Sigma Literary Society Serenaders provided entertainment in Old Central and in Stillwater during the 1890s. Standing left to right are Thomas J. Hartman, Cora A. Miltimore, Norris T. Gilbert, Willa M. Adams, George W. Bowers, and Minnie A. Dysert. Seated left to right are S. Earl Myers and Jessie O. Thatcher.

and decided to stuff it into a small hole in the side of a large bass drum used by the recently organized college band. It took quite a while to push the rope through the hole, but it took even longer for the drum player to determine the problem and eliminate the rope by removing the head of the drum.[36]

Years passed, and one bright morning a group of students belonging to the class of 1914 passed near Old Central and observed the colors of the business class flying from the belfry and some of its majors "fortified in the steeple." Immediately the members of the class of 1914 nailed shut the door to the belfry, only to find themselves being hauled down the steps of Old Central by the heels.[37] After additional years ebbed away, another Halloween brought more action in the Old Central belfry. The ghosts again looked like a group of men students from the college. They headed straight for the Dairy Barn and soon returned with two prize bovines, one of which ended up on the second floor of the Engineering Building, presently Gundersen Hall. Another intended for the Old Central belfry simply would not fit. Undaunted, reported the *Daily O'Collegian,* one of the ghostly students went to the Sheep Barn and brought back "a cute creature that seemed to be made to fit the opening."[38] It stayed in the belfry until daylight brought the janitor and assistance from the sheep herders. The same morning turkeys and bicycles decorated the tops of Whitehurst and Murray halls.[39]

When additional permanent buildings went up near Old Central, the bell rang at the beginning and ending of every class period. This ceased in September 1908, when the blowing of a bugle, in the military tradition of the college, opened and closed classes. This impractical method lasted only briefly, and soon an electric bell system rang simultaneously at the opening and closing of classes in all buildings on the campus. Meantime, the bell in Old Central lapsed into disuse and mechanical disrepair. After several years, students knew little of Old Central's bell until the Orange and Black in 1913 printed a letter to the editor suggesting that the broken wooden supports of the bell carriage be repaired so that the bell could be rung to call students to athletic pep meetings and all other gatherings of the student body. Eventually this suggestion resulted in the needed repairs, and in September 1916, for the first time in years, the Old Central bell rang again calling the freshman and sophomore classes together for the annual class fight in the old cottonwood tree west of Old Central.[40]

Intercollegiate athletics would eventually focus much attention on the Old Central bell and clapper. Sports development in an organized way came at about the same time to the Oklahoma A. and M. College and to similar institutions in Oklahoma Territory and nationwide. President Angelo C. Scott announced at the daily chapel meeting in the Old Central assembly hall one winter morning in early 1900 that the colleges of the territory had organized the Oklahoma Intercollegiate Athletic Association. This group included Oklahoma A. and M. College at Stillwater, Northwestern Normal School at Alva, Kingfisher College at Kingfisher, Central Normal School at Edmond, and University of Oklahoma at Norman. After Scott energized the students by urging that they prove their supremacy in athletics, an enthusiastic group of men students organized the Oklahoma A. and M. College Athletic Association. Fortunately, the railroad reached Stillwater just in time to run an excursion train to Guthrie, the scene of the first territorial field meet in early May 1900. The college won this event for three consecutive years, thus permanently keeping the Douglas Cup, the trophy for the meet.[41]

With this vigorous and successful adventure into athletics at the college, the Old Central bell and clapper began to play a part in the sports scene. Overall, however, few athletic victories, including National Collegiate Athletic Association championships, were celebrated by ringing the bell, and these scattered occasions recognized game wins and various championships in a variety of sports, including wrestling, basketball, and football.

President Angelo C. Scott announced at the daily chapel meeting in the Old Central assembly hall one winter morning in early 1900 that the colleges of the territory had organized the Oklahoma Intercollegiate Athletic Association. This resulted in the Stillwater college receiving the Douglas Cup in 1902 for winning the territorial meet for three consecutive years. It was the first championship team trophy won by the college and launched the spirited "Bedlam Series" with the University of Oklahoma.

The Old Central bell and clapper soon figured most prominently in the Oklahoma A. and M. College victory celebrations in football with the University of Oklahoma. Just after repairs had been completed on the cradle of the bell, the college in 1917 defeated the university on the gridiron by a score of 9-0, its first win since the annual game series began in 1904.[42] Although seven months earlier the United States had entered World War I, the students and residents of Stillwater set aside their cares the moment the news of this upset reached town by telegraph. The bell in Old Central, said the *Orange and Black,* brought "the glad tidings to those who had not heard. Immediately whistles, bells and gunshots made the Battle of Verdun seem like a small boy's Fourth of July." Bonfires dotted Stillwater while the merrymaking continued until the early morning hours. When the special train returned to Stillwater with the team and fans at 3:00 A.M., 300 students and townspeople met it, and the celebrating persisted, with even larger bonfires for the rest of the night.[43]

Following the weekend, a gigantic pep rally celebrating the occasion took place in the College Auditorium on Monday evening. Many Stillwater townspeople also attended. "It is customary," said President James W. Cantwell to the audience, "for a country to celebrate with much pomp a great victory, and we feel more jubilant than ever before, for we have conquered a foe which has held us powerless in years past." Cantwell then predicted that the enrollment of the college would increase due to an improved athletic record. Immediately after the meeting the rooters invaded the business district of Stillwater, collected all the old lumber and boxes possible, and carried them to Lewis Field on the campus. While the huge bonfire raged, an immense snake dance took place. Amid the cheering of the fans, the Old Central bell rang constantly and the shrill whistle of the campus power plant blew persistently. The festivities continued until late in the night, and President Cantwell declared the next day a holiday to complete the jubilee. "Never before in the history of the College," observed the *Orange and Black*, "has such an enthusiastic celebration been held."[44]

Student opinion and tradition at the Oklahoma A. and M. College soon reserved the Old Central bell for the special purpose of celebrating football victories over the University of Oklahoma. Students dubbed it the Victory Bell. The wins, usually upsets in the long game series, came infrequently and by 1987 numbered only twelve, with but six ties. Seven years passed after the 1917 win before victory came again. In 1924, after a victory score of 6-0 on Lewis Field, the Old Central bell rang more than an hour. Student leaders took turns at clanging it, and President Bradford Knapp climbed to the belfry to participate also. Then in 1927, victory smiled again in another upset, this time with a score of 13-7. Students had made for Old Central's bell and "began its wild clanging" during a giant pep rally the evening before the game. After the game, the bell rang again to celebrate the first Aggie win in Owen Stadium at Norman.[45]

With the arrival of football coach Lynn O. Waldorf at the Oklahoma A. and M. College in 1929, the gridiron fortunes of the institution improved dramatically. That year the Aggies played the University of Oklahoma to a 7-7 tie in Norman, and a year later won by a score of 7-0 on Lewis Field. The Old Central bell rang and rang, much to the irritation of the visiting Sooners. All seemed well until the following Tuesday, when Otis S. Wile, a journalist alumnus of the college in Stillwater, received a telephone call from Eugene Peach, the state editor of the *Daily Oklahoman*, desiring verification of the clapper removal from the Old Central bell. Peach had received a news story from Norman reporting that the clapper had been taken by the University of Oklahoma students during the night following the game. A group of Aggie students climbed to the belfry only to find the clapper gone. The clapper, demanded the *Daily O'Collegian*, "must be rescued from the pilfering Sooners and restored lest Aggies of bygone days shall turn restlessly in their beds and Aggies of nowadays squirm at constant jibes and jests of unsympathetic Sooners . . . .Aggie students will not sit idly by and see so precious an object as old Victory's ,clapper go unrescued."[46]

In a little while two students from the Stillwater campus, Hugh "Hudie" Haston and Gerald T. "Cowboy" Curtin, rescued the captured clapper from a fraternity house at the University of Oklahoma and replaced it in the bell. Soon a press dispatch from Norman announced that the clapper found by Haston and Curtin in the fraternity house came from a church bell in Norman and not from the Old Central bell. Five men students from the Stillwater campus appointed themselves an unofficial group of clapper experts, according to the *Daily O'Collegian*, and "assembled in the cupola of Old Central and declared the now historic relic to be the one and original."[47] Curtin, president of the Oklahoma A. and M. College "O" Club, the organization of student athletic lettermen, planned to have a committee of lettermen take charge of the clapper.[48]

The controversy over the Old Central bell clapper finally settled down when athletes from the two institutions agreed that in the future the clapper would go to the team winning the annual gridiron classic. Haston and Curtin likely originated the idea, although Peyton Glass Jr. of the class of 1933 was credited with it at the time. In case of a tie, the institution with the last win would keep the clapper. This happened in 1931 when Waldorf's team held the Sooners to a 0-0 tie in Owen Stadium in Norman.[49] Then in 1932 the Aggies defeated them by a score of 7-0 in Stillwater. "The victory occasioned no little shouting among the Cowboys' friends," reported the *Daily O'Collegian*, "and the grand old Victory Bell that hangs high in Old Central received a none to[o] gentle thrashing by the Clapper that caused hallowed sounds to reverberate throughout Aggieland."[50]

Again in 1933 Waldorf's team won the annual classic with the Sooners in Norman by a score of 13-0. Shortly before noon on the following Monday, when the students had returned to the campus after the Thanksgiving holiday, the Old Central bell rang out the points scored at Norman in a ceremony. A year later, in 1934, during a losing season coached by Waldorf's successor, the Aggies managed to hold the Sooners to a scoreless tie on Lewis Field in Stillwater. The Old Central bell did not ring, but the clapper remained. Meantime, Waldorf, with five years of stellar service as head football coach for the Oklahoma Aggies, moved on to an outstanding coaching career at the Northwestern University and the University of California. At the Oklahoma A. and M. College, Waldorf's teams won 34 games, lost 10, and tied 7. His overall career record stood at 170 wins, 94 losses, and 22 ties, an achievement that earned induction into the National Football Foundation Hall of Fame.[51]

Beginning in 1935, the Aggies commenced another losing streak in the annual gridiron games with the Sooners. That year the clapper of the Old Central bell went to the University of Oklahoma, and reports in Stillwater had it kept in the president's office. It did, in fact, remain there until the following year when L. Whitley Cox Sr. of the University of Oklahoma class of 1936 and president of the athletic lettermen club, transferred it to his house in Tulsa. He kept the clapper in a trunk in his attic and took it to the Aggie-Sooner football game each year. Annually the desire of the students of the Oklahoma A. and M. College

When the Aggies lost the annual gridiron game with the Sooners in 1935, the Old Central bell clapper was placed in the hand of L. Whitley Cox Sr. of the University of Oklahoma class of 1936 and president of the athletic lettermen club. For a week he carried it to his classes and had himself photographed with it in front of the Alpha Sigma Phi fraternity house.

to win the contest centered around regaining the clapper. Confusion entered the situation when word reached Stillwater that the clapper had never been in the office of the University of Oklahoma president, but had been located in Cox's trunk.[52] A student in Stillwater complained that "if we don't hurry up and beat O.U. again, there will not be any object in trying. The clapper will have rusted away completely."[53]

Although the Aggies played the Sooners to a scoreless tie in 1942, a suggestion from several residents of Norman and Stillwater that the Old Central bell and clapper should be contributed to the national scrap metal drive of World War II brought scorn from the Oklahoma A. and M. College campus. It also produced the recommendation that only otherwise useless metal be given to the scrap drive.[54]

The evening before the 1944 Aggie-Sooner classic in Oklahoma City, three young men came to the house of Cox in Tulsa. They identified themselves as being from the *Oklahoma Daily,* the student newspaper of the University of Oklahoma, and brought with them a press-quality camera. They asked to see the Old Central bell clapper and to take a picture of Cox and his wife holding it in front of their fireplace. After Cox got the clapper from his trunk in the attic, the three young men asked to hold it to get a closer look. Cox readily consented, but while the three men looked at the trophy they suddenly turned and ran out of the house to their car backed up in the driveway. "I ran after them as they drove from the driveway," said Cox, "and jumped on their running board to retrieve the clapper. I could not get a hand on the clapper because it was under their feet, so I grabbed their expensive press camera belonging to the *Daily O'Collegian* and returned to my house." Soon the three young men rang the doorbell of the Cox house and asked to have their camera. "I told them if they would be gentlemen enough to return the clapper I would give them the camera," explained Cox. "They agreed. I assured them that if the Aggies won the game the next day I would surrender the clapper."[55]

The following day, the Aggie football team of Coach Edwin M. "Jim" Lookabaugh, with but one season loss, romped over the Sooners at Taft Stadium in Oklahoma City with a score of 28-6 and went on to the Cotton Bowl for another victory. Following the win over the University of Oklahoma, the clapper was returned on the playing field to Robert D. "Bob" Fenimore, the Aggie star of the game, so that the victory, the first in eleven years, could be appropriately celebrated on the Stillwater campus. Some six hundred students rang the bell for several days and nights, often counting out the score by twenty-eight fast rings for the Cowboys and six slow tolls for the Sooners.[56]

The Aggies played even better football under Lookabaugh in 1945, the year World War II concluded, when they had no losses for the season, including the Sugar Bowl game. The Old Central bell and clapper joyfully rang again and again when the Aggies won the annual classic, held in Norman, by a score of 47-0.[57]

The following year, in 1946, the University of Oklahoma roared back on the gridiron in Stillwater with a crushing 73-12 defeat, a pattern that would continue, without even a tie, for the next nineteen years. Meanwhile, the Old Central bell clapper remained in the possession of the Sooners, who almost forgot about it. Leonard H. Haug, the band director at the University of Oklahoma, kept the clapper in his possession from 1946 until his retirement in the early 1960s. After Haug retired, Gene A. Braught became the University of Oklahoma Band director and also the custodian of the clapper. Each year during the nineteen-year interval, Hiram H. Henry, the director of the Oklahoma A. and M. College Band, sent orange and black ribbons and a friendly note to the director of the University of Oklahoma Band to remind him to have the clapper readily available for presentation if the Cowboys won. During this nineteen-year period the clapper was never placed on public display at the annual games, nor had it been exhibited during the previous eight-year period Cox had it in his trunk in Tulsa.[58]

The Aggie longing to rewin the clapper trophy remained undiminished over the years the Sooner team appeared invincible. In 1950 the clapper tradition received national recognition when it surfaced in an article in the *Ethyl News* along with other intercollegiate football trophies such as the noted Little Brown Jug used to record the scores of the Minnesota-Michigan grid games since 1903 and the Old Oaken Bucket of Indiana-Purdue rivalry.[59]

At the Oklahoma A. and M. College the validity of the trophy began to be doubted, and administrators of the two institutions even discussed the substitution of another memento for the winner of the annual classic, but took no action because they concluded that the students of both institutions wanted the clapper to continue as the trophy. By the time of the 1959 game only a few people at the University of Oklahoma knew the location of the clapper, and on the Oklahoma State University campus the bell itself could not be readily located. A year later the bell turned up in storage in the Old Library, where it had been kept for two years, almost forgotten.[60] "The bell was removed from the tower of Old Central because it was feared that its weight might cause the bell to fall," explained Abe L. Hesser, the Student Union director. He said that the bell would be placed in the Student Union tower, where it could be rung by students whenever the Cowboys won the annual football game with the Sooners.[61]

Then in 1961, under the direction of Wesley W. Watkins, the president of the Oklahoma State University Student Senate, a plan developed with the student leadership of the University of Oklahoma to make the Old Central bell clapper one-half of a new trophy proposed for the winner of the annual football game between the two universities. In this transaction, the Sooners would have returned the bell clapper to the Stillwater campus in exchange for the recently returned Big Red shotgun to the Norman campus. The University of Oklahoma student leadership eventually rejected the idea of a joint trophy as did much sentiment in the Oklahoma State University student body. At that point Watkins and the student senate proposed to establish the clapper as the "official" football trophy, already firmed up by tradition, as the annual symbol of the Oklahoma-Oklahoma State game. Nothing came of this effort, and the clapper remained on the Sooner campus.[62]

Finally in 1965, the Cowboys, in a losing season, upset the Sooners in Norman by a score of 17-16. In a ceremony on the playing field after the game, Band Director Hiram H. Henry of the Oklahoma State University accepted the clapper from Band Director Gene A. Braught of the University of Oklahoma. At last the clapper had come home, together with the second clapper reputedly liberated years earlier from a Norman church. Meanwhile, the Old Central bell had been hung in the tower of the Student Union, and immediately after the close of the 1965 classic the original clapper was installed in the bell in such a way that it could not be readily unbolted, and a long rope attached to the bell. Students crowded into the Circus Room on the top floor of the Student Union to ring the bell throughout the evening and night following the game. The next year, in 1966, the Cowboys again upset the Sooners on

After a nineteen-year losing streak in football, the Cowboys upset the Sooners in 1965 in Norman by a score of 17-16. In a ceremony on the field after the game, Band Director Hiram H. Henry (*right*) of the Oklahoma State University accepted the Old Central bell clapper, together with the second clapper reputedly liberated years earlier from a Norman church, from Band Director Gene A. Braught of the University of Oklahoma.

the gridiron in Stillwater by a tight score of 15-14. Once more Cowboy students kept the bell clanging for many hours to celebrate the victory.[63]

The 1966 Cowboy win over the Sooners on Lewis Field brought what appeared to be the beginning of another revised football tradition between the two institutions. That year following the game the Sooner's Little Red in an unplanned goodwill ceremony surrendered his Indian headdress to Robert B. Bird, the president of the Oklahoma State University Student Senate. It looked on the surface as though a joint trophy of the headdress and the bell clapper had been established for the winner of the annual gridiron classic. Most spectators in the stadium probably came to this conclusion. As soon as the post-game ceremony ended, the headdress was returned to Little Red and the president of the Sooner student body when they explained that Little Red needed it for other athletic events of the University of Oklahoma at which he regularly appeared. About a month later the University of Oklahoma Student Senate sent a similar Indian headdress, according to Murl R. Rogers, the Oklahoma State University Alumni Association executive director, and for a brief period it appeared on display in the Student Union on the

Immediately after the Cowboy win over the Sooners in the 1965 gridiron classic, the clapper was reinstalled in the Old Central bell then hanging in the Student Union tower. Students rang it for hours. Dwain Gindra, Cashion, steadies the clapper, and Paul K. Rodman, Corpus Christi, Texas, gets set to ring out the news of the victory.

Cowboy campus. The next year, in 1967, the Sooners overcame the Cowboys in Norman by a score of 38-14. At the close of the football game the substitute Indian headdress was returned to the Sooners along with the bell clapper from an early-day Norman church. With the original clapper back in the Old Central bell and the original headdress back on Little Red's head, the bell clapper trophy tradition of thirty-six years came to an end, probably to the relief of both institutions.[64]

Although the clapper custom remained but a memory, an incident concerning the clapper occurred nine years later reminiscent of the origin of the tradition. In 1975, when Old Central was being restored to its original 1894 condition, Stephen R. Ward, a *Daily O'Collegian* staff writer, published an article on the bell clapper gridiron tradition in which he mentioned that the original clapper hung in the bell recently returned to the Old Central belfry. His research for the article brought him in contact with students on both the Sooner and Cowboy campuses.[65] The day following the publication of the article, an anonymous male called the *Daily O'Collegian* office long-distance and told a secre-

In 1966 the Cowboys again upset the Sooners in football at Stillwater by a tight score of 15-14. That year the Sooner's Little Red surrendered his Indian headdress to Robert B. Bird, the president of the Oklahoma State University Student Senate. It looked as though a joint trophy of the headdress and the Old Central bell clapper had been established for the winner of the annual gridiron classic, but this did not occur.

tary: "I've got a tip for you. The clapper in the bell is gone."[66] When *Daily O'Collegian* reporters and campus police investigated Old Central, they found a shattered basement window, a locked door forced open, and the clapper missing, much in the original pattern of the removal of the clapper by the University of Oklahoma students forty-five years earlier.[67] Seven days later another anonymous long-distance telephone call reached the *Daily O'Collegian* office: "I have a tip for you," said a male voice. "It's about the Old Central bell up there. The clapper is back in it." Again the call could not be traced through the Oklahoma State University switchboard. When *Daily O'Collegian* reporters and campus police investigated, they quickly found the clapper securely in place in Old Central's bell.[68]

"There is no doubt in my mind," commented Ward, "that the theft was prompted by my story about the lost [church bell] clapper at the University of Oklahoma. I had told at least one University of Oklahoma student in the course of doing the story what the University of Oklahoma had was not the original. The theft could have been hatched at the University of Oklahoma or it could have been plotted at Oklahoma State University . . . .I am satisfied that the . . . caper ended with the return of the clapper because someone was convinced . . . they had . . . a historical artifact."[69]

The next year, in 1976, when the Cowboys defeated the Sooners in Owen Stadium in Norman, the score concluded at 31-24. No one on either campus publicly mentioned the Old Central bell clapper tradition before the game, and after the victory apparently no one gave serious thought about ringing the bell on the Cowboy campus. Not even student pranksters broke into the building to ring the bell. The *Daily O'Collegian* did not even comment that the bell was not rung to recognize the victory.[70] A *Daily Oklahoman* reporter managed but a cryptic comment: "And even staid Old Central tower on the Oklahoma State University campus shook its ancient masonry in time to the chimes of its never-rung bell."[71] Perhaps the student tradition of ringing the bell when winning the annual gridiron classic had died like the bell clapper trophy custom.

If anyone in 1976 following the gridiron win over the Sooners had desired to ring the Old Central bell, special arrangements would have been necessary. Following the disappearance and return of the clapper in 1975, it was removed from the bell and placed in safekeeping in the custody of the Oklahoma State University Architectural Services. It remained there until the restoration of Old Central was completed in 1983, when James L. Showalter, the curator of the Oklahoma Museum of Higher Education in Old Central, replaced it in the bell.[72]

In the early years of little public entertainment on the campus and in Stillwater, students in and around Old Central improvised their own diversions, sometimes spontaneous and sometimes planned. Even the daily morning chapel service in the assembly hall had its moments of

Old Central's bell and clapper presently hang in the building for which they were originally intended. The new bell cradle of steel beams is anchored to the reinforced belfry, an improvement made during the restoration of the structure.

humor, hilarity, and ingenuity, as did the unscheduled entertainment and coeducational social activity in the chemistry laboratory. Student pranks also took place in the classrooms of the building. Romance likewise flourished in the structure, and especially when the south steps and entrance became a location for making and breaking social engagements.

Graduation class identity proved to be a powerful rallying force among students in the early days of Old Central. Social events revolved around each class, and peer pressures kept the relationships strong through the collegiate years and for decades after graduation. The class of 1903 party, duplicated many times in other homes in Stillwater, symbolized class organization, as did the flagpole incident on the roof of Old Central and the annual class fights held in the battered cottonwood tree west of the structure. Efforts to substitute pole fights and pushball contests for tree fights at Old Central were less successful. The Old Central bell and clapper became a long-term symbol of athletic success, especially in the annual football competition between the Oklahoma State University and the University of Oklahoma.

Endnotes

1. *Stillwater Messenger*, 2 November 1894, p. 3.

2. Stillwater *Eagle-Gazette*, 15 November 1894, p. 1.

3. Alfred E. Jarrell to Berlin B. Chapman, 9 April 1956, Alfred E. Jarrell File, Berlin B. Chapman Collection, Special Collections, Edmon Low Library, Oklahoma State University, Stillwater, Oklahoma.

4. Alfred E. Jarrell to Berlin B. Chapman, 9 April 1956, Alfred E. Jarrell File, Berlin B. Chapman Collection.

5. William A. Worley to Willa Adams Dusch, 20 February 1951, Old Central Centennial History Collection, Special Collections, Edmon Low Library.

6. Oklahoma A. and M. *College Paper*, March 1906, p. 79.

7. *College Paper*, 1 May 1900, p. 32.

8. *College Paper*, 1 May 1900, p. 32.

9. Oklahoma A. and M. College, *Some Graduates of the A. and M. College and What They Are Doing* (Stillwater: Oklahoma A. and M. College, 1905), unpaged; *Annual Catalog, Oklahoma A. and M. College, 1901-1902*, p. 4; *Annual Catalog, Oklahoma A. and M. College, 1905-1906*, p. 4; Berlin B. Chapman, editor, *Old Central in the Crisis of 1955* ([Orlando, FL: Golden Rule Publishing Company, 1964]), pp. 18-19; *Stillwater NewsPress*, 15 February 1984, p. 1B, 21 January 1987, pp. 1-2B, 4 February 1987, p. 1B.

10. Author interview with Elizabeth Oursler Taylor, 2 November 1985, Old Central Centennial History Collection.

11. *College Paper*, 28 November 1902, p. 113.

12. Olin W. Jones, "Aggieland's First Collegiates," *Oklahoma A. and M. College Magazine*, vol. 1, no. 6 (February 1930), p. 24. A variation of this incident appeared in the Oklahoma A. and M. College *Daily O'Collegian*, 29 October 1938, p. 2.

13. R. Morton House, ''The Class of 1903 at Oklahoma A. and M. College,'' *Chronicles of Oklahoma,* vol. 44, no. 4 (Winter 1966-1967), pp. 397-398. A variation of the House account is in the letter of William A. Worley to Willa Adams Dusch, 20 February 1951, Old Central Centennial History Collection. James L. Showalter, ''Oklahoma A. and M. College Territorial Student Survey,'' typescript, Old Central Centennial History Collection.

14. House, p. 398.

15. *1916 Redskin,* p. 220, Oklahoma A. and M. College Yearbook.

16. Oklahoma A. and M. College *Orange and Black,* 11 October 1915, p. 2.

17. *Stillwater Gazette,* 26 September 1895, p. 2; House, pp. 403, 405; Paul G. Crouse, ''Reminiscences,'' typescript, Paul G. Crouse File, Berlin B. Chapman Collection.

18. House, p. 405.

19. *Orange and Black,* 10 September 1913, p. 1; *1915 Redskin,* p. 108.

20. *Orange and Black,* 10 September 1913, p. 1.

21. *1915 Redskin,* p. 146.

22. *1915 Redskin,* p. 146.

23. *Orange and Black,* 13 September 1915, p. 1.

24. *Orange and Black,* 16 September 1916, p. 1; *1917 Redskin,* p. 274.

25. *Orange and Black,* 22 September 1917, p. 1.

26. *Orange and Black,* 29 September 1917, p. 2.

27. *Orange and Black,* 24 September 1919, p. 1; *1920 Redskin,* p. 258.

28. *Orange and Black,* 24 September 1919, pp. 1, 2, 4.

29. Stillwater *Advance-Democrat,* 30 September 1920, p. 1; *Orange and Black,* 6 October 1921, p. 1.

30. Oklahoma A. and M. College *O'Collegian,* 2 May 1925, p. 1.

31. Alfred E. Jarrell to Berlin B. Chapman, 9 April 1956, 1 September 1958, Alfred E. Jarrell File, Berlin B. Chapman Collection; *Tulsa Sunday World Magazine,* 14 December 1958, p. 6; *Stillwater NewsPress,* 28 August 1975, p. 5; *Daily O'Collegian,* 22 September 1938, p. 4.

32. Alfred E. Jarrell to Berlin B. Chapman, 10 July 1958, Alfred E. Jarrell File, Berlin B. Chapman Collection.

33. Author interview with James L. Showalter, 27 February 1986, Old Central Centennial History Collection; *Stillwater Messenger,* 16 November 1894, p. 3; Alfred E. Jarrell to Berlin B. Chapman, undated questionnaire enclosed with letter of 27 June 1954, and Alfred E. Jarrell to Berlin B. Chapman, 9 April 1956, Alfred E. Jarrell File, in Berlin B. Chapman Collection.

34. Stillwater *Payne County Populist,* 30 November 1894, p. 4.

35. *College Paper,* March 1906, p. 80.

36. *College Paper,* March 1906, p. 80.

37. *1913 Redskin,* p. 69.

38. *Daily O'Collegian,* 2 November 1938, p. 4.

39. *Daily O'Collegian,* 2 November 1938, pp. 2, 4, 2 November 1939, p. 2.

40. *Orange and Black,* September 1908, p. 45, 26 November 1913, p. 2, 16 September 1916, p. 1; Oklahoma City *Daily Oklahoman,* 22 April 1914, p. 41.

41. House, pp. 393-397. Intercollegiate athletics at Oklahoma State University are discussed in another volume of the Centennial Histories Series entitled *A History of the Oklahoma State University Intercollegiate Athletics* by Doris Dellinger.

42. Oklahoma State University, *Oklahoma State Football 1986* (Stillwater: Oklahoma State University, 1986), pp. 80-88. Hereinafter all citations relating to annual football statistics will come from the all time Oklahoma State University scores included in this book.

43. *Orange and Black,* 1 December 1917, p. 1.

44. *Orange and Black,* 8 December 1917, p. 1.

45. *Daily O'Collegian,* 18 November 1927, pp. 1-2, 22 November 1927, p. 1.

46. *Daily O'Collegian,* 26 November 1930, pp. 1-2.

47. *Daily O'Collegian,* 6 January 1931, p. 1.

48. *Daily O'Collegian,* 7 January 1931, p. 1.

49. *Daily O'Collegian,* 5 December 1933, p. 1; Author interview with Peyton Glass Jr., 2 October 1986, Old Central Centennial History Collection.

50. *Daily O'Collegian,* 1 November 1932, p. 1.

51. *Daily O'Collegian,* 5 December 1933, p. 1; Ronald L. Mendell and Timothy B. Phares, *Who's Who in Football* (New Rochelle, NY: Arlington House, 1974), p. 360.

52. *Daily O'Collegian,* 4 December 1935, p. 1, 18 November 1936, p. 3, 19 November 1937, p. 1; Author interview with L. Whitley Cox Sr., 22 October 1986, Old Central Centennial History Collection.

53. *Daily O'Collegian,* 27 October 1939, p. 2.

54. *Daily O'Collegian,* 29 September 1942, p. 2, 8 October 1942, p. 2.

55. Cox interview.

56. *Daily O'Collegian,* 29 November 1944, pp. 1, 2, 4; *Tulsa World,* 30 November 1985, p. 1D; Cox interview; Author interview with Robert D. "Bob" Fenimore, 26 October 1986, Old Central Centennial History Collection.

57. *Daily O'Collegian,* 21 November 1945, p. 1.

58. Author interviews with Hiram H. Henry, 22 October 1986 and 28 October 1986, Old Central Centennial History Collection.

59. "Touchdown Trophies," *Ethyl News,* no volume, no number (October 1950), pp. 10-11; *Daily O'Collegian,* 7 November 1950, p. 6.

60. *Daily Oklahoman,* 18 November 1953, p. 13; *Daily O'Collegian,* 24 November 1959, p. 8.

61. *Daily O'Collegian,* 22 November 1960, p. 7.

62. *Daily O'Collegian,* 4 January 1961, p. 2, 13 January 1961, p. 8, 17 January 1961, p. 1, 3 March 1961, pp. 1, 4.

63. Author interview with David E. Jafek, 27 January 1986, Author interview with Thomas A. Casey, 26 January 1986, and Author interview with Albert E. Jones, 26 January 1986, in Old Central Centennial History Collection; *Daily O'Collegian,* 1 December 1965, p. 1, 8 December 1965, p. 1; Otis Wile, "The Bell Clapper Comes Home," *Oklahoma State Alumnus Magazine,* vol. 7, no. 1 (January 1966), pp. 4-8.

64. *Daily O'Collegian,* 6 December 1966, p. 1, 30 November 1967, p. 1; Author interview with Leo Elwell, 19 October 1986, and Author interview with Robert B. Bird, 22 October 1986, in Old Central Centennial History Collection; Jafek interview; Henry interview, 22 October 1986.

65. *Daily O'Collegian,* 31 October 1975, p. 1.

66. *Daily O'Collegian,* 1 November 1975, p. 1.

67. *Daily O'Collegian,* 4 November 1975, p. 7.

68. *Daily O'Collegian,* 5 November 1975, p. 8.

69. Author interview with Stephen R. Ward, 20 September 1986, Old Central Centennial History Collection.

70. Author interview with Ernest B. Tye, 22 October 1986, Old Central Centennial History Collection; Records, Oklahoma State University Security Department, Stillwater, Oklahoma.

71. *Daily Oklahoman,* 24 October 1976, p. 1A.

72. *Tulsa World,* 30 November 1985, p. 11D.

9 Decline and Renewal

The physical life of Old Central is an account of not only decline and renewal, but also of controversy and survival. The soil on which the building stands has always threatened its survival, as has its sandstone foundation construction and heavy use across the years. Although these conditions soon caused the building's future to be in question, at the same time they tended to emphasize its historical significance. Considering these factors, the building has been a relatively low-cost maintenance structure for its size and the volume of service rendered. Old Central stands as the sole survivor of the sandstone foundation first generation buildings and the material patriarch of the Oklahoma State University and the land-grant college movement in Oklahoma.

Within a few months after the completion of Old Central in 1894, a roof-like cover called a portico took shape over the south basement-level entry to the building. Attached to the building on two sides, the portico had two posts supporting it on the other sides. A Victorian ornamentation garnished the entire portico above as well as under its exposed roofline. The portico had the purpose of deflecting rainwater from the steps and other low levels of the basement entry. Other changes to the building followed.[1]

Nearly a year after the opening of Old Central, newly-arrived President George E. Morrow had a flagpole placed on the east gable end of its roof. Extending about twenty feet above the roof and its lanyard reaching to a second story window frame below, the flagstaff remained operable until 1902, when a sophomore student cut the rope on the pole from the roof of the building to remove the freshman class colors. The flagpole, never practical in this roof location and now rendered unusable, was removed and eventually replaced with a flagstaff at ground level in front of the building.[2]

The 1901 building appropriation of $54,000 for the college made by the legislative assembly did more than provide adequate money for new structures. It also made funds available, as tax revenues accumulated, for the extensive improvement and modernization of Old Central from 1901 to 1903. The painting of the inside and outside of the building was completed in 1901, and at the same time a "purifying bucket-pump" was placed on the well north of the structure.[3] This made the water "more fit to drink than it has been in the past."[4]

Meanwhile, utility services developed for all campus buildings. The president's office in Old Central had a telephone by 1900, and in 1901 pipes were laid to connect the college with the new city waterworks.[5] "A trial . . . with direct pressure threw a stream over the assembly building," reported the *College Paper*. "This practically insures us against fire."[6] At the same time a septic tank sanitary sewer system went into operation on the campus, although the city did not operate a sewer service until 1909. Also in 1901 a dynamo in the engineering department began to supply limited quantities of electricity for lighting purposes. Not until 1905 did the municipal power plant provide electricity for the campus. In 1902 a centralized heating system began to function on the

In this campus view taken from the west about 1904, the 1902 Engineering Building is to the immediate left, while the north and south ends of the Library Building are evident to the east of Old Central. In the background is the residential area of Stillwater fronting on Knoblock Street and beyond. In the foreground are the brick sidewalks connecting the campus buildings with brick sidewalks leading to the Stillwater business district. The semicircular road in front of Old Central joins Knoblock and Hester streets.

campus following the construction of a new powerhouse. Early in 1903 work commenced on brick sidewalks connecting all permanent buildings on the campus with brick sidewalks leading to the business district of Stillwater.[7]

The refurbishing of Old Central in 1903 updated the structure, only nine years of age, and also attempted to correct a major moisture and water problem in the basement. This problem in the basement resulted from inadequate drainage around the building, three doorway entrances into the basement, window wells at all basement windows, and an unusually porous foundation made of uncut sandstone rock. The Permian red clay, on which the building stands, expands when wet, and this produced cracks in the wall through which water could flow into the basement.[8]

The basement work took the major share of the money and time spent on reworking Old Central in 1903. First, workmen removed all woodwork in the basement, including the wainscoting, and the concrete floor. Then, an excavation was made in the center of the basement hallway to accommodate a brick sump tunnel 37 inches in diameter. The tunnel started about twelve feet north of the south basement wall and followed the centerline of the hall to the crossing of the north inside stairwell. At this point it turned west at a right angle, ending in a bank of soil under the northwest outside stairwell. This water collection system, intended to drain the under-floor areas of the basement, had brick feeder lines draining into the top of the tunnel coming from under every room in the basement. Next, soil was installed to raise the unfinished floor level by nearly a foot, thus decreasing the moisture and water problem. On top of this a one-inch layer of concrete was poured, followed by a thicker concrete slab shaped by boards laid in it to which a tongue and groove yellow pine floor was nailed.[9]

The window wells were eliminated except for the pair in the southeast room overlooking the basement entry. Likely the old window frames were cut back, and the window panes reworked rather than new windows being installed. New plaster went into place where needed, and apparently the wainscoting was not resituated. Simultaneously the old boiler was removed, and the steam heating system of the building was connected with the central power plant of the campus. Probably additional heating radiators were installed at the time.[10]

With the new campus central water and sewer system in place, one or more toilets went into service about 1903 in the former steam boiler room located in the northwest corner of the Old Central basement, and at the same time workmen removed the carbide gas machine. The renovation included installation of an electrical lighting system, likely with wires exposed on the inside walls, in much of the building. As was the custom of the time, the old gas lighting fixtures were probably converted to electrical lighting fixtures. With this work completed, Old Central's physical condition in quality and modernization appeared to equal that of the newest structures on the campus.[11]

When the new agricultural and administration building, Morrill Hall, was completed in 1906, Old Central no longer remained the center of attention. The edifice had not yet become a symbol or antique, nor was it good enough structurally to be valued highly for functional reasons. While students and faculty crowded into it as always, it received virtually no maintenance attention for more than a decade, likely due to inadequate funding. A plaster fall or two occurred during these years, the moisture problem likely continued to a much lesser degree in the basement, and the exterior woodwork probably needed minor repairs as well as paint. The greatest problem of all resulted from the sandstone rubble foundation interacting with the Permian red clay on which the building stood. By 1914 this had resulted in slight movement of the massive brick and stone walls, and the subsequent deterioration of the masonry. At that time the building had reached its twentieth year of service.[12]

Permian red clay is found in sections of Oklahoma and Texas and is unusually heavy in the Stillwater area and notably so on the campus of Oklahoma State University. Although slow to absorb water, as the clay becomes saturated it expands, displacing walls inward, usually causing cracks in the masonry. When the clay dries out, it shrinks away from the walls, leaving an open space between the walls and the soil. With the next rain, the cracks fill with water, exerting hydrostatic pressure to force water into the basement. Interior footings and floors of buildings constructed on saturated clay remain fixed acceptably well, but exterior footings and walls may be displaced further each time as loose soil and debris are accumulated with changes in water content in the soil. Exterior walls go up, down, and sideways, and this heaving results in masonry damage, a severe problem for not only Old Central over the years, but also for the other early sandstone foundation buildings that once stood on the campus. Even more modern structures at the institution have experienced similar problems due to shifting clay.[13]

Old Central's sandstone foundation was not substandard at the time of construction. Probably nothing could have been done in the central area of the United States to devise a more durable foundation. Reinforced concrete for use in construction was not patented until 1867 in France, and some years passed before it became widely used in the United States. But reinforced concrete foundations alone could not overcome the wrenching capabilities of Permian red clay. Finally, the problems began to be understood when the science of soil mechanics developed in the 1920s, and from it grew an awareness in the 1930s of the special difficulty caused by the shrink-swell behavior of the red clay. Not until after World War II were foundation construction methods devised that can

Elizabeth Oursler Taylor of the class of 1912 moved to Stillwater in 1905 and lived in a house across College Avenue within sight of Old Central. Her class was the first in the history of the college to wear academic robes for graduation. Stillwater honored the class by staging a downtown parade in which the graduates marched in their academic robes.

largely overcome the problems caused by Permian red clay.[14]

In the years between 1903 and 1914, people reacted to Old Central in various ways. Elizabeth Oursler Taylor of the class of 1912,who first came to know Old Central in 1905 when she lived in a house across College Avenue from the building, viewed it favorably: "Old Central belonged to me," she recalled. "It awed me, including its big auditorium. The condition of the building was good."[15] Randle Perdue, a freshman in 1911, said: "I was not particularly impressed by the building, which then had no particular import . . . .It was just another classroom building, in apparent good condition."[16] A news writer for the *Daily Oklahoman*, however, found it to be both historic and obsolete: "The central building, first permanent structure on the campus and yet in use, was a magnificent building . . . .Today it stands, small and dingy, among its neighbors of newer architecture. The bell tower that once housed the gong that called classes to duty is silent and an electric system rings the changing periods at the same second in every building on the campus."[17]

Old Central continued to be occupied fully and generally acceptable to both students and faculty until 1914. Even the printing department found the 1903 reconditioning of the basement satisfactory when they occupied it from 1906 to 1920. But in 1914 faculty offices in the building suddenly became unpopular and were sometimes even refused.

This occurred when college authorities took a highly visible and drastic measure to stabilize the cracked masonry of the structure. Two large tie rods, complete with turnbuckles designed to take up slack, were installed just beneath the first floor ceiling of the building and extended through the east and west walls, where the tie-rod heads, made like large six-pointed iron stars, could be seen. Oil well pump sucker rods were likely modified and used for the procedure.[18] The *Orange and Black* detailed the reason for the repair work: "The walls of Central building are cracking in several places. Beginning in the pressroom and running upward between the mathematics room on the east is a crack an inch wide which has appeared in the last year. The cracks in the recitation rooms have been plastered, but in the pressroom they remain open."[19] Other reconditioning repairs of substance on the building remained for a later date.

Before long, politics and fear psychology endangered the future of Old Central. O. W. Killam, a state senator from Locust Grove in Mayes County, visited the college to review the need for a new gymnasium in January 1915, soon after the legislature met.[20] During his stay on the campus he said he hoped for an appropriation large enough to demolish Old Central, "as it had become unsafe." At the same time the *Orange and Black* also commented that "the walls of this building have large cracks in them which were plastered over last fall, and large brace rods

In the mid-1910s, deer grazed peacefully in a grove of trees that once grew where the Student Union and Paul Miller Journalism and Broadcasting Building presently stand. Old Central can be seen in the background. To the immediate left is the Chemistry Building and to the east of it is the 1902 Engineering Building.

run from one side to the other. If one of these should break, perhaps there would be lost much more than the cost of a new building, as there are classes in this building nearly every hour in the day.''[21]

An unsigned editorial in the *Orange and Black* printed just before the 1915 legislature adjourned opened caustically: '''The loss of a few hundred Subs [preparatory department students] is as nothing compared to the expenditure of a few thousand dollars which would necessarily need be expended for the tearing down and rebuilding of the Old Central Building at A. and M.,' is what seems to be the thought of the majority of men who have the power to tear it down and rebuild it.'' With this barb aimed at the legislature, the editorialist explained that filling the large cracks in the walls of Old Central with plaster did not add to its structural strength as did the large brace rods running from side to side of the building, but, the viewpoint continued, ''if the rods should break and the building collapse then there would certainly be a loss of many lives.''

Moreover, the editorialist viewed Old Central as very unsightly in appearance. ''The outside walls are old and are far from beautiful,'' the comment maintained. ''On the inside the floors, [and] also the stairs, are of wood and badly worn. The stairs are very narrow and builded in such a way as it is very hard for one to get up and down them, and it is not at all an uncommon thing for some one to fall down them.'' In conclusion, if the building caught fire, it would be very rapidly destroyed, ''and it would be almost impossible to extinguish the fire.''[22]

Old Central won support a few months later in 1915 when another unsigned editorial appeared in the *Orange and Black*. The article spoke of a determination by some to destroy the building and replace it with a modern structure. These same people, observed the editorial, ''say the beauty of the proposed rectangle of buildings will be marred if it is left on its present site.'' A few hundred dollars, the reasoning continued, ''would put those massive stone and brick walls in perfectly safe condition. Since the anchoring rods were put in, a little over a year ago, the cracked walls have ceased to spread, and they appear to have conquered that trouble.'' Next came the question, why destroy the building?

The editorialist then called Old Central the oldest building on the campus and the oldest college building in the state. ''The rectangle can be completed on all sides with it left standing,'' said the editorial, ''and it will then be truly 'Central Building.' The contrast will be unique.'' If the interior of the building is unsatisfactory for class use, the thinking concluded, ''why not establish and maintain a museum in it?'' The suggestion followed that the college librarian should have charge of the museum, thereby holding maintenance costs to the minimum. Finally, said the editorial, ''a historical museum stored in a historical building would be a grand thing for the College and Oklahoma.''[23] Little new

President James W. Cantwell, who served from 1915 to 1921, worked to retain Old Central throughout his administration. He took steps to improve the physical condition of the building and opposed its condemnation in 1921.

would be added to the Old Central controversy, now fully rounded out, in the decades ahead.

President James W. Cantwell agreed that Old Central should be retained, perhaps because it could not be replaced because of the lack of funds as much as for its cultural and historical significance. Of the many physical plant improvements carried out on the campus during the summer of 1916, the most extensive appeared to be the work done on Old Central. On the inside, replastering took place as required, and then some walls were repainted while others had new wallpaper applied. Even the blackboards were refinished and the furnishings revarnished. Likely exterior masonry cracks were filled and the woodwork repaired as needed. Also on the outside, new steam lines replaced the old leaky ones between Old Central and Morrill Hall. "Old Central is no longer a dingy looking building," declared an *Orange and Black* reporter.[24]

Over the twenty-two years of its life, Old Central had miraculously escaped fire. Other buildings on campus were not as fortunate. Morrill Hall burned to the ground in August 1914, and two months later, immediately to the east, the Women's Building, presently the Bartlett Center for the Studio Arts, partly burned. Both fires started near the top of the buildings, and the cause was never determined. A campus fire protection system involving wards and fire calls from the whistle of the campus power plant went into service a few months later.[25]

Two years to the month after fire struck the Women's Building, a fire began in a desk on the second floor of Old Central. A night watch-man discovered it at 1:00 A.M. making his rounds next door in the Library Building. After turning in the alarm, he hurried to the fire, and with the aid of a crowd that had assembled, extinguished it before the city fire department arrived. The blaze destroyed only one desk and burned a small hole in the floor. "The origin of the fire is not known," said the *Orange and Black*, "but as the desks in the room where the fire began are of an old style that contained a place for waste paper, it is probable that it was started by the activities of mice in contact with matches, or by spontaneous combustion of trash that had accumulated there."[26] Again the cause was never determined.

The Old Central fire brought about a revised campus plan, which depended on the military cadet corps. Appointed faculty and staff would serve as fire marshals and army staff as assistants until the chief of the city's fire department arrived to take command. In case of fire, student musicians of the regiment would repeatedly sound the fire call on bugles or trumpets, while other student cadet companies carried out assigned tasks during a fire. The cadets experienced frequent fire drills after the Old Central blaze.[27]

Attention continued to focus on Old Central. In 1917 Frederick W. Redlich, a professor in the architecture department of the college and also the campus planner, presented plans and specifications for the construction of a new science building to the Oklahoma State Board of Agriculture, the institution's governing body. Redlich planned for the proposed building, presently a part of the Paul Miller Journalism Building, to conform to the campus quadrangle as it would be shaped, he said "when Old Central is removed." The south side of the original quadrangle would be open.[28]

The first aerial photograph of the Oklahoma A. and M. College campus, made in 1919, shows Old Central and the road in front of it connecting with Knoblock and Hester streets.

About three years later, Redlich, then head of the architecture department, designed a new Library Building for the campus to fit into his proposed campus quadrangle design. With a major colonnaded portico entrance on the east end of the building, the library would overlook the quadrangle unobstructed by Old Central. Again intending to remove Old Central, he located the new building near the west side of Old Central.[29]

When Old Central seemed threatened by the new Library Building, the Alumni Association of the college at its May 1920 board of directors meeting voted to urge the state board of agriculture to retain Old Central. Within a month the founders of Stillwater and their families circulated a petition to save Old Central. After many scores of townspeople and alumni of the college signed the document, it went to John A. Whitehurst, the president of the state board of agriculture. James W. Cantwell, the president of the college, received a copy, intended for the administrative officials and the faculty of the institution.[30]

The petitioners desired "to most heartily and strenuously protest against the destruction, razing, or removal of 'Old Central' building." After reviewing the efforts of Stillwater to construct it, the petition took up the continuing significance of the structure: "The building stands as a monument to the foresight and courage of those early pioneers who are fast leaving the land they have builded into a glorious state and many of whom can no longer look upon the magnificent institution resulting from their works of courage and their one great sacrifice for the future education of the citizenship of the coming state."

Not only did Old Central stand as a monument to the founding fathers of the college, the petition emphasized, but the continuing support of the institution by Stillwater citizens "throughout years . . . to come will depend on these memories and the pride of their achievements, the only fitting monument to which is 'Old Central' standing upon the campus." If the building could no longer be used for classes and similar collegiate purposes, the petitioners reasoned, it should be assigned to the alumni association or a similar organization and converted to a historical museum. "It is almost unthinkable," added the *Stillwater Gazette*, "that a building of the historic value which Old Central has in Oklahoma's civic and educational life, should be razed because it has passed the sphere of usefulness in which it originally served."[31]

Soon after receiving the petition, Whitehurst wrote the Alumni Association without officially bringing the petition to the attention of the Oklahoma State Board of Agriculture. "The Board," he said, "had no inclination to destroy a land-mark, but rather desires to preserve it for some useful purpose." It would take a special act of the legislature, he pointed out, to provide the money to recondition Old Central. If this was agreeable to the Alumni Association after an architect determined the cost of reconditioning the building, he would recommend to the next

In 1917 Frederick W. Redlich, a professor of architecture at the college and also the campus planner, indicated that Old Central should be removed because it blocked the south end of the original campus quadrangle.

legislature that funds be appropriated to refurbish the structure and place it in the hands of the Alumni Association. He asked the association to "consider seriously such a proposition."[32]

The next month, at its August 1920 meeting, the board of directors of the Alumni Association of the college voted to request the state board of agriculture to have Old Central inspected by an architect with a view to having it turned over to the Alumni Association. The alumni board specified an architect from Oklahoma City to prevent Frederick W. Redlich from again recommending the removal of Old Central. This request did not officially come to the attention of the state board of agriculture, nor did the 1921 Oklahoma Legislature appropriate money for refurbishing Old Central.[33]

Meanwhile, Philip A. Wilber of the class of 1919 went to work for the college as an instructor in the architecture department. He had studied architecture with Redlich, who favored the removal of Old Central. Wilber had also assisted Redlich with campus planning, and both worked together in 1920 supervising the construction of the Library Building and the Home Economics Building. Wilber, an able and dynamic instructor and administrator, later served as head of the architecture department from 1927 to 1947, and as college architect from 1947 until retirement in 1964. Throughout his forty-five years of work at the college, he became closely associated with Old Central and its future.[34]

Wilber entered the 1920 Old Central controversy by sending a letter to the editor of the alumni magazine. "No thought," he pointed out, "seems to have been given to the future development of our campus, whose progress is blocked by the position Old Central now commands. The development and beautification of our campus seems to me a much more noble and worthy task . . . than . . . defeating . . . [it] simply on the grounds of sentiment." Then Wilber asked: "What is sentiment which stifles progress? . . . Will the accommodations Old Central is capable of offering as a Student Union serve as such in five years? . . . Surely our hopes are larger than this." Wilber thought "that if the alumni are to decide the fate of Old Central, which means at the same time the fate of the future campus," the question of retaining Old Central should be voted on by the entire Alumni Association. Surely, he emphasized, there were ways of preserving memories associated with Old Central other than keeping the building and "arresting the future of our campus which in its present form will soon be the laughing stock for schools greater and older than our own."[35]

Although few alumni agreed with Wilber, Raymond A. Larner of the class of 1920 suggested that an exact model of Old Central, about four or five feet in height, be constructed and kept "for all time to come" in the Alumni Association headquarters. This would permit the removal of the building but at the same time retain its physical features, including its cracked walls, tie rods, "worn steps," and "rickety stairways." Larner explained that the idea was not original with him, "as models of old historical buildings are to be seen in many of the great

SPECIAL COLLECTIONS, OSU LIBRARY

Philip A. Wilber studied architecture at the college under Frederick W. Redlich, the campus planner, who taught him that Old Central should be removed. Wilber, the successor to Redlich as campus planner, persisted in this belief for many years.

museums."[36] Pauline C. Thompson of the class of 1916 also liked the thought of a model to replace Old Central.[37]

Redlich and Wilber persisted in their desire to remove Old Central. Several months later, on February 4, 1921, the Oklahoma State Board of Agriculture ordered President James W. Cantwell to vacate Old Central for class use, after having advice from Albert C. Kreipke of the Kreipke-Schaefer Construction Company and Redlich that the building could not be safely used for class work. The order went into effect on February 15, 1921, but Cantwell pleaded that it would take until April 15 to vacate the building. Meanwhile, on March 18, Cantwell resigned the presidency of the college effective on the following July 1. With the formal condemnation of Old Central by the state board of agriculture and Cantwell's subsequent resignation, the building ceased to house classes beginning with the autumn semester of 1921 and continuing until the spring semester of 1930.[38]

The physical condition of Old Central received little attention from 1916, when its exterior and interior underwent complete renewal, to 1927, when all occupants moved from the building. Its heating facilities, however, were improved during these years by adding at least one steam radiator and two gas space heaters. For a period, Old Central did not receive steam heat from the campus central power plant and had to depend solely on gas space heaters. Following a major hail storm in the early 1920s, the roof needed extensive repair. When Raymond E. Bivert came to the campus in 1922 as a freshman student, he found the building usable and normal in appearance for its age.[39]

In 1924 the belfry of Old Central suffered damage from a bolt of lightning which sent shingles flying in a cloud of dust. Even a part of the belfry framework became disjointed. Tower and roof repairs followed.[40] Two weeks later, when President Bradford Knapp had a request from students for permission to ring the Old Central bell during an *O'Collegian* subscription campaign in 1924, he responded that he could not authorize it due to the condemnation of the building. "I would consider such an act untrue to myself," said Knapp to the student request, "to the board of agriculture, and to the state if I permitted a person to ascend to the belfry tower."[41]

With Old Central condemned and with Redlich and Wilber in the college architecture department planning to remove it, people viewed it as a doomed structure that had given its best to the college, but must soon be replaced. The institution, with a shortage of space, continued to use the building, but only in part, suggesting that it contained poor-quality housing. For a college so underfunded, it could not afford the luxury of keeping an old building in repair for symbolic, sentimental, and historic reasons.[42]

From 1906, when Morrill Hall was completed, little major change

The *Redskin* staff of the college for 1924-1925 was housed in Old Central. James W. Bradley, seated at the rolltop desk, served as editor, and Jess R. Keeth, seated at the flattop desk, worked as business manager. After 1921, following the condemnation of the building for classroom use, the *O'Collegian* and the *Redskin* staffs occupied office space in Old Central until the building was condemned for all uses in 1927.

The *O'Collegian* staff of the college for 1923-1924 occupied a room in Old Central. Madeline L. Bradley, seated at the center desk, served as editor during the fall and winter quarters, and Harold A. Matkin, standing near the window, worked as editor during the spring quarter. At the time the *O'Collegian* was published semiweekly.

Centennial Histories Series

occurred in the uses of Old Central for some years. The college printing office occupied the entire basement of the building until 1920. Meantime, the offices and most classrooms of mathematics, English, and business inhabited the first and second floors. The mathematics department office, an original occupant, stayed on until 1923. The English office departed in 1914, but the dean's office of the School of Commerce and Marketing remained until 1917. The preparatory department office returned to Old Central in 1914 and stayed until 1922. After the tie-rod installation of 1914 and subsequent concern, classes remained the primary use of the building until the state board of agriculture condemned the building in 1921 and prohibited its use for classes. The college physician had temporary housing in the structure in 1922 and 1923.[43]

The publications department office moved to Old Central as early as 1921, and two years later all student publications, including the *O'Collegian*, the *Redskin*, and the *Aggievator*, as well as the student senate, occupied office space in the building. The Alumni Association also had offices in the structure, and the college physical plant department used the basement as a repair shop. Over the years, many student meetings and organizations met in Old Central's classrooms and assembly hall, even after classes ceased to be held in the structure.[44]

Meanwhile, President Knapp, who came to the campus in September 1923, soon focused additional public attention on Old Central. With a desire to increase building space to accommodate greater numbers of students, he advised at length with Redlich and Wilber, the campus planners in the architecture department. At the annual meeting of the Alumni Association in May 1924, Knapp proposed a plan calling for the removal of Old Central and using the material in the building to construct a memorial to the Oklahoma A. and M. College veterans of World War I. The memorial, Knapp said, would be built upon the site of Old Central and contain a clock tower "with a special chapel and rooms for the exclusive use of the alumni organization."[45]

The following year, in January 1925, in a major address to the student body at a chapel meeting, President Knapp again proposed to remove Old Central and construct in its place a World War I memorial. This, as the *O'Collegian* viewed it, proved to be "the most notable change" in the building program proposed by Knapp in which he called on the legislature then in session for funds to construct five new structures, including a large combination administration and agricultural building of three floors, the beginning of the present Whitehurst Hall. Curiously, noted the *O'Collegian*, Knapp had not requested an appropriation to demolish Old Central, relocate its occupants, and construct the World War I memorial in its place. The legislature responded with about two-thirds of the funding Knapp requested.[46]

Some months later, in June 1925, the Alumni Association board of directors voted to replace Old Central with a freestanding campanile bell tower dedicated to the students of the college who served in World War I. A committee on replacement was appointed at the same meeting, but the members went unannounced pending acceptance by those appointed. The board of directors consisted of Emma A. Chandler, Stillwater, president; W. L. Hubler, Fairfax, vice president; A. Frank Martin, Stillwater, secretary; Clarence H. McElroy, Stillwater, treasurer; and Thomas J. Hartman, Tulsa, a member.[47] The alumni of the college, at least on the surface, seemed resigned to the demise of Old Central when Charles Kilpatrick, the state chairman of the Alumni Association membership committee, announced in late October 1925 in a ten point circular letter to the alumni of the college: ''OLD CENTRAL MUST COME DOWN. We want to build a campanile on the spot so that in the future the chimes will peal out memories of Old Central and A. and M. history.''[48]

The *O'Collegian* accepted but lamented the planned destruction of Old Central in a series of editorials.[49] The grief became poignant when the Alumni Association voted to remove the building: ''Old Central's death warrant is signed. Let's lose little time in carrying out the execution.''[50] Soon a stay of the death penalty occurred when President Knapp announced that the building was in no immediate danger of being destroyed. He explained that action to raze it must first be authorized by the state board of agriculture, and unless the structure became dan-

Bradford Knapp served as president of the college from 1923 to 1928. Upon the recommendation of Frederick W. Redlich and Philip A. Wilber, the campus planners in the architecture department, Knapp approved a plan to remove Old Central and erect in its place a student union and a campanile honoring students of the college who served in World War I.

gerous, nothing would be done for some time. Knapp concluded by commenting that if the building became dangerous, all occupants would be vacated.[51]

Although no written evidence remains, it is likely that Knapp received requests from students, alumni, and friends of the college to repair Old Central. At the same time, the building maintenance funds appropriated by the 1925 Oklahoma Legislature proved inadequate to refurbish the structure. Moreover, because of the lack of classroom space on the campus for the student body, Old Central needed to be retained and reconditioned because of the ever-increasing number of students. At this time Redlich resigned his position at the college, and Wilber became the chief campus planner in the architecture department. Wilber soon volunteered his services to the state board of agriculture as chairman of an alumni memorial committee of architects to plan a suitable structure to replace Old Central, such as a campanile.[52]

Less than a year later by October 1926, Wilber produced a major plan for campus expansion. President Knapp liked it. Sensing that the legislature would not agree to finance it, Knapp decided to underwrite it with a private subscription of $500,000 from students, alumni, citizens of Stillwater, and other supporters of the institution. He took the plan to the state board of agriculture for approval. In addition to a student union, a football stadium, and a gymnasium, the proposal asked for $100,000 to remove Old Central and build a campanile in its place for a memorial to all World War I veterans from the college, but, said Knapp, "especially to those who gave their lives for their country." The proposed tower, Knapp continued, "should be also a memorial to the first building erected upon the campus and to those who made this possible." At the top of the campanile there would be a clock and chime of bells. Overall, Knapp concluded, the structure would "be a thing of beauty and usefulness in calling students to class by the chime of . . . bells instead of the discordant notes of a factory whistle," then in use for the purpose in the campus power house.[53] The plan was approved by the board the following day, and a commercial fund raising firm took over the task of soliciting the money from the public. The campaign ebbed away, due in part to Knapp's deteriorating situation as president, and the little money raised went to construct a permanent portion of the south stands of the football stadium.[54]

Life went on as usual inside Old Central until 1927. While Raymond E. Bivert, a graduate student and general manager of student publications, sat at his rolltop desk in the northwest room of the second floor of the building early in the afternoon of February 7, small pieces of plaster hit his head and shoulders. A major chunk of plaster, the size of a dinner plate, barely missed him and landed on the working surface of his desk. He had a minimal headache for several hours from the bump.

In 1927 Philip A. Wilber, the campus planner of the college in the architecture department, prepared this representation of the proposed campanile and student union building. The plan had the approval of President Bradford Knapp, the Alumni Association, and the Oklahoma State Board of Agriculture, the governing body of the college.

Since he did not have a visible injury, he did not go to a physician, but went instead to his room at the Acacia Fraternity house, where he rested. Soon President Knapp's office called to inquire about his injury, which he described as insignificant. As requested, Bivert called on Knapp the next day and also felt well enough to attend class.[55]

Clement E. Trout, the college publications department head, who sat near Bivert when the plaster fell, ordered a wire fence constructed at once around the south side of Old Central to protect people while passing by on the brick sidewalk in front of the building from falling exterior masonry. Danger signs went up on the fence. Meanwhile, a crowd of students and faculty gathered to view the activity, including an inspection of the building by President Knapp, engineering professors, and DeWitt T. Hunt, the shops department head. Knapp immediately ordered all persons and offices removed from the structure as soon as possible.[56]

Old Central again went through informal condemnation. The day after the plaster incident, President Knapp held a two-hour conference with college officials to relocate the Old Central offices. This effort proved to be a complicated matter due to crowded conditions in all campus buildings. The college publications department moved into an unfurnished room intended for the college administrative council in the new Whitehurst Hall; the *O'Collegian* occupied the waiting room downstairs in the College Cafeteria Building; the *Redskin* and *Aggievator* used the second floor room of the College Cafeteria Building, together with the student senate; and Mable Caldwell, editor of the *A. and M. Boomer*, the alumni magazine, retreated to her English department office in the English and History Building.[57]

Clearly, no one desired to occupy Old Central in its hazardous and dilapidated condition in 1927, but in spite of efforts to remove it, it developed a uniqueness of character as well as providing much needed housing so indispensable because of increasing student enrollment. The extreme difficulty Knapp faced in locating campus accommodations for those removed from Old Central in 1927 suggested the usefulness of the sixteen rooms in the building if only it could be refurbished and returned to service and the glaring need for new academic and administrative housing. Letters reached President Knapp from alumni, such as Elizabeth Oursler Taylor of the class of 1912, requesting that the building be retained, and at the same time no pressure developed from the state board of agriculture or alumni to remove it. Two major feature articles in the *Daily Oklahoman* brought statewide attention to it. Even a legislative delegation inspecting the campus had a look at the deserted building under the direction of President Knapp.[58]

Raymond E. Bivert, a graduate student and general manager of student publications at the college, was hit on his head by a piece of falling plaster while sitting at a rolltop desk in Old Central in 1927. This incident caused the building to be condemned a second time and closed to all uses.

Old Central stood condemned and deserted. Without occupants, it languished even more. Students imagined stones and bricks easing out of position in the structure, and people looked at its walls with apprehensive stares. Dejected loneliness seemed to consume the building. Vandals removed or broke holes in the huge window panes one by one. The hastily erected wire fence in front of the building began to break down from students climbing over it to use the brick sidewalk in front of the building during the heavy spring rains and avoid the muddy detour on the lawn around the fence. Almost a year later the fence around the south side of the building remained unrepaired, and debris cluttered the entrance to its poorly secured south doors. A wooden obstruction blocked the portico entrance itself.[59]

As the 1927 Christmas season approached, President Knapp asked people to be kind to Old Central until an appropriate memorial could be erected in its place. "The other day I looked the south side of 'Old Central' over carefully," Knapp said. "The heavy hand of time is showing. Brick and stone are gradually falling away and the danger of ultimate collapse is there." Then he explained what he had probably heard from some alumni and students in recent months: "To the old graduates and to many of the student body this old building is a sort of shrine; they think of it with reverence and affection; hallowed memories crowd round about it."

Next Knapp spoke of the current pillaging problem: "Now if that is true and if we have any regard for this old building, why do we let small boys and thoughtless people break out the windows and commit acts of depredation without and within the building?" The plea continued: "The college cannot afford to hire a watchman to watch this building in the day time. Could we not organize enough sentiment and public opinion in this matter to prevent these acts. If these young boys or their parents knew that the whole student body was against such acts, I believe the acts would stop." The college needed time, he said, to work out a suitable replacement for the building: "Let us keep this old relic until the new plans of the student body for a memorial can be worked out and we can erect something of beauty to replace the old 'Old Central.'"[60]

Both the students and President Knapp continued to be concerned about Old Central. Collegians sensed or knew the cultural and historical significance of the building, and many, even among those last housed in it, wanted it preserved. One such student said: "We leave, with regretfulness on our part; with appreciation for its part—Old Central. May it forever stand as a marker, for ages to come, of those generations before."[61]

Two students published poems in the O'Collegian lamenting the plight of Old Central. Meantime, President Knapp's decision to remove

This stone, according to the *1927 Redskin*, fell from a wall of Old Central. "Ere long," said the *Redskin*, "others must follow."

the building became an increasing problem for Knapp's administration. There seemed little basic support from either students or alumni to demolish the structure, even with the approval of the state board of agriculture. The popular subscription money to remove the building and construct a campanile in its place did not eventuate, nor did the legislature appropriate money for the purpose. As a result, the building remained forsaken but basically intact while the chaotic political conditions of Governor Henry S. Johnston's administration brought about Knapp's resignation as president effective on June 30, 1928.[62]

Henry G. Bennett, a man of unusual talents, became the new president of the Oklahoma A. and M. College the day after Knapp's administration concluded. Bennett, described by Robert S. Kerr Sr. as "a dreamer of no little dreams," had ably served nine years as president of the Southeastern State Teachers College at Durant. During this period he had also earned the doctor of philosophy degree in education at Columbia University in New York City. He soon proved he could establish academic and administrative stability at the Oklahoma A. and M. College in the middle of a mammoth sea of turbulent Oklahoma politics. Although he never lost the common touch, he promptly became a man of uncommon achievement.

Bennett accomplished mightily during the twenty-three years he served as president of the Oklahoma A. and M. College. Although he worked miracles in enlarging the physical plant, increasing enrollment, and developing educational services, perhaps his greatest achievement was to shelter the institution politically. He accomplished this in three ways, all developed and confirmed in his thinking by his applied collegiate administrative experience and his doctoral studies. First, he selected a group of able young leaders for the major administrative divisions of the college and promoted faculty morale by recognizing and rewarding their noteworthy services. This increased loyalty to Bennett, enhanced his leadership strength and magnetism, and developed a dynamism of purpose for the faculty and staff heretofore unknown to the college. Second, he established modern tenure for the faculty, thus making it possible for academic personnel to achieve long-term teaching and research distinction free from the fear of political patronage removal. Finally, he succeeded in 1944 in establishing, after more than a decade of concentrated effort, a non-political constitutional board of regents for the college and the other agricultural and mechanical institutions statewide. In the process he guided the reworking of the regent structure of all higher educational institutions in the state and established

When Henry G. Bennett became president of the college in 1928, he announced on his first day in office his intention to save and refurbish Old Central. He secured a $40,000 appropriation from the 1929 Oklahoma Legislature to accomplish this task. He proudly points to an architect's drawing of his proposed plan for campus expansion and development over a twenty-five year period.

Centennial Histories Series

a coordinating agency known as the Oklahoma State Regents for Higher Education.[63]

On President Bennett's first day in office, he told a *Daily O'Collegian* reporter that he intended to save and refurbish Old Central. He viewed the building as a landmark of exceptional value and had plans to "make it useful as well as ornamental."[64] He believed it could be converted into a fireproof structure at a nominal cost and be furnished as a recreational center. When Bennett addressed the student body of the college for the first time, he announced that he would recommend to the state legislature and the state board of agriculture that Old Central be preserved for the alumni. Reinforced, fireproofed, and redecorated, it could be used by students as a recreational center.[65]

About the same time, Bennett addressed the Kay County alumni of the college in Ponca City. There he said he hoped to create in Old Central a "memorial to the sacrifices of a pioneer people in the cause of higher education." He favored "gathering there everything that pertained to the early development of higher education that might be displayed, and would refurnish the inside of the building as nearly as possible as it was when it was the only building on the campus."[66] Immediately support for the project developed among alumni and friends of the college. Among others, Thomas J. Hartman of the class of 1898, and Harry E. Thompson, a member of the first faculty of the college, urged Bennett to secure a legislative appropriation to recondition the structure.[67]

Two months later, in September 1928, Bennett determined that a legislative appropriation of $40,000 would restore, fireproof, and redecorate Old Central. Philip A. Wilber, the campus planner and new head of the architecture department, and R. L. Santee, an engineering graduate of the college, agreed that Old Central could be restored. The new president himself, much interested in old collegiate buildings and campus planning, had recently visited in North Carolina and observed two rehabilitated university buildings, one dating from 1792. A retired Oklahoma City building contractor, E. C. Ross, who had wide experience restoring Spanish missions in California, assured Bennett that Old Central could easily be refurbished and that $40,000 would cover the cost. Upon Bennett's recommendation, the state board of agriculture also approved this amount.[68] This figure would be practical, said Bennett, and the building "can be restored to service at a lower cost than a new building its size can be built." He also added that Old Central "would help to perpetuate many college traditions which have their origin within its walls."[69]

When President Bennett completed the preparation of the Oklahoma A. and M. College budget request for the 1929 legislative session, it included the $40,000 item to rehabilitate Old Central, and altogether came to more than twice the amount appropriated by the 1927 legislature. Bennett requested money for six new buildings. The Old Central money survived a substantial pruning by the state budget officer of more than a million dollars even before the legislature met. The legislature cut the total appropriation of the college even more, but the $40,000 for Old Central remained intact as did $75,000 for the construction of the Infirmary Building when the bill became law on July 13, 1929.[70]

Little time passed before work began on the refurbishing of Old Central. The state board of agriculture required that the Oklahoma City architectural firm of Layton, Hicks, and Forsyth, best known for designing the Oklahoma Capitol Building, prepare the refurbishing plans and specifications for Old Central and do the architectural work for the construction of the Infirmary Building. Bruce W. Berry Jr. of Oklahoma City, a junior student in the architecture department at the college, drew up the renovation plans and specifications for Old Central while employed by the firm during the summer of 1929. Berry also served as the architectural superintendent of construction for the remodeling of Old Central. The Albert C. Kreipke Construction Company of Oklahoma City bid in the general contract on the building, and M. F. Fischer and Sons of Norman won the heating and plumbing contract. William E. Jewell, a stone mason of Oklahoma City, served as the general superintendent of con-

1917 REDSKIN

By 1917 ivy had covered most of the north wall and windows of Old Central. Students posed at the windows not yet covered. The ivy did much to deteriorate the masonry and wooden trim.

struction. Wilber, the campus planner, did not participate actively in the renovation that ensued.[71]

Refurbishing and restoration work on Old Central commenced in September 1929 and concluded early in 1930. Likely at the request of President Bennett, a large labor force moved the work rapidly to have the building ready for use by the next Founders' Day meeting of the alumni scheduled for December 14, 1929. The plans and specifications, no longer known to exist, called for a general reconditioning of the structure. Traditional aspects of the building would remain intact, such as the design of the building on the inside and outside. Even the inscriptions on the exterior sandstone would be retained. When the untrue rumor started that the $40,000 cost of refurbishing the building would be the same as its original cost, Berlin B. Chapman of the history department faculty corrected it by reporting that original records revealed it cost $25,000 when furnished and equipped in 1894.[72]

By the time the renewal of Old Central began, it had stood unused and vandalized for two and one-half years, truly a used-up building. Interior work consisted of the removal of the wood floor in the basement and the installation of a concrete floor. During this work the sump tunnel installed in 1903 under the hallway floor in the basement came to light, much to the surprise of everyone. Its purpose was unknown, and confused workmen thought it to be part of a proposed heating system never put in use. No one at the time even suspected that it served a drainage purpose by collecting water. It remained undisturbed under the new concrete floor awaiting rediscovery during the restoration of the building a half-century later.[73]

Other work on the interior of Old Central included the removal of the original plaster and wooden laths and their replacement by new heavy-duty metal lathing and plaster. All original door frames, baseboards, and wainscoting were reinstalled wherever possible. New interior doors, with small upper panes of glass and modern black hardware, replaced all original doors throughout the building. The fireplace in the old president's office on the first floor was partially dismantled and new firebricks installed. A part of the interior renovation also consisted of an entirely new steam heating system involving replacement pipes and radiators. In addition, the old sanitary plumbing facilities in the basement were removed and new plumbing fixtures installed in two rest rooms made from a part of the northwest room on the first floor of the building. A new electrical system, including modern light fixtures and concealed electrical wiring run through pipe, were installed. New maple floors, providing an unusually durable surface, likewise went into the reconditioning process. Even the chimney in the old steam boiler room, long useless, was eliminated. Finally, the interior walls and woodwork received a complete repainting. New venetian blinds, much like original, went into place.[74]

The exterior of Old Central also sustained extensive reworking in 1929 and 1930. The primary structural improvement involved the installation of the remaining tie rod and turnbuckle system designed to retard exterior wall movement. Three additional tie rods went into place north and south through the building, and four others supplemented the two already in position running east and west. Two entries to the basement were closed. The entrance to the original steam boiler room on the northwest corner of the building had long since ceased to serve a functional purpose, and the dual northeast doors had little use as well. The elimination of both entrances substantially decreased the possibility of water entering the basement. At the same time, the portico over the south basement doorway was removed.[75]

Masons replaced all cracked brick and reset the loose stonework. Workers reshaped the exposed roof section of the chimney serving the old president's office to more modern vertical lines by removing its original bell design. All exterior window frames and doors were repaired or replaced as needed, as was the decayed wood in the roof overhang. The railing in the belfry reappeared for the first time in many years, and the wood portion of the bell cradle went through repair. Then the original embossed metal roof of the building was removed for a fireproof pressed asbestos shingle cover with a guaranteed life expectancy of over a hundred years. The final exterior work consisted of painting. A new set of twenty musical bell chimes would be placed in the belfry, said college officials, but these did not appear. By December 14, 1929, the date of the second annual Founders' Day, the only work remaining on the interior of the building consisted of installing electric light fixtures and heating equipment. The college administration invited both students and alumni to visit the structure, and for this purpose the general contractor gave it a cleaning by removing construction debris.[76]

While the refurbishing of Old Central neared completion, Layton, Hicks, and Forsyth, the architectural firm in charge of the work, recommended to the state board of agriculture that the outside of the basement wall below the surface of the ground be excavated and thoroughly cleaned and two coats of cement bonding and waterproofing applied, followed by a heavy coat of portland cement plaster. In order to prevent the new interior gypsum plaster from becoming wet, the work should be done immediately. Although the board recommended that President Bennett have the work accomplished, it was not done because of a lack of funds.[77]

A year later an inspection of the Old Central basement revealed that the interior gypsum plaster from near the ground level and below was deteriorating and falling off. The senior member of the architectural firm in charge, Solomon A. Layton, recommended to the state board of agriculture that the foundation plantings be removed from around Old Central because he believed they primarily caused the moisture problem. Albert C. Kreipke of the Kreipke Construction Company, the general contractor for the building renovation, suggested that the repair department of the college could waterproof the foundation for less money than he could do it. President Bennett, also at the meeting, said the repair department would do the work if possible. There is no known record that the foundation was waterproofed.[78]

President Bennett did much more than bring about the refurbishing of Old Central. He ably transformed its character for the alumni and the people of Oklahoma. His action to save the building recognized its historic value as a symbol for the college and likewise gave the campus tradition. He did this because he believed history to be of considerable significance in the development of the college. For this purpose he desired a strong Alumni Association, and he saw in Old Central the one structure on the campus known to all former students and graduates of the college. He planned to make the building crucial in their association with the institution. He needed their support. Many of the graduates at the time had reached the height of their influence as business and professional leaders. Bennett used Old Central to build a strong alliance with the alumni to strengthen and develop the institution for a dominant educational role in the state, nation, and world.[79]

As a part of this effort, during his first year as president, Bennett established Founders' Day, an annual commemorative program for the alumni on December 14 of each year. On that day in 1891 the first students had enrolled in the college, a day that also coincided with Bennett's birthday in 1886. He carefully centered Founders' Day activities in Old Central after its renewal and also located the rejuvenated Alumni Association there. Berlin B. Chapman of the history department ably assisted him in turning the annual December meetings into historical commemorations concerning the origin and development of the college. Former presidents, early faculty, and prominent alumni returned to speak at the gatherings in Old Central. In 1928 Bennett gave each alumnus attending the annual meeting a leaflet by Chapman titled *Early History of Oklahoma Agricultural and Mechanical College* and a year later a paperweight made in part of wood salvaged from the renovation of Old Central. He even had the campus Student Self-Help Industries construct a miniature model of Old Central for alumni banquet table and similar meeting purposes.[80]

Controversy, survival, and developing historical significance characterized Old Central during the years from its completion in 1894 to its renewal in 1929 and 1930. Controversy first surrounded the building when the initial tie rods went into its walls in 1914 and continued intermittently until President Henry G. Bennett renewed the structure when he came to office in 1928. Survival forces entered the scene when Frederick W. Redlich and Philip A. Wilber, campus planners, determined that Old Central should be destroyed to improve the architectural design and layout of the institution. Even President Bradford Knapp adopted their concept. Meanwhile, the Oklahoma State Board of Agriculture followed this pattern by formally condemning the building when it ordered all classes from it in 1921 for safety reasons, and again in 1926 when it authorized the construction of a campanile to replace the structure.

Old Central survived these onslaughts because of the lack of funds to remove it; inadequate student, alumni, Stillwater, and public support to carry through on removal plans; and the pressing need for the classroom and office space in it. Finally, while the controversy over retaining the structure raged, student, alumni, and public support developed to recondition it. The moving force behind the growing sentiment to renew Old Central proved to be a developing awareness of its historical significance in the founding of the college and its role in higher education throughout Oklahoma. President Bennett saw in the structure an inexpensive source of classroom and office space, an artifact of educational history and tradition well worth preserving, and a means of developing strong alumni support for the present and future development of the institution.

Endnotes

1. Robert E. Cunningham, *Stillwater: Where Oklahoma Began* (Stillwater, OK: Arts and Humanities Council of Stillwater, 1969), p. 145.

2. *Stillwater Gazette*, 26 September 1895, p. 2; James L. Showalter, "A Structural History of Old Central," p. 37, Old Central Centennial History Collection, Special Collections, Edmon Low Library, Oklahoma State University, Stillwater, Oklahoma; R. Morton House, "The Class of 1903 at Oklahoma A. and M. College, *Chronicles of Oklahoma*, vol. 44, no. 4 (Winter 1966-1967), pp. 403, 405.

3. *Stillwater Gazette*, 25 July 1901, p. 4; Oklahoma A . and M. *College Paper*, 1 October 1901, p. 82, 2 December 1901, p. 145; Oklahoma A. and M. College *Daily O'Collegian*, 8 October 1946, p. 1.

4. *College Paper*, 1 October 1901, p. 82.

5. Showalter, p. 29; *College Paper*, 1 November 1901, p. 109.

6. *College Paper*, 1 November 1901, p. 109.

7. Showalter, pp. 29-31; Cunningham, pp. 82-87; *Stillwater Gazette*, 12 September 1901, p. 8; *College Paper*, 1 October 1899, p. 58, October 1902, pp. 70-71, November 1902, p. 109, 28 January 1903, pp. 197-198; Stillwater *Peoples Press*, 26 August 1909, p. 1, 9 September 1909, p. 1; Stillwater *Advance-Democrat*, 9 September 1909, p. 1.

8. Showalter, pp. 32-33.

9. Showalter, pp. 33-36; *College Paper,* 15 October 1903, p. 100.

10. Showalter, pp. 34-35; *College Paper,* 15 October 1903, p. 100.

11. Showalter, pp. 30-32.

12. Showalter, pp. 36-37; *College Paper,* February 1906, p. 71.

13. R. E. Means, W. H. Hall, and James V. Parcher, *Foundations on Permian Red Clay of Oklahoma and Texas* (Stillwater: Oklahoma Engineering Experiment Station Publication, Oklahoma Agricultural and Mechanical College, 1950), pp. 1-26; Author interview with James V. Parcher, 7 November 1986, Old Central Centennial History Collection.

14. Parcher interview; Means, Hall, and Parcher, pp. 13-26.

15. Author interview with Elizabeth Oursler Taylor, 2 November 1985, Old Central Centennial History Collection.

16. Author interview with Randle Perdue, 21 November 1983, Old Central Centennial History Collection. For a similar viewpoint see also Author interview with DeWitt T. Hunt, 7 November 1985, Old Central Centennial History Collection.

17. Oklahoma City *Daily Oklahoman,* 22 April 1914, Special Supplement, p. 41.

18. *College Paper,* October 1906, p. 14; Oklahoma A. and M. College *Orange and Black,* 10 June 1920, p. 2, 19 September 1914, p. 1; "First Issue Delayed," *A. and M. Boomer,* vol. 1, no. 1 (1 October 1920), p. 12; "Calendar of Uses of Old Central," Old Central Centennial History Collection.

19. *Orange and Black,* 19 September 1914, p. 1.

20. Oklahoma Election Board, *Directory State of Oklahoma, 1915* (McAlester, OK: News-Capital Print, 1915), p. 12.

21. *Orange and Black,* 30 January 1915, p. 2.

22. *Orange and Black,* 6 March 1915, p. 2.

23. *Orange and Black,* 4 October 1915, p. 2.

24. *Orange and Black,* 8 September 1916, p. 1.

25. Philip Reed Rulon, *Oklahoma State University—Since 1890* (Stillwater: Oklahoma State University Press, 1975), pp. 147-148; *Orange and Black,* 27 March 1915, p. 2.

26. *Orange and Black,* 9 October 1916, p. 1.

27. *Orange and Black,* 2 December 1916, p. 6.

28. *Orange and Black,* 7 May 1917, p. 1; Minutes, Oklahoma State Board of Agriculture, 3 July 1917, p. 12, Oklahoma Archives and Records Division, Oklahoma Department of Libraries, Oklahoma City, Oklahoma.

29. *Orange and Black,* 18 June 1920, p. 1.

30. Minutes, 22 May 1920, Oklahoma A. and M. College Alumni Association, Secretary's Book, December 18, 1905-May 16, 1923, Files, Oklahoma State University Alumni Association, Oklahoma State University; Clarence Roberts, "Three Things to Do," *A. and M. Boomer,* vol. 1, no. 1 (1 October 1920), p. 10; *Stillwater Gazette,* 9 July 1920, p. 1.

31. Copy of petition in *Stillwater Gazette,* 9 July 1920, p. 1.

32. John A. Whitehurst to Alumni Association, July 1920, "Whitehurst Writes About Old Central," *A. and M. Boomer,* vol. 1, no. 1 (1 October 1920), p. 19; Minutes, Oklahoma State Board of Agriculture, July-December 1920, no discussion or action, Oklahoma Archives and Records Division, Oklahoma Department of Libraries.

33. Minutes, 25 August 1920, Oklahoma A. and M. College Alumni Association, Secretary's Book, December 18, 1905-May 16, 1923; Minutes, Oklahoma State Board of Agriculture, July-December 1920, no discussion or action, Oklahoma Archives and Records Division, Oklahoma Department of Libraries; Oklahoma State Legislature, *Oklahoma Session Laws, 1921, Eighth Legislature, Regular Session, [Convened January 4, 1921, Adjourned April 2, 1921], and Extraordinary Session, [Convened April 25, 1921, Adjourned May 21, 1921]* (Oklahoma City, OK: Harlow Publishing Company, 1921), no discussion or action.

34. Minutes, Oklahoma State Board of Agriculture, 4 February 1921, p. 1, Oklahoma Archives and Records Division, Oklahoma Department of Libraries; *Annual Catalog, Oklahoma A. and M. College, 1928-1929*, p. vii; *Annual Catalog, Oklahoma A. and M. College, 1946-1947*, p. xxvi; *Stillwater NewsPress*, 2 August 1977, p. 2.

35. Philip A. Wilbur to Alumni Association, October 1920, "What Is Your Idea About Old Central?" *A. and M. Boomer*, vol. 1, no. 2 (1 November 1920), pp. 14-15.

36. Raymond A. Larner to Alumni Association, November 1920, "What About Small, Exact Model of Old Central?" *A. and M. Boomer*, vol. 1, no. 3 (1 December 1920), p. 2.

37. Pauline C. Thompson to Alumni Association, December 1920, "Mark Up Another Vote for Model of Central," *A. and M. Boomer*, vol. 1, no. 4 (1 January 1921), p. 11.

38. Minutes, Oklahoma State Board of Agriculture, 4 February 1921, p. 2, 1 March 1921, p. 8, 18 March 1921, p. 1, Oklahoma Archives and Records Division, Oklahoma Department of Libraries; *Annual Catalog, Oklahoma A. and M. College, 1923-1924*, p. 27; *Annual Catalog, Oklahoma A. and M. College, 1925-1926*, p. 11; *Annual Catalog, Oklahoma A. and M. College, 1926-1927*, p. 12; *Annual Catalog, Oklahoma A. and M. College, 1928-1929*, p. 12; "Old Central Calendar of Uses," Old Central Centennial History Collection.

39. Showalter, p. 38; Author interview with Raymond E. Bivert, 30 October 1983, Old Central Centennial History Collection; *Orange and Black*, 10 May 1923, p. 1; Oklahoma A. and M. College *O'Collegian*, 14 September 1924, p. 3, 14 January 1925, p. 1, 13 October 1925, p. 1.

40. *O'Collegian*, 4 September 1924, p. 1.

41. *O'Collegian*, 18 September 1924, p. 1. See also *O'Collegian*, 14 September 1924, p. 1.

42. Showalter, pp. 38-39.

43. *College Paper*, October 1906, p. 14; *Orange and Black*, 5 September 1914, p. 3, 8 September 1917, p. 4, 17 May 1919, p. 4, 10 June 1920, p. 2; *Stillwater NewsPress*, 13 December 1967, p. 3; *Daily O'Collegian*, 15 December 1932, p. 3; *Annual Catalog, Oklahoma A. and M. College, 1894-1895*, pp. 98-102; *Annual Catalog, Oklahoma A. and M. College, 1911-1912*, p. 10; *Annual Catalog, Oklahoma A. and M. College, 1913-1914*, p. 12; *Annual Catalog, Oklahoma A. and M. College, 1921-1922*, p. 25; *Annual Catalog, Oklahoma A. and M. College, 1922-1923*, p. 27; "Calendar of Uses of Old Central," Old Central Centennial History Collection.

44. *Annual Catalog, Oklahoma A. and M. College, 1921-1922*, p. 25; *Orange and Black*, 8 March 1922, p. 1, 7 September 1922, p. 1; *O'Collegian*, 5 July 1924, p. 1, 14 January 1925, p. 1, 30 September 1925, p. 1, 14 October 1925, p. 1; "Calendar of Uses of Old Central," Old Central Centennial History Collection.

45. *O'Collegian*, 22 May 1924, p. 1.

46. *O'Collegian*, 14 January 1925, p. 1; Oklahoma State Legislature, *Oklahoma Session Laws, 1925, Tenth Legislature, Regular Session, [Convened January 6, 1925, Adjourned March 28, 1925]* (Oklahoma City, OK: Harlow Publishing Company, 1925), pp. 23, 263.

47. *O'Collegian*, 7 June 1925, p. 1; "Alumni Program," *A. and M. Boomer*, vol. 4, no. 1 (September-October 1925), p. 2.

48. *O'Collegian*, 29 October 1925, p. 1; Charles Kilpatrick, Circular Letter, Files, Oklahoma State University Alumni Association.

49. *O'Collegian*, 11 June 1925, p. 4, 20 September 1925, p. 2, 13 January 1926, p. 2, 25 May 1926, p. 2.

50. *O'Collegian*, 29 October 1925, p. 2.

51. *O'Collegian*, 14 November 1925, p. 1.

52. Rulon, p. 190; *O'Collegian*, 14 November 1925, p. 1.

53. Minutes, Oklahoma State Board of Agriculture, 4-5 October 1926, pp. 5-6, 37, Special Collections, Edmon Low Library; *O'Collegian*, 8 October 1926, pp. 1, 3; *Stillwater Gazette*, 15 October 1926, p. 9.

54. Author interview with Raymond E. Bivert, 1 December 1986, Old Central Centennial History Collection; Rulon, pp. 193-198; *O'Collegian,* 15 July 1927, pp. 1, 4.

55. Bivert interview, 30 October 1983; *O'Collegian,* 8 February 1927, p. 1, 9 February 1927, p. 1, 11 February 1927, pp. 1, 4; *Stillwater Democrat,* 10 February 1927, p. 1.

56. *O'Collegian,* 8 February 1927, p. 1.

57. *O'Collegian,* 9 February 1927, p. 1.

58. Bivert interview, 30 October 1983; *O'Collegian,* 8 February 1927, p. 2, 9 February 1927, p. 2, 22 February 1927, p. 1; Taylor interview; *Daily Oklahoman,* 20 February 1927, p. 6C, 24 April 1927, pp. 1D, 8D.

59. *O'Collegian,* 1 April 1927, p. 1; *Daily O'Collegian,* 13 December 1927, p. 2; *1927 Redskin,* p. 398, Oklahoma A. and M. College Yearbook; Berlin B. Chapman, "Old Central of Oklahoma State University," *Chronicles of Oklahoma,* vol. 42, no. 3 (Autumn 1964), p. 281; Berlin B. Chapman to LeRoy H. Fischer, 14 December 1983, Old Central Centennial History Collection.

60. *Daily O'Collegian,* 20 December 1927, p. 1.

61. *O'Collegian,* 10 February 1927, p. 2.

62. *O'Collegian,* 13 February 1927, p. 2, 22 July 1927, p. 2; Bivert interview, 30 October 1983; *Daily Oklahoman,* 20 February 1927, p. 6C; Berlin B. Chapman to LeRoy H. Fischer, 14 December 1983, Old Central Centennial History Collection; Rulon, pp. 195-197.

63. Rulon, pp. 219-238, 265-269; Berlin B. Chapman, "Dr. Henry G. Bennett as I Knew Him," *Chronicles of Oklahoma,* vol. 33, no. 2 (Summer 1955), pp. 159-168.

64. *O'Collegian,* 2 July 1928, p. 1.

65. *O'Collegian,* 13 July 1928, p. 1; *Daily O'Collegian,* 17 October 1928, pp. 1-2.

66. *O'Collegian,* 13 July 1928, p. 4.

67. Thomas J. Hartman to Jessie Thatcher Bost, 12 February 1955, and Harry E. Thompson to Thomas J. Hartman and Mary Jarrell Hartman, 17 February 1955, Buildings and Building Programs—Old Central File, in Berlin B. Chapman Collection; "Invitation Letters," *Oklahoma A. and M. College Magazine,* vol. 9, no. 7 (April 1938), p. 4; *Stillwater NewsPress,* 21 January 1987, p. 1B; Berlin B. Chapman, editor, *Old Central in the Crisis of 1955* ([Orlando, FL: Golden Rule Publishing Company, 1964]), p. 17.

68. *Daily O'Collegian,* 16 October 1928, p. 1; Minutes, Oklahoma State Board of Agriculture, 4-5 September 1928, p. 29, Special Collections, Edmon Low Library.

69. *Daily O'Collegian,* 16 October 1928, p. 1.

70. *Daily O'Collegian,* 27 November 1928, pp. 1, 4, 6 December 1928, p. 1; Oklahoma State Legislature, *Harlow's Session Laws of 1929 Enacted by the Regular Session of the Twelfth Legislature of the State of Oklahoma, Convened January 7, 1929, Adjourned March 30, 1929, and Special Session, Convened, May 16, 1929, Adjourned July 5, 1929* (Oklahoma City, OK: Harlow Publishing Company, 1929), p. 289.

71. *Daily O'Collegian,* 4 October 1929, p. 1, 15 September 1929, pp. 1, 4, 3 October 1929, p. 1; Minutes, Oklahoma State Board of Agriculture, 16-17 July 1929, p. 3, 2-3 September 1929, pp. 28, 30, 32-34, 2-3, 7 October 1929, p. 28, 4-5 November 1929, p. 21, 3 January 1930, p. 35, 5 February 1930, p. 35, 5 March 1930, p. 38, Special Collections, Edmon Low Library.

72. *Daily O'Collegian,* 15 September 1929, pp. 1, 4, 19 September 1929, p. 1; Bill Peavler to LeRoy H. Fischer, 21 January 1987, Old Central Centennial History Collection.

73. *Daily O'Collegian,* 30 October 1929, p. 1.

74. *Daily O'Collegian,* 29 September 1929, p. 4, 16 October 1929, p. 1, 27 November 1929, p. 1; Helen Johnson, "Old Central Has New Lease on Life," *Oklahoma A. and M. College Magazine,* vol. 1, no. 1 (September 1929), p. 9; Showalter, pp. 43-45; Minutes, Oklahoma State Board of Agriculture, 3-4 December 1929, p. 31, 30 June 1930, p. 25, Special Collections, Edmon Low Library.

75. Showalter, pp. 41-42; Minutes, Oklahoma State Board of Agriculture, 3-4 December 1929, p. 31, Special Collections, Edmon Low Library; Author interview with James L. Showalter, 11 December 1986, Old Central Centennial History Collection.

76. *Daily O'Collegian,* 29 September 1929, p. 4, 16 October 1929, p. 1, 27 November 1929, p. 1, 14 December 1929, p. 1; Johnson, p. 9; Showalter, pp. 42-43, 45.

77. Minutes, Oklahoma State Board of Agriculture, 3-4 December 1929, p. 31, Special Collections, Edmon Low Library.

78. Minutes, Oklahoma State Board of Agriculture, 6-7 October 1930, p. 7, 31 October 1930, pp. 1-2, 8, Special Collections, Edmon Low Library.

79. Showalter, pp. 41, 46; Taylor interview; Bivert interview, 30 October 1983; Author interview with Berlin B. Chapman, 14 December 1983, and Author interview with J. Lewie Sanderson, 21 September 1983, in Old Central Centennial History Collection.

80. Henry G. Bennett, "A Message From the President," *Oklahoma A. and M. College Magazine,* vol. 1, no. 1 (September 1929), p. 4; [Berlin B. Chapman], *Early History of Oklahoma Agricultural and Mechanical College* ([Stillwater: Oklahoma Agricultural and Mechanical College, 1928]); Chapman, "Dr. Henry G. Bennett as I Knew Him," pp. 160-161; Minutes, Oklahoma State Board of Agriculture, 3 April 1930, p. 12, Special Collections, Edmon Low Library.

10 Decline and Retirement

President Henry G. Bennett was a true champion of Old Central. He continually emphasized the building's potential as a future higher education museum. His presidential term began the renewal of the building in 1929, and he managed to convert the structure into a public higher education memorial and historic landmark for the campus and the state. He made a spiritual resource of the building for living and future generations, and at the same time assured its continued existence.

Although President Bennett succeeded in transforming Old Central into a historic symbol, he could not change it into a historical museum because of the shortage of instructional and office housing at the college. In the spring of 1930, the Former Students Association, previously the Alumni Association, opened its offices on the second floor of Old Central. In this location the organization would be adjacent to former students' meetings centered in the assembly hall, now renamed the Old Central auditorium. The alumni offices also contained the new Student Placement Bureau and space for the editorial work of the college magazine. Photographs of the institution's outstanding athletes and track and football teams decorated the walls of the offices. Other pictures showed scenes of the campus since its beginning. A plan also developed to preserve trophies and relics of the college for eventual display in the Old Central auditorium, but this did not work out because the Former Students Association needed space for meetings, as did professors and students. Soon a complete set of framed photographs of all presidents of the college appeared on a wall of the Old Central auditorium. Each photograph had an indentifying brass plate with name and dates of the administration.[1]

At the same time, the newly-established Graduate School under the direction of Daniel C. McIntosh moved into two rooms on the first floor of Old Central once occupied by the early presidents of the college. The agricultural education department also located in the structure as soon as the renewal work on the building reached completion in 1930. Next came the geology department, housed in the basement, together with its geology museum, ultimately containing 20,000 mineral and fossil specimens.[2]

The publications department moved in likewise and shared space on the second floor in the Former Students Association offices. As a result, Clement E. Trout, the head of the publications department, again occupied the building he helped vacate in 1927. All other space in the structure, including its auditorium, began in 1930 to serve as classrooms for a wide assortment of courses and also for student meetings.[3] President Bennett soon reported to the Oklahoma State Board of Agriculture that the remodeling of Old Central gave "some relief to overcrowded conditions" and that supporters of the institution "have been outspoken in their appreciation of its preservation."[4]

With the refurbishing of Old Central completed, President Bennett emphasized the annual use of the building by alumni at commencement,

In 1930 the Former Students Association opened its offices on the second floor of Old Central. This 1940 photograph shows the staff and assistants, together with alumni wall displays and housing for the Student Placement Bureau and the *Oklahoma A. and M. College Magazine*. Seated at the left is Bess Allen, magazine associate editor, and standing at the right front is Archie O. Martin, secretary-treasurer of the association.

Centennial Histories Series

homecoming, and Founders' Day. "Plenty of chairs and space will be available in the chapel room of Old Central," the Former Students Association secretary pointed out, "for meeting and greeting friends, and an alumni register will be maintained in the F.S.A. offices."[5] Former students, the suggestion continued, should view the photographs of old and recent athletic teams posted on the walls of the alumni headquarters. Thus in Old Central, graduates and former students of all ages would feel at home.[6]

For the 1930 Founders' Day dinner, Bennett arranged for replicas of the Old Central bell to be made of clay from the college campus in the ceramics plant, one of the Student Self-Help Industries. Each former student attending the annual Founders' Day dinners statewide that year also received a bell as a favor. James H. Adams, a member of the first graduating class of the college, served as toastmaster. Freeman E. Miller, an early faculty member, spoke on "Sons of the Founders." Then President Bennett talked on "A. and M. Today," a pattern he usually followed. He commented on the past and present services and programs of the college and predicted a thriving future. Next the Old Central bell rang at length. The small replica of the building made by one of the Student Self-Help Industries stood near the diners, as did several small covered wagons, all designed to carry out the idea of Founders' Day. Even the music of the evening consisted of old-time melodies. Radio Station KVOO of Tulsa broadcast most of the program live so that the county units of the Former Students Association holding simultaneous banquets in their towns throughout the state could hear the campus commemoration.[7]

The next year, in 1931, the fortieth anniversary of the founding of the college was celebrated. Founders' Day followed much the same pattern, with headquarters again in the Former Students Association offices in Old Central. Tradition and history of the college continued to be emphasized at the banquet. Attention centered on honoring James L. Mathews, a member of the first territorial legislature, credited as the chief founder of the college. Former state governor James B. A. Robertson related his early association with the institution and told of its significance in the development of Oklahoma. When President Bennett spoke, he predicted the doubling of student enrollment at the college in less than a decade. "This institution will command the respect of the nation," he said. "The people of Oklahoma will come to feel more and more that Oklahoma's future is wrapped up in this college." A small grandfather clock was then presented to Bennett by the faculty in honor of his birthday, which also occurred on Founders' Day. Just before the banquet concluded, Elsie D. Hand, the librarian of the college, announced that Mable Caldwell of the English department would prepare an illustrated history of the institution (but this did not take place).

Favors for the banquet were block prints of Old Central suitable for framing.[8]

Later Founders' Day commemorations continued to emphasize the historical significance of Old Central. The offices of the Former Students Association in the building did much to encourage this development, with many of its meetings held there. A past president of the college, Angelo C. Scott, spoke in 1933 at Founders' Day activities. He explained how a light in Old Central guided him into Stillwater in 1899 from Orlando during a raging January blizzard. He also told of his notable executive achievements while housed in the building. A new tradition began in 1933 at the Founders' Day banquet when Dean Nora A. Talbot of the School of Home Economics presented President Bennett with a huge birthday cake. That same day a morning convocation for students took place in the College Auditorium concerning the history and traditions of Founders' Day, and once more Old Central entered the scene. For the first time the student body heard speeches on the history of Old Central and the college, and this became another annual tradition. In 1936 past president Bradford Knapp spoke at Founders' Day. Not only had Founders' Day become a tradition to be celebrated annually, but student, staff, and faculty writing on the history of Old Central and the college became an accepted and appreciated activity.[9]

With Old Central as the historical point of departure to measure the growth of the college, an unknown writer in 1936 captured the significance of the Founders' Day commemorations: "With the celebration . . . , those in attendance become more and more conscious of the rewards which the pioneers of the institution are reaping." The first and second generations have harvested immense benefits, and the college "will soon be starting on its third, and is thriving on the stability which the founders gave. Only by a comparison of figures can those of recent years most thoroughly appreciate the progress, in the face of difficulty in many instances, which the institution has made. Each celebration of this type gives evidence that the college is steadily progressing into one of the greatest educational institutions in the southwest."[10] In this way Old Central finally assumed, with the passing years, its rightful place in the hearts and minds of former and current students of the college.

Meantime, in 1929, President Bennett called for the development of a master plan for campus construction and beautification. The state board of agriculture approved the idea and employed a Denver, Colorado, firm which had served as a campus planning consultant for about thirty other colleges in the Southwest. Philip A. Wilber, the campus planner and head of the architecture department at the college, and his associate, Donald A. Hamilton, did not approve of the plan submitted, so they revised it. The finished design, made public in 1930, was known informally as the Twenty-Five Year Plan. It called for a uniform architecture, one never officially named, but generally known as Williamsburg Georgian. President Bennett liked the distinctive architectural styles of Old Central and Gardiner Hall, formerly the Women's Building and presently the Bartlett Center for the Studio Arts. He planned to blend them into his "Williamsburg of the West."[11.]

The Twenty-Five Year Plan tersely announced that the "Old Central building will become a museum."[12] Again Bennett had prevailed in long-range planning over the expedient classroom and office uses for the building following the completion of its renovation in 1930. His pledge to make Old Central a museum in the years ahead, just as he had said in his first days in office, underwent restatement in his Twenty-Five Year Plan. He also forecast the preservation of the building. The plan created much speculation concerning the length of Bennett's tenure, brought considerable publicity, and firmly fixed the idea in the public mind of converting Old Central into a museum.[13]

President Bennett's campus plan also called for beautification through improved streets, landscaping changes, and sidewalk construction. For years the treacherous, slick, and sloping brick sidewalks serving Old Central needed replacing, and this occurred in part during the Great Depression in 1934 with money provided by the Federal Emergency Relief Administration. Landscaping came first to the Old Central

The brick sidewalk constructed in 1903 in front of Old Central became hazardous over the years, but remained until replaced by a concrete sidewalk in 1946. This photograph shows its condition in 1931.

quadrangle area in 1938 because of the settled condition of that portion of the campus. This included foundation plantings around Old Central, a newly sodded bermuda grass lawn, and trees planted under the direction of Bryan Thompson, the new college landscape gardener.[14]

Somehow, the hazardous brick sidewalk in front of Old Central remained throughout the Great Depression years. "The bricks," wrote a *Daily O'Collegian* reporter, "which come in all stages of repair, from those cracked into atoms to a few whole ones, double the height of the normal ridges in the ground and turn curves into angles. Don't quote us, but we have heard it rumored that there was once a senior who finally learned how to walk on the sidewalk in front of Old Central without stumbling or losing his balance."[15] Not until after World War II, in 1946, did a nine foot wide sidewalk of concrete replace the one of bricks in front of Old Central. This, too, gave way to a new system of concrete sidewalks encompassing all sides of Old Central in the early 1970s.[16]

President Bennett's Twenty-Five Year Plan for campus expansion and beautification called for the replacement of antiquated and obsolete buildings on an estimated time schedule. With the pressures of increasing enrollment, the need for additional classrooms and faculty offices also became readily apparent. All of the first-generation buildings remained intact because of the lack of funds for their replacement caused by the Great Depression. Even the jolt of a small gas explosion in the Animal Husbandry Building in 1932 and a severe gas explosion in 1936 under President Bennett's office in Whitehurst Hall did not bring action to begin the removal of old buildings.[17]

The break finally came in 1937 when 455 school children and teachers died in an explosion in New London, Texas. Accumulated gas under the basement floor of the school caused the blast. Four days later the Oklahoma State Board of Agriculture in an emergency session ordered the Music and Arts Building and the English and History Building at the Oklahoma A. and M. College vacated of classes. The state fire marshall had termed them "a menace to life."[18]

In 1930 the state fire marshall originally had condemned the Music and Arts Building, a structure erected for chemistry in 1899 and 1900, and later included the English and History Building, constructed for engineering in 1902. College Architect Philip A. Wilber said it would be impossible to repair the buildings for future use. He explained that the structures had not been evacuated earlier because increasing enrollments made their use necessary. They did not have steam heating systems like Old Central, but only gas stoves.[19]

Adequate classroom housing could not be found on the campus for the students from the two vacated buildings. President Bennett seized upon the situation by requesting permission from the state board of agriculture to erect tents for instructional purposes. The tents, with wooden floors and sides, electric lights, and gas stoves, went up on the lawn between Hanner Hall and Thatcher Hall. A ridgepole supported the roof of each tent, and one of the tents, larger in size than the others, served as a library reading room. Photographs of the tents, as well as news items concerning them, soon appeared in many state newspapers. The legislature, in session at the time, had little choice except to appropriate funds for two new large buildings and their equipment. At the same time, more maintenance and repair money also became available for the college.[20]

The additional state appropriated funds, when combined with self-liquidating bond issue money and federal Public Works Administration allocations, financed the construction of six permanent campus buildings underway by the spring of 1938. These included the Fieldhouse, Engineering South, Life Sciences East, an extension on the Industrial Arts Shops, the Agronomy Barn, and the Campus Fire Station. Bennett had earlier pioneered the self-liquidating bond issue method for the construction of public higher education buildings in Oklahoma. Murray Hall, a women's dormitory begun in 1933, became the first public higher education building in the state erected with self-liquidating bonds. With the use of these techniques, the modern building program at the col-

With Old Central and other early-day structures of the original campus quadrangle in the background, students await the arrival of the homecoming parade in 1939. The newly-erected Campus Fire Station is in the right foreground.

lege began, and soon the institution became known as the fastest growing school west of the Mississippi River.[21]

Meanwhile, other events also influenced the physical condition and future of Old Central. In 1931 the college had a report prepared by the Stillwater Fire Department and a private firm, the Oklahoma Inspection Bureau of Oklahoma City, on life and fire hazards on the campus. Improvements recommended for Old Central included the removal of dead pigeons, feathers, and droppings from the unused attic area and belfry and also the use of screen or other repairs to prevent the entrance of birds. Due to the historic significance of the building, the report recommended, an automatic sprinkler system should be placed in the structure. Other proposals mentioned the installation of approved chemical fire extinguishers, stairway partitions of incombustible construction, and panic bars on the outside doors. Unlike the other old buildings on the campus, the report listed no immediate dangers for Old Central. The college soon installed the recommended fire extinguishers, but did not set in place panic bars or construct stairway partitions of incombustible materials.[22]

Several years later fire threatened to destroy Old Central. About daybreak on October 20, 1938, a student noticed smoke rolling from its belfry as he walked across the campus near the new fire station, which had been completed about six weeks earlier. The student hastily reported the fire, and immediately two trucks responded from the campus station, just over a hundred yards distant, as did a truck from downtown, a mile away. The fire started in trash sacks, likely from a match or cigarette, under the south stairway leading from the first floor to the second floor. The fire gained headway rapidly, working its way upward along the stairway and the walls, but had not spread much. The firemen, mostly students from the new School of Fire Protection at the college, quickly brought the flames under control. The students gained their first practical experience at quenching a campus fire in Old Central. The only casualties were a large number of pigeons, the victims of carbon monoxide, nesting in the belfry. "We almost lost Old Central this morning," said J. Ray Pence, the Stillwater fire chief. "The new station on the campus paid for itself this morning. But for the nearness of the station to the building, we would have lost Old Central."[23]

Eight years later in 1946 with World War II concluded, the college began active planning to equip Old Central with an automatic sprinkler system, as recommended in 1931. More than a year passed in 1946 and 1947 before a contract to install the system was let, due to the lack of funding caused by huge increases in war veteran campus housing. Fortunately, farsighted people, such as Raymond J. Douglas of the School of Fire Protection, provided Old Central with automatic sprinklers. No other collegiate building in Oklahoma had such a system, and Old Central probably would not have survived without the sprinklers.[24]

Due to the freezing areas it served in the attic and belfry, the automatic state-of-the-art sprinkler system installed in Old Central in 1947 had dry pipes and covered the entire building. Air under constant pressure filled the dry pipes of the system. If a fire occurred, a soft metal alloy in the sprinkler heads would melt where the fire broke out, allowing the air to escape. When the air pressure in the pipes dropped, the master control valve of the sprinkler system allowed water to fill the pipes but flow only from the sprinkler heads opened by heat from the fire.[25]

Nothing about the Old Central fire sprinkler system at the time of installation could be called experimental. Soon Douglas changed that by developing a research problem to replace the air in the dry pipe system in Old Central with nitrogen to keep corrosive scale from forming in the pipes when filled with air. Previously such air-filled systems nationwide often had scale break loose and block the sprinkler heads, thus decreasing reliability. Moreover, cleaning procedures proved costly and ineffective. The test demonstrated conclusively that nitrogen in dry

The controls of the 1947 automatic fire retardant sprinkler system were located at the foot of the basement stairway in Old Central. No other collegiate building in Oklahoma had such a system. Old Central probably would not have survived without it.

pipe systems prevented corrosion. When the 1947 sprinkler system became obsolete and was finally replaced, no evidence of internal corrosion could be found.[26]

Soon after the sprinkler system filled with nitrogen began to attract national attention, virtually the entire ceiling in the northeast basement room rumbled, paused a few seconds, and collapsed on January 10, 1950. Only moments before, an estimated thirty-five students and their psychology instructor, Solomon L. Reed, escaped from the room. Students at first dived under tables, but when the ceiling failed to fall at once, they began rushing for the three windows and two doors of the room. An aluminum sprinkler pipe, a part of the Douglas nitrogen corrosion reduction experiment, broke under the impact of the falling plaster and water flooded the room until personnel from the nearby fire station shut off the sprinkler system. It was determined that the metal lathing holding the plaster had too few nails to support it, a casualty of the 1929-1930 renewal of the building.[27]

Students reacted both seriously and humorously to the Old Central plaster fall. One suggested that constant safety evaluations be made of old buildings on the campus for needed repairs and that some of them should be removed regardless of their sentimental value. Another recommended replacing Old Central with a replica, and said other colleges should remove their first building soon after construction so as to establish a precedent for their destruction with only a moderate uproar from the alumni.[28] The fairy tale novel, *Alice's Adventures in Wonderland,* provided the setting for an additional student's comments when White Rabbit took Alice on a tour of the old campus quadrangle. "'And what is that building to the left of us?' inquired Alice. 'It's Old Central,' replied White Rabbit, 'which survives only because the Aggies believe in ancestor worship. The ceilings fall down, which sets off a sprinkler system . . . . It is said they raise fish in the basement.'"[29]

Less than a year later, on December 14, 1950, fire again struck Old Central. It began in an open recessed area on the first floor just inside and north of the south entrance. The recess contained a large canvas trash sack suspended in a metal rack. Apparently someone carelessly threw a lighted cigarette or match in the sack in the evening. No one happened to be in the building at the time. The fire spread up the wood wall trim and entered the ceiling, where it inched its way along interior supporting beams of the ceiling and walls, and also ate a path up the south wooden staircase to the second floor, including the small stairway room once occupied by the night watchman. Soon the rising heat had set off three automatic sprinklers, which successfully retarded the fire, except where it burned in concealed areas between the first and second floors.[30]

Meantime, the large automatic sprinkler fire alarm bell attached to

194

the north side of Old Central rang and rang. It was heard at the fire station, just over a hundred yards away. No one took it seriously because the classroom bell system in Williams Hall, adjacent to Old Central as well as the fire station, rang erratically and incessantly from time to time due to malfunctions.[31] Finally a person passing by Old Central heard the bell, rushed into the fire station, and exclaimed: "Hey! That bell outside Old Central has been ringing quite a spell."[32]

With an estimated delay of thirty to forty minutes fire trucks responded from the Campus Fire Station as did units from the fire stations in Veterans Village and downtown. Although the sprinkler system had effectively contained the fire in visible areas, it had not done so in concealed spaces. By use of "fog" fine spray water for quenching fires in concealed areas, the firemen had the situation quickly under control. Not even the firefighters at the time recognized the extent of the fire or the effectiveness of the "fog" they used. Years later during the restoration of the building, it was discovered that the fire had spread in the concealed space between the first and second floors to the east wall of the building and upwards within the east wall towards the attic.[33]

Stillwater Fire Chief Everett S. Hudiburg reported soon after the fire that the automatic alarm bell, installed in both Old Central and the Campus Fire Station at the time of the sprinkler system, had never been connected, despite repeated requests. After viewing the fire damage, Hudiburg commented: "The only thing that saved this building was the automatic sprinkler system Dr. Bennett had installed a couple of years back."[34]

Years passed, and finally in 1957 a leased telephone line connected the Campus Fire Station alarm with the Old Central sprinkler system. Several weeks later on July 25, a mid-morning fire alarm sent three fire trucks hurrying to Old Central, but no fire could be found. A large section of ceiling plaster in the second floor auditorium had collapsed, breaking a sprinkler system pipe, which in turn activated the alarm. Luckily, no one was in the auditorium, unused during the summer session then in progress. Fire personnel had the water shut off in about a minute after the alarm sounded, consequently preventing much water damage. Restoration work on the auditorium ceiling in later years determined that the supporting framework of the ceiling had been improperly made during the construction of the building.[35]

Although the idea of chimes for the belfry of Old Central had surfaced soon after President Bennett announced his plan for the preservation of the building, twenty years passed before they were installed. A senior memorial contributed by the classes of 1947, 1948, and 1949, midget electronic carillons were installed in a small room with glass walls constructed on the first floor of Old Central. Also placed in service was a master time control clock to ring them automatically, a keyboard to play them manually, and an amplifying system with three speakers mounted on the bell tower. The carillons could be heard within a radius of a mile of Old Central. Campus planners indicated that there would be little resemblance between the electronic carillons in Old Central and the forty-foot long manually-operated carillons scheduled to be placed in the tower of the new library. The huge expensive carillons would be used only for special occasions, while the Old Central chimes rang hourly from eight in the morning until ten in the evening.[36]

On May 4, 1949, the Student Association in a ceremony on the lawn north of Old Central presented the chimes to the college in memory of the students of the institution who had lost their lives in World War II. President Bennett accepted the chimes for the college and described the gift as "fitting and proper as a memorial to those who gave their lives in World War II." He commented that through the years an age-old tradition of bells developed "to express gaiety, happiness, meditation, and sadness."[37]

Chime concerts at Old Central began on a daily basis in 1950 by organ students in the music department. These continued with a wide variety of music, including fraternity and sorority songs, until 1953 when the new library opened. After all the planning, the giant hand-operated carillonic chimes did not materialize in the library tower. Instead, high-quality English and Flemish electronic bells took their place. By striking the hours mechanically, as did the Old Central chimes, they quickly displaced the smaller and less adequate system. In 1955 the Student Association, responsible for placing the chimes in Old Central in 1949, attempted to sell them to the Oklahoma Panhandle A. and M. College at Goodwell, but nothing came of this effort. For the first time, the accelerated building program successfully launched by President Bennett had challenged and jolted Old Central.[38]

Following the death of President Bennett in 1951, the board of regents elected Oliver S. Willham president of the college in 1952. After graduating from the college in 1923 with a major in agriculture and a superior academic record, Willham obtained employment at the Oklahoma Panhandle A. and M. College, where he soon became second in administrative authority. He spent the summers doing graduate study in animal husbandry at the Iowa Agricultural College, where he earned both the master of science and the doctor of philosophy degrees by 1935. He joined the animal husbandry faculty at the Oklahoma A. and M. College in 1935 and four years later was named vice dean of agriculture. When Bennett became President Harry S. Truman's Assistant Secretary of State of the Technical Cooperation Administration (Point Four) Program in 1950, Willham served in his absence as the executive vice president of the college.[39]

Although President Willham had the confidence and good will of

Oliver S. Willham, who served as president of the university from 1952 to 1966, continued and enlarged the Henry G. Bennett building program to renovate campus structures and construct new buildings for thousands of additional students soon to come.

almost all Oklahomans, no one in his position at the college had a more difficult period of service than his first years in office. His early presidency was transitional following the long tenure of President Bennett; in addition he had to make the changes needed to convert the institution to a university. The building program in progress had to be refinanced and completed, and new planning and funding needed to be worked out to renovate campus structures and construct new buildings for thousands of additional students soon to come. Willham also had to implement the institution's contract with the Technical Cooperation Administration to develop a modern educational system in Ethiopia. Whatever problems he faced as president, he always maintained his composure, his sense of humor, and his ability to inspire confidence in others. He traveled and spoke widely throughout Oklahoma, and soon developed a high degree of personal popularity.[40]

In 1953, the same year the new college library went into use, the Oklahoma State Regents for Higher Education established its budget council. As this group planned the physical modernization and expansion of state-owned and operated collegiate institutions in anticipation of rapidly increasing student enrollments, another situation developed to challenge the future of Old Central. Not only did the budget council prepare a statement of immediate state collegiate physical plant needs for the Oklahoma Legislature meeting in 1955, but it also supervised the preparation of a list of similar long-term needs for the decade from 1957 to 1967. In addition, the budget council called for a detailed survey of all existing state collegiate buildings as of February 1, 1954.[41]

Less than a year before, during the spring commencement in 1953, a group of early-day graduates and former students of the college met in the new Student Union to form the Half-Century Club. Thomas J. Hartman, of the class of 1898 and a prominent retired Tulsa banker, organized the club and served as its first president.[42] At the initial annual dinner of the club during the spring commencement of 1954, Berlin B. Chapman of the history department was named historian of the group and received a certificate inscribed for "perseverance in preserving the early history of the college."[43] Beginning with his return to the college history faculty in 1941, Chapman had worked closely with the early graduates and first teachers of the college. He kept in touch with them and took many on tours through Old Central, soon to be challenged by the campus renewal and expansion program. Chapman saw similarities to

Mary Jarrell Hartman, class of 1903, and Thomas J. Hartman, class of 1898, celebrated their golden wedding anniversary in 1953, the year they formed the Alumni Association Half-Century Club. In 1955, when Old Central appeared to be threatened with destruction, Hartman organized the early graduates of the institution to urge the preservation of the building because of its historic significance.

Harvard Hall in which he had studied while a graduate student at Harvard University. He was intrigued by the building's historic significance over the years, such as when troops of General George Washington used it as a barracks during the American Revolution.[44]

Campus planning developed rapidly during the 1950s when President Willham and his staff moved to comply with the recommendations for physical plant updating made by the state regents for higher education. Many Quonset buildings and old military-type housing of wood used to shelter and instruct the returning veterans of World War II needed to be replaced. In addition, Philip A. Wilber, who had been active in proposals to remove Old Central in 1920, now served as college architect and director of building supervision and planning. Now under consideration were the demolition of all remaining first-generation buildings constructed on sandstone foundations with complete wooden interiors. Overall, these buildings were generally inadequate and could not economically be brought up to modern standards. Wilber's list also included Old Central.[45]

President Willham, as had former presidents Bradford Knapp and Henry G. Bennett, depended on the office of the campus architectural planner for information and advice concerning the structural and physical condition of older buildings on the campus. Willham drew upon this information, together with other materials channeled to him from his administrative staff, for a series of annual articles on the academic achievements and physical needs of the institution published for the information and reaction of the alumni in the *Oklahoma A. and M. College Magazine*. One such article involved Old Central and appeared in the February 1955 issue of the monthly. It carried the title "Looking to the Future."

After relating the enrollment growth, praising the quality of the faculty, and reporting on the land-grant educational venture of the college in Ethiopia, President Willham told of the research function of the institution. He spoke of the personnel needs of the faculty and the quest for adequate new buildings to house the students and teachers.[46] Finally, he used information from the Wilber list of sandstone foundation buildings, and wrote: "We invite your inspection at any time of our older buildings. We believe you should know that several will not last many years longer." He cited four examples of such structures in the following order: Old Central, Williams Hall, Old Library, and Student Publications. He said of Old Central: "It has a sandstone foundation and wooden floors, stairwell, and framework interior."

Overall, President Willham wrote: "These buildings will continue to be used by A & M college as long as it is possible for us to economically keep them in repair. It is said that 50 years is the life of such a building. If so, most of our older buildings are past retirement age."

Berlin B. Chapman, professor of history at the university, assisted the members of the Alumni Association Half-Century Club in urging the preservation of Old Central. He holds a copy of his *Old Central in the Crisis of 1955* at the time of his retirement in 1966.

He added in conclusion: "Your continued interest as alumni and former students in building a greater Oklahoma A & M College is most sincerely welcomed. Our success in carrying out plans for future needs . . . will be reflected in no small measure by the degree of support and coopera- tion you give to these worthwhile goals." Although Willham did not write of replacing Old Central, a three-line description of a photograph of it and Williams Hall on the same page of the magazine contained a statement that both "must be replaced in the very near future."[47]

The comments in the Willham article concerning Old Central deeply disturbed Berlin B. Chapman. When Hartman and his wife visited with Chapman in the Student Union on February 10, 1955, he told them of the statements in the magazine, which they had not yet read, concern- ing Old Central.[48] The next day Hartman sent Willham the following telegram: "I am distressed to read in the *College Magazine* where you advocate wrecking of Old Central because it has already stood fifty years on a sandstone foundation. Why so soon after Dr. Bennett endeared him- self to all the Old Grads by obtaining funds for her repair? It would be a crime to wreck Oklahoma's first College Building so long as time endures. The first Church erected in the United States in 1565 still stands on a foundation of sand. Old Central will stand long after you and I have passed. Repair and use as a museum."

A day later Hartman sent President Willham a letter concerning the preservation of Old Central, which read in part: "Old Central is a fix- ture . . . . If I have learned anything during the Eighty Years thus far allotted to me, it has been how easy it is to destroy something . . . .

Centennial Histories Series

You have the ability to continue her usefulness if you apply it in the right way . . . . Like a person grown old, her faults should be endured.

"Thou too! Live on! Old Central—Great; Live on! Live on! Whate'er thy state. Arise! Old Friends in every State, Destruction must not be her fate.

"It is better that you use much time to preserve her usefulness and very little to plan her destruction. Then, and only then, will you win the support that it is your right to expect from those who have supported you since enrolling in A. and M. College."[49]

On the day Hartman wrote this hard-hitting letter, he also contacted Jessie Thatcher Bost, the president of the Half-Century Club, a member of the class of 1897, and the first woman graduate of the college. She approved of Hartman's efforts, appointed him chairman of the Committee to Save Old Central, and authorized him to choose the members of the committee. Hartman had his letter to President Willham and the article in the *Oklahoma A. and M. College Magazine* duplicated and sent to the members of the Half-Century Club. He also urged each club member to write President Willham requesting that Old Central be saved. In less than a week Hartman visited Stillwater again to win support for the preservation of Old Central. He contacted Archie O. Martin, the secretary of the Former Students Association, former Lieutenant-Governor James E. Berry, Mayor A. B. Alcott, and J. Herbert Loyd, the president of the Chamber of Commerce. He also conversed with President Willham, who assured him that when Old Central was no longer needed for classes, he would recommend that it be turned over to the alumni for use as a museum.[50]

Meantime, President Willham replied to Hartman in a letter not yet received before the above conversation: "I have your wire and letter, for which I want to thank you. I believe, however, that you misunderstood my statement in the A. and M. Magazine concerning Old Central. I have no intention of tearing Old Central down. We are still using it and plan to use it so long as it can safely be done. Even after it is condemned, we can let it stand as a landmark or museum.

"I work very closely with our architects and engineers relative to our buildings and the safety of our students. The statement was made about the sandstone foundation and wooden interior merely to point out that we might have to give up the use of the building for students rather quickly. I have Mr. C. K. Bullen, our campus engineer and an alumnus of the College, watching campus buildings closely. He and Mr. Wilber, our architect, who is also an alumnus, assure me that we have done all that we can to preserve Old Central.

"Again thanking you for your interest and assuring you that I am just as concerned as you are in seeing Old Central stand for many years, I am sincerely yours."[51]

President Willham received many letters from members of the Half-Century Club requesting that Old Central be preserved. He carefully replied to each with much of the same information and consideration contained in his letter to Hartman. Most of the early alumni responded to Hartman's request for copies of their letters to Willham and his responses to them. Hartman gave them to Chapman for preservation and future use, if needed. Chapman published many of the letters in an edited book titled *Old Central In the Crisis of 1955.* The letters contain much important information on the significance of Old Central.[52]

A public response from President Willham concerning his Old Central comments in February 1955, came the next month in the *Oklahoma A. and M. College Magazine.* According to the magazine, "Fears of any former students that Old Central is to be destroyed . . . can be put to rest, . . . [and] the oldest of the college buildings will be where it stands for many years to come." Welden Barnes, the college director of public information, stated: "Between what the article did say, and what was in a three-line description over a campus scene pictured, some of our former students got a mistaken impression. I hope this explanation will clear up any misunderstanding."[53]

At the alumni banquet of May 1955, President Willham said in his address: "We have no idea of tearing down Old Central."[54] This pleased the crowd immensely and produced an enthusiastic applause. When the occasion presented itself, he reassured members of the Half-Century Club that Old Central would remain. He wrote to Alfred E. Jarrell, the last survivor of the first graduation class: "You may be sure that we will keep Old Central."[55] The dynamic leadership efforts of Hartman and the members of the Half-Century Club, together with the understanding support of President Willham, had turned the tide of alumni opinion in 1955 in favor of retaining Old Central regardless of its structural problems and repair costs. Chapman, the historian of the Half-Century Club, also played a major role in the preservation of the building in 1955, and the early graduates revered him for it.[56]

Old Central no longer appeared on the list of first-generation buildings recommended for removal following the appeal of the Half-Century Club in 1955. President Willham recommended to the state regents for higher education in September 1955 a line item of $5,000 for general repairs to Old Central. Pressure continued, however, from the state regents for higher education and the college architect's office to replace seven first-generation buildings (excluding Old Central) and the temporary Quonsets and old military-type housing with modern structures.[57]

The old first-generation sandstone foundation buildings of wood and brick became a focal point again when President Willham explained in 1959 that the recently renamed Oklahoma State University would perhaps be just five years away from a crisis in the use of the structures.

He said that the older buildings had been retained far beyond their intended lifetimes because of housing shortages. He pointed out that Old Central also should be closed to classes but be maintained as a museum when the university no longer needed it for classrooms and offices. "It is a great worry every time we must schedule classes in Old Central," explained Willham, "but the space is needed."[58]

The next year, 1960, brought new emphasis at the Oklahoma State University for the removal of obsolete permanent-type structures, and the list increased from seven to eleven. Old Central still did not appear on the list. "In many instances the yearly maintenance and repairs needed on these buildings exceeds their original cost," said President Willham. "The reason most of them need to be replaced by modern standards is that many are wood structures with wood floor joists, and just stone or brick veneer trim."[59]

In 1962 the announcement came that Old Central would soon undergo repairs, including a new roof. Several hail storms had severely damaged the roof of pressed asbestos shingles, installed in 1929, with a hundred year life expectancy. In 1963, with money from a bond issue, Old Central received a new roof of asphalt shingles, and the exterior northwest staircase underwent reconstruction. The steam and electrical systems were repaired as well, and new paint went on the building. Chapman passed on to members of the Half-Century Club news of the

In 1963 Old Central underwent repair and painting work. Early graduates of the university were encouraged by the refurbishing effort and circulated this photograph among themselves.

Old Central renewal and supplied a photograph of work on the roof. The early graduates welcomed the improvements.[60]

Despite the repairs made on Old Central, the building did not return to its earlier physical status and dignity. Like the other old structures on the campus, it did not have central mechanical air conditioning for the comfort of students and faculty during the summer months. Moreover, the radiator steam heating system in Old Central also grew obsolete when forced air heating and cooling replaced radiators in the newer structures on the campus. Window air conditioning units went into several rooms of Old Central, and an unsightly air conditioning device appeared in front of the building to cool a portion of the second floor.

The largely unused auditorium on the second floor of Old Central underwent conversion in part in the early 1960s. Harry K. Brobst, the director of the Tests and Measurements Bureau housed in the building, obtained money from the United States Office of Education to construct four counseling cubicles in the north side of the auditorium which were utilized for three or four years in the training of school counselors. At least five other rooms had temporary partitions installed. Ceilings were lowered in several rooms with fiber tile suspended on metal framework, while others had dropped plaster areas covered by similar fiber tile nailed

SPECIAL COLLECTIONS, OSU LIBRARY

This view of the south entrance and stairwell of Old Central is representative of the interior of the building as it appeared in 1970 following its retirement from classroom and administrative uses. New exterior and interior doors with small glass panes had replaced the original doors in the refurbishing of 1929-1930. All interior woodwork was painted white soon after World War II.

to wood strips attached directly to the old damaged ceiling itself. About the same time, Old Central's bell went into storage in the unoccupied Old Library because campus architectural planners considered the belfry unsafe to support it. Even Old Central's turf appeared to be violated several years later when a parking lot intended to serve the Student Union went into use in 1964 on the lawn southwest of the antique structure. At this point the lawn south of the building first underwent consideration for major building purposes.[61]

Meanwhile, Old Central found itself an anxious bystander in the years from 1961 to 1971, a decade-long period of the greatest building construction in the history of the university. This occurred during the last five years of the Oliver S. Willham administration and the first five years of the Robert B. Kamm administration. With rapidly expanding enrollments, the need was clearly established for new construction and the updating of existing facilities. Adequate financial resources to meet the challenge became available through several channels: by the federal government's "Great Society" financial commitment for substantial campus construction; by state building bond monies generously voted and provided; by private funding which became available once the Oklahoma State University Foundation was established in the early 1960s and resulted in structures like the Seretean Center for the Performing Arts; by self-liquidating bond issue funds used to construct revenue-producing buildings, such as several residential halls; and finally, by student fee money which underwrote in part such buildings as the Colvin Physical Education Center, as did non-earmarked university funds.

During the decade from 1961 to 1971, a total of thirty permanent buildings and complexes were erected on the Stillwater campus. The new structures sometimes involved the removal of first generation sandstone foundation buildings such as Old Central. The new buildings erected, in addition to those previously mentioned, included seven residential halls ranging in height from five to fourteen stories; College of Business Administration Building; Engineering North; Life Sciences West; Mathematical Sciences; Student Union Parking Garage; Agricultural Engineering; Live Animal Evaluation Center; Motor Pool; Printing Services; and Central Food Services. Additions were made to the College of Veterinary Medicine Building, Agricultural Hall, Edmon Low Library, and Student Union. Major renovation included Gundersen Hall, Life Sciences East, and Engineering South. In addition, other major campus improvements involved streets, sidewalks, parking, lighting, and landscaping. Thus Old Central witnessed an amazing transition in the size and appearance of the university between 1961 and 1971.[62]

With the construction of many new buildings during the Bennett and Willham administrations from 1928 to 1966, the uses of Old Central experienced much change. This pattern of transformation for Old Cen-

Old Central looked on while the 1920-1921 Library Building underwent destruction in early 1962. Before long the 1902 Engineering Building and Auditorium, seen to the left of Old Central, would be razed as would the original turreted Library Building, evident to the right.

A turret and wall of the original Library Building gives way to the incessant pounding of the demolition machinery not long before Old Central was closed to student and administrative uses in September 1969. The Seretean Center for the Performing Arts was soon to be erected where the Auditorium and the original Library Building once stood.

tral also continued unabated during the administration of President Kamm, who served from 1966 to 1977. The completion of the Student Union in 1950 began a major departure of offices from Old Central. The Former Students Association and the Student Placement Bureau, both original occupants of the building following its refurbishing in 1929 and 1930, moved to offices in the Student Union in 1950. The Graduate School, also an inhabitant of Old Central since 1930, moved to new quarters in 1954 in Whitehurst Hall. Other administrative units, also in the building since 1930, likewise moved out at various times. The geology department, with its rock and fossil museum displays, in 1947 moved into a World War II era temporary-frame building of two stories located between Whitehurst Hall and Life Sciences East. The agricultural education department moved out in 1943, while the publications and journalism department stayed only until 1932, when it switched to Whitehurst Hall.[63]

Offices continued to crowd into Old Central, suggesting the persistent need for space and the growth of the student body. The English department moved into the rooms vacated by the publications and journalism department in 1932 and remained for most of the decade. The psychology department, later including educational psychology, occupied the offices vacated by the geology department in 1947 and remained in the building until 1966, although much of its class and laboratory work continued there until the university closed the building for conventional uses in 1969. Both the philosophy department and the religious education department had offices in the building from 1955 through 1958.[64]

Non-departmental offices in Old Central included the agricultural division of the Oklahoma State Department of Vocational-Technical Education from 1933 to 1937 under the direction of J. B. Perky. Both President Henry G. Bennett and Philip S. Donnell, dean of the School of Engineering, worked actively with the Boy Scouts of America, and the offices of the Cimarron Valley Council of the Boy Scouts occupied one room in Old Central from 1941 to 1947. At that point the Cimarron Valley Council merged to form the present Will Rogers Council, and the office moved to Ponca City. A gift of music records, music scores, and music books, together with sound equipment from the Carnegie Foundation of New York, flourished in Old Central from 1942 to 1947 in what was known as the Carnegie Music Room. No other library like it could be found in Oklahoma. The Tests and Measurements Bureau, under the direction of Harry K. Brobst, moved into Old Central in 1947 and remained until early 1970 when it moved to the remodeled Hanner Hall. By early 1971, the vocational rehabilitation division of the Oklahoma State Department of Vocational-Technical Education vacated the room it had occupied since 1968. For the first time since 1930, a period of

Although Old Central was closed to student and administrative uses in September 1969, the vocational rehabilitation division of the Oklahoma State Department of Vocational-Technical Education did not vacate the building until early 1971. It was the last occupant to leave the structure before restoration began.

forty years, Old Central had no offices.[65]

In the years following the major renewal of Old Central in 1929 and 1930, a wide variety of classes, student organizations, faculty committees, and alumni groups met in the building. Its auditorium, as always, continued to be especially popular for meetings, lectures, recitals, and similar events. During much of World War II, the structure's auditorium and classrooms housed training activities of the Women Accepted for Volunteer Emergency Service (WAVES). But when the Student Union opened in 1950 with ample student and faculty activity facilities, the building ceased to be the hub for extensive campus meetings.[66]

Berlin B. Chapman took a special interest in Old Central following his return to the history faculty in 1941. He found within its walls and atmosphere the historic beginnings of Stillwater and the college. He frequented the building for enjoyment and sometimes relaxed on its south steps with a sandwich. He also promoted the structure for student meetings and programs of the Payne County Historical Society. From this association he worked out two memorable events, each historically significant, held in its auditorium.[67]

In 1949 Chapman arranged for the annual meeting of the Oklahoma Historical Society to assemble in the Old Central auditorium. This proved to be the only annual meeting of the society held in Stillwater. Approximately two hundred people from all parts of Oklahoma attended the gathering. Addresses included a discussion of archives and archival records for the study of Oklahoma history and the initial presentation on Payne County's claim to the site of the Battle of Round Mountains, the first Civil War military engagement in present Oklahoma. An array of historic documents was also displayed in the Old Central auditorium.[68]

A year later, in 1950, Chapman held the first public examination in the history of the Graduate School at Oklahoma A. and M. College in the Old Central auditorium. Amos D. Maxwell took the final examination on his master of arts thesis in history prepared under the direction of Chapman. Maxwell's topic was "The Sequoyah Constitutional Convention." Former Governor William H. "Alfalfa Bill" Murray, who as a young man served as vice president of the Sequoyah Constitutional Convention when it met in Muskogee in the Creek Nation, attended the Maxwell examination, as did his son, Johnston Murray, who later in the year would be elected governor of Oklahoma.[69]

Daniel C. McIntosh, the dean of the Graduate School, opened the examination with a capacity crowd present. Chapman served as chairman of the examining committee consisting of Muriel H. Wright, the associate editor of the *Chronicles of Oklahoma,* and Angie Debo and Norbert R. Mahnken, both history professors. Following the examination, President Bennett presented former Governor Murray for comments on the Sequoyah Constitutional Convention. Then Wright announced that the entire thesis would be published in two parts in the *Chronicles*

The first public examination for a graduate degree in the history of Oklahoma State University was held in the Old Central auditorium in 1950. Former Oklahoma Governor William H. "Alfalfa Bill" Murray pins a badge worn at the Sequoyah Constitutional Convention in 1905 on Amos D. Maxwell, the recipient of the degree. Others left to right are Muriel H. Wright, Oklahoma Historical Society editor; Daniel C. McIntosh, Graduate School dean; and Berlin B. Chapman, history professor and advisor.

of Oklahoma. The thesis was later republished as a book. It seemed fitting that the examination occurred in Old Central, at the time the headquarters of the Graduate School.[70]

Due to the deteriorating physical condition of Old Central, university authorities made the decision to close it for conventional student and faculty uses in September 1969. Extensive remodeling of the University Auditorium was underway in preparation for the construction of the Seretean Center for the Performing Arts, and immediately to the south, Williams Hall, a first-generation structure, was also demolished to make way for the Seretean Center. The massive brick walls of old Williams Hall slowly gave way to the incessant pounding of the demolition machinery. A student reported being told by a university employee that the wrecking of Williams Hall hastened the deterioration of Old Central's physical condition.[71]

The decision to move all occupants from Old Central came after E. Edward Davidson, the university vice president for business and finance, accompanied by Chaplin E. Bills, the university architect, and James J. Thorne, the director of the university physical plant department, toured the building. When the report to close the structure reached the press, Davidson acted as spokesman for the university. He said the building had "developed some good cracks in the last several weeks and 'appears dangerous.'" He explained that experts would be asked to determine the condition of the building, decide on the repairs needed, and estimate the cost of refurbishing it. He emphasized that "there is no talk of tearing down the structure."[72] To a reporter from the alumni magazine he said much the same: "We are not planning to tear down Old Central." Then he added that barriers would be placed around the building for safety.[73] And to Chapman, who inquired of the fate of the structure, he replied: "We at Oklahoma State University are interested in preserving this building."[74]

How much had the physical condition of Old Central deteriorated? Despite the new roof, the northwest exterior staircase reconstruction, and the inside and outside paint applied in 1963, the signs of severe exterior masonry degeneration were evident to even the casual observer. The north wall had a large crack in the bricks, the east wall had a medium-size brick crack, but the south wall at the main entrance portico had a highly menacing brick and stone separation. A huge rift occurred in the brickwork under the bell tower above the entrance to the portico, and this caused the large wedge-shaped piece of rock at the crown of the portico arch, known as the keystone, to hang dangerously, as if to collapse and take the complete arch with it, if not a large portion of the wall itself.

Brobst, the head of the Tests and Measurements Bureau in Old Central, remarked that the structure had "shown considerable deterioration

With the demolition of much of the Auditorium and all of the original Library Building, the masonry of Old Central apparently deteriorated rapidly. Especially severe was the crack above the south entrance to the building, where the keystone hung precariously as if ready to collapse and take much of the wall with it.

in the last month . . . after pounding down the walls of Williams Hall." An element of fear and high humor soon entered the situation. Edward E. Goldenberg, a graduate assistant in psychology, conducting an experiment on rats in the basement of Old Central, said its condition had reached the danger zone, but he also convinced himself that "nothing will happen. Of course, they said that about the Titanic, too." He added that the building settled more every day, and that cracks in the floor grew larger. "I know the cracks are getting bigger," he explained. "One day I walked over them, and the next I tripped and almost broke my leg."[75]

By early 1971, Old Central again stood empty in a continually deteriorating condition, but unlike years in the past, it was not in danger of being destroyed. After physically renewing the structure in 1929 and 1930, President Bennett continued to use Old Central as the point of departure for understanding the historical development and perspective of the Oklahoma A. and M. College throughout his administration from 1928 to 1951. He emphasized its historic significance in the life of the college through its daily use and during the annual Founders' Day commemorations. In addition, he successfully chartered its future as the Oklahoma Museum of Higher Education.

Ironically, the building program Bennett launched would in later years threaten the future of Old Central. The structure ceased to be the hub of student and faculty activities with the completion of the Student Union in 1950, and the physical existence of Old Central itself appeared threatened by the effort to remove the remaining first-generation campus buildings in the 1950s and 1960s. A rousing reaction in 1955 to save the structure by members of the Half-Century Club of alumni and former students ensured its survival, and from that point forward, people no longer seriously questioned the preservation of the building, not even when it ceased to be needed in 1969 for conventional student and faculty uses. History and tradition have always been the bodyguards of Old Central.

Endnotes

1. Oklahoma A. and M. College *Daily O'Collegian,* 12 March 1930, p. 1, 19 March 1930, p. 1, 22 March 1930, p. 4; Genevieve Braley, "Classes Resumed in Old Central," *Oklahoma A. and M. College Magazine,* vol. 1, no. 8 (April 1930), p. 5; "Classes Again Convene in 'Old Central' Rooms," *Oklahoma A. and M. College Magazine,* vol. 2, no. 2 (October 1930), p. 46; Author interview with Murl R. Rogers, 15 September 1985, Old Central Centennial History Collection, Special Collections, Edmon Low Library, Oklahoma State University, Stillwater, Oklahoma; *Annual Catalog, Oklahoma A. and M. College, 1930-1931,* p. 11.

2. *Daily O'Collegian,* 12 March 1930, p. 1, 31 December 1942, p. 1; Braley, p. 5; *Annual Catalog, Oklahoma A. and M. College, 1930-1931,* p. 11; "Classes Again Convene in 'Old Central' Rooms," p. 46.

3. *Annual Catalog, Oklahoma A. and M. College, 1930-1931,* p. 11; *Daily O'Collegian,* 12 March 1930, p. 1, 14 March 1930, p. 2, 22 March 1930, p. 4; Braley, p. 5; "Classes Again Convene in 'Old Central' Rooms," p. 46.

4. [Henry G. Bennett], "Brief Survey of the Year's Progress Oklahoma A. and M. College," unpaged, with Minutes, Oklahoma State Board of Agriculture, 3 June 1930, Special Collections, Edmon Low Library.

5. "Reunion at Commencement," *Oklahoma A. and M. College Magazine,* vol. 1, no. 8 (April 1930), p. 10.

6. "Reunion at Commencement," p. 10; *Daily O'Collegian,* 17 September 1930, p. 1, 22 November 1930, p. 2.

7. *Daily O'Collegian,* 5 December 1930, p. 1, 16 December 1930, p. 1, 17 December 1930, pp. 1, 4.

8. "President Bennett is Honored in Fourth Annual Founders' Event Celebrating Fortieth Anniversary of the College," *Oklahoma A. and M. College Magazine,* vol. 3, no. 3 (December 1931), p. 3.

9. Otis Wile, "Sixth Founders' Day Celebration Is Best Yet," *Oklahoma A. and M. College Magazine,* vol. 5, no. 4 (January 1934), pp. 3, 13, 15; *Daily O'Collegian,* 23 November 1934, pp. 1, 4, 13 December 1936, pp. 1-2, 7, 14 December 1943, p. 1, 24 July 1947, p. 2, 5 January 1949, p. 3, 8 February 1949, p. 2; John W. Hamilton, "Saga of a Little Red Schoolhouse," *Oklahoma A. and M. College Magazine,* vol. 19, no. 3 (December 1947), p. 2; *Stillwater NewsPress,* 24 May 1950, p. 4.

10. "Founders' Day," *Oklahoma A. and M. College Magazine,* vol. 8, no. 3 (December 1936), p. 5.

11. Minutes, Oklahoma State Board of Agriculture, 5-6 March 1929, p. 28, 6-7 October 1930, p. 5; Philip Reed Rulon, *Oklahoma State University—Since 1890* (Stillwater: Oklahoma State University Press, 1975), pp. 230-231.

12. Oklahoma A. and M. College, *Equity of Chance* (Stillwater: Oklahoma A. and M. College, 1930), p. 4.

13. *Daily O'Collegian,* 18 October 1930, pp. 1, 4, 1 February 1956, p. 1, 12 July 1957, p. 3; "Oklahoma A. and M. of the Future," *Oklahoma A. and M. College Magazine,* vol. 2, no. 3 (November 1930), pp. 80-81.

14. *Daily O'Collegian,* 6 March 1934, p. 1, 14 December 1937, p. 3, 7 June 1938, p. 4, 25 September 1938, p. 1, 26 November 1938, p. 1; Ruth Randolph Oakes, "A. and M. Building Program Progressing," *Oklahoma A. and M. College Magazine,* vol. 9, no. 6 (March 1938). p. 5.

15. *Daily O'Collegian,* 28 September 1939, p. 2.

16. *Daily O'Collegian,* 18 June 1946, p. 1.

17. Oklahoma A. and M. College, *Equity of Chance,* pp. 1-2; Rulon, p. 232.

18. *Daily O'Collegian,* 23 March 1937, p. 1; Minutes, Oklahoma State Board of Agriculture, 3-4 March 1937, p. 63, 22 March 1937, pp. 1-4.

19. *Daily O'Collegian,* 23 March 1937, pp. 1-2; Campus Structures File, Oklahoma State University, Old Central Centennial History Collection.

20. Minutes, Oklahoma State Board of Agriculture, 26 March 1937, p. 1; *Stillwater Gazette,* 26 March 1937, p. 1, 9 April 1937, p. 1; *Daily O'Collegian,* 24 March 1937, pp. 1-2, 31 March 1937, p. 1, 2 April 1937, p. 1; Author interview with Joseph R. Norton, 2 February 1987, Author interview with Julius A. Pattillo, 2 February 1987, and Author interview with James E. Webster, 2 February 1987, in Old Central Centennial History Collection; Oklahoma State Legislature, *Oklahoma Session Laws, 1936-1937, Sixteenth Legislature, Extraordinary Session, Convened November 24, 1936, Adjourned January 4, 1937, Regular Session, Convened January 5, 1937, Adjourned May 11, 1937* (Oklahoma City, OK: Harlow Publishing Corporation, 1937), p. 529.

21. *Daily O'Collegian,* 21 April 1938, p. 1, 29 May 1938, p. 1, 23 October 1938, p. 4; Minutes, Oklahoma State Board of Agriculture, 5 February 1930, p. 36; *Stillwater Gazette,* 17 April 1931, p. 1, 29 September 1933, p. 1.

22. Stillwater Fire Department and the Oklahoma Inspection Bureau, "Tentative Report on the Conditions Relating to the Life and Fire Hazard of the Oklahoma A. and M. College, Stillwater, Oklahoma [1931-1932]," Building 7, Old Central, Special Collections, Edmon Low Library; *Daily O'Collegian,* 4 December 1932, p. 1.

23. *Stillwater Daily Press,* 20 October 1938, p. 1. Other accounts of the fire are in the *Daily O'Collegian,* 21 October 1938, p. 1, Stillwater *Payne County News,* 21 October 1938, p. 1, *Tulsa Daily World,* 21 October 1938, p. 5, and Phil Perdue, "Higher Education for Firemen at the Oklahoma A. and M. College," *Fire Engineering,* vol. 92, no. 12 (December 1939), p. 578.

24. Philip S. Donnell to Automatic Sprinkler Corporation of America, 17 June 1946, 12 March 1947, 23 September 1947, and Author interview with Richard W. Giles, 29 November 1985, in Old Central Centennial History Collection.

25. Author interview with Richard W. Giles, 10 November 1985, Old Central Centennial History Collection.

26. Raymond J. Douglas File, Fire Protection and Safety Technology Department, Oklahoma State University; Giles interview, 10 November 1985; Mary Jane Warde, "Fifty Years of Fire Protection at Oklahoma State University" (Master of Arts thesis, Oklahoma State University, 1981), pp. 69-70; *Firemen,* vol. 15, no. 3 (March 1948), p. 5; Major Jesse Townshend, "Fire Protection Careers," *Oklahoma A. and M. College Magazine,* vol. 25, no. 5 (January 1954), pp. 11-12.

27. *Stillwater Daily News Press,* 10 January 1950, p. 1; *Daily O'Collegian,* 11 January 1950, p. 1, 12 January 1950, p. 1; Giles interview, 10 November 1985.

28. *Daily O'Collegian,* 11 January 1950, p. 2, 13 January 1950, p. 2.

29. *Daily O'Collegian,* 16 February 1950, p. 2.

30. Giles interview, 10 November 1985; Author interview with Everett S. Hudiburg, 10 October 1985, Old Central Centennial History Collection.

31. Giles interview, 10 November 1985.

32. Hudiburg interview.

33. *Daily O'Collegian,* 16 December 1950, p. 1; Giles interview, 10 November 1985; Oklahoma City *Daily Oklahoman,* 15 December 1950, p. 1; Richard W. Giles to Ann Carlson, 16 November 1987, Old Central Centennial History Collection.

34. *Daily O'Collegian,* 16 December 1950, p. 1.

35. *Daily O'Collegian,* 26 July 1957, p. 1; *Stillwater Daily News Press,* 25 July 1957, p. 1; Giles interview, 10 November 1985.

36. *Daily O'Collegian,* 15 February 1929, p. 1, 28 January 1949, p. 1, 26 April 1949, p. 1, 3 May 1949, p. 1.

37. *Daily O'Collegian,* 5 May 1949, pp. 1-2.

38. *Daily O'Collegian,* 24 October 1950, p. 1, 16 November 1950, p. 1, 26 October 1951, pp. 1, 6, 24 April 1952, p. 3, 27 September 1952, p. 6, 15 September 1954, p. 9, 15 December 1955, p. 1, 16 December 1955, p. 1.

39. Rulon, pp. 203-204, 278, 281-282; *Who's Who in America,* vol. 28 (Chicago, IL: Marquis Who's Who, 1954), p. 2871.

40. Rulon, pp. 282-283.

41. Minutes, Budget Council, Oklahoma State Regents for Higher Education, 3 November 1953, 12 January 1954, Oklahoma State Regents for Higher Education File, 1952-1959, Oliver S. Willham Collection, Special Collections, Edmon Low Library.

42. Archie O. Martin to Thomas J. Hartman, 29 May 1953, Old Central Centennial History Collection; *Stillwater NewsPress,* 8 May 1977, p. 8, 2 May 1979, pp. 8-9, 7 September 1980, pp. 7B-8B.

43. *Stillwater NewsPress,* 7 September 1980, p. 7B.

44. Berlin B. Chapman, editor, *Old Central in the Crisis of 1955* ([Orlando, FL: Golden Rule Publishing Company, 1964]), pp. 14-16, 43; Author interview with Berlin B. Chapman, 14 December 1983, Old Central Centennial History Collection.

45. Annual Catalog, Oklahoma A. and M. College, 1948-1949, p. xxxii; Oliver S. Willham to Mell A. Nash, 20 September 1955, Oklahoma State Regents for Higher Education File, 1952-1959, Oliver S. Willham Collection; *Daily O'Collegian,* 5 April 1955, p. 3, 29 April 1978, p. 1.

46. Author interview with Ray E. Dryden, 5 November 1985, Old Central Centennial History Collection; Oliver S. Willham, "Looking to the Future," *Oklahoma A. and M. College Magazine,* vol. 26, no. 6 (February 1955), pp. 5-7.

47. Willham, "Looking to the Future," p. 7.

48. Chapman, editor, *Old Central in the Crisis of 1955,* pp. 16-17.

49. Chapman, editor, *Old Central in the Crisis of 1955,* pp. 19-22.

50. Chapman, editor, *Old Central in the Crisis of 1955,* pp. 22-23, 28-30.

51. Oliver S. Willham to Thomas J. Hartman, 17 February 1955, Buildings and Building Programs—Old Central File, Berlin B. Chapman Collection, Special Collections, Edmon Low Library.

52. See letters in full written in response to the Old Central comments of Oliver S. Willham in his "Looking to the Future" article in the Buildings and Building Programs—Old Central File, Berlin B. Chapman Collection. See also extensive selections from the same letters published in Chapman, editor, *Old Central in the Crisis of 1955,* pp. 18-75.

53. "Live On, Old Central," *Oklahoma A. and M. College Magazine,* vol. 26, no. 7 (March 1955), p. 23.

54. Chapman, editor, *Old Central in the Crisis of 1955,* p. 40.

55. Oliver S. Willham to Alfred E. Jarrell, 25 June 1958, Alfred E. Jarrell File, Berlin B. Chapman Collection. See also Alfred E. Jarrell to Berlin B. Chapman, 2 June 1958 and Alfred E. Jarrell to Oliver S. Willham, 15 June 1958, Alfred E. Jarrell File. The same sentiment is in Clarence R. Donart to Berlin B. Chapman, 21 March 1959, Buildings and Building Programs—Old Central File, and Mary J. Hartman to Berlin B. Chapman, 23 March 1966, Mary Jarrell Hartman File, in Berlin B. Chapman Collection.

56. Mary Nielsen Taylor to Berlin B. Chapman, 31 July 1966, Berlin B. Chapman to Angie Debo, 12 June 1981, Author interview with Warren E. Shull, 19 September 1983, and Author interview with J. Lewie Sanderson, 21 September 1983, in Old Central Centennial History Collection; Mrs. Thomas M. Hartman to Berlin B. Chapman, 29 September 1969, Alfred E. Jarrell File, Berlin B. Chapman Collection; *Stillwater NewsPress*, 12 February 1986, p. 1B.

57. Oliver S. Willham to Mell A. Nash, 20 September 1955, and Attachment, Oklahoma State Regents for Higher Education File, 1952-1959, Oliver S. Willham Collection; *Daily O'Collegian*, 13 March 1959, p. 4.

58. *Stillwater NewsPress*, 15 March 1959, p. 11.

59. "A Close Look at the 'Back Door,'" *Oklahoma State Alumnus Magazine*, vol. 1, no. 1 (January 1960), p. 6.

60. Gregg Bond, "Major Building Projects for 1962," *Oklahoma State Alumnus Magazine*, vol. 3, no. 3 (March 1962), p. 9; Oliver S. Willham, "OSU Faces a Financial Crossroad," *Oklahoma State Alumnus Magazine*, vol. 4, no. 3 (March 1963), p. 8; *Stillwater NewsPress*, 8 December 1963, p. 14; *Tulsa Sunday World*, 14 December 1969, Magazine Section, p. 6; Oklahoma State University, *Financial Report for the Year Ended June 30, 1963* (Stillwater: Oklahoma State University, 1963), p. 77; Mary J. Hartman to Berlin B. Chapman, 24 October 1963, Mary Jarrell Hartman File, and William L. English to Berlin B. Chapman, 17 December 1963, Buildings and Building Programs—Old Central File, in Berlin B. Chapman Collection; Berlin B. Chapman, "Historic Photo of Old Central, 1963," and Mary Nielsen Taylor to Berlin B. Chapman, 31 July 1966, in Old Central Centennial History Collection.

61. Author interview with Harry K. Brobst, 20 September 1983, James L. Showalter, "A Structural History of Old Central," p. 50, and Author interview with Robert W. MacVicar, 13 May 1985, in Old Central Centennial History Collection; Otis Wile, "The Bell Clapper Comes Home," *Oklahoma State Alumnus Magazine*, vol. 7, no. 1 (January 1966), p. 4; *Daily O'Collegian*, 16 December 1964, p. 2.

62. Author interview with Robert B. Kamm, 5 November 1987, Old Central Centennial History Collection.

63. *Annual Catalog, Oklahoma A. and M. College, 1930-1931*, p. 11; *Annual Catalog, Oklahoma A. and M. College, 1948-1949*, p. 11; *Annual Catalog, Oklahoma A. and M. College, 1942-1943*, p. 16; "That's Geology at A. & M.," *Oklahoma A. and M. College Magazine*, vol. 21, no. 12 (August 1950), p. 4; *Oklahoma A. and M. College Class Schedule, Second Semester, 1954-1955*, p. 64; A. O. Martin, "The Secretary's Corner," *Oklahoma A. and M. College Magazine*, vol. 22, no. 7 (March 1951), p. 37; *Daily O'Collegian*, 9 September 1932, p. 1; Minutes, Board of Directors, Oklahoma State University Alumni Association, 2 December 1950, Files, Oklahoma State University Alumni Association, Oklahoma State University, Stillwater, Oklahoma; "Calendar of Uses of Old Central," Old Central Centennial History Collection.

64. *Daily O'Collegian*, 9 September 1932, p. 1, 21 January 1934, p. 3, 24 June 1947, p. 1, 10 October 1958, p. 3; *Oklahoma A. and M. College Class Schedule, First Semester, 1937-1938*, p. 1; *Oklahoma State University Class Schedule, Second Semester, 1966-1967*, p. 52; *Oklahoma State University Class Schedule, Second Semester, 1962-1963*, p. 24; *Oklahoma A. and M. College Class Schedule, Second Semester, 1954-1955*, pp. 48, 64; *Oklahoma State University Class Schedule, First Semester, 1958-1959*, p. 49; "Calendar of Uses of Old Central," Old Central Centennial History Collection.

65. *Annual Catalog, Oklahoma A. and M. College, 1933-1934*, pp. 11-12; *Annual Catalog, Oklahoma A. and M. College, 1936-1937*, p. 13; *Daily O'Collegian*, 20 June 1933, p. 1, 12 October 1941, p. 2, 17 June 1943, p. 1, 24 June 1947, p. 1, 2 October 1947, p. 1, 27 April 1968, p. 5, 19 December 1968, p. 4; "The Cover," *Oklahoma A. and M. College Magazine*, vol. 13, no. 3 (December 1941), p. 1; *Annual Catalog, Oklahoma A. and M. College, 1942-1943*, p. 16; *Oklahoma City Times*, 27 October 1955, p. 13; Ray R. Matoy, *Thunderbird Tracks: Early History of Will Rogers Council, Boy Scouts of America* (Stillwater, OK: Prairie Imprints, 1988), p. 88; Author interview with Harry K. Brobst, 3 March 1987, E. Edward Davidson to James J. Thorne, 30 December 1971, and "Calendar of Uses of Old Central," Old Central Centennial History Collection.

66. *1944 Redskin,* p. 11, Oklahoma A. and M. College Yearbook; ''Calendar of Uses of Old Central,'' Old Central Centennial History Collection.

67. Chapman interview.

68. *Daily O'Collegian,* 20 May 1949, p. 8; *Stillwater NewsPress,* 22 May 1949, p. 4, 21 April 1976, p. 5, 6 February 1985, p. 10B; *Stillwater Gazette,* 3 June 1949, p. 1; Berlin B. Chapman to LeRoy H. Fischer, 23 October 1984, 31 October 1984, and 3 December 1984 and Attachments, in Old Central Centennial History Collection.

69. *Stillwater NewsPress,* 11 January 1950, p. 2, 15 January 1950, p. 7; *Tulsa Daily World,* 12 January 1950, p. 10; *Stillwater Gazette,* 13 January 1950, p. 7; *Daily O'Collegian,* 13 January 1950, p. 1.

70. *Stillwater NewsPress,* 16 January 1950, pp. 1-2, 24 April 1966, p. 3, 29 May 1977, p. 3, 28 April 1982, p. 1B; *Daily O'Collegian,* 17 January 1950, p. 8, 21 October 1954, p. 6; *Stillwater Gazette,* 20 January 1950, p. 2. See also Amos DeZell Maxwell, ''The Sequoyah Constitutional Convention'' (Master of Arts thesis, Oklahoma Agricultural and Mechanical College, 1950). The thesis was also published in the *Chronicles of Oklahoma* as Amos Maxwell, ''The Sequoyah Convention,'' *Chronicles of Oklahoma,* vol. 28, no. 2 (Summer 1950), pp. 161-192 and Amos Maxwell, ''The Sequoyah Convention,'' (part 2) *Chronicles of Oklahoma,* vol. 28, no. 3 (Autumn 1950), pp. 299-340. The thesis also was published as a book as Amos DeZell Maxwell, *The Sequoyah Constitutional Convention* (Boston, MA: Meador Publishing Company, 1953).

71. *Stillwater NewsPress,* 12 September 1969, p. 1; *Daily O'Collegian,* 13 September 1969, p. 1.

72. *Stillwater NewsPress,* 12 September 1969, p. 1. See also *Daily O'Collegian,* 13 September 1969, p. 1, *Daily Oklahoman,* 21 September 1969, p. 8A, and Author interview with E. Edward Davidson, 26 February 1987, Old Central Centennial History Collection.

73. ''Old Central Preservation,'' *Oklahoma State Alumnus Magazine,* vol. 10, no. 9 (December 1969), p. 4.

74. E. Edward Davidson to Berlin B. Chapman, 24 September 1969, Old Central Centennial History Collection.

75. *Daily O'Collegian,* 27 September 27, 1969, p. 7; Brobst interview, 3 March 1987. Years later, Harry K. Brobst remained convinced that the destruction of Williams Hall severely deteriorated the masonry of Old Central.

11 Beginning the Restoration

At last the Oklahoma State University had reached the point of no longer needing Old Central for conventional instructional and administrative uses. Enough housing could be found for these purposes in new and remodeled campus structures, but by the time the last occupant moved from Old Central in early 1971, the building appeared to be used up on both the interior and exterior. The structure, although rescued and safe from destruction, emerged from the building expansion program dilapidated and hazardous. "The last time I visited Old Central," explained Mary Nielsen Taylor of the class of 1903, "the interior was so uncared for it seemed that an old friend was gradually passing away."[1]

From 1955, no one seriously questioned keeping the structure intact, including its physical renewal. At the same time, no one also seemed to doubt the future use of Old Central as a museum of higher education, a suggestion which was first made in 1915 a year after tie rods appeared in the massive walls of the structure. President Henry G. Bennett supported the concept in his Twenty-Five Year Plan for campus development in 1930, and in 1940 the Alumni Association passed a resolution calling for the conversion of Old Central to a museum and established a committee for the purpose.[2]

Throughout his administration President Bennett continued to be committed to converting Old Central into a museum, as was Oliver S. Willham, who became president in 1952. Early graduates of the institution also promoted the use of the building for a museum, and the editorial page and the feature article columns of the *Daily O'Collegian* again voiced the same sentiment. Finally in 1969 after the administration of President Robert B. Kamm ordered the removal of all occupants from

Old Central as soon as possible because of the deteriorated and hazardous condition of the building, assurances came immediately from E. Edward Davidson, the university vice president for business and finance, that the structure would be preserved and refurbished. President Kamm welcomed the challenge of leading the effort to renew Old Central and prepare it for service as a museum of higher education.[3]

President Kamm took over the leadership of the Oklahoma State University upon the retirement of President Willham in 1966. Kamm had completed his undergraduate training in English and speech at the University of Northern Iowa, and then attended the University of Minnesota, where he earned the master of arts and doctor of philosophy degrees in higher education administration and student personnel. After working as dean of students at Drake University and dean of the basic division and student personnel services at the Texas Agricultural and Mechanical University, he became dean of the College of Arts and Sciences at the Oklahoma State University in 1958. He served in this position until 1965, when he became vice-president for academic affairs.

Robert B. Kamm, president of the university from 1966 to 1977, initiated and promoted the restoration of Old Central when it was no longer needed for classroom and administrative uses.

In 1966 he was elevated to the presidency of the institution, a position he held until 1977, when he retired from the office and began service as University Professor.

President Kamm has served widely in many leadership positions in civic and academic organizations, including the presidency of the American College Personnel Association, the chairmanship of the Council of Presidents of the National Association of State Universities and Land-Grant Colleges, and as the United States delegate to the Executive Board of the United Nations Educational, Scientific, and Cultural Organization. His honors include being named to the Oklahoma Hall of Fame and as the "Oklahoman of the Year" by the Oklahoma Broadcasters Association.[4]

Many achievements characterized the administration of President Kamm. His steady and dynamic leadership guided the university during a difficult period in higher education when campuses in the United States experienced more than usual unrest. Through these years he saw to it that the Oklahoma State University remained a stable campus where teaching, research, extension, and student services continued without interruption. Simultaneously, freedom and responsible dissent, so essential to a creative and constructive university, were retained and increased. This dual focus prompted some to refer to the Oklahoma State University as both a progressive and conservative institution. In keeping with this guideline, President Kamm encouraged and promoted change, but at the same time stressed values, structures, and services that had stood the test of time and had proven fundamental for a modern land-grant university.

President Kamm's "people emphasis" program guided and motivated the faculty and staff to serve students and other constituents more effectively, and these management principles soon became deeply embedded in collegiate-level educational psychology nationwide. He frequently said: "Students are the reason a university exists. They're Number One!"[5] As the institutional leader, he also used and encouraged the team approach involving new ideas and suggestions in dealing with the innumerable and complex problems of a comprehensive university. Finally, he encouraged the enlargement of the curriculum in the humanities, in the social and behavioral sciences, and in the applied areas of business and education to stand side-by-side with traditional land-grant institutional strengths in the biological and physical sciences and in their applied areas of agriculture, engineering, home economics, and veterinary medicine. In this way he developed the institution into a university in the fullest sense.[6]

President Kamm's concern about Old Central dated from his arrival on the campus. "A strong believer in acknowledging the past, and in tradition," he explained, he became interested in Old Central soon after coming to Stillwater in 1958. Upon becoming president in 1966, he became actively involved with the building. "I had watched the deterioration of something very dear to many and was troubled. We needed our somewhat restricted monies for other purposes, however, and were unable to divert available funds for the restoration of Old Central."[7]

In keeping with the promise of the Kamm administration to refurbish and restore Old Central at the time the decision was reached to remove its occupants in 1969, steps were soon taken by the university architect's office to determine the needs and costs of the work. By the autumn of 1970, even before the last office moved from Old Central, tests were made and recommendations compiled on the building's foundation, long a major problem. The findings then went to a leading structural engineer, Warren E. Sullivan of Oklahoma City, for evaluation and recommendations on stabilizing the foundation to prevent further movement and deterioration of the exterior and interior masonry walls. With this information, the Harmon Construction Company of Oklahoma City and the university architect's office estimated that the building could be underpinned, the masonry reworked, and the interior and the roof renewed for a cost of $361,800. They also prepared an estimate covering the demolition of the building and reconstructing it with a concrete reinforced frame, reusing the exterior brick and stone, for a cost of $379,500.[8]

Also during the autumn of 1970, President Kamm visited with LeRoy H. Fischer, a professor of history at the university, concerning the possibility of arranging for the Oklahoma Historical Society to refurbish and restore Old Central and then develop and operate it as a museum of higher education. Fischer, a member of the board of directors of the Oklahoma Historical Society, considered the suggestion workable and indicated he would explore it with the leadership of the Oklahoma Historical Society. Soon President Kamm appointed the Old Central Committee, an ad hoc group of university personnel, consisting of E. Edward Davidson, the vice president for business and finance; E. Moses Frye, the legal counsel; Homer L. Knight, the head of the history department; Murl R. Rogers, the executive director of the Alumni Association; and LeRoy H. Fischer, the chairman.[9]

The Old Central Committee held its first meeting on December 7, 1970, and agreed unanimously that the Oklahoma Historical Society seemed ideal for Old Central since it already funded and operated eleven historical facilities statewide. The committee likewise recommended unanimously that a lease-contract should be drawn up with the Oklahoma Historical Society for the restoration, development, and operation of Old Central as a museum of higher education. Possible provisions of a proposed lease-contract were considered briefly. In response to a suggestion that a meeting be held with George H. Shirk, the president of the Oklahoma Historical Society, and H. Milt Phillips, the vice president, President Kamm arranged a luncheon meeting in the Student Union on December 15, 1970, where a mutual decision by both parties to work toward a lease-contract resulted.[10]

While negotiations moved along to work out a lease-contract for Old Central with the Oklahoma Historical Society, plans developed to nominate the building for the National Register of Historic Places. Congress created the national register in the Historic Preservation Act of 1966 and placed its administration in the National Park Service of the United States Department of the Interior. The register is the official list of the nation's cultural property worth saving and is a protective inventory of irreplaceable resources spread across the face of the country. Listing on the register also makes a historic site or structure eligible for federal dollar-for-dollar matching funds, then becoming available for the first time. Murl R. Rogers, Kent R. Ruth, and LeRoy H. Fischer prepared the nomination form for Old Central and submitted it in February 1971 to George H. Shirk, the Oklahoma state historic preservation officer, and to the Oklahoma State Historic Preservation Review Commission. Following approval by the commission, the nomination underwent appraisal by the keeper of the National Register of Historic Places in the

Odie B. Faulk (*left*) and LeRoy H. Fischer (*right*) join Murl R. Rogers (*second left*) to present the certificate from the state of Oklahoma recognizing the enrollment of Old Central on the National Register of Historic Places to OSU President Robert B. Kamm in 1976. Faulk served as professor and head of the history department; Rogers worked as executive director of the Alumni Association; and Fischer was Oppenheim Regents professor of history and chairman of the Old Central Committee.

National Park Service. After approval, the Secretary of the Interior placed Old Central on the National Register of Historic Places on July 27, 1971.[11]

Negotiations continued between the Oklahoma State University and the Oklahoma Historical Society. E. Moses Frye, legal counsel for the university, prepared a draft of a lease-contract and submitted it to George H. Shirk, president of the historical society. Shirk and the executive committee of the historical society generally found little to change in the lease-contract but voiced an abiding concern over the provision for the historical society to raise capital funds for the restoration of Old Central. The historical society leadership believed capital monies for restoration should be raised by the university because funds as extensive as those needed for Old Central had never been approved when requested from the Oklahoma Legislature by the historical society. The historical society leadership thought it would be no problem convincing the legislature to increase appropriations for its annual budgets to develop, maintain, and staff the Old Central museum of higher education following its restoration.[12]

With no procedure yet determined to finance the cost of the Old Central restoration, the lease-contract for the building remained unsigned. The Old Central Committee requested that Senator Robert M. Murphy and Representative Daniel D. Draper Jr., both members of the legislature from Stillwater, insert an appropriation of $50,000 as a line item in the 1971 appropriation bill of the Oklahoma Historical Society. This approach to raising capital improvement money for Oklahoma Historical Society historic sites had developed apace during several years before 1971, when it included funding for thirteen historic sites. This appeared to be a satisfactory procedure for financing the capital improvements needed for Old Central. Although the 1971 Old Central line item of $50,000 underwent reduction to $25,000 by the end of the legislative session, federal money soon became available to match it dollar-for-dollar, a pattern that would continue almost until the restoration of the building reached completion in 1983.[13]

Now that a workable procedure for raising funds for the restoration of Old Central was functional, President Kamm appointed a permanent Old Central Committee of university personnel to serve indefinite terms at his pleasure. He chose E. Moses Frye, Murl R. Rogers, and LeRoy H. Fischer, chairman, from the previous committee, and added Bill D. Halley, the university architect. Kamm recommended that the committee begin work immediately with the Oklahoma Historical Society.[14]

Convinced that the Oklahoma State University had a workable procedure for raising funds for the restoration of the building, the board of directors of the Oklahoma Historical Society approved the lease-contract on July 22, 1971, and two days later, on July 24, the board of regents of the Oklahoma State University also signed.[15]

Under terms of the Old Central lease-contract, the university agreed to provide utilities at cost, to supply and maintain a lawn and landscaping program, to furnish adequate fire safety and fire protection for the structure, and to establish and maintain the Old Central Committee. This body was obligated to advise and work closely with the Oklahoma Historical Society on the reconditioning and restoration of the structure, the assembling and arrangement of its displays, and the operation of its museum of higher education.

The Oklahoma Historical Society agreed in the lease-contract to recondition and restore Old Central externally and internally to its original condition at the time of its completion in 1894, including the reequipping and refurnishing of at least one laboratory and one classroom. The historical society also promised to depict other aspects of Oklahoma higher education history through artifact, photographic, and descriptive displays on a permanent basis. The historical society likewise consented to provide a full-time curator and other professional staff as needed, including janitorial service, to carry out the terms of the contract. In addition, the historical society agreed to supply funds as necessary to maintain the building in the condition to which it was restored. Finally, the historical society promised to advise with the Old Central Committee on all matters concerning the structure and its operation. The lease-contract extends for fifty years, subject to renewal for the same amount of time.[16]

The $25,000 legislative appropriation for the restoration of Old Central, the signing of the lease-contract for its restoration, development, and operation as a museum of higher education, and its placement on the National Register of Historic Places occurred in approximately a month in mid-1971. The building almost immediately burst into the limelight of news media publicity and became the center of public attention. It seemed as though not enough could be published or spoken about the structure's past, its restoration, and its future as a museum of higher education. Letters highly favorable to the project arrived frequently, and early graduates of the institution viewed the effort with much enthusiasm. Because the state and federal money needed for the task would only become available in small amounts over a long time period, it was estimated that about three to five years would be required to complete the restoration.[17]

Considering the complex problems involved, planning for the restoration of Old Central moved rapidly. The Old Central Committee met with Oklahoma Historical Society officials George H. Shirk, president, and Verlin R. Easterling, newly appointed executive director, on December 15, 1971, to tour and study in detail the exterior and interior of the building. The group planned procedures to raise the state and federal money needed for the project. It also considered placing a new foundation under the structure by means of cribbing and underpinning, and looked into the possibilities of completely demolishing the building and then rebuilding it to its original appearance.[18]

The committee agreed unanimously, and President Kamm concurred, that total demolition, rebuilding, and restoration would be the preferable procedure to follow. The committee also agreed that research on the source of federal restoration funds should be conducted through the offices of United States Senator Henry L. Bellmon and Speaker of the United States House of Representatives Carl Albert. The committee designated one of its members, E. Moses Frye, the university legal counsel, to carry out the contacts and investigations needed for the project.[19]

During the months of January and February 1972, the Old Central Committee and the Oklahoma Historical Society leadership determined, after extensive research, advisement, and consultation that the total demolition, rebuilding, and restoration of Old Central would be cost prohibitive. As a result, the committee and the society decided to refurbish and restore Old Central to the highest standards permitted by available state and federal funding. Then attention centered on stabilizing the foundation of the building, its major structural problem. The committee and the university architect's office consulted at length with Raymond E. Means and James V. Parcher, soil mechanics engineers at the university, and also with Veldo H. Brewer, David N. Martin, and Warren E. Sullivan, structural engineers, concerning a satisfactory procedure for underpinning the Old Central foundation.[20]

With the 1972 Oklahoma Legislature in session and approval of an additional sum of $25,000 for the restoration of Old Central, E. Moses Frye, assisted by other members of the committee, concentrated attention on raising federal matching funds. Money appeared to be available for the Old Central restoration in the United States Department of Housing and Urban Development, and an application for a grant of $125,000 in matching funds from the Oklahoma City office of the Department of Housing and Urban Development was prepared and submitted with the approval of the Oklahoma Historical Society. The document consisted of fifty pages. The announcement of the grant came on June 9, 1972, followed by a state-wide press release prepared by the Oklahoma Historical Society.[21]

By late July 1972, the Old Central plans and specifications for all foundation, brick, and stone refurbishing and restoration were completed by the university architect's office and submitted for approval to the Oklahoma Historical Society, to the Oklahoma State Board of Public Affairs, the contracting agent for the Oklahoma Historical Society, and to the Department of Housing and Urban Development. Following approval, the low bid by contractors came in at $199,354, including alternate units, and went to the firm of Walter A. Nashert and Sons Construction Company of Oklahoma City. At this point the money deficiency rested in state funding for Old Central, which totaled but $50,000.[22]

After much negotiation with the construction company, the contractor agreed to extend the bid until the spring of 1973 when it was anticipated that the Oklahoma Legislature would appropriate $50,000 additional for Old Central restoration purposes. The money became available on July 1, 1973, and these funds, when combined with $25,000 in-kind state services of those working on the project, such as the members of the Old Central Committee, fully qualified the state for the $125,000 in federal matching money provided by the Department of Housing and Urban Development. The contract with Nashert underwent revision downward, as provided by the alternate unit arrangement, in March and April 1973, and caused the basic amount of the contract to be $122,862, subject to contingency needs and alternate units of work that could be added to the contract after the refurbishing and restoration of the building began. The selection of the Walter A. Nashert firm pleased the Old Central Committee, because Nashert had a deep interest in early Oklahoma buildings and had written a book on the history of building construction in the state.[23]

George H. Shirk, president of the Oklahoma Historical Society, accepts the Old Central key from Armon H. Bost, chairman of the Oklahoma State University Board of Regents, at the Old Central restoration groundbreaking ceremonies on May 12, 1973. The Oklahoma Historical Society leased Old Central for restoration, development, and museum purposes in 1971.

Wielding orange and black shovels in the Old Central restoration groundbreaking ceremonies on May 12, 1973, were left to right: Armon H. Bost, chairman, OSU Board of Regents; George H. Shirk, president, Oklahoma Historical Society; Robert B. Kamm, president, OSU; Verlin R. Easterling, executive director, Oklahoma Historical Society; L. E. "Dean" Stringer, president, OSU Alumni Association; Murl R. Rogers, executive director, OSU Alumni Association; Senator Robert M. Murphy; Representative Daniel D. Draper Jr.; and Walter A. Nashert Sr., Walter A. Nashert and Sons Construction Company.

With restoration work on Old Central about to begin, ceremonies commemorating the event took place during the 1973 spring commencement day on May 12. Alumni and friends of the Oklahoma State University assembled on the lawn south of Old Central at 10:00 o'clock in the morning, and LeRoy H. Fischer, the chairman of the Old Central Committee, acted as master of ceremonies. The invocation was given by A. Frank Martin, the president of the Half-Century Club and a member of the class of 1920. President Robert B. Kamm gave the welcome and appreciation, followed with the introduction of distinguished guests and alumni by Fischer.

Nine persons wielded orange and black shovels for the groundbreaking part of the ceremonies: Armon H. Bost, chairman, Oklahoma State University Board of Regents; George H. Shirk, president, Oklahoma Historical Society; Robert B. Kamm, president, Oklahoma State University; Verlin R. Easterling, executive director, Oklahoma Historical Society; L. E. "Dean" Stringer, president, Oklahoma State University Alumni Association; Murl R. Rogers, executive director, Oklahoma State University Alumni Association; Senator Robert M. Murphy; Representative Daniel D. Draper Jr.; and Walter A. Nashert Sr., Walter A. Nashert and

Sons Construction Company. Next came the symbolic transfer of the Old Central key from the Oklahoma State University to the Oklahoma Historical Society by Bost and Shirk. Fischer concluded with comments on "The Future of Old Central." The ceremonies created additional public interest in the restoration of the building.[24]

The intent of the Old Central foundation stabilization effort and expense was to stop the detrimental movement of the structural support of the building. Much evidence for this need could be seen by viewing the cracked masonry of the exterior walls prior to the refurbishing of the foundation. The foundation had to be stabilized and strengthened first before other restoration could be accomplished satisfactorily for the years ahead. Only then would the building be stabilized and its movement minimized.

The Walter A. Nashert and Sons Construction Company ran into immediate problems when it began excavation work on Old Central to underpin the foundation with reinforced concrete as required by the

Alumni and friends of the university gathered on the lawn south of Old Central for restoration groundbreaking ceremonies on May 12, 1973. The restoration work reached completion ten years later.

architectural plans and specifications. The decision to underpin the foundation with reinforced concrete resulted when a hole dug in October 1970 by structural engineers at the center of the west foundation wall revealed that the original foundation consisted of large sandstone pieces held together by mortar and resting on the earth. A total of five test holes were drilled to a depth of sixteen feet around the building. The underpinning method required that the existing foundation be divided into four foot lengths consecutively numbered one, two, and three, and then repeated again and again until the entire foundation was numbered. Then all four foot lengths of the foundation with the same number would be excavated and underpinned with reinforced concrete. This allowed only four foot sections of the foundation to be exposed, with eight foot lengths of earth on each side of the four foot excavations to support the wall. After permitting the concrete to harden, each four foot excavation would be filled with tamped earth. Then the next similar numbered sections would be excavated and reinforced concrete inserted, until the entire foundation had been underpinned.[25]

When the contractor began the excavation to underpin the foundation, the extreme deterioration of the original sandstone and mortar footing was fully revealed for the first time. The sandstone actually fell in pieces into the opening made for the initial four foot length of concrete underpinning. Over the many years that the sandstone and mortar had been in place, the sub-soil moisture had turned the mortar into wet sand and made the sandstone unstable. Although this procedure had long been successfully used in the construction industry, immediately the foundation underpinning procedure was abandoned, and meetings were held concerning other foundation renewal techniques. A major conference convened on the campus on May 15, 1973, and a new procedure emerged concerning the Old Central foundation problem. Nine persons, representing the university architect's office, the contractor, foundation consultants, and structural engineers, composed the group. They were Ray E. Dryden, Bill D. Halley, William Kaiser, John McElwain, Raymond E. Means, Walter A. Nashert, Walter A. "Jack" Nashert Jr., Warren E. Sullivan, and John Wells.[26]

The new foundation stabilization procedure for Old Central called for a wraparound support of steel and gunite concrete against the existing foundation without disturbing the soil beneath it. The design required that the new support be tied to the old foundation with twelve inch diameter steel reinforced portland cement concrete plugs every ten feet through the old foundation, with the opposite end of the plug enlarged to create a ball to hold the plug securely in place. Four continuous heavy steel reinforcing bars surrounded the old foundation, and on top of these bars a super-strength reinforcing wire mesh of highway construction size covered the surface of the old foundation.

The foundation stabilization procedure for the Old Central restoration called for a wraparound support of steel and gunite concrete against the existing foundation without disturbing the soil beneath it. A workman sprays the gunite concrete under high pressure through and around the heavy steel apron tied to the foundation of Old Central.

Then gunite concrete, used for years in the construction industry, was blown under high pressure through and around the heavy steel apron tied to the foundation of Old Central. The gunite concrete, applied with an average thickness of five inches, completely covered the reinforcing steel. Because of the high portland cement content of gunite concrete and its dense nature, it prevented moisture penetration from further deteriorating the sandstone foundation and helped to waterproof the basement. In addition, gunite concrete has two to three times greater strength than standard mixed portland cement concrete.[27]

The gunite concrete foundation stabilization process was used for the exterior walls on most of Old Central. One exception to this was the newly poured reinforced concrete footing under the north stairway exterior walls and the south arched entryway and steps. In addition, all structurally supporting interior walls were stabilized in the basement with the same gunite concrete process.[28]

The decision to rebuild the north, east, and west walls of the stairway enclosure on the north side of Old Central resulted from major cracks in the masonry walls and the number of openings in the three wall sur-

SPECIAL COLLECTIONS, OSU LIBRARY

The south entrance portico and surrounding wall areas of Old Central required restoration primarily because of extensive masonry deterioration, causing the unsafe condition of the arch over the entryway. Some observers also maintained that the demolition of the nearby Auditorium and Williams Hall contributed to the deterioration of the masonry of Old Central.

faces. The minimal lateral support of the walls, essentially freestanding for two and three stories in height, also influenced the decision to remove them and rebuild. The same determination was made for the south entrance portico and walls. The primary cause for rebuilding this area of the south wall was the unsafe condition of the arch over the entryway. The keystone hung precariously in the arch.

The faulty walls of Old Central underwent removal with extreme care. Stones from the walls were numbered and measured to be reset in exactly the same location. Bricks were also salvaged and cleaned for reuse in the walls, and only a minimal number of replacements were needed. The new walls matched the old walls in texture due to laying the carefully cleaned brick in the same coursing pattern, but they did not exactly match the original in color even though much effort went into adding appropriate color tinting to the new mortar. To correct this, a light stain was sprayed on the entire masonry surface, and this made the color of the building aesthetically pleasing to the eye. In the restoration of the walls, the tie rods were tightened, and a new one installed running north and south. The two east-west tie rods at the ceiling level of the second floor, no longer functional, were removed. Their heads, made like large six-pointed iron stars, remain in place for historic and aesthetic reasons.[29]

When the north, east, and west walls on the north side of Old Central were being rebuilt and restored, bracing held up the interior staircase and windows in their exact positions. On the remaining walls,

Centennial Histories Series

The decision to rebuild the north, east, and west walls of the stairway enclosure on the north side of Old Central resulted from major masonry cracks caused by inadequate lateral support for the walls. During restoration bracing held the interior staircase and windows in their proper positions.

almost an inch of old mortar was removed from between the bricks and replaced, a procedure that both strengthened and beautified the structure. A few blocks of native sandstone were needed to replace broken window sills and renew entrance openings. Sandstone for this purpose came from an early-day farmhouse cellar near Stillwater. The fabricated limestone concrete steps used to restore the stairway on the northwest side of the building, as well as the front staircase, came from Kansas, the source of considerable material used to construct the building in 1893 and 1894. Workers reshaped the exposed roof section of the chimney serving the old president's office to restore the original bell design. Even the chimney to the old steam boiler room, removed in the 1929 and 1930 refurbishing, underwent complete rebuilding and emerged on the roof with the same bell pattern.[30]

When Old Central underwent retirement from conventional university uses in 1969, no one seriously questioned the effort to refurbish and restore the building. The same sentiment prevailed to convert it into a museum of higher education. President Kamm took steps to promote its restoration even before the last occupant moved from the structure and recommended that the Oklahoma Historical Society restore, develop, and operate it as a museum of higher education.

Endnotes

1. Mary Nielsen Taylor to Berlin B. Chapman, 31 July 1966, Old Central Centennial History Collection, Special Collections, Edmon Low Library, Oklahoma State University, Stillwater, Oklahoma.

2. Oklahoma A. and M. College *Orange and Black,* 4 October 1915, p. 2; Oklahoma A. and M. College, *Equity of Chance* (Stillwater: Oklahoma A. and M. College, 1930), p. 4; Resolution, June 1, 1940, Files, Oklahoma State University Alumni Association, Oklahoma State University; "Alumni Hear Talks and Report," *Oklahoma A. and M. College Magazine,* vol. 11, no. 9 (June 1940), p. 9.

3. Philip S. Donnell to Automatic Sprinkler Corporation of America, 17 June 1946, Author interview with Murl R. Rogers, 15 September 1985, and Mary Nielsen Taylor to Berlin B. Chapman, 31 July 1966, in Old Central Centennial History Collection; Clarence R. Donart to Thomas J. Hartman, 6 April 1956, Alfred E. Jarrell to Berlin B. Chapman, 7 July 1958, Alfred E. Jarrell File, and Clarence R. Donart to Berlin B. Chapman, 21 March 1959, Building and Building Programs—Old Central File, in Berlin B. Chapman Collection, Special Collections, Edmon Low Library; "Buildings in Unsatisfactory Condition," Buildings 1965 File, Oliver S. Willham Collection, Special Collections, Edmon Low Library; Oklahoma A. and M. College *Daily O'Collegian,* 8 March 1956, p. 4, 29 June 1956, p. 4, 17 July 1956, pp. 1, 4, 31 January 1957, p. 2, 30 July 1957, p. 2; Author interview with Robert B. Kamm, 3 June 1982, Old Central Centennial History Collection.

4. *Who's Who in America, 1986-1987* (2 vols., Wilmette , IL: Marquis Who's Who, 1986), vol. 1, p. 1466.

5. Robert B. Kamm, *They're No. One!: A People-Oriented Approach to Higher Education Administration* (Oklahoma City, OK: Western Heritage Books, 1980), back cover.

6. Author interview with Richard W. Poole, 12 April 1987, Old Central Centennial History Collection; Philip Reed Rulon, *Oklahoma State University—Since 1890* (Stillwater: Oklahoma State University Press, 1975), pp. ix-xi; Kamm, *They're No. One!,* throughout.

7. Kamm interview.

8. Author interview with Bill D. Halley, 1 February 1986, and Chaplin E. Bills to E. Edward Davidson, 7 January 1971, in Old Central Centennial History Collection.

9. Records of Meeting, Old Central Committee, 7 December 1970, Old Central Centennial History Collection.

10. [Elmer L. Fraker], "Along the Trail," 16 July 1970, Records of Meeting, Old Central Committee, 7 December 1970, and Robert B. Kamm to LeRoy H. Fischer, 9 December 1970, in Old Central Centennial History Collection; Oklahoma State Legislature, *Oklahoma Session Laws, 1970, Thirty- second Legislature, Second Regular Session, Convened January 6, 1970, Adjourned April 15, 1970* (St. Paul MN: West Publishing Company, 1970), pp. 527-528.

11. United States Department of the Interior, National Park Service, *The National Register of Historic Places* (Washington, DC: United States Department of the Interior, National Park Service, 1969); Inventory-Nomination Form for Old Central, National Register of Historic Places, Approved July 27, 1971, Old Central Centennial History Collection; Oklahoma Historical Society, *Handbook: Historic Sites Preservation in Oklahoma* (Oklahoma City, OK: Oklahoma Historical Society, May 1971), throughout.

12. George H. Shirk to E. Moses Frye, 31 December 1970, Old Central Centennial History Collection; "Minutes of the Quarterly Meeting of the Board of Directors of the Oklahoma Historical Society, January 28, 1971," *Chronicles of Oklahoma,* vol. 49, no. 1 (Spring 1971), p. 136.

13. Murl R. Rogers and LeRoy H. Fischer to Representative Bill Willis, Representative Daniel D. Draper Jr., Senator Clem McSpadden, Senator George A. Miller, Senator Herschal H. Crow, Senator James E. Hamilton, Senator Robert M. Murphy, and Representative Rex Privett, 10 May 1971, in Old Central Centennial History Collection (separate letters were written to each of these legislators); Oklahoma State Legislature, *Oklahoma Session Laws, 1971, Thirty-third Legislature, First Regular Session, Convened January 5, 1971, Adjourned June 11, 1971. First Extraordinary Session, Convened July 1, 1971, Adjourned July 1, 1971* (St. Paul, MN: West Publishing Company, 1971), p. 807.

14. Elmer L. Fraker to Robert B. Kamm, 7 July 1971, Robert B. Kamm to LeRoy H. Fischer, 12 July 1971, Robert B. Kamm to Elmer L. Fraker, 13 July 1971, and LeRoy H. Fischer to Robert B. Kamm, 14 July 1971, in Old Central Centennial History Collection.

15. "Minutes of the Quarterly Meeting of the Board of Directors of the Oklahoma Historical Society, July 22, 1971," *Chronicles of Oklahoma*, vol. 49, no. 3 (Autumn 1971), p. 397; Minutes, Board of Regents of the Oklahoma Agricultural and Mechanical Colleges, 23-24 July 1971, pp. 36-37, Special Collections, Edmon Low Library; Old Central Lease-Contract between the Oklahoma Historical Society and Oklahoma State University, July 24, 1971, Old Central Centennial History Collection.

16. Old Central Lease-Contract between the Oklahoma Historical Society and Oklahoma State University, July 24, 1971. Section IIIB of the lease-contract underwent minor revision in 1972 and was approved by both contracting parties, "Minutes of the Quarterly Meeting of the Board of Directors of the Oklahoma Historical Society, October 26, 1972," *Chronicles of Oklahoma*, vol. 50, no. 4 (Winter 1972-1973), p. 519.

17. *Stillwater NewsPress*, 25 July 1971, p. 1, 3 August 1971, p. 1, 8 August 1971, p. 11, 15 September 1971, p. 22, 1 December 1971, p. 16; *Daily O'Collegian*, 27 July 1971, p. 1, 10 September 1971, p. 8, 15 December 1971, p. 1; Oklahoma City *Daily Oklahoman*, 25 July 1971, p. 4A, 18 September 1971, p. 11; *Tulsa Tribune*, 18 September 1971, p. 2B; LeRoy H. Fischer, "Historic Old Central to Serve Again: Preserved for Posterity," *Oklahoma State Alumnus Magazine*, vol. 12, no. 8 (November 1971), pp. 3-6; examples of letters are Edward E. Dale to LeRoy H. Fischer, 18 November 1971, Mary Nielsen Taylor to LeRoy H. Fischer, 13 August 1971, and Berlin B. Chapman to LeRoy H. Fischer, 8 October 1971, and 11 November 1971, in Old Central Centennial History Collection; "Minutes of the Quarterly Meeting of the Board of Directors of the Oklahoma Historical Society, October 28, 1971," *Chronicles of Oklahoma*, vol. 49, no. 4 (Winter 1971-1972), p. 533.

18. Minutes, Old Central Committee, 15 December 1971, Old Central Centennial History Collection.

19. E. Moses Frye to LeRoy H. Fischer, 31 December 1971, and LeRoy H. Fischer to George H. Shirk, and Verlin R. Easterling, 30 December 1971, in Old Central Centennial History Collection.

20. Minutes, Old Central Committee, 10, 19 and 25 January 1972, 8 February 1972, and David N. Martin to Members of Old Central Committee, 7 February 1972, in Old Central Centennial History Collection; LeRoy H. Fischer to Berlin B. Chapman, 29 January 1972, Berlin B. Chapman Collection.

21. Oklahoma State Legislature, *Oklahoma Session Laws, 1972, Thirty-third Legislature, Second Regular Session, Convened January 4, 1972, Adjourned March 31, 1972* (St. Paul, MN: West Publishing Company, 1972), p. 177; George H. Shirk to LeRoy H. Fischer, 15 February 1972, LeRoy H. Fischer to Bill D. Halley, 3 May 1972, LeRoy H. Fischer to E. Moses Frye, 8 May 1972, Robert H. Breeden to George Shirk, 2 June 1972, LeRoy H. Fischer to Verlin R. Easterling, 9 June 1972, and Old Central Press Release from Oklahoma Historical Society, in Old Central Centennial History Collection; "Minutes of the Quarterly Meeting of the Board of Directors of the Oklahoma Historical Society, February 17, 1972," *Chronicles of Oklahoma*, vol. 50, no. 1 (Spring 1972), p. 133; "Funds Received for Restoration of Old Central as a Museum, Historical Sight," *Oklahoma State Alumnus Magazine*, vol. 13, no. 7 (September-October 1972), p. 10.

22. R. D. Schultz to Michael Bureman, 25 July 1972, 1 August 1972, R. D. Schultz to E. Moses Frye, 17 October 1972, William Kaiser to University Architect, 18 October 1972, and R. D. Schultz to Verlin R. Easterling, 23 October 1972, in Old Central Centennial History Collection; "Minutes of the Quarterly Meeting of the Board of Directors of the Oklahoma Historical Society, July 27, 1972," *Chronicles of Oklahoma*, vol. 50, no. 3 (Autumn 1972), p. 388.

23. Verlin R. Easterling to Robert H. Breeden, 14 November 1972, William Kaiser to University Architect, 5 December 1972, R. D. Schultz to Files of University Architect, 6 December 1972, R. D. Schultz to Verlin R. Easterling, 11 December 1972, William Kaiser to R. D. Schultz, 7 March 1973, R. D. Schultz to Verlin R. Easterling, 14 March 1973, Ray E. Dryden to Walter Nashert and Sons, 13 April 1973, and Verlin R. Easterling to John Ivey, 17 April 1973, in Old Central Centennial History Collection; Oklahoma State Legislature, *Oklahoma Session Laws, 1973, Thirty-fourth Legislature, First Regular Session, Convened January 2, 1973, Adjourned May 17, 1973* (St. Paul, MN: West Publishing Company, 1973), p. 392; Walter Nashert, *Tepees to Towers: The Story of Building the Sooner State* ([Oklahoma City, OK; Walter Nashert, 1969]).

24. Old Central Restoration Ceremonies Program, Oklahoma State University, May 12, 1973, Old Central Centennial History Collection; *Stillwater NewsPress,* 11 May 1973, p. 1, 13 May 1973, p. 1; *Daily O'Collegian,* 5 June 1973, p. 7, 4 September 1973, pp. 1, 5; *Tulsa World,* 11 June 1973, p. 20D, 26 August 1973, p. 1B; *Oklahoma State* University *News,* 4 June 1973, p. 3; Oklahoma Historical Society *Mistletoe Leaves,* August 1973, p. 2; Warren E. Shull, "Ceremony Launches Renovation of Old Central," *Oklahoma State Alumnus Magazine,* vol. 14, no. 6 (June-July 1973), pp. 10-11.

25. Old Central Restoration Plans and Specifications, Phase I, Special Collections, Edmon Low Library; Halley interview; Author interview with Ray E. Dryden, 5 November 1985, and Raymond E. Means to LeRoy H. Fischer, 28 May 1973, in Old Central Centennial History Collection.

26. Halley interview; Dryden interview; Raymond E. Means to LeRoy H. Fischer, 28 May 1973, Old Central Centennial History Collection.

27. Halley interview; Dryden interview; Raymond E. Means to LeRoy H. Fischer, 28 May 1973, and Warren E. Sullivan to Bill D. Halley, 23 June 1973, in Old Central Centennial History Collection.

28. Halley interview; Warren E. Sullivan to Bill D. Halley, 23 June 1973, Old Central Centennial History Collection.

29. Halley interview; Old Central Restoration Plans and Specifications, Phase 1 and Phase 3, Special Collections, Edmon Low Library; Author interview with James L. Showalter, 11 December 1986, Old Central Centennial History Collection.

30. "Old Central: Painstaking Job," *Oklahoma State University Outreach,* vol. 14, no. 8 (November 1973), p. 4; Old Central Restoration Plans and Specifications, Phase 1.

12 Completing the Restoration

The primary exterior contract for the restoration of Old Central began a construction program that would continue periodically for a decade. A total of eight contracts finally brought the work to completion because available state and federal money came in small amounts with relatively brief time expiration limits, thus making it impossible to stockpile funds for a single contract. Coordination of the total effort became extremely difficult for this reason, but the process provided time for the long and tedious planning always needed for historic preservation at its best. The total cost of the restoration was greater, but the restoration of Old Central turned out better than if money had been available for a single contract. Double digit inflation in construction throughout the decade-long work on the building also increased the total money needed.

As work on the major exterior contract for Old Central came to a close in 1974, plans moved forward to raise additional funds to finance the remaining restoration of the building. The appropriation bill of the Oklahoma Historical Society for 1974 contained a line item for $50,000 for Old Central, and it appeared likely to be approved by the legislature. In the last hours of the 1974 legislative session when the Oklahoma Historical Society bill was up for final consideration, confusion entered the situation because the 1973 Old Central line item appropriation of $50,000 had the wording "final appropriation" following the dollar figure. As a result, no money was appropriated for Old Central. The intent behind the wording "final appropriation" was to indicate the concluding money of a three-year funding plan from 1971 to 1973 in cooperation with the United States Department of Housing and Urban Development.[1]

The most urgent concern for the restoration of Old Central continued to be fund raising. The primary responsibility for this effort rested with two members of the Old Central Committee, E. Moses Frye, the university legal counsel, and LeRoy H. Fischer, the chairman of the committee. In 1974 it became evident that the Department of Housing and Urban Development could no longer be counted on for additional federal money due to the lack of funding by the Congress. Smaller amounts of federal money then became available to the states through the Historic Conservation and Recreation Office of the National Park Service, a division of the United States Department of the Interior. From this point forward, state appropriated money was matched as long as possible dollar-for-dollar by funds from this source, administered in Oklahoma by the state historic preservation office of the Oklahoma Historical Society. Oklahoma State Historic Preservation Officers George H. Shirk, Harry L. Deupree, H. Glenn Jordan, and C. Earle Metcalf cooperated fully by approving the federal matching funds needed to restore Old Central. Others at the Oklahoma Historical Society who provided executive assistance to expedite the use of federal funds were Verlin R. Easterling and Jack Wettengel.[2]

The quest for state money for the restoration of Old Central became urgent. Because $50,000 did not materialize in the 1974 Oklahoma Legislature, an effort developed to raise $100,000 in the 1975 legislature for Old Central to complete the entire restoration project when matched with federal funds. In an effort to control state spending and reduce line-item expenditures, David L. Boren, the new governor of Oklahoma, met with George H. Shirk, the historical society president, and H. Milt Phillips, its vice president. Upon their advice, thirty-two of the approximately eighty line items of the Oklahoma Historical Society appropriation bill were deleted. Old Central remained in the bill, but for $20,000 only. The board of directors of the Oklahoma Historical Society allocated $34,000 of funds to Old Central from discretionary money for state historic sites capital improvements in the same legislation. Thus $54,000 in state money became available in 1975, and when matched dollar-for-dollar with federal funds the total came to $108,000.[3]

A small amount of exterior work, other than paint restoration, remained to be completed following the major outside contract. With this in mind, and also with the purpose of commencing minimal work on the interior of Old Central, a mini-contract was let to the Continental Contracting Company of Midwest City, on March 24, 1975, for the sum of $9,850. Funding came from the residue of state and Department of Housing and Urban Development monies remaining after the major exterior contract. The new contract included interior bracing of the ventilation cupola; the removal of specified ceilings and partitions installed since the construction of the building; the fabrication and installation

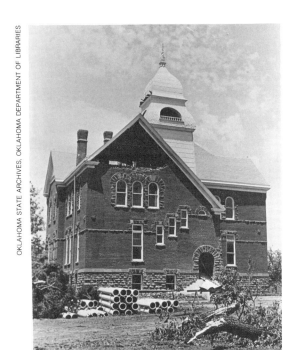

In 1975 a tornado struck Old Central, blowing out the gable of the south masonry wall and the ventilation cupola on the roof ridge over the assembly hall. The large pipes stacked in front of Old Central at the time of the tornado later supplied chilled water for the building's air conditioning system.

of facsimile roof ridge ornaments; the purchase and installation of gutter downspout extensions and splash blocks; the reinforcement of the belfry; and the removal of the original bell and clapper from the Student Union tower and its reinstallation in the Old Central belfry. In addition, the belfry needed other repairs due to deteriorating materials and the lack of adequate maintenance over the years. The wood railings within the outside openings were replaced; the floor of the belfry was rebuilt and waterproofed; and the hatch opening to the belfry access ladder was reconditioned. At last the exterior of the building was fully restored, and a beginning at reconditioning commenced on the interior.[4]

While this work proceeded, disaster struck Old Central and the campus of the Oklahoma State University as well as the city of Stillwater. In the early evening of Friday, June 13, 1975, a tornado traveled in a northwest to southeast direction, hitting Old Central and twenty-eight other buildings on the campus. The top or gable of the south masonry wall of Old Central was destroyed, together with its circular window; the ventilation cupola on the high roof ridge of the building over the auditorium was blown off and demolished; most windows on the west side were either cracked or blown out; and the roof and exterior painting were also substantially damaged. Amazingly, no structural injury occurred to the building.[5]

No evidence remained as to why only these parts of Old Central received damage. Cyclonic currents within the tornado could have totally demolished the structure. Adjacent buildings sustained major devastation: to the north the antique copper standing seam roof of Morrill Hall was rolled up like a carpet and blown off the building; to the southeast the tower of the Campus Fire Station was tipped over and wrecked. Weather experts speculated that the tornadic velocity winds passing over the Old Central roof from northwest to southeast sucked out the south masonry gable of the building. Gable walls like this, sometimes described as curtain walls, are freestanding above the top story of the structure and are susceptible to being toppled because of having no side or lateral support.[6]

Soon after the tornado struck Old Central, the question arose as to whether the restoration of the building would continue. "The project will definitely continue," said LeRoy H. Fischer, the chairman of the Old Central Committee. "The renovation will move along a little slower than we had planned, but it will continue."[7] Fischer noted that the restoration would be delayed until repairs could be made to the building, and that funds being used for the project would go for patching. Fol-

When a tornado hit Old Central in 1975, most windows on the west side of the building were either cracked or blown out, but amazingly no structural damage occurred to the edifice.

OKLAHOMA STATE ARCHIVES, OKLAHOMA DEPARTMENT OF LIBRARIES

Centennial Histories Series

lowing the tornado, temporary repairs were made to seal off the damaged parts of Old Central and make them weatherproof. The Lambert Construction Company of Stillwater refurbished the tornado damage to the building at the contract price of $21,499.[8]

Attention turned next to planning the interior restoration of Old Central. Thomas A. Hazell, a graduate student in history, conducted research for photographs of the exterior doorways and the interior of the building, including furnishings and equipment, students working in classes and laboratories, and organizational groups. Picture files in the Edmon Low Library and photographs in old *Redskins* proved especially helpful. At the same time, a news release appealed to the public for similar materials. Kenny L. Brown, another graduate student in history, continued the research work for the interior restoration of Old Central, including a thorough search for photographs in Stillwater newspapers. With the use of these materials, the university architect's office completed the plans and specifications for the restoration of the interior.[9]

The Oklahoma Historical Society and the Old Central Committee wanted a major contract to do all restoration work on the interior of Old Central, but the amount of money available did not make this possible. The purpose then turned to raising as much state and federal matching money as feasible to get the maximum restoration return on the dollar at a time of double-digit inflation in the construction industry. By early 1976 the campaign for additional funding moved into high gear when the Oklahoma Historical Society placed a $50,000 line item in its budget request to the Oklahoma Legislature. With some state and federal money already available for interior restoration, the anticipated $50,000 of state funds would then be matched with a like amount of federal money for $100,000, thus bringing the total amount for the interior restoration contract to slightly over $100,000. Although the legislature appropriated the requested $50,000 in 1976, the Oklahoma State Historic Preservation Review Commission allocated only $35,000 of the $50,000 requested.[10]

The Oklahoma Historical Society appropriation bill in the 1977 Oklahoma Legislature contained a line item for $50,000 for the interior restoration of Old Central. New state money appropriated for the building came to but $30,000, although $20,000 in funds for the structure about to lapse were reappropriated and added to existing state money. Altogether, old and new state funding available totaled approximately $100,000, and allocated federal funds to match it amounted to but $60,000. Thus, $40,000 in federal matching money remained to be acquired to let a contract for approximately $200,000, the optimum amount planned. The Oklahoma State University administration and the Old Central Committee made a special appeal that $40,000 in federal matching money under the jurisdiction of the Oklahoma State Historic

Preservation Review Commission not being utilized be allocated to Old Central. Fortunately, the request was fully funded, although federal historic preservation money for Oklahoma appeared to be decreasing. The total federal money used for the Old Central restoration eventually came to $277,756.[11]

Even with $200,000 available for the restoration of the interior of Old Central, several months would elapse before a contract could be arranged. The plans and specifications for the entire interior of the building, prepared by the renamed architectural services of the Oklahoma State University, readily won the approval of the National Park Service in the Department of the Interior, but the estimated cost came to $550,710. The administration of the Oklahoma Historical Society then requested that the total cost of the entire interior of the building be no more than $350,000, which required a complete revision of the plans and specifications. The cost reduction was accomplished mainly by eliminating individual room fan coil units for steam heating and chilled water cooling, by reactivating the existing steam radiator heating system, and by installing a cooling method connected with the central chilled water campus system.[12]

The Oklahoma Historical Society and the National Park Service approved and expedited the revised Old Central plans and specifications. These went next to the Oklahoma State Board of Public Affairs, the contracting agency of the Oklahoma Historical Society, for contractor bid letting. The J. Edwin Thomas Construction Company of Oklahoma City, specialists in interior refurbishing, submitted the low bid of $187,468 in December 1977. On January 27, 1978, the base bid and five of the eight alternates were accepted, at a cost of $165,813. Remaining funds were reserved for contingency problems as work progressed. This approach permitted the latitude required to maximize efficient utilization of construction money in order to secure as much work as possible for each dollar expended. Although the renovation and restoration work concentrated on the first floor, carpentry, plumbing, electrical, heating, and air conditioning work also went on elsewhere in the building. Most of the first floor, including the stairwells to the second floor, underwent restoration during the contract. Altogether, the contract completed about 60 percent in dollar cost of the total interior renovation and restoration of the building. The contractor had until February 1979 to complete his work.[13]

Meantime, from the beginning of restoration activity on Old Central in 1971 by the Oklahoma Historical Society, early-day artifacts for possible use in the building kept turning up on the campus and in Stillwater, as well as in other parts of Oklahoma. These items would perhaps be used in the refurnishing and reequipping of the structure, as well as for the development of its museum displays. When Bryan P. Glass, the director of the Oklahoma State University Museum of Natural and Cultural History, became a member of the Old Central Committee in 1975, he inventoried these gift materials and supervised their safety and security. The furniture-type items occupied a part of the storage area in the Oklahoma State University Research Foundation Electronics Laboratory, a World War II temporary frame structure, located at 1203 West Sixth Avenue. The artifacts there appeared to be protected adequately, although the building was not equipped with smoke detectors or automatic sprinklers. Smaller items were kept in the Oklahoma State University Museum of Natural and Cultural History, located in a permanent fireproof structure.[14]

Then tragedy struck the electronics laboratory, including the storage area containing the furniture-type items for possible use in Old Central. The structure burned beyond repair when struck by lightning in the early morning hours of May 31, 1977. Visual inspection by representatives of the Old Central Committee indicated that the items stored for Old Central had burned beyond likely use. Only the metal parts remained

In 1977 a fire in the university electronics laboratory damaged beyond repair furnishings for possible use in Old Central. Involved were early-day chemistry laboratory tables and large, high rolltop desks probably used in Old Central when the building went into service.

from the antique opera seats collected for the Old Central auditorium, but these conceivably could have been used with new bentwood parts. Aside from this, there was but a possibility that one of the three early-day chemistry laboratory tables may not have been burned beyond repair. All other furniture pieces burned to a crisp, including two large high rolltop desks probably used in Old Central when the building first went into service.[15]

About a month after the equipment and furniture intended for Old Central burned, a new president, Lawrence L. Boger, reached Stillwater to administer the university, beginning June 15, 1977. An Indiana native, he earned the bachelor of science degree in agricultural economics at Purdue University, and the master of arts degree in economics and the doctor of philosophy degree in agricultural economics at the Michigan State University. He served on the agricultural economics faculty of the Michigan State University from 1948 to 1977. He moved through the various academic ranks until he became professor and head of the agricultural economics department, a position he held from 1954 to 1969. Then he served as dean of the Michigan State University College of Agriculture and Natural Resources from 1969 to 1976, when he held the position of university provost for a year before becoming president of the Oklahoma State University. He has in addition served as a consultant on many state, national, and international commissions and boards, both private and public.[16]

President Boger's administration at the Oklahoma State University can best be characterized by three interrelated words: quality, innovation, and planning. He has made quality a trademark of his administration and has caused administrators, faculty, and staff to think quality through the institution's instruction, research, and service activities during periods of severe financial reverses for Oklahoma. He has consistently refused to let the state's negative financial environment become an excuse, has budgeted unusually well, and has conveyed a sense of calm, optimism, and strength even during the most difficult conditions.

During President Boger's administration, the Oklahoma State University emerged as a national leader in educational telecommunications. His administration also developed and implemented a unique institutional centennial program involving three time periods: the Centennial Decade (1980-1989), the Centennial Year (1990), and the Pre-21st Century Decade (1991-2000). Similarly, it implemented a process involving all units of the institution in developing rolling five-year plans subject to annual review and updating. President Boger's administration also arranged a major capital campaign for the construction of the Noble Research Center for Agriculture and Renewable Natural Resources, and it likewise doubled the research grants and contracts of the university.[17]

242

Lawrence L. Boger, who served as president of the university from 1977 to 1988, addresses the university's Centennial Advisory Commission in the Old Central assembly hall in 1985 during the group's first campus meeting. President Boger faithfully promoted the restoration of Old Central and its development as the Oklahoma Museum of Higher Education.

Soon after President Boger reached the campus, he was briefed about the restoration of Old Central and immediately voiced support for seeking state and federal funding for the continuation of the renewal effort.[18] "Restoring and preserving this historic edifice is very important to all of us," he said.[19] "We look forward to the day it will be fully restored and open to local people and visitors to the campus."[20]

In the months and years ahead, additional funding needed to be raised and four contracts would be necessary before the restoration of Old Central could be completed. During this period in the construction industry, double digit inflation occurred annually. Meanwhile, the federal government attempted to blunt rising prices and towering budget deficits by reducing and soon eliminating, among innumerable other appropriation items, all money for historical restoration construction. Fortunately for the Old Central project, the economy of Oklahoma remained strong until the work reached completion.

The 1978 Oklahoma Legislature appropriated $30,000 for Old Central, and the following year supplemented this amount with $50,000. Using this money, plus remaining state dollars and residual federal funds, a contract in the amount of $125,361 went to the Metro Construction Company of Oklahoma City in early 1980 to refurbish and restore completely the first and second floors of Old Central. The mechanical work needed in the attic was also completed. The 1980 Oklahoma Legislature provided $60,000 in new money for Old Central, and reappropriated $30,000 about to lapse, making a total of $90,000 for the year. In 1981 the legislature added $90,000 in new money due to the lack of federal matching funds. The same year the Oklahoma Diamond Jubilee Commission, under the chairmanship of Jack T. Conn, granted $30,000 for the Old Central restoration effort.[21]

This funding made possible three contracts to complete the refurbishing and restoration of Old Central. The J. Edwin Thomas Construction Company of Oklahoma City bid the basement contract, including the construction of the chemistry lecture and demonstration classroom bench, for $121,615. The exterior contract for the repair of the roof cornice and the repainting of all wood on the exterior of the building went to the L. F. Downey Construction Company of Oklahoma City for $17,800. The fabrication of replicas of the brass gaslight fixtures that first illuminated Old Central went out for contract also, and the low bidder was the Washington House of Reproductions in Washington, Virginia, for $9,992.74.[22]

The goal of the restoration was to reproduce visually the exterior and interior as nearly as possible to represent the building as it appeared when completed in 1894. At the same time, modern cooling, heating, plumbing, electrical, fire protection, and security systems, concealed where practicable, were installed. Early photographs of the exterior and interior identified original 1894 features of the building that did not exist at the time restoration commenced, and these were restored if at all feasible. External basement items of significance not restored consisted of window wells, the steam boiler room entrance, and the northeast entrance. These features underwent removal early in the life of the structure because of severe water flooding problems, a condition that would return if their restoration had taken place. Also changing the exterior is a well-drained access ramp to the basement entrance for the physically disabled. Luckily, the various building modifications performed through the years did not change other basic building elements.

On the interior restoration of Old Central, the decision was reached because of cost and/or practical considerations to use the original steam boiler room in the basement as a non-public space to house the mechanical and electrical control systems serving the building. Likewise, the steam radiator heating system, as improved with new radiators in the 1929-1930 refurbishing of the building, would be retained and updated. Finally, the restrooms and adjacent office, built in the first floor northwest original classroom in the 1929-1930 remodeling, remained. The restrooms underwent reconstruction using present-day plumbing fixtures and room finishes. The National Park Service required that the restrooms have a modern look so as not to imply by design that they dated from the opening of the building. The next-door office, although restored in most details like the other rooms, was intended for the building's curator. The room has a central lighting control panel, a self-contained heating-cooling unit, and a refrigerated drinking fountain.[23]

The planning for the Old Central restoration called for air conditioning the building with forced air and connecting to the campus-wide chilled water distribution system. For this purpose two air-handling units with chilled water cooling coils were installed in the attic of the building directly above the open two-story stairwells with the intent of moving large quantities of chilled air into the stairwells. Doors on the first and second floors must remain open to permit the cool air to fill the rooms. The air is returned to the attic air handling units through the original outside wall vent shafts and new sheet metal return air ducts in the attic.

In the basement of Old Central, individual room units for both cooling and heating are concealed in wooden housings built to replicate the original ceiling-hung radiator units. The individual basement assemblies supply air to the rooms through metal grilles in the sides of wood housings at the ceiling level and return it through replicated wood ductwork enclosures with air grille openings near the basement floor. The cooling and heating systems for the entire building perform well despite their concealment within original physical features.[24]

Air handling units with chilled water cooling coils were installed in the attic of Old Central during its restoration to cool the building in warm weather. The air is returned to the attic air handling units through the original outside wall air shafts and new sheet-metal air ducts.

The fire safety sprinkler system installed in Old Central in 1948 underwent complete reconstruction and modernization. Although the original installation was a dry pipe system designed to fill with water only when a fire began, the new sprinkler layout also utilized the more efficient wet pipe system filled with water at all times. Of necessity, the attic, bell tower, and the second floor have dry sprinklers because the pipes serving them are subject to freezing temperatures. In addition, the new system has a better water supply than the old due to a new connection with a larger water supply pipe which includes an outside firehose connection with modern control valves near the building.

Unlike the old fire safety sprinkler system in Old Central, the new setup has concealed piping and sprinkler heads on the three floors of the building. Because the sprinkler system is hidden virtually from view, the interior appearance of the building when constructed is preserved. The pipes and sprinkler heads are above the ceiling, and each sprinkler head opening is covered by a metal plate. The plate is designed to drop off at 135 degrees Fahrenheit and expose the sprinkler which will then drop down from the recess. The sprinkler itself operates at 165 degrees Fahrenheit. The sprinkler plates have a small gap between the ceiling and the plate to let heat enter above the plate to activate its release. The plates were painted the color of the ceiling at the factory to gain Underwriters Laboratories approval. The painter's helper was instructed not to paint them, but desiring to do a good job, he filled the small gap between the ceiling and the plates with a caulking compound. This made the sprinkler system inoperative. This honest error proved costly to the contractor. All plates had to be removed and replaced with new ones to assure proper operation of the sprinkler system. Old Central will always have a degree of fire hazard due to its combustible wooden interior, but as long as the new electrical and fire sprinkler protection systems are well maintained and wholly operational, it is relatively safe from fire.[25]

A completely new concealed electrical distribution system also was installed in Old Central during the restoration. All wiring is in metal conduit piping inside the walls and between the floors. On the first and second floors electrical receptacles are concealed at designated locations beneath removable floor panels and in the basement are located at predetermined points behind removable wainscoting. The electric brass light fixtures in the building are reproductions. The lighting was originally gas, and the gas pipes are still concealed in the walls and ceilings. Except for four rooms and a stairwell which had no lights, all light fixtures are in their original places.

The light fixtures in Old Central have historically correct light-weight shades with light frosting and clear glass. All brass fittings, including the simulated turn-on turn-off gas valves, are authentic. The only lights

This view of the restored Old Central assembly hall shows the replicated gaslight fixtures made of brass and presently wired for electricity. All light fixtures are in their original places except for four rooms and a stairwell which had no lights.

that show in early photographs are the president's three-shaded light and the three-armed light attached to the vertical gas pipe-feeding burners on the chemistry lecture and demonstration classroom bench. These are reproduced, but the design of the other lights is patterned after the original gas lights in ''The Castle,'' the first permanent building at the Northwestern Oklahoma State University in Alva, constructed soon after Old Central. Bulbs of low wattage in Old Central simulate the low glow of light from gas fixtures.[26]

Other systems provided for in Old Central at the time of restoration included fire, smoke, and sprinkler alarms, and fire extinguishers. An elaborate electronic security system, connected with the Oklahoma State University Security Department, protects against unauthorized access to the building. In order to restore the structure faithfully, it could not fully comply with current building and life safety codes. Every effort, however, was made to conform with the intent of the codes.[27]

The restoration of Old Central revealed several unusual features. Some of the rooms had slate blackboards on all walls, although the originals without exception had undergone removal over the years. The blackboards were no problem to duplicate, for they were still manufactured. During the demolition of the various layers of flooring in the auditorium, a cast-iron floor grille was discovered in its original location, thus making their duplication possible. Also in the auditorium, a full-scale drawing of the lecture platform appeared on the original subfloor, including step locations and numbers. Although evidence indicated that the lecture platform was not originally built as drawn, a new platform was constructed of the exact size and design, for no indications could be found of the dimensions and pattern of the platform built.[28]

Other exceptional situations also occurred in the restoration of Old Central. The sump tunnel for collecting water under the basement hallway floor, constructed in the revamping of the basement in 1903 and discovered in the refurbishing of the structure in 1929 and 1930, again appeared when a workman crashed his air hammer into it while removing the old concrete basement floor. The 37 inch diameter tunnel of brick and limestone went through repairs to serve again for collecting water and to house the basement sump pump.[29]

Even the restoration repainting of the non-masonry exterior surfaces of Old Central involved unusual problems. Over the years the colors of the wood had changed to all-white with the style of the times. Early photographs revealed a typical late-Victorian color scheme, with a dark hue for windows, doors, and a part of the bell tower; middle tones for the eaves and the belfry enclosure; and light tints for the middle of the belfry, shingled parts of the gables, door panels, and the ornaments on the belfry and ventilation cupola. Older people remembered coloration based on green. Preliminary tests confirmed these opinions, as did the microscopic examination of paint samples taken from all areas of the building. Thus the non-masonry exterior of the restored building is painted with dark, medium, and olive green, the colors that graced the building until about 1915. The paint suggests that the structure is a survivor from another era very different from our own. Much distinction is added to both the style and feel of the building by its exterior paint colors.[30]

In July 1980, James L. Showalter, a member of the staff of the Oklahoma Historical Society, became the curator of the Oklahoma Museum of Higher Education located in Old Central. His initial work involved the completion of the restoration of the building. His special interests in both construction and historical restoration proved especially helpful in this effort. He worked closely with contractors in the restoration of the basement and the wood surfaces on the exterior. He personally carried out demolition labor in the basement to reduce the cost of the contract, initiated and supervised the work on an improved lawn drainage system around the building, and contributed significantly in many other ways to the completion of the restoration of the structure. Perhaps his most noteworthy restoration efforts involved the designing and replication of the brass light fixtures, as well as elaborate research and detailed planning to return the exterior painted surfaces to their original late-Victorian green colors. In early 1982, Marcia G. Davis became assistant

The university centennial-year class of 1990 assembled for its photograph south of Old Central upon arrival on the campus in August 1986. By this time the non-masonry exterior of the restored building had been changed from the all-white of more recent years to dark, medium, and olive green, the Victorian colors that graced the structure following completion in 1894.

curator and worked with Showalter in completing the restoration work.[31]

The dedication of the restoration of Old Central took place on June 12, 1982, eighty-eight years to the month after the dedication of the opening of the building, and in the year of the diamond jubilee commemoration of Oklahoma statehood. The ceremony occurred on the annual alumni weekend at the Oklahoma State University and was held in the Old Central assembly hall, formerly the auditorium, where the 1894 dedication took place. The capacity crowd of alumni and out-of-town visitors seemed in a festive mood.[32] "Today's dedication is meant to be a quiet recognition of the renewed life of Old Central and the birth of the Oklahoma Museum of Higher Education," said Curator James L. Showalter as he welcomed the alumni, faculty, staff, and Oklahoma Historical Society officials.[33] Many of those present had worked for ten years or more to see Old Central restored.

Next, LeRoy H. Fischer expressed the appreciation of the Old Central Committee to those who had supported the restoration effort. Then, James H. Boggs, the university vice president for academic affairs and research, reviewed highlights of Old Central history and thanked the Oklahoma Historical Society for its high-quality work in restoring the building. Melvena K. Thurman, the deputy state historic preservation officer of the Oklahoma Historical Society, told of the contribution of her office in providing federal matching money for the restoration of Old Central. C. Earle Metcalf, the executive director of the Oklahoma Historical Society, spoke of the work and pleasure of his agency in heading the effort to restore the building. Fittingly, Speaker of the Oklahoma House of Representatives Daniel D. Draper Jr. and Oklahoma Senator Bernice Shedrick, both of Stillwater, related the long and tedious struggle to raise money to restore Old Central. Both were pivotal figures in eventually securing a total of $494,000 in state funds for the project. In conclusion, Jack T. Conn, the president of the Oklahoma Historical Society and also the chairman of the Oklahoma Diamond Jubilee Commission, spoke on behalf of the commission which provided $30,000 to complete the restoration of the building.[34]

During the restoration dedication program, the Old Central Committee extended gratitude to several institutions, groups, and many persons for their assistance with the restoration of Old Central. The Oklahoma Historical Society and its able staff assisted mightily, especially C. Earle Metcalf, the executive director, and Mac R. Harris, the director of sites and museums. Also over the years, the society's presidents, George H. Shirk, W. D. "Jim" Finney, and Jack T. Conn vigorously supported the Old Central project. Two of the society's staff, James L. Showalter, the curator of Old Central, and Marcia G. Davis, the assistant curator, capably and tirelessly worked at the restoration process.

The Stillwater legislative delegation, composed of Daniel D. Draper Jr., the speaker of the Oklahoma House of Representatives, and Bernice Shedrick of the Oklahoma Senate, vigilantly labored to secure funds for the restoration of Old Central. Earlier, former Senator Robert M. Murphy energetically helped to acquire the money needed annually. Finally, the restoration would not have been possible without the continuing support of the Oklahoma Legislature for more than a decade.

The Oklahoma Diamond Jubilee Commission also received praise for its monetary contribution to the restoration of Old Central, as did its chairman, Jack T. Conn, and Michelle K. Lefebvre, its executive director, for making the structure an Oklahoma Diamond Jubilee project. Thanks and appreciation also went to the federal agencies providing matching funds for the undertaking, namely the Department of Housing and Urban Development and the Historic Conservation and Recreation Office of the National Park Service. These grants were made possible when the Secretary of the Interior named Old Central to the National Register of Historic Places.

Strictly speaking, the Oklahoma State University administration, faculty, staff, alumni, and friends of the institution saved Old Central from destruction over the years. Three presidents, Henry G. Bennett, Oliver S. Willham, and Robert B. Kamm, served at times when they

When the Old Central restoration dedication ceremonies took place on June 12, 1982, in the assembly hall, those attending sat on antique bentwood chairs. They are like the original chairs in the assembly hall. They date from the 1890s and were probably used in the Oklahoma Consitutional Convention Hall in Guthrie in 1906-1907.

could have ordered its demolition, but chose to preserve it, and it was President Kamm who commenced the most recent effort to restore it for use as the Oklahoma Museum of Higher Education. President Lawrence L. Boger continued to promote the restoration and museum development work.

Berlin B. Chapman, emeritus professor of history, for more than a half-century reminded us again and again of the lasting historical significance of Old Central. Students and alumni, as well as townspeople, early perceived the importance of the building and also rallied to its support in moments of peril. Without the nearby Campus Fire Station, the structure would likely have been destroyed twice by fire. Al Tyson, the supervising architect of the restoration, should be given special recognition for his accurate and thorough planning, as well as the entire staff of the university architectural services, and particularly its director, Bill D. Halley. In conclusion, each member of the Old Central Committee, composed of E. Moses Frye, Bryan P. Glass, Bill D. Halley, Murl R. Rogers, Roscoe Rouse, and Raymond D. Sharp, received thanks and appreciation for their faithful work, support, and enthusiasm over the years.[35]

When the restoration dedication ceremonies ended, Old Central settled down to its new life as the Oklahoma Museum of Higher Educa-

The Old Central interior and exterior restoration doorknobs and ornamental keyhole plates of cast bronze were patterned after an original Old Central set in the Oklahoma State University Museum of Natural and Cultural History. The doorknobs and ornamental keyhole plates feature an agricultural motif dominated by wheat.

tion. In it is portrayed the history of collegiate level education in Indian and Oklahoma territories and the state of Oklahoma. The largest artifact of the museum is Old Central itself. The statewide higher education theme of the museum is not only one-of-a-kind in Oklahoma and the Southwest, but is one-of-a-kind in the United States. It is highly appropriate that Oklahoma should develop a museum of higher education because of the fact that it has long had a higher percentage of its population of college age enrolled in higher education than any other state in the nation.[36]

The goal of the Old Central restoration was to reproduce visually the exterior and interior of the building when completed in 1894. Although accomplished in large part, notable exceptions became necessary at the basement level due to the pressing need for moisture and water control, as well as cost containment. Basement features eliminated from restoration planning included window wells, an exterior entrance to the steam boiler room, and also a northeast entrance to the hallway at the same level. These features had undergone removal early in the life of the structure. Also to preserve the visual integrity of 1894, the modern cooling, heating, plumbing, electrical, fire protection, and security systems in the building were faithfully concealed whenever possible. The steam heating system of 1894 underwent no significant changes in the restoration to jeopardize visual integrity, and remains the method of heating the structure.

State and federal fund raising continued to be a persistent problem throughout the decade-long restoration of Old Central. The availability of state money through legislative line item appropriations remained constant but sometimes elusive during the years of the refurbishing, and conveniently increased when federal funds no longer continued available. At the beginning of the project, federal money for the task had recently become obtainable on a dollar-for-dollar matching basis, but this funding faded away about three years before the restoration reached completion. Neither before nor after the project could state and federal money have been matched to accomplish some of the undertaking. As indicated, state funds amounted to $494,000, while the federal figure reached $277,756. Thus the total cost of the restoration came to $771,756, including architectural fees, maintenance during restoration, and various contingency expenses.

Endnotes

1. LeRoy H. Fischer to Bill D. Halley, 18 April 1974, Jack Wettengel to Robert M. Murphy, 19 June 1974, and Preliminary Draft, House of Representatives Bill 1531, March 4, 1974, Oklahoma Legislature, in Old Central Centennial History Collection, Special Collections, Edmon Low Library, Oklahoma State University, Stillwater, Oklahoma; *Stillwater NewsPress,* 3 June 1974, p. 2; Oklahoma State University *Daily O'Collegian,* 21 June 1974, p. 1; Oklahoma State Legislature, *Oklahoma Session Laws, 1974, Thirty-fourth Legislature, Second Regular Session, Convened January 8, 1974, Adjourned May 17, 1974* (St. Paul, MN: West Publishing Company, 1974), pp. 685-689.

2. LeRoy H. Fischer to E. Moses Frye, 27 March 1974, E. Moses Frye to LeRoy H. Fischer, 29 March 1974, 19 February 1975, Carl Albert to E. Moses Frye, 4 April 1974, and LeRoy H. Fischer to Jack Wettengel, 22 July 1974, in Old Central Centennial History Collection.

3. E. Moses Frye to Jack Wettengel, 31 October 1974, LeRoy H. Fischer to Robert M. Murphy, 31 December 1974, LeRoy H. Fischer to Daniel D. Draper Jr., 31 December 1974, H. Milt Phillips to E. Moses Frye, 3 February 1975, LeRoy H. Fischer to Old Central Committee, 25 September 1975, and Minutes, Old Central Committee, 22 October 1975, in Old Central Centennial History Collection; Oklahoma State Legislature, *Oklahoma Session Laws, 1975, Thirty-fifth Legislature, First Regular Session, Convened January 7, 1975, Adjourned June 6, 1975* (St. Paul, MN: West Publishing Company, 1975), pp. 700-701.

4. LeRoy H. Fischer to Bill D. Halley, 22 March 1974, 3 September 1974, Elena M. Hildenbrand to R. D. Schultz, 22 November 1974, Robert H. Breeden to Elena M. Hildenbrand, 21 November 1974, Robert H. Breeden to Jack Wettengel, 18 December 1974, Bid Notice, 24 January 1975, Oklahoma State Board of Public Affairs, Periodic Estimate for Partial Payment, Continental Contracting Company, June 14, 1975, to July 22, 1975, and Author interview with Bill D. Halley, 1 February 1986, in Old Central Centennial History Collection; Old Central Restoration Plans and Specifications, Phase 2, Special Collections, Edmon Low Library.

5. Halley interview, 1 February 1986, and Bill D. Halley to Jack Wettengel, 17 June 1975, in Old Central Centennial History Collection; Gregg Bond, "A Close Call," *Oklahoma State University Outreach,* vol. 16, no. 7 (September-October 1975), pp. 13-14.

6. Halley interview, 1 February 1986.

7. *Daily O'Collegian,* 19 June 1975, p. 1.

8. *Daily O'Collegian,* 19 June 1975, p. 1, 20 January 1976, p. 5; *Oklahoma State* University *News,* 6 October 1975, p. 2; Jack Wettengel to Robert H. Breeden, 25 June 1975, LeRoy H. Fischer to Old Central Committee, 25 September 1975, Minutes, Old Central Committee, 22 October 1975, in Old Central Centennial History Collection; Old Central Tornado Damage Plans and Specifications, Special Collections, Edmon Low Library.

9. Minutes, Old Central Committee, 22 October 1975, 30 January 1976, 7 July 1976, Newspaper Release, "Old Central Photographs Urgently Needed," and LeRoy H. Fischer to Bill D. Halley, 26 February 1976, in Old Central Centennial History Collection.

10. Minutes, Old Central Committee, 30 January 1976, LeRoy H. Fischer to Robert M. Murphy, 11 February 1976, LeRoy H. Fischer to Daniel D. Draper Jr., 11 February 1976, LeRoy H. Fischer to George L. Cross, 19 February 1976, Daniel D. Draper Jr. to LeRoy H. Fischer, 17 May 1976, and George H. Shirk to Oklahoma State Historic Preservation Review Commission, 24 June 1976, in Old Central Centennial History Collection; Oklahoma State Legislature, *Oklahoma Session Laws, 1976, Thirty-fifth Legislature, Second Regular Session, Convened January 6, 1976, Adjourned June 9, 1976, and First Extraordinary Session, Convened July 19, 1976, Adjourned July 23, 1976* (St. Paul, MN: West Publishing Company, 1976), p. 393.

11. LeRoy H. Fischer to Robert M. Murphy, 5 April 1977, 19 July 1977, LeRoy H. Fischer to Daniel D. Draper Jr., 5 April 1977, 19 July 1977, LeRoy H. Fischer to Jack Wettengel, 5 July 1977, 26 July 1977, LeRoy H. Fischer to George L. Cross, 26 July 1977, LeRoy H. Fischer to Harry L. Deupree, 26 July 1977, C. Earle Metcalf to LeRoy H. Fischer, 3 June 1987, and Allocations List for Fiscal Years 1976 and 1977, Oklahoma State Historic Preservation Review Commission, in Old Central Centennial History Collection; Oklahoma State Legislature, *Oklahoma Session Laws, 1977, Thirty-sixth Legislature, First Regular Session, Convened January 4, 1977, Adjourned June 8, 1977, and First Extraordinary Session, Convened June 13, 1977, Adjourned June 17, 1977* (St. Paul, MN: West Publishing Company, 1977), pp. 1040, 1042, 1043.

12. Cost Breakdown, Old Central Restoration, Phase 3, Architectural Services of Oklahoma State University, Al Tyson to Howard L. Meredith, 28 August 1977, and Minutes, Old Central Committee, 1 December 1977, in Old Central Centennial History Collection.

13. Old Central Restoration Plans and Specifications, Phase 3, Special Collections, Edmon Low Library; C. Earle Metcalf to Allie O. Isom, 7 December 1977, Bid Tabulation, 13 December 1977, Old Central Restoration Phase 3, Robert C. Reynolds to C. Earle Metcalf, 20 December 1977, State of Oklahoma, Notice of Award of Contract, Old Central Restoration, Phase 3, 27 January 1978, LeRoy H. Fischer to Lawrence L. Boger, 30 March 1978, and Minutes, Old Central Committee, 17 October 1978, in Old Central Centennial History Collection.

14. Minutes, Old Central Committee, 22 October 1975, 30 January 1976, 7 July 1976, and LeRoy H. Fischer to Clarence Banks, 1 July 1976, in Old Central Centennial History Collection.

15. *Stillwater NewsPress,* 31 May 1977, p. 1; *Tulsa Daily World,* 1 June 1977, pp. 1A, 1C; Oklahoma City *Daily Oklahoman,* 2 June 1977, p. 31; Bryan P. Glass to G. D. Shepherd, 1 July 1977, Old Central Centennial History Collection.

16. *Who's Who in America, 1986-1987* (2 vols., Wilmette, IL: Marquis Who's Who, 1986), vol. 1, p. 277.

17. Author interview with Richard W. Poole, 12 April 1987, Old Central Centennial History Collection.

18. LeRoy H. Fischer to Lawrence L. Boger, 22 July 1977, Old Central Centennial History Collection.

19. Lawrence L. Boger to LeRoy H. Fischer, 27 July 1977, Old Central Centennial History Collection.

20. Lawrence L. Boger to LeRoy H. Fischer, 31 May 1978, Old Central Centennial History Collection.

21. Minutes, Old Central Committee, 28 November 1979, 12 May 1980, 9 July 1981, Al Tyson to C. Earle Metcalf, 25 January 1980, LeRoy H. Fischer to Bernice Shedrick, 10 July 1981, LeRoy H. Fischer to Daniel D. Draper Jr., 10 July 1981, LeRoy H. Fischer to Lawrence L. Boger, 23 July 1981, James L. Showalter to Old Central Committee, 22 April 1982, and LeRoy H. Fischer, "Old Central Committee Comments at the Time of the Rededication of Old Central," throughout, in Old Central Centennial History Collection; Old Central Restoration Plans and Specifications, Phase 4, Special Collections, Edmon Low Library; Oklahoma State Legislature, *Oklahoma Session Laws, 1978, Thirty-sixth Legislature, Second Regular Session, Convened January 3, 1978, Adjourned April 28, 1978* (St. Paul, MN: West Publishing Company, 1978), pp. 722, 725-726; Oklahoma State Legislature, *Oklahoma Session Laws, 1979, Thirty-seventh Legislature, First Regular Session, Convened January 2, 1979, Adjourned July 2, 1979* (St. Paul, MN: West Publishing Company, 1979), p. 857; Oklahoma State Legislature, *Oklahoma Session Laws, 1980, Thirty-seventh Legislature, Second Regular Session, Convened January 8, 1980, Adjourned June 16, 1980, and First Extraordinary Session, Convened July 7, 1980, Adjourned July 11, 1980* (St. Paul, MN: West Publishing Company, 1980), pp. 1006, 1161, 1165-1166; Oklahoma State Legislature, *Oklahoma Session Laws, 1981, Thirty-eighth Legislature, First Regular Session, Convened January 6, 1981, Adjourned July 20, 1981, and First Extraordinary Session, Convened August 31, 1981, Adjourned September 4, 1981* (St. Paul, MN: West Publishing Company, 1981), p. 1213; "Old Central: Safe at Last," *Oklahoma State University Outreach,* vol. 53, no. 4 (Summer 1982), p. 35.

22. Minutes, Old Central Committee, 9 July 1981, 3 September 1981, 3 May 1982, 22 July 1983, James L. Showalter to LeRoy H. Fischer, 3 March 1982, 7 May 1982, 24 July 1982, and James L. Showalter to Old Central Committee, 22 April 1982, in Old Central Centennial History Collection; Old Central Restoration Plans and Specifications, Phase 5, Special Collections, Edmon Low Library.

23. Author interview with Al Tyson, 24 October 1985, Old Central Centennial History Collection.

24. Tyson interview, 24 October 1985.

25. Author interviews with Richard W. Giles, 10 November 1985 and 29 November 1985, and Author interview with Everett E. Hudiburg, 10 October 1985, in Old Central Centennial History Collection.

26. Tyson interview, 24 October 1985; James L. Showalter, "The Restoration of Old Central," *Outlook in Historic Conservation* (September-October 1982), unpaged; *Stillwater NewsPress,* 9 February 1983, p. 22.

27. Tyson interview, 24 October 1985.

28. Author interview with Al Tyson, 3 January 1986, Old Central Centennial History Collection.

29. Showalter, "The Restoration of Old Central"; *Stillwater NewsPress,* 23 May 1982, p. 9A.

30. James L. Showalter to LeRoy H. Fischer, 7 September 1982, Old Central Centennial History Collection; Showalter, "The Restoration of Old Central"; *Stillwater NewsPress,* 7 November 1982, p. 1G; Oklahoma State University *Oklahoma Stater,* October 1982, p. 7.

31. James L. Showalter to Old Central Committee, 3 September 1981, 22 December 1981, James L. Showalter to LeRoy H. Fischer, 21 September 1981, 26 February 1982, 24 June 1982, 19 July 1982, and 18 August 1982, in Old Central Centennial History Collection; *Oklahoma Stater,* April 1982, p. 2.

32. Program, Dedication of Old Central and the Museum of Higher Education, June 12, 1982, Old Central Centennial History Collection; "Old Central: Safe at Last," p. 35; *Stillwater NewsPress,* 16 June 1982, p. 6.

33. "Old Central: Safe at Last," p. 35.

34. Program, Dedication of Old Central and the Museum of Higher Education, June 12, 1982; "Old Central: Safe at Last," p. 35. For the total appropriation of the Oklahoma State Legislature, see the *Oklahoma Session Laws for 1971-1981,* and C. Earle Metcalf to LeRoy H. Fischer, 3 June 1987, and attachments, in Old Central Centennial History Collection.

35. LeRoy H. Fischer, "Old Central Committee Comments at the Time of the Rededication of Old Central," throughout, and LeRoy H. Fischer to Robert M. Murphy, 22 June 1982, in Old Central Centennial History Collection.

36. Showalter, "The Restoration of Old Central"; LeRoy H. Fischer to Lawrence L. Reger, 1 November 1985, and Clare Bouton to LeRoy H. Fischer, 6 December 1985, in Old Central Centennial History Collection.

13 Significance

The importance of Old Central is a developmental and ever-changing process. The building became consequential even before construction, and over the years new meanings and values emerged. As with any restored historic structure, its import will always be subject to interpretation and question. Higher education in particular and society in general will also regroup, refine, and add to the significance presently attributed to the edifice, a procedure ultimately assisted by additional research and study. The considerations that follow deal with the building's architecture, its time of construction among the early collegiate buildings in present Oklahoma, distinctive points of its history, its sentimental and symbolic values, and finally its role in launching the land-grant collegiate movement in Oklahoma.

Over the years the architectural design of Old Central has baffled casual onlookers, even though most considered it distinctive. The motif seemed to defy easy architectural classification when its significance went unexamined. Because of the shape and decoration of the bell tower and the ventilation cupola, wrote a viewer, "The building itself looks like it might have been moved from a city square in Moscow."[1]

"That building is undoubtedly the best specimen of its style of architecture among old buildings in this part of the country," said Samuel A. McReynolds of the class of 1902. "I believe this is a modified Byzantine architecture, but whatever the name, it adds great distinction to our campus."[2] "As long as there is a romantic sentimental side to the nature of man," added another, "structures such as . . . Old Central will always be a necessary and beautiful part of our lives."[3]

Still another individual thought Old Central to be an "archaic mon-

The ponderous stone window arches (*upper left*) are distinctively Roman Empire. The building's overall heaviness of style in brick and stone treatment is characteristic of Richardsonian Romanesque Revival architectural design, as is the bell tower (*upper right*) topped with an intricately foliated metal ornament. The six-pointed star (*lower left*) serves as one of several heads for turnbuckle tie rods intended to stabilize the structure. The tie rods were installed in 1914 and 1929. The heavy stone arch over the cavernous main entrance to Old Central (*lower right*) is also distinctively Roman Empire.

strosity," and to one more it looked like a castle on the open prairie when first constructed.[4] The fairy tale novel, *Alice's Adventures in Wonderland,* provided the setting for an additional opinion concerning the architectural design of Old Central. Alice and White Rabbit reportedly toured the old campus quadrangle, and when they reached Old Central, Alice inquired, "What style of architecture is Old Central?" With no more than a pause White Rabbit replied: "God only knows."[5]

The architect of Old Central, Herman M. Hadley, had fifteen years of wide and somewhat distinguished building design experience before he planned the college structure, and this became apparent as the building took shape. Considering the low budget restraints involved in the construction, unusual and desirable features still resulted, such as the heating, cooling, and ventilating systems, all relatively efficient and modern for the time. Hadley undoubtedly intended to design a building utilizing local materials whenever possible and suitable for the comfort and convenient use of the students and faculty it would serve. At the same time, he planned to make it architecturally distinctive, and unknowingly forecast the uncommon architectural composition of the university in the years ahead.[6]

The exterior and interior architectural design of Old Central relates to European origins, as do many United States buildings of the period of Queen Victoria's reign (1837-1901) in Great Britain. No European construction style dominates in Old Central, so its design cannot be typed except to call it eclectic, which is to indicate that it is made up of several architectural patterns. Even so, the design beginnings of the structure go back many hundreds of years in the history of both western and eastern Europe. The Richardsonian Romanesque Revival patterns in the United States in the late 19th century developed by Henry H. Richardson are evident in the building and were drawn on liberally by Hadley in designing it. The cavernous heavy stone arch over the main entrance on the south is distinctively Roman Empire, as are the ponderous stone window arches on the second floor and the brick eave supports, known as corbels, extending upward and outward to carry the weight of the gables. The overall heaviness of style in the brick and stone treatment of Old Central is characteristic of Richardsonian Romanesque Revival architectural design.

The Old Central bell tower and ventilation cupola, both topped with intricately foliated metal ornaments, called finials, are also earmarks of Richardson's architectural plans. He likewise developed window placement as an integral part of interior design, with their size and location determined by internal need rather than external regularity. Accordingly, a group of windows on the south side of Old Central follow the stairwell precisely, as do those on the north stairwell elevation. Even the south-side arched half window in Old Central is designed to meet the

The Old Central ventilation cupola, with its metal ornament, is typically Victorian, as are the caps and swans' necks on the roof ridge.

lighting needs of the night watchman's room.[7]

Byzantine architectural design, based on classical patterns traced from Greece through Rome, provided a basis for buildings as far apart as Russia and Italy, and also remotely influenced the appearance of Old Central. The belfry shape, and also its metallic ornament, suggest the domes of the Cathedral of St. Mark in Venice, as do the onion-shaped domes of the Cathedral of the Annunciation in Moscow and the adjacent Cathedral of the Archangel Michael. The massive brick and stone walls of Old Central likewise imply Byzantine architecture.[8]

Jacobean architectural forms, important in England from 1603 to 1625, during the reign of King James I, directly influenced the style of Old Central. Brick with stone trim dominated this design, but included large windows, steep pitched roof lines, decorative gables, and bell towers topped with garnished metalwork, all characteristic of Old Central. In Jacobean interiors, plaster, rather than wood, was commonly used for the ceilings and sometimes for the upper part of the walls, with paneling below, as is the pattern in Old Central. More remotely, even a touch of Gothic design can be noted in the graceful vault of the auditorium ceiling and the plaster offsets in its walls, while below in the first floor hallway a glimpse of both Romanesque and Byzantine architecture can be found in the two arches.[9]

Alongside the eclectic architecture of the 19th century, and in part from it, there developed a style unique to the English-speaking world known as Victorian architecture, which also drew heavily on the past. The roof level of Old Central reflects this pattern with its decorative fish-scale wood shingles on the bell tower, and another wood shingle design on the east, north, and west gables. The fancy sheet metal detail of the bell tower topped with a metal ornament, the capped roof ridge terminating with swans' necks and hip knobs, and the embossed metal shingles of the roof itself, are other Victorian representations, as are the high-pitched roof lines. Inside the building, the woodwork, and especially the paneled doors, the wainscot, and the stairwells, complete to ornamented stair posts, are also typically Victorian.[10]

Old Central underwent designing when eclecticism in western world architecture reached its peak. Eclecticism in building implies freedom on the part of the architect or client or both to choose from the styles of the past the features that seem most appropriate. This is precisely what Hadley did in designing Old Central. For whatever reasons, the administration, faculty, and board of regents of the Oklahoma A. and M. College did not participate to a noticeable degree in the planning process. The eclectic architectural movement commenced about the middle of the nineteenth century and continued into the twentieth century in the

SPECIAL COLLECTIONS, OSU LIBRARY

This Victorian wood-shingled pattern is found on the east, north, and west gables of Old Central. The design of the building's two bell-shaped chimneys is also Victorian.

United States and abroad. For many years the architects who created eclectic designs were held in low esteem and considered to be without intellectual respectability. Eclectic work has been severely criticized as being irrelevant, dishonest, unfitted to its purposes, sentimental, and even undemocratic. What makes eclectic architecture so difficult to understand is the incongruous appearance it produces when compared with unlike surrounding eclectic structures. But whatever the eclectic design of Old Central, it has retained its distinctive appearance even in its eclectic structural environment.[11]

However Old Central is viewed architecturally, it should not be labeled as being of vernacular design. The word vernacular as used in recent years generally applies to structures native to a particular locale or region. These often are pioneer buildings such as houses, farm structures, and village storerooms. Such constructions combine inherited ideas common to the general public with local building materials and do not conform to any established style or period. Moreover, vernacular structures are almost without exception never planned by formally educated architects. The architectural credentials and long experience of Hadley when designing Old Central precludes the building from being

Inside Old Central, the woodwork, and especially the paneled doors, the wainscot, the stairwells, and the ornamental stair posts, are typically Victorian. Also shown are window locations determined by internal need rather than external regularity, a pattern characteristic of Richardsonian Romanesque Revival architectural design.

Jacobean architectural forms, dominant in England during the reign of King James I (1603-1625), directly influenced the interior design of Old Central. This is reflected in the ceilings and upper walls of plaster and the lower walls of paneling. A glimpse of Romanesque and Byzantine architectural forms can be found in the archways located on the first floor. The gaslight fixtures are Victorian representations.

styled vernacular even without internal evidence of the structure strongly suggesting it to be of eclectic design.[12]

In another area of Old Central historic significance, uncertainty has also prevailed. Through much of the life of the building, students and alumni of the institution considered it to be the first higher education building erected in the present state of Oklahoma. This idea was repeated as a fact again and again until many people accepted it as truth. For several decades the idea went unchallenged, and frequently it appeared in print, especially in the student newspaper. The statement seemed logical and gave greater prestige to Old Central. No one took time to research the question in the records of Oklahoma educational history.[13]

The question of the first college building in Oklahoma came to the forefront in 1933 when the *Daily Oklahoman* published an article concluding that Old North at the Central State University in Edmond, Oklahoma, reached completion first. The *Daily Oklahoman* stated that Old North went into operation on January 2, 1893, while Old Central did not undergo use until its dedication on June 15, 1894, nearly a year and a half later. At the University of Oklahoma in Norman, the first permanent building went into service in September 1893, but fire destroyed it completely in January 1903. As a result, the structure at Norman did not enter the dispute. On the Stillwater campus soon after World War II the question began to be raised frequently about Old Central's claim as the oldest college building in Oklahoma. Further clarification did not come until 1971 when work reached completion to place both Old Central and Old North on the National Register of Historic Places. Old North seemed to win the controversy.[14]

Meantime, in 1969, Robert E. Cunningham, a Stillwater businessman, writer, and historian, contended that the University of Oklahoma completed a permanent building earlier than Old Central "but that the Norman edifice burned." He also maintained that the Central State University "occupied [only] a partially finished building somewhat sooner," and thus "the A. and M. structure [was] the oldest in the state now in use" devoted to higher education.[15] Not to be outdone by Old North, Cunningham again restated his claim for Old Central in 1971 soon after it went on the National Register of Historic Places: "In other words, the oldest building devoted to higher learning in Oklahoma is the one

At the University of Oklahoma in Norman, the first permanent building went into service in September 1893, but fire destroyed it completely in January 1903. As a result, the structure did not enter the dispute to determine the oldest permanent college building still standing in Oklahoma.

The original section of Old North at the Central State University in Edmond reached completion in August 1893, almost a year in advance of Old Central. The north wing of the addition to Old North was not finished until January 1898, however, more than three years after all work on Old Central ceased. Although not restored like Old Central, Old North continues in use for classroom and administrative purposes.

known as Old Central, at Stillwater. Norman lost its claim to first place by fire, and Edmond was building wings to its candidate for the oldest structure after Old Central was fully operative.''[16]

Repeatedly, research reveals that Old North at the Central State University underwent collegiate use when classes were first held in it on January 2, 1893, although it was not until August of that year that the original section of the building reached completion. By comparison, Old Central went into use at the time of dedication on June 15, 1894, although its heating and ventilation system did not reach completion until the winter of 1894-1895, thereby concluding all construction work. The $15,000 in bond issue money for Old North authorized by the Oklahoma Legislative Assembly became available in early 1894 and funded the construction of the wings and tower of the building. On June 3, 1894, closing exercises for the school year were held in the auditorium, but work on the north wing did not reach completion until January 1898.[17] The original section of Old North reached completion almost a year in advance of Old Central. The north wing of the addition to Old North was not finished until more than three years after all work on Old Central ceased. Old Central, unlike Old North, never had an addition, nor were its exterior walls ever seriously altered. Old North presently has an updated interior and serves as housing for the College of Education at the Central State University.

In addition to Oklahoma Territory, where the University of Oklahoma, the Oklahoma A. and M. College, and the Oklahoma Normal School were founded by the legislative assembly in 1890, Indian Territory also became a part of the state of Oklahoma. The Indian University, first located at Tahlequah and later at Muskogee, was the one higher educational institution in Indian Territory. The school offered, in addition to elementary and secondary instruction, four years of collegiate-level training, and was attended by Indians from the Five Civilized Tribes and the West in general. The Indian University building at Tahlequah was constructed in 1867 as part of the Baptist Mission and served the Indian University, the present Bacone College, until it moved to Muskogee in 1885. The building still stands and is of brick construction with porches, cornices, and trim of wood. It has, however, been enlarged since its original construction. The Indian University building is undoubtedly the oldest higher education building in Oklahoma. The Secretary of the Interior enrolled the structure on the National Register of Historic Places in 1976. Seminary Hall, a large brick edifice at the Northeastern Oklahoma State University in Tahlequah, dates from 1888 and was originally the Cherokee Female Seminary, but postdates the Indian University building. Seminary Hall has an updated interior and a modified exterior.[18]

Although Old Central is by no measurement the oldest higher education building in Oklahoma, it is the only restored higher education structure in the state. Other aspects of the history of Old Central also reveal much about the significance of the building. As the answer to the aspirations of the first students, faculty, and people of Stillwater for a permanent building to house the college, it immediately became their pride and joy. The $10,000 raised by the residents of Stillwater to capture the land-grant college of Oklahoma Territory was invested in the construction of Old Central and permanently secured the institution for the town. With the construction costs totalling but $14,948, the building was largely Stillwater's creation. The Oklahoma Legislative Assembly made up the difference in price to meet the contract cost. No longer was there serious likelihood that the town, about twenty miles from a railroad, would lose the college. The importance of the security brought about by the Old Central contract let on June 20, 1893, became evident when on September 16, 1893, the Cherokee Outlet opened to settlement. Stillwater lost about half of its population, and the most advanced class of the college lost about half of its students.

Very little seemed routine about the construction of Old Central. Initially, the ability to finance the structure determined the town near which the college would be located. Then its placement decided the location

The Indian University building at Tahlequah was constructed in 1867 as part of the Baptist Mission and served the Indian University, the present Bacone College, until it moved to Muskogee in 1885. The building is undoubtedly the oldest college building still standing in Oklahoma. It presently serves educational needs of the Northeastern Oklahoma State University.

of the campus on the 200 acres of land provided by the citizens of Stillwater for the use of the institution. It also pioneered major building construction not only on the campus but throughout Stillwater. It created the need for the first bond issue of the town and proved to be its most difficult bond issue ever carried through to completion. Even when adequate money authorized by the Oklahoma Legislative Assembly appeared in sight to complete the building, nearly a year elapsed before the funding reached the contractor to place a roof on it. By contrast, the first permanent buildings at the University of Oklahoma and the Oklahoma Normal School were already in use. In this perspective, little about the construction of Old Central appeared commonplace.

In another relationship, partisan politics and Stillwater's lack of adequate population severely impacted the construction of Old Central. In the beginning, politics held up the location of the structure at Stillwater and caused it to be placed only in Payne County, providing money was raised locally to construct it. This led to an unsuccessful effort by the people of Stillwater to have Payne County underwrite bonds to construct the building at the town. Then Stillwater tried twice before it successfully issued and sold the bonds required to construct the building, and thus win the institution for the town. It took an act of the Oklahoma Legislative Assembly to legalize the second effort, due to the use of dubious population and property evaluation procedures. Finally, a change in the political party of presidents in the White House led directly to a political circumstance in Oklahoma Territory that held up funds for nearly a year to complete the construction of the building.

Even the effort to adjust and complete the furnishings and cabinet work in Old Central immediately following the conclusion of its construction in 1894 took on unusually broad implications in a lawsuit filed by Charles F. Willis and William R. Bradford, the carpenters involved. Not only did the verdict of the Oklahoma Supreme Court improve the contracting system used by the college, but it also bettered the contracting procedures used by all public institutions in the territory and later the state of Oklahoma. The lawsuit likewise established the important legal principle that the territory and later the state of Oklahoma could not be sued except by its consent. In addition, the verdict of the lawsuit severely limited the jurisdiction of the court system of Oklahoma regarding cases for services and sales claims against public territorial and later state institutions. The broad legal implications of the Oklahoma Supreme Court decision in the Willis and Bradford lawsuit remain undiminished in their effect with the passage of time.

During the years when Old Central housed the president's office, several enduring patterns, both planned and unplanned, emerged. The tenures of President George E. Morrow and President Angelo C. Scott brought a certain stability to the executive office, although party politics regularly intruded to impact both the administration and the faculty, as it would in the future. At the same time, the political leadership as well as the citizenry of Oklahoma Territory grew into an understanding of the nature and potential of the land-grant institution. Both the legislative assembly and the people finally realized that the federal funds of the college needed to be used almost exclusively for salary and teaching aids. Then, after much reluctance, the legislative assembly began to increase slowly appropriated funds for general operating budget purposes and for periodic building construction, a pattern continued through the years.

Old Central remained the nerve center for the physical and academic development of the college from the completion of its construction in 1894 until the administrative offices of the college moved to Morrill Hall in the autumn of 1906. Executive planning in Old Central during these years resulted in seven permanent first generation buildings of brick and stone construction. Even though Old Central was built with no thought of making it the south centerpiece of the original campus quadrangle, it assumed that role with the construction of the first Library Building, the 1902 Engineering Building, and Morrill Hall. Several years after the administrative offices moved to Morrill Hall, the initial campus quadrangle reached completion, but its pattern had been set in the executive offices of Old Central.

At one period or another while Old Central housed the administrative offices of the college, it contained elements of the instruction and laboratory work of the college academic departments and the Agricultural Experiment Station. During these years the building also housed the beginnings of the modern College of Agriculture, the College of Arts and Sciences, the College of Business Administration, the College of Home Economics, and the College of Veterinary Medicine. It also sheltered the origins of the present Edmon Low Library, the School of Architecture, the School of Journalism, the Public Information Office, the Registrar's Office, and such present academic departments as English, history, mathematics, chemistry, and physics, as well as the whole or parts of other scholastic fields tracing their origins to the first years of the college. In a related but different respect, the Oklahoma State University Foundation also traces its origin and purpose to Old Central through its concept of giving. The foundation points out that the building rests on land donated to the institution. In addition, leading Stillwater citizens loaned money at interest to the town of Stillwater to construct Old Central by making up the difference between the $10,000 discounted bond issue and the sum of $10,000 itself.[19]

The Old Central belfry and bell continued to lure students over the years. Access to the spire became so popular that the second floor doorway to it remained locked at all times. By various means students undid the door lock or removed the battered door itself for the hazardous climb to the belfry. Sometimes students were caught in it, but many more escaped undetected. When the bell concluded its academic role on the campus in 1908, it announced student activities, but not until its cradle of wood and iron underwent extensive repairs in 1916. The first use in its new function called freshmen and sophomores together for the annual class fight in the aged cottonwood tree west of Old Central.

Almost immediately the athletic side of student life focused much attention on the Old Central bell and clapper. But overall a low percentage of athletic victories were celebrated by ringing the bell. Even in football, the sport that attracted the most student and public attention, the bell did not celebrate all wins, but soon came to be reserved almost exclusively for the elusive gridiron victories over the University of Oklahoma.

The Old Central bell clanged vigorously to celebrate but four football wins out of the first twenty-five football games played with the Sooners. Then students from the Norman campus removed the bell clapper during the night immediately following the 1930 Aggie win. With Coach Lynn O. Waldorf bringing championship level football to the Stillwater campus during a five-year period of service from 1929 to 1933,

Aggie athletes suggested that the bell clapper be made a trophy for the winner of the annual classic.

If the Oklahoma-Oklahoma State football teams had performed on the same achievement level, the Old Central bell clapper trophy tradition would have been satisfactory, but in the eighty-two games of the series through 1987, the Oklahoma State University won only twelve and tied six. Despite the long-term agony caused by the missing bell clapper on the Aggie campus, it did much to encourage football athletic competition at the Oklahoma State University for the annual game with the Sooners, and also in the Missouri Valley and the Big Eight athletic conferences.

So few Aggie wins occurred in the thirty-six year Old Central bell clapper tradition that the public almost forgot about the custom and the student leadership of the two institutions sometimes lost track of the trophy. The bell clapper should have been publicly exhibited as a reminder of its existence at all football games between the two universities. When the bell clapper tradition concluded somewhat abruptly in 1966, the student bodies and administrations of both institutions did not regret its passing. Since then the bell clapper has quietly remained on the Cowboy campus. In more recent years it has hung in the Old Central bell of which it was originally a part.

In a related area, Old Central took on sentimental and symbolic significance to a wide variety of people, especially faculty and former students. "Really," explained Harry E. Thompson, a member of the first faculty, "it seemed we had reached the top, for no one could go up into that immense tower . . . and see the whole world at his feet, without thinking that the utopian of an education had been realized."[20] Freeman E. Miller, also an early teacher at the college, said of Old Central: "May it stand for decades to come as a reminder of the days when men dared much and accomplished more—when out of poverty they beheld great visions and adventured forth with brave hearts to achieve the victories they coveted . . . . To them be the homage of good men and women forever!"[21]

Mary Jarrell Hartman of the class of 1903 had a special relationship with Old Central. She was the daughter of Alfred N. Jarrell who had given forty acres of his homestead to help meet the legal requirements for locating the college at Stillwater. She said: "To me, Old Central represents the struggles and hardships to get an education in those pioneer days. The students were as raw and undeveloped as the country. Even the teachers were fresh out of Eastern colleges and trying to carve out fame and fortune for themselves as best they could. This shiny new building was the soil of the Institution. It represented the best in building construction at the time. We all tried to live up to it."[22]

Frank D. Northup, the editor of the *Stillwater Gazette*, came to Stillwater in 1893 in time to see Old Central under construction on various occasions. In 1899 he became superintendent of printing at the college. He wrote in 1955: "I sincerely hope Old Central . . . is preserved for future generations. In time . . . it will be a priceless shrine. It clearly represents the pinched purses, the hopes and the high aspirations of those who struggled there in the days that carried little more than hope. Its presence will give a lift to many students and visitors long after those early grads, and those of us who still live are gone."[23]

Thomas J. Hartman of the class of 1898, and a member of the college's board of regents before statehood, thought that Old Central should "serve for all time as a monument to those early pioneers who believed in education."[24] The idea of Old Central as a historic monument to education also surfaced from time to time in the mind of Alfred E. Jarrell, who graduated in 1896 in the first class of the college. He was also the last survivor of the class. In 1958, as he reflected on the recent graduates of the institution who saw the new campus quadrangle develop and experienced the use of the Student Union and the Edmon Low Library, he wrote: "Your college faculty can always point out to each generation of students where the college expects to go! But I want them to preserve Old Central to show each generation of students where the college came from! Then the new students should be better prepared to take advantage of their many educational blessings."[25]

This 1987 aerial view of the Oklahoma State University campus shows Old Central nestled among the structures it spawned nearly a century ago.

Although no one developed the historic monument to education idea of Old Central as uniquely as Jarrell, students and alumni over the years looked upon the building with pride and reverence for the past it represented. They did not forget to remind the Stillwater people of later generations that the building held the key to the future of the town and college for a number of years. The people of Stillwater obligated themselves beyond their true worth to help build it, but anyway they looked at it, they got a bargain. Here the early settlers, often discouraged but never defeated, went to find strength and inspiration. "It gradually became a monument of courage and fortitude," wrote historian and alumnus Robert E. Cunningham, "to a little band of settlers who had but a puny grip on the future in this remote place called Stillwater. Here was proof to them, and to their friends and opponents in the new country, that they could build and hold a college where it could find and relay the answers to newcomers who needed every help they could get."[26]

The idea of Old Central as an historic monument continued to develop over the years. With the passage of time, however, the significant role of the people and municipal government of Stillwater in the launching of the college and its first permanent structure came largely to be overlooked. Each college generation, nonetheless, produced reverence and admiration for the historic significance and sentimental contributions of Old Central. From the first graduates to the coming of Henry G. Bennett to the institution's presidency in 1928, supportive sentiment for Old Central flourished.[27] More than a year before Bennett reached the campus, a student reflected on Old Central's past: "Here this sperm [of education] progressed, swelled, grew, overran, and strengthened until a new building was necessary. And now look at the buildings which are here and think of those which are needed . . . . Old Central. May it forever stand as a marker, for ages to come, of those generations before."[28]

When Bennett came to the college as its executive head, he immediately announced his intention to refurbish Old Central and make it a "memorial to the sacrifices of a pioneer people in the cause of higher education."[29] He favored gathering in the building everything that pertained to the early development of higher education that could be displayed, and he proposed to refurbish it as nearly as possible to its form when completed in 1894. He was the first president of the college to recognize the value of the structure as an educational shrine and symbol, and its rebuilding by his action gave the college tradition. To Bennett, Old Central was a gift on a platter. He needed it, he grabbed it, and he used it fully. The building provided a common project with the alumni, and together they approached the community, the state, and the legislature as a unit. Bennett also used Old Central to build an alliance with the alumni that reached not only into his Twenty-Five Year Plan for campus development, but also served throughout his administration. He renewed and broadened the structure as a spiritual resource and revived it as a memorial to those who established the college and the public higher education system in Oklahoma.[30]

With the renewed emphasis that Bennett brought to Old Central as a historic symbol, interest continued to develop in the building. "A greater memorial is being made than merely the bare work of reconstruction . . .," wrote a student, "the greatest work is the saving for posterity the vision and the ideals of those early day educators, men whose lives are a part and soul of the red and worn sandstone of the aged structure. A host of memories lie heavily on this time-worn building . . . memories of students who have gone before, to pave the way for a greater college. It is only fitting and proper that this building should be preserved to become a solid realization of the vision of those pioneer educators and students . . . . The making of Old Central into this symbol gives to us all a concrete realization of those ideals."[31]

The view of Old Central as a symbol of the past recognizing the founders of the college and the beginning of higher education in present Oklahoma continued through the years after President Bennett reached the campus. In this respect, a variety of viewpoints emerged. One person saw it as a monument to the development of the campus and a cherished souvenir of those who used it.[32] Another writer called it a "cradle of traditional sentiment" and "the taproot from whence A. and M.'s sturdy boughs of knowledge have sprung."[33] Similarly, it was viewed as a landmark and "an old and cherished friend to the hearts of the passing parade of students."[34] An additional person found it to mean to students what the Alamo means to Texans.[35] Perhaps one of the earliest students of the college captured a significant symbolic meaning of Old Central when she requested nearly a year in advance of the 1953 commencement a reservation in the Student Union Hotel: "Be sure to save my room for me—the one that looks out on Old Central."[36]

As the last half of the twentieth century unfolded, the faculty, staff, and administration found additional significance for Old Central. It provides perspective, they suggested, for the institution and the people of past and present generations who relate to it. It helps us to be humble and challenges us to do well in the present to build a better future. It reminds us of struggles, labors, and accomplishments as well as causes us to recognize that we are a part of a significant past which will continue long after we have moved from the scene of life. The past as portrayed by Old Central stands in vivid contrast to our present achievements as a university, a state, and a nation. Thus in several respects, the building is an unfathomable spiritual resource.[37]

Similarly, as new meaning came to Old Central from those who held that it serves as a significant reminder of past achievements, other early permanent campus structures nationwide underwent review for comparison. Harvard Hall still stands on the campus of the oldest college in the country. Within its walls troops of General George Washington camped during the American Revolution, and there notable literary greats, such as Henry Wadsworth Longfellow, James Russell Lowell, and Oliver Wendell Holmes Sr., once taught. Nassau Hall, still in use at Princeton University, housed troops of the English as well as the rebels of General Washington during the American Revolution.

Yale University has Hale Hall and the University of Arkansas reveres its Old Main, as does Drake University with a building of the same name. The University of Virginia proudly displays its old quadrangle court designed by Thomas Jefferson and constructed during his lifetime. At the Iowa State University, Old Botany is the center of attention, and at the Oregon State University the institution's eye is fixed on Benton Hall, its first structure on the Corvallis campus. What these buildings are to their institutions, Old Central is to the Oklahoma State University. For each generation Old Central is more than a mental impression because it is an original physical reality. It is also the only landmark on the campus known to all former students and graduates of the university.[38]

Although Old Central ties the past to the present, it also has the glamour of an early day at the Oklahoma State University. It contrasts strikingly on both the interior and exterior with the newer and more modern buildings on the campus. It is the one structure representing the beginning of the institution. It shows what it was like when it started, and no other building illustrates so well the growth of its physical plant. It is the beginning of the university's extensive building program.[39]

Old Central also has other importance. It is recognized as the building representing the total history of the Oklahoma State University. It became the first physical symbol of the institution. It is also the object of the attempts over the years of many students, alumni, faculty, administrative officials, townspeople, the Oklahoma Historical Society, and the Oklahoma Legislature to preserve it as a significant historic site. It is related in one way or another to every important movement on the campus since its construction. Although it is the only restored higher education building in Oklahoma, it is likewise one of the most carefully refurbished buildings in the state. In addition, it houses the Oklahoma Museum of Higher Education, one-of-a-kind in Oklahoma and the nation. Old Central's future is of great benefit in saving the educational heritage of Stillwater, the Oklahoma State University, and the state of Oklahoma. Old Central is more than this, more than the wood, stone, and brick that compose it, for it reflects in many ways the spirit and soul of the Oklahoma State University.[40]

Perhaps the transcendent significance of Old Central is that in it a sense of land-grant college identity and purpose emerged soon after it reached completion in 1894. This pattern appeared initially in the brief administration of Henry E. Alvord, the first president to be housed in the building, and then continued apace under the executive leadership of George E. Morrow and Angelo C. Scott. By the time President Scott moved his office in 1906 from Old Central to the newly-constructed Morrill Hall, the framework of land-grant collegiate organization and leadership was firmly understood and applied by the institution's leadership on all levels—staff, faculty, administrative, and governing body.

Then public opinion and politics at the time of Oklahoma statehood in 1907 caused the land-grant college concept to take hold statewide. William H. Murray, who chaired the Constitutional Convention, organized this movement, established agricultural education, and hastened the development of the Oklahoma A. and M. College. This caused practical agriculture to be taught soon in a wide range of elementary schools, high schools, and most public institutions of higher learning statewide, all by legislative mandate. Under Murray's leadership as speaker of the house of representatives, the first state legislature provided for five area agricultural and mechanical secondary schools in Lawton, Warner, Helena, Broken Arrow, and Tishomingo, all under the direction of the Oklahoma State Board of Agriculture, also the governing body

ARCHIVES, OKLAHOMA HISTORICAL SOCIETY

Under the political leadership of William H. "Alfalfa Bill" Murray in the first Oklahoma State Legislature of 1907-1908, the influence of the Oklahoma A. and M. College spread rapidly statewide. Murray led the movement to establish agricultural education in all levels of teaching throughout the new state.

of the Oklahoma A. and M. College. The legislature later created a sixth area agricultural and mechanical secondary school at Goodwell.

This caused the Stillwater institution to gain statewide ascendancy at the time of Oklahoma statehood, a pattern that continues in the authority of the Board of Regents for the Oklahoma Agricultural and Mechanical Colleges. This body presently governs not only the Oklahoma State University but also Cameron University, Lawton; Langston University, Langston; Oklahoma Panhandle State University, Goodwell; Connors State College, Warner; and Northeastern Oklahoma A. and M. College, Miami. These institutions, presently junior or senior level collegiate establishments, have a sense of land-grant college identity and purpose, and together have caused Oklahoma to make a major contribution towards developing in the United States the world's highest agricultural productivity. This development across Oklahoma became initially structured within the walls of Old Central.[41]

Not only did applied agricultural science and education have their statewide beginnings in Old Central, but the other characteristics of the land-grant college concept as worked out in Oklahoma first developed in the building as well. These include the idea of public higher education at low cost; research as a legitimate function of higher education; public extension service; continuing education; and the elevation of the practical arts, sciences, and professions to academic respectability. Following World War II, the land-grant institutions took the lead among United States colleges in international cooperative educational programs, especially in agriculture, in the emerging nations. This proved to be the international application of the extension concept first developed for Oklahoma in Old Central and brought to full flower by the Oklahoma State University in its elaborate educational programs for agriculture, science, and technological improvements in Ethiopia, Pakistan, Thailand, Costa Rica, Guatemala, Brazil, and other nations. For these reasons, the Oklahoma State University and the other land-grant institutions are often cited as the single greatest contribution of the United States to higher education.[42]

The concepts and goals of the Oklahoma State University have not changed fundamentally since the faculty and administration prepared the first comprehensive annual catalog soon after moving into Old Central. In the catalog they expressed appreciation for the generous financial support of the territorial and federal governments, and for "the great work committed" to the college, and invited young men and women to enter the institution to "learn the great lessons for a life of usefulness such as she has to teach." Although the college had passed the period of "adversity and discouragement and vexatious limitations," they would not be forgotten, but would be a source of strength "to fill with enlarged effort . . . her labor and occupation. Those who toiled to lay the foundation of a great and powerful institution have not labored without result. Their endeavors have already borne the rich fruitage of success. It remains for the present and future to fill each passing year with achievements all its own, in order that the sacrifices made, the treasures expended, and the labors of heart and head and hand shall not have been put forth in vain."[43] This is the legacy of Old Central.

Endnotes

1. Bonnie Power, "Historical Vignettes of A. and M.," *Oklahoma A. and M. College Magazine*, vol. 17, no. 5 (February 1945), p. 4.

2. Samuel A. McReynolds to Oliver S. Willham, 3 March 1955, Buildings and Building Programs—Old Central File, Berlin B. Chapman Collection, Special Collections, Edmon Low Library, Oklahoma State University, Stillwater, Oklahoma.

3. Oklahoma A. and M. College *Daily O'Collegian,* 21 February 1950, p. 2.

4. *Daily O'Collegian,* 29 July 1958, p. 4, 11 December 1958, p. 1.

5. *Daily O'Collegian,* 16 February 1950, p. 2.

6. See Chapter 3, "Constructing the College Building"; Philip Reed Rulon, *Oklahoma State University—Since 1890* (Stillwater: Oklahoma State University Press, 1975), pp. 230-231.

7. John C. Poppeliers, S. Allen Chambers Jr. and Nancy B. Schwartz, *What Style Is It? A Guide to American Architecture* (Washington, DC: Preservation Press, 1983), pp. 62-65; *Encyclopedia of Modern Architecture* (New York, NY: Harry N. Abrams, 1964), pp. 242-243; Doreen Yarwood, *Encyclopedia of Architecture* (New York, NY: Facts on File Publications, 1986), pp. 307-310; Author interview with W. George Chamberlain, 4 February 1986, and Author interview with Bill E. Peavler, 12 June 1985, in Old Central Centennial History Collection, Special Collections, Edmon Low Library; United States Department of the Interior, National Park Service, *The National Register of Historic Places Supplement 1974* (Washington, DC: United States Department of the Interior, National Park Service, 1974), p. 171.

8. Yarwood, pp. 84-88.

9. Yarwood, pp. 224-226; Peavler interview.

10. Peavler interview; Chamberlain interview; Carole Rifkind, *A Field Guide to American Architecture* (New York, NY: New American Library, 1980), pp. 193-216; Noreen I. K. Humphreys, *Victorian Architects Builders Carpenters Catalog* (Carson City, NV: Noreen I. K. Humphreys, 1976), pp. 195, 199, 201, 213-215, 288; Marcus Fayette Cummings and Charles Crosby Miller, *Victorian Architectural Details: Two Pattern Books* (Watkins Glenn, NY: American Life Foundation and Study Institute, 1978), throughout; J. Mordaunt Crook, *Victorian Architecture: A Visual Anthology* (New York, NY: Johnson Reprint Corporation, 1971), pp. 269-270; A. J. Bicknell and William T. Comstock, *Victorian Architecture: Two Pattern Books* (Watkins Glenn, NY: American Life Foundation and Study Institute, 1978), Comstock volume, Plates 31, 35, 44, 47, 61.

11. William Dudley Hunt Jr., *Encyclopedia of American Architecture* (New York, NY: McGraw-Hill Book Company, 1980), pp. 151-154; Walter C. Kidney, *The Architecture of Choice: Eclecticism in American, 1880-1930* (New York, NY: George Braziller, 1974), throughout; Peavler interview; *Stillwater NewsPress Weekender,* 18 September 1981, p. 2.

12. See Chamberlain interview for opposing viewpoint.

13. Examples of this claim are found in Harry E. Thompson, "1892—A. and M. College—1930," *Oklahoma State University Outreach,* vol. 51, no. 4 (March 1980), pp. 12, 21; Mary J. Hartman to Berlin B. Chapman, 17 November 1962, Buildings and Building Programs—Old Central File, Berlin B. Chapman Collection; Hays Cross, "Homecoming Recalls Memories," Oklahoma A. and M. College Magazine, vol. 13, no. 1 (October 1941), p. 3; Vick Lindley, "The Aggie Campus Reminds Me," *Oklahoma A. and M. College Magazine,* vol. 22, no. 3 (November 1950), p. 10; Author interview with J. Lewie Sanderson, 21 September 1983, and Leaflet, *Museums in Stillwater, Oklahoma,* in Old Central Centennial History Collection; Oklahoma A. and M. College *Orange and Black,* 9 November 1922, p. 2; *Daily O'Collegian,* 18 September 1929, p. 2, 14 March 1930, p. 2, 21 June 1960, pp. 1, 6, 9 March 1968, p. 1.

14. Oklahoma City *Daily Oklahoman,* 10 September 1933, p. 8A; Roy Gittinger, *The University of Oklahoma, 1892-1942* (Norman: University of Oklahoma Press, 1942), pp. 14-16, 37-38; *Daily O'Collegian,* 24 July 1947, p. 2; "Is Old Central Really Oldest?" *Oklahoma A. and M. College Magazine,* vol. 22, no. 9 (May 1951), p. 42; Short Course Department, *This Is Your Oklahoma A. and M. College* ([Stillwater: Oklahoma A. and M. College, 1952]), unpaged; Sanderson interview; Stan Hoig to LeRoy H. Fischer, 5 January 1971, Garland Godfrey to LeRoy H. Fischer, 26 October 1972, and Program, Dedication of Old North Tower as a National Historic Site, November 9, 1972, in Old Central Centennial History Collection.

15. Robert E. Cunningham, *Stillwater: Where Oklahoma Began* (Stillwater, OK: Arts and Humanities Council of Stillwater, Oklahoma, 1969), p. 143.

16. *Stillwater NewsPress,* 20 December 1971, p. 3.

17. Stan Hoig and Reba Collins, *In the Shadow of Old North Tower* (Edmond, OK: Central State University, 1972), pp. 5-6; Stan Hoig, "Old North Tower—Monument to Higher Education," *Outlook in Historic Conservation* (July-August 1979), unpaged; Robert A. Martin, compiler, *The Statutes of Oklahoma, 1893, Being a Compilation of All Laws in Force in the Territory of Oklahoma* (Guthrie, OK: State Capital Printing Company, 1893), p. 129.

18. John Williams and Howard L. Meredith, *Bacone Indian University: A History* (Oklahoma City, OK: Western Heritage Books, 1980), p. 18; Indian University Nomination Form, National Register of Historic Places, and Author interview with C. Earle Metcalf, 16 August 1987, in Old Central Centennial History Collection; Rudia Halliburton Jr., "Northeastern's Seminary Hall," *Chronicles of Oklahoma,* vol. 51, no. 4 (Winter 1973-1974), p. 393.

19. Oklahoma State University Development Foundation, *Report '77,* Table of Contents Page, Special Collections, Edmon Low Library.

20. Thompson, p. 21.

21. Freeman E. Miller, *The Founding of Oklahoma Agricultural and Mechanical College* (Stillwater, OK: Hinkel and Sons, 1928), p. 24.

22. Mary J. Hartman to Berlin B. Chapman, 17 November 1962, Buildings and Building Programs—Old Central File, Berlin B. Chapman Collection.

23. Frank D. Northup to Oliver S. Willham, 18 February 1955, Buildings and Building Programs—Old Central File, Berlin B. Chapman Collection.

24. Thomas J. Hartman to Jessie Thatcher Bost, 12 February 1955, Buildings and Building Programs—Old Central File, Berlin B. Chapman Collection.

25. Alfred E. Jarrell to Oliver S. Willham, 15 June 1958, Alfred E. Jarrell File, Berlin B. Chapman Collection. See also Alfred E. Jarrell to Berlin B. Chapman, 10 July 1958, Alfred E. Jarrell to Berlin B. Chapman, undated, and Alfred E. Jarrell Radio Speech, 27 May 1951, in Alfred E. Jarrell File, Berlin B. Chapman Collection.

26. *Stillwater NewsPress,* 20 December 1971, p. 3.

27. C. Vincent Jones to Robert B. Kamm, 21 September 1972, Author interview with Elizabeth Oursler Taylor, 2 November 1985, and Author interview with Raymond E. Bivert, 30 October 1983, in Old Central Centennial History Collection; *Orange and Black,* 10 January 1916, p. 2, 19 May 1921, p. 2, 9 November 1922, p. 2, 23 November 1922, p. 2; Oklahoma A. and M. College *O'Collegian,* 27 October 1926, p. 1; *Daily O'Collegian,* 27 July 1956, p. 8.

28. *O'Collegian,* 10 February 1927, p. 2.

29. *Daily O'Collegian,* 13 July 1928, p. 4.

30. *Daily O'Collegian,* 13 July 1928, p. 4. See also *Daily O'Collegian,* 17 October 1928, pp. 1-2; James L. Showalter, "A Structural History of Old Central," pp. 41, 48, and Author interview with Berlin B. Chapman, 14 December 1983, in Old Central Centennial History Collection.

31. *Daily O'Collegian,* 18 September 1929, p. 2. See also Helen Johnson, "Old Central Has a New Lease On Life," *Oklahoma A. and M. College Magazine,* vol. 1, no. 1 (September 1929), p. 9.

32. *Daily O'Collegian,* 23 November 1934, p. 1.

33. Richard M. Caldwell, "Founders Day," *Oklahoma A. and M. College Magazine,* vol. 18, no. 4 (January 1947), p. 8.

34. Power, p. 4.

35. Dean Boston, "From the Prairies to Campus Towers," *Oklahoma A. and M. College Magazine,* vol. 23, no. 4 (December 1951), p. 20.

36. Amie Neal Jamison to Berlin B. Chapman, 9 June 1952, Old Central Centennial History Collection.

37. Author interview with Robert B. Kamm, 3 June 1982, Old Central Centennial History Collection; Lawrence L. Boger, "The Start of Something Big!" *Oklahoma State University Outreach,* vol. 56, no. 4 (July 1985), pp. 4-6.

38. Berlin B. Chapman to LeRoy H. Fischer, 14 December 1983, Old Central Centennial History Collection; Kamm interview; Berlin B. Chapman, "Oklahoma Territory and the National Archives: A Historian's Paradise," *Chronicles of Oklahoma,* vol. 60, no. 4 (Winter 1982-1983), p. 403; Henry Lyttleton Savage, editor, *Nassau Hall, 1756-1956* (Princeton, NJ: Princeton University, 1956), pp. 92-94; Iowa State University *Iowa Stater,* November 1986, p. 3; Oregon State University *Oregon Stater,* June 1987, p. 7; *Daily O'Collegian,* 10 October 1970, p. 4; *Stillwater NewsPress,* 7 November 1982, p. 1G.

39. Author interview with Warren E. Shull, 19 September 1983, Author interview with Harry K. Brobst, 20 September 1983, and Author interview with Randle Perdue, 21 November 1983, in Old Central Centennial History Collection; Bivert interview; *Daily O'Collegian,* 27 June 1972, p. 5.

40. Author interview with Murl R. Rogers, 15 September 1985, Old Central Centennial History Collection; Kenny L. Brown and LeRoy H. Fischer, "Old Central: A Pictorial Essay," *Chronicles of Oklahoma,* vol. 55, no. 4 (Winter 1977-1978), p. 409; *Daily O'Collegian,* 10 October 1970, p. 4; LeRoy H. Fischer, "Historic Old Central to Serve Again: Preserved for Posterity," *Oklahoma State Alumnus Magazine,* vol. 12, no. 8 (November 1971), p. 5.

41. Rulon, pp. 123-124, 127-130; *Directory of Oklahoma, 1985-1986* (Oklahoma City, OK: Oklahoma Department of Libraries, 1986), p. 320; Oklahoma State Legislature, *Session Laws of 1907-1908 Passed at the First Session of the Legislative Assembly of the State of Oklahoma, Convened December 2, 1907, [Adjourned May 26, 1908]* (Guthrie, OK: Oklahoma Printing Company, 1908), p. 5, 13-20; Oklahoma State Legislature, *Session Laws of 1909 Passed at the First Session of the Second Legislature of the State of Oklahoma, Convened January 5, 1909, [Adjourned March 12, 1909]* (Oklahoma City, OK: Oklahoma Engraving and Printing Company, 1909), pp. 16-18, 82-83; Oklahoma State Legislature, *Session Laws of 1910-1911 Passed at the Extraordinary Session and at the Regular Session of the Third Legislature of the State of Oklahoma, Convened November 28, 1910, [Adjourned December 16, 1910], Convened January 3, 1911, [Adjourned March 11, 1911]* (Guthrie, OK: Leader Printing Company, 1911), p. 374.

42. Russell I. Thackrey, "The Land-Grant Heritage," *Oklahoma A. and M. College Magazine,* vol. 24, no. 4 (December 1952), pp. 8-11; Jerry Leon Gill, *The Great Adventure: Oklahoma State University and International Education* (Stillwater: Oklahoma State University Press, 1978), throughout.

43. *Annual Catalog, Oklahoma Agricultural and Mechanical College, 1894-1895,* pp. 18, 21.

Appendices

Appendix 1

Old Central Roof Plan

1894

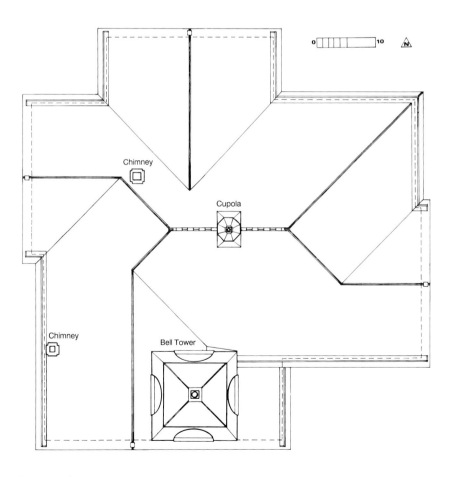

Appendix 2

Old Central Basement Floor Plan
1894

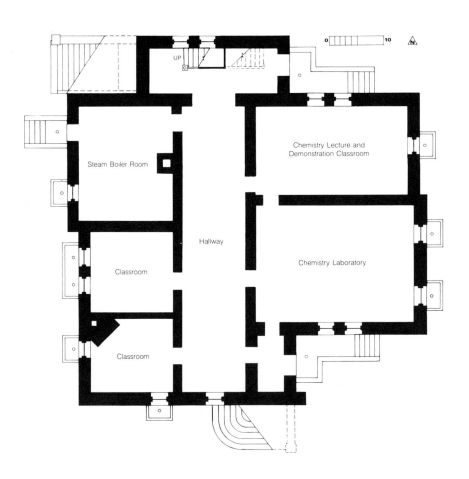

Old Central First Floor Plan
1894

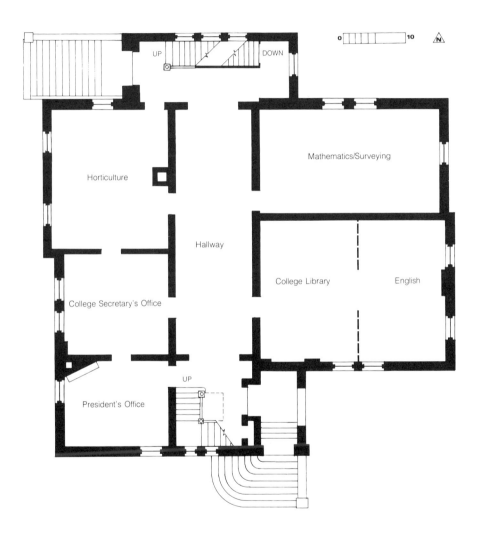

Old Central Second Floor Plan
1894

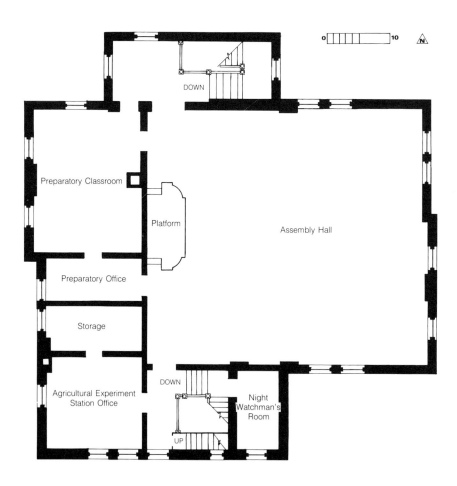

Bibliography

COLLECTIONS

Fort Smith Public Library, Fort Smith, Arkansas.

Kansas State Historical Society, Topeka, Kansas.

Oklahoma Department of Libraries, Oklahoma Archives and Records Division, Oklahoma City, Oklahoma:

    Oklahoma State Board of Agriculture Minutes.

Oklahoma Historical Society, Oklahoma City, Oklahoma:

    Manuscript Census of 1890, Payne County, Oklahoma Territory.

    Photographic Archives.

Oklahoma Museum of Higher Education, Stillwater, Oklahoma.

    Photographic Collection

Oklahoma State University, Alumni Association, Stillwater, Oklahoma:

    Files.

Oklahoma State University, Fire Protection and Safety Engineering Technology Department, Stillwater, Oklahoma:

    R. J. Douglas File.

Oklahoma State University, Museum of Natural and Cultural History, Stillwater, Oklahoma:

    One Thousand Dollar Bond Presented to Oklahoma A. and M. College.

Oklahoma State University, Public Information Services, Stillwater, Oklahoma:

    Files.

Oklahoma State University, Registrar's Office, Stillwater, Oklahoma:

    Files.

Oklahoma State University, Security Department, Stillwater, Oklahoma:

    Files.

Oklahoma State University, Edmon Low Library, Special Collections, Stillwater, Oklahoma:

Board of Regents for the Oklahoma Agricultural and Mechanical Colleges Minutes.

Berlin B. Chapman Collection.

Chapman, Berlin B., compiler. Papers Concerning Oklahoma State University and Vicinity.

Robert E. Cunningham Newspaper Collection.

Robert E. Cunningham OSU History Material Collection.

Willa Adams Dusch Collection.

Alexander C. Magruder Medal Collection.

James Clinton Neal Collection.

Oklahoma Agricultural and Mechanical College Class Schedules, 1914-1957.

Oklahoma Agricultural and Mechanical College Commencement and Baccalaureate Programs.

Oklahoma Agricultural and Mechanical College Faculty. "Minutes of the First Faculty, March 17, 1892, to June 2, 1899." Typed manuscript in two volumes.

Oklahoma State Board of Agriculture Minutes.

Oklahoma State University Class Schedules, 1958-1970.

Oklahoma State University Development Foundation. *Report '77.*

Oklahoma State University Vertical Files.

Old Central Centennial History Collection.

Old Central Restoration Plans and Specifications, Phases 1, 2, 3, 4, 5.

Old Central Tornado Damage Plans and Specifications.

One Thousand Dollar Bond Presented to Hays Hamilton.

Photographic Collection.

Record Book Committee, compiler. "Selections from the Record Book of the Oklahoma Agricultural and Mechanical College, 1891-1941. Compiled on the Occasion of the Fiftieth Anniversary of the Founding of the College." Vols. 1-2. Copy 2.

Angelo C. Scott Collection.

"Sigma Literary Society Minutes—February 8, 1895, to November 28, 1896." Manuscript book.

Stillwater Fire Department and the Oklahoma Inspection Bureau. "Tentative Report on the Conditions Relating to the Life and Fire Hazard of the Oklahoma A. and M. College, Stillwater, Oklahoma [1931-1932]."

Trimble, Harvey M. "Fifty Years of Chemistry at Oklahoma Agricultural and Mechanical College." Unpublished typed manuscript, 1942.

"Webster Literary Society Minutes—October 16, 1893 to October 3, 1896." Manuscript book.

Oliver S. Willham Collection.

Payne County Courthouse, Payne County Court Clerk's Office, Stillwater, Oklahoma:

Case Number 489, *Willis and Bradford vs. Oklahoma Agricultural and Mechanical College.*

Payne County Historical Society, Stillwater, Oklahoma.

Sheerar Cultural and Heritage Center, Stillwater, Oklahoma.

Stillwater Municipal Building, Stillwater City Clerk's Office, Stillwater, Oklahoma:

"Record of the Minutes of the Board of Trustees of the Town of Stillwater, April 7, 1891, to June 30, 1901." Manuscript book.

University of Oklahoma, Western History Collection, Norman, Oklahoma:

Photographic Archives.

INTERVIEWS

Oklahoma Historical Society, Archives Division, Oklahoma City, Oklahoma:
Indian Pioneer Papers, vol. 137, p. 312.
Ida A. Merwin interview with J. D. E. Owen, 19 August 1937.

Oklahoma State University, Edmon Low Library, Special Collections, Stillwater, Oklahoma:
Old Central Centennial History Collection:
Author interview with Robert B. Bird, 22 October 1986.
Author interviews with Raymond E. Bivert, 30 October 1983 and 1 December 1986.
Author interviews with Harry K. Brobst, 20 September 1983 and 3 March 1987.
Author interview with Thomas A. Casey, 26 January 1986.
Author interview with W. George Chamberlain, 4 February 1986.
Author interview with Berlin B. Chapman, 14 December 1983.
Author interview with L. Whitley Cox Sr., 22 October 1986.
Author interview with E. Edward Davidson, 26 February 1987.
Author interview with Ray E. Dryden, 5 November 1985.
Author interview with Leo Elwell, 19 October 1986.
Author interview with Robert D. "Bob" Fenimore, 26 October 1986.
Author interviews with Richard W. Giles, 10 November 1985 and 29 November 1985.
Author interview with Peyton Glass Jr., 2 October 1986.
Author interview with Bill D. Halley, 1 February 1986.
Author interviews with Hiram H. Henry, 22 October 1986 and 28 October 1986.
Author interview with Everett E. Hudiburg, 10 October 1985.
Author interview with DeWitt T. Hunt, 7 November 1985.
Author interview with David E. Jafek, 27 January 1986.
Author interview with Albert E. Jones, 26 January 1986.
Author interviews with Robert B. Kamm, 3 June 1982 and 5 November 1987.
Author interview with Robert W. MacVicar, 13 May 1985.
Author interview with C. Earle Metcalf, 16 August 1987.
Author interview with Joseph R. Norton, 2 February 1987.
Author interview with James V. Parcher, 7 November 1986.
Author interview with Julius A. Pattillo, 2 February 1987.
Author interview with Bill E. Peavler, 12 June 1985.
Author interview with Randle Perdue, 21 November 1983.
Author interview with Richard W. Poole, 12 April 1987.
Author interview with Murl R. Rogers, 15 September 1985.
Author interview with J. Lewie Sanderson, 21 September 1983.
Author interviews with James L. Showalter, 27 February 1986 and 11 December 1986.
Author interview with Warren E. Shull, 19 September 1983.
Author interview with Elizabeth Oursler Taylor, 2 November 1985.
Author interview with Ernest B. Tye, 22 October 1986.
Author interviews with Al Tyson, 24 October 1985 and 3 January 1986.
Author interview with Stephen R. Ward, 20 September 1986.
Author interview with James E. Webster, 2 February 1987.

THESES

Clemence, Eldon L. "A History of the Democratic Party in Oklahoma Territory." Master of Arts thesis, Oklahoma State University, 1966.

Maxwell, Amos DeZell. "The Sequoyah Constitutional Convention." Master of Arts thesis, Oklahoma Agricultural and Mechanical College, 1950.

Warde, Mary Jane. "Fifty Years of Fire Protection at Oklahoma State University." Master of Arts thesis, Oklahoma State University, 1981.

NEWSPAPERS

Blackwell Rock-Record. 1893.

Cushing Herald. 1895-1900.

Edmond Sun-Democrat. 1894.

Guthrie *Daily Oklahoma State Capital.* 1893-1894.

Guthrie *Oklahoma State Capital.* 1891-1892.

Iowa State University *Iowa Stater,* 1986.

Oklahoma A. and M. College *New Education.* 1910-1915.

Oklahoma City *Daily Oklahoman.* 1893-1894, 1897, 1899, 1901, 1905, 1914, 1927, 1933, 1950, 1953, 1959, 1960, 1969, 1971-1972, 1977-1978, 1985.

Oklahoma City Times. 1955.

Oklahoma Historical Society *Mistletoe Leaves.* 1973.

Oklahoma State University *News.* 1973, 1975, 1982.

Oklahoma State University *Oklahoma Stater.* 1982.

Oklahoma State University Student Newspaper:

    Oklahoma A. and M. College Mirror. 1895-1898.

    College Paper. 1899-1907.

    Brown and Blue. 1908.

    Orange and Black. 1908-1924.

    O'Collegian. 1924-1927.

    Daily O'Collegian. 1927-1987.

Oregon State University *Oregon Stater.* 1987.

Perkins Bee. 1893-1894.

Perkins Journal. 1892-1902, 1950.

Perkins *Payne County Democrat.* 1894-1895.

Stillwater Advance. 1901, 1905.

Stillwater *Advance-Democrat.* 1905, 1908-1909, 1920.

Stillwater Conder. 1894.

Stillwater *Daily Democrat.* 1894-1906.

Stillwater Daily Press. 1929, 1938-1939.

Stillwater Democrat. 1898, 1901-1904, 1927.

Stillwater *Eagle-Gazette.* 1894-1895.

Stillwater Gazette. 1892-1893, 1895-1901, 1903, 1905, 1907, 1909, 1913-1914, 1920, 1925-1933, 1937, 1949-1950.

Stillwater Messenger. 1894-1895.

Stillwater NewsPress. 1949-1952, 1956-1959, 1963-1988.

Stillwater *Oklahoma Hawk.* 1893.

Stillwater *Oklahoma State.* 1898.

Stillwater *Oklahoma State Sentinel.* 1893-1897.

Stillwater *Payne County News.* 1928, 1936, 1938.

Stillwater *Payne County Populist.* 1893-1900.

Stillwater *Payne County Republican.* 1893.

Stillwater *Peoples Press.* 1907-1909.

Stillwater *Peoples Progress.* 1906-1907.

Stillwater *Shop 'n Swap.* 1982.

Topeka Capital Commonwealth. 1889.

Topeka Daily Capital. 1904.

Topeka State Journal. 1904.

Tulsa Tribune. 1930, 1969, 1971.

Tulsa World. 1928, 1929, 1938, 1950, 1958, 1963, 1969, 1973, 1977, 1985.

GOVERNMENT DOCUMENTS

Biographical Directory of the American Congress, 1774-1971. Washington, DC: Government Printing Office, 1971.

Burford, John H., compiler. *Reports of the Cases Argued and Determined in the Supreme Court of the Territory of Oklahoma.* Vol. 6. Muskogee, OK: Muskogee Printing Company, 1898.

Directory of Oklahoma, 1985-1986. Oklahoma City, OK: Oklahoma Department of Libraries, 1986.

Martin, Robert A., compiler. *Statutes of Oklahoma, 1890.* Guthrie, OK: State Capital Printing Company, 1891.

Martin, Robert A., compiler. *The Statutes of Oklahoma, 1893, Being a Compilation of All Laws in Force in the Territory of Oklahoma.* Guthrie, OK: State Capital Printing Company, 1893.

Oklahoma Agricultural Experiment Station. Bulletin No. 1: General Information, Organization and History. Stillwater, Oklahoma, December, 1891. Guthrie, OK: Daily News Print, 1891.

Oklahoma Decisions: Cases Decided in the Supreme Court, Court of Criminal Appeals, and Court on the Judiciary. Vol. 638. St. Paul, MN: West Publishing Company, 1982.

Oklahoma Educational Institutions: Biennial Reports of the Board of Regents, Clerk and Treasurer of the Territorial Agricultural and Mechanical College, 1897-1898. Guthrie, OK: State Capital Printing Company, 1899.

Oklahoma Election Board. *Directory State of Oklahoma 1915.* McAlester, OK: News-Capital Print, 1915.

Oklahoma State Legislature. *Session Laws of 1907-1908 Passed at the First Session of the Legislative Assembly of the State of Oklahoma, Convened December 2, 1907, [Adjourned May 26, 1908].* Guthrie, OK: Oklahoma Printing Company, 1908.

Oklahoma State Legislature. *Session Laws of 1909 Passed at the First Session of the Second Legislature of the State of Oklahoma, Convened January 5, 1909, [Adjourned March 12, 1909].* Oklahoma City, OK: Oklahoma Engraving and Printing Company, 1909.

Oklahoma State Legislature. *Session Laws of 1910-1911 Passed at the Extraordinary Session and at the Regular Session of the Third Legislature of the State of Oklahoma, Convened November 28, 1910, [Adjourned December 16, 1910], Convened January 3, 1911, [Adjourned March 11, 1911].* Guthrie, OK: Leader Printing Company, 1911.

Oklahoma State Legislature. *Oklahoma Session Laws, 1921, Eighth Legislature, Regular Session, [Convened January 4, 1921, Adjourned April 2, 1921], and Extraordinary Session, [Convened April 25, 1921, Adjourned May 21, 1921].* Oklahoma City, OK: Harlow Publishing Company, 1921.

Oklahoma State Legislature. *Oklahoma Session Laws, 1925, Tenth Legislature, Regular Session, [Convened January 6, 1925, Adjourned March 28, 1925].* Oklahoma City, OK: Harlow Publishing Company, 1925.

Oklahoma State Legislature. *Harlow's Session Laws of 1929 Enacted by the Regular Session of the Twelfth Legislature of the State of Oklahoma, Convened January 7, 1929, Adjourned March 30, 1929 and Special Session, Convened May 16, 1929, Adjourned July 5, 1929.* Oklahoma City, OK: Harlow Publishing Company, 1929.

Oklahoma State Legislature. *Oklahoma Session Laws, 1936-1937, Sixteenth Legislature, Extraordinary Session, Convened November 24, 1936, Adjourned January 4, 1937, and Regular Session, Convened January 5, 1937, Adjourned May 11, 1937.* Oklahoma City, OK: Harlow Publishing Corporation, 1937.

Oklahoma State Legislature. *Oklahoma Session Laws, 1970, Thirty-second Legislature, Second Regular Session, Convened January 6, 1970, Adjourned April 15, 1970.* St. Paul, MN: West Publishing Company, 1970.

Oklahoma State Legislature. *Oklahoma Session Laws, 1971, Thirty-third Legislature, First Regular Session, Convened January 5, 1971, Adjourned June 11, 1971, and First Extraordinary Session, Convened July 1, 1971, Adjourned July 1, 1971.* St. Paul, MN: West Publishing Company, 1971.

Oklahoma State Legislature. *Oklahoma Session Laws, 1972, Thirty-third Legislature, Second Regular Session, Convened January 4, 1972, Adjourned March 31, 1972.* St. Paul, MN: West Publishing Company, 1972.

Oklahoma State Legislature. *Oklahoma Session Laws, 1973, Thirty-fourth Legislature, First Regular Session, Convened January 2, 1973, Adjourned May 17, 1973.* St. Paul, MN: West Publishing Company, 1973.

Oklahoma State Legislature. *Oklahoma Session Laws, 1974, Thirty-fourth Legislature, Second Regular Session, Convened January 8, 1974, Adjourned May 17, 1974.* St. Paul, MN: West Publishing Company, 1974.

Oklahoma State Legislature. *Oklahoma Session Laws, 1975, Thirty-fifth Legislature, First Regular Session, Convened January 7, 1975, Adjourned June 6, 1975.* St. Paul, MN: West Publishing Company, 1975.

Oklahoma State Legislature. *Oklahoma Session Laws, 1976, Thirty-fifth Legislature. Second Regular Session, Convened January 6, 1976, Adjourned June 9, 1976, and First Extraordinary Session, July 19, 1976, to July 23, 1976.* St. Paul, MN: West Publishing Company, 1976.

Oklahoma State Legislature. *Oklahoma Session Laws, 1977, Thirty-sixth Legislature, First Regular Session, Convened January 4, 1977. Adjourned June 8, 1977, and First Extraordinary Session, Convened June 13, 1977, Adjourned June 17, 1977.* St. Paul, MN: West Publishing Company, 1977.

Oklahoma State Legislature. *Oklahoma Session Laws, 1978, Thirty-sixth Legislature, Second Regular Session, Convened January 3, 1978, Adjourned April 28, 1978.* St. Paul, MN: West Publishing Company, 1978.

Oklahoma State Legislature. *Oklahoma Session Laws, 1979, Thirty-seventh Legislature, First Regular Session, Convened January 2, 1979, Adjourned July 2, 1979.* St. Paul MN: West Publishing Company, 1979.

Oklahoma State Legislature. *Oklahoma Session Laws, 1980, Thirty-seventh Legislature, Second Regular Session, Convened January 8, 1980, Adjourned June 16, 1980, and First Extraordinary Session, Convened July 7, 1980, Adjourned July 11, 1980.* St. Paul, MN: West Publishing Company, 1980.

Oklahoma State Legislature. *Oklahoma Session Laws, 1981, Thirty-eighth Legislature, First Regular Session, Convened January 6, 1981, Adjourned July 20, 1981, and First Extraordinary Session, Convened August 31, 1981, Adjourned September 4, 1981.* St. Paul, MN: West Publishing Company, 1981.

Oklahoma Territorial Assembly. *Journal of the First Session of the Legislative Assembly of Oklahoma Territory Beginning August 27, 1890.* Guthrie, OK: Oklahoma News Publishing Company, 1890.

Oklahoma Territorial Board of Agriculture. *First Biennial Report of the Oklahoma Territorial Board of Agriculture, 1903-1904.* Guthrie, OK: State Capital Company, 1905.

Oklahoma Territorial Council. *Journal of the Council Proceedings of the Third Legislative Assembly of the Territory of Oklahoma, Beginning January 8, 1895, Ending March 8, 1895.* Guthrie, OK: Daily Leader Press, 1895.

Oklahoma Territorial Council. *Journal of the Council Proceedings of the Sixth Legislative Assembly of the Territory of Oklahoma, Beginning January 8, 1901, Ending March 8, 1901.* Guthrie, OK: State Capital Printing Company, 1901.

Oklahoma Territorial Council. *Journal of the Council Proceedings of the Eighth Legislative Assembly of the Territory of Oklahoma Beginning January 10, 1905, Ending March 10, 1905.* Guthrie, OK: State Capital Company, 1905.

Oklahoma Territorial House of Representatives. *Journal of the House Proceedings of the Third Legislative Assembly of the Territory of Oklahoma, Beginning January 8, 1895, Ending March 8, 1895.* Guthrie, OK: Daily Leader Press, 1895.

Oklahoma Territorial House of Representatives. *Journal of the House Proceedings of the Sixth Legislative Assembly of the Territory of Oklahoma, Beginning January 8, 1901, Ending March 8, 1901.* Guthrie, OK: State Capital Printing Company, 1901.

Oklahoma Territorial House of Representatives. *Journal of the Proceedings of the House of Representatives of the Eighth Legislative Assembly of the Territory of Oklahoma, Beginning January 10, 1905, Ending March 10, 1905.* Guthrie, OK: State Capital Company, 1905.

Oklahoma Territorial Legislature. *Session Laws of 1895 Passed at the Third Regular Session of the Legislative Assembly of the Territory of Oklahoma.* No place: no publisher, 1895.

Oklahoma Territorial Legislature. *Session Laws of 1897 Passed at the Fourth Regular Session of the Legislative Assembly of the Territory of Oklahoma.* Guthrie, OK: Leader Company, 1897.

Oklahoma Territorial Legislature. *Session Laws of 1899 Passed at the Fifth Regular Session of the Legislative Assembly of the Territory of Oklahoma.* Guthrie, OK: State Capital Printing Company, 1899.

Oklahoma Territorial Legislature. *Session Laws of 1901, Passed at the Sixth Regular Session of the Legislative Assembly of the Territory of Oklahoma.* Guthrie, OK: State Capital Printing Company, 1901.

Oklahoma Territorial Legislature. *Session Laws of 1903 Passed at the Seventh Regular Session of the Legislative Assembly of the Territory of Oklahoma.* Guthrie, OK: State Capital Company, 1903.

Oklahoma Territorial Legislature. *Session Laws of 1905 Passed at the Eighth Regular Session of the Legislative Assembly of the Territory of Oklahoma.* Guthrie, OK: State Capital Company, 1905.

Oklahoma Territorial Legislature. *Wilson's Revised and Annotated Statutes of Oklahoma, 1903.* Two volumes, by W. F. Wilson. Guthrie, OK: State Capital Company, 1903.

Parker, Howard, compiler. *Oklahoma Reports: Cases Determined in the Supreme Court of the State of Oklahoma, May 13-November 9, 1909.* Vol. 24. Guthrie, OK: State Capital Printing Company, 1910.

Report of Oklahoma Educational Institutions, 1902. Guthrie, OK: State Capital Company, [1902].

Report of the President of the Board of Regents, Oklahoma Agricultural and Mechanical College of the Territory of Oklahoma, 1901-1902. Guthrie, OK: State Capital Company, [1902].

Report of the President of the Oklahoma Agricultural and Mechanical College to the Secretary of the Interior and the Secretary of Agriculture for the Year Ending June 30, 1894, and the Biennial Report to the Governor of Oklahoma, December 31, 1894. Guthrie, OK: Representative Print, 1895.

Report of the Secretary of the Interior Being Part of the Message and Documents Communicated to the Two Houses of Congress at the Beginning of the First Session of the Fifty-fourth Congress in 5 Volumes. Vol. 3. Washington, DC: Government Printing Office, 1895.

United States Congress. *The Statutes at Large, Treaties and Proclamations of the United States of America From December 5, 1859, to March 3, 1863.* Edited by George P. Sanger. Vol. 12. Boston, MA: Little, Brown and Company, 1863.

United States Congress. *The Statutes at Large of the United States of America From December, 1885, to March, 1887, and Recent Treaties, Postal Conventions and Executive Proclamations.* Vol. 24. Washington, DC: Government Printing Office, 1887.

United States Congress. *Statutes of the United States of America Passed at the First Session of the Fifty-first Congress, 1889-1890 and Recent Treaties and Executive Proclamations.* [Vol. 26, Part 1]. Washington, DC: Government Printing Office, 1890.

United States Congress. *Supplement to the Revised Statutes of the United States, 1874-1891,* 2nd edition, revised and continued. Vol. 1. Washington, DC: Government Printing Office, 1891.

United States Congress. *The Statutes at Large of the United States of America, from December, 1901, to March, 1903, Concurrent Resolutions of the Two Houses of Congress, and Recent Treaties, Conventions, and Executive Proclamations.* Vol. 32, Part 1. Washington, DC: Government Printing Office, 1903.

United States Congress. *The Statutes at Large of the United States of America, From November, 1903, to March, 1905, Concurrent Resolutions of the Two Houses of Congress, and Recent Treaties, Conventions, and Executive Proclamations.* Vol. 33, Part 1. Washington, DC: Government Printing Office, 1905.

United States Congress. *The Statutes at Large of the United States of America from March, 1913, to March, 1915, Concurrent Resolutions of the Two Houses of Congress, and Recent Treaties, Conventions and Executive Proclamations.* Vol. 38, Part 1. Washington, DC: Government Printing Office, 1915.

United States Department of Agriculture, Office of Experiment Stations. *Bulletin No. 51: Statistics of the Land-Grant Colleges and Agricultural Experiment Stations in the United States for the Year Ending June 30, 1897.* Washington, DC: Government Printing Office, 1898.

United States Department of the Interior, Census Office. *Report on the Population of the United States at the Eleventh Census: 1890.* [Vol. 1], Part 1. Washington, DC: Government Printing Office, 1895.

United States Department of the Interior, National Park Service. *The National Register of Historic Places.* Washington, DC: United States Department of the Interior, National Park Service, 1969.

United States Department of the Interior, National Park Service. *The National Register of Historic Places Supplement 1974.* Washington, DC: United States Department of the Interior, National Park Service, 1974.

ARTICLES

Adams, James Homer. "Some Lines From History." *Oklahoma A. and M. College Magazine,* vol. 1, no. 4 (December 1929), pp. 12, 16.

"Alumni Hear Talks and Report." *Oklahoma A. and M. College Magazine,* vol. 11, no. 9 (June 1940), p. 9.

"Alumni Program." *A. and M. Boomer,* vol. 4, no. 1 (September-October 1925), p. 2.

Bennett, Henry G. "A Message From the President." *Oklahoma A. and M. College Magazine,* vol. 1, no. I (September 1929), p. 4.

Boger, Lawrence L. "The Start of Something Big." *Oklahoma State University Outreach,* vol. 56, no. 4 (July 1985), pp. 4-6.

Bond, Gregg. "Major Building Projects for 1962." *Oklahoma State Alumnus Magazine,* vol. 3, no. 3 (March 1962), pp. 6-9.

Bond, Gregg. "A Close Call." *Oklahoma State University Outreach,* vol. 16, no. 7 (September-October 1975), pp. 12-15.

Boston, Don. "From the Prairies to Campus Towers." *Oklahoma A. and M. College Magazine,* vol. 23, no. 4 (December 1951), pp. 18-22.

Braley, Genevieve. "Classes Resumed in Old Central." *Oklahoma A. and M. College Magazine,* vol. 1, no. 8 (April 1930), p. 5.

Brown, Kenny L. and Fischer, LeRoy H. "Old Central: A Pictorial Essay." *Chronicles of Oklahoma,* vol. 55, no. 4 (Winter 1977-1978), pp. 403-423. This article was reprinted under the title, "Historic Old Central," in the *Payne County Historical Review,* vol. 1, no. 4 (April 1981), pp. 22-33.

Caldwell, Richard M. "Founders Day." *Oklahoma A. and M. College Magazine,* vol. 18, no. 4 (January 1947), pp. 8-9.

Chapman, Berlin B. "Founding the College." *Oklahoma A. and M. College Magazine,* vol. 1, no. 4 (December 1929), pp. 7, 21.

Chapman, Berlin B. "The Men Who Selected Stillwater as the College Site for A. and M." *Oklahoma A. and M. College Magazine,* vol. 2, no. 4 (December 1930), pp. 108-109.

Chapman, Berlin B. "Dr. Henry G. Bennett as I Knew Him." *Chronicles of Oklahoma*, vol. 33, no. 2 (Summer 1955), pp. 159-168.

Chapman, Berlin B. "Old Central of Oklahoma State University." *Chronicles of Oklahoma*, vol. 42, no. 3 (Autumn 1964), pp. 273-290.

Chapman, Berlin B. "Oklahoma Territory and the National Archives: A Historian's Paradise." *Chronicles of Oklahoma*, vol. 60, no. 4 (Winter 1982-1983), pp. 400-411.

"Classes Again Convene in 'Old Central' Rooms." *Oklahoma A. and M. College Magazine*, vol. 2, no. 2 (October 1930), p. 46.

"A Close Look at the 'Back Door.'" *Oklahoma State Alumnus Magazine*, vol. 1, no. 1 (January 1960), pp. 4-7.

"The Cover." *Oklahoma A. and M. College Magazine*, vol. 13, no. 3 (December 1941), p. 1.

Cross, Hays. "Memories to Be Revived." *Oklahoma A. and M. College Magazine*, vol. 11, no. 3 (December 1939), pp. 4, 13.

Cross, Hays. "Homecoming Recalls Memories." *Oklahoma A. and M. College Magazine*, vol. 13, no. 1 (October 1941), p. 3.

Ewing, Amos A. "The First Board of Regents." *Oklahoma A. and M. College Magazine*, vol. 1, no. 4 (December 1929), pp. 4, 30.

"First Issue Delayed." *A. and M. Boomer*, vol. 1, no. 1 (1 October 1920), p. 12.

Fischer, LeRoy. "Historic Old Central to Serve Again: Preserved for Posterity." *Oklahoma State Alumnus Magazine*, vol. 12, no. 8 (November 1971), pp. 3-6.

"Founders' Day." *Oklahoma A. and M. College Magazine*, vol. 8, no. 3 (December 1936), pp. 4-5.

"The Founding and Struggle for Survival." *Oklahoma State Alumnus Magazine*, vol. 10, no. 5 (May 1969), pp. 12-15.

"Funds Received for Restoration of Old Central as a Museum, Historical Sight." *Oklahoma State Alumnus Magazine*, vol. 13, no. 7 (September-October 1972), p. 10.

Guthrey, E. Bee. "Early Days in Payne County." *Chronicles of Oklahoma*, vol. 3, no. 1 (April 1925), pp. 74-80.

Halliburton, Rudia Jr. "Northeastern's Seminary Hall." *Chronicles of Oklahoma*, vol. 51, no. 4 (Winter 1973-1974), pp. 391-398.

Hamilton, John W. "Saga of a Little Red Schoolhouse." *Oklahoma A. and M. College Magazine*, vol. 19, no. 3 (December 1947), p. 2.

Hastings, James K. "Oklahoma Agricultural and Mechanical College and Old Central." *Chronicles of Oklahoma*, vol. 28, no. 1 (Spring 1950), pp. 81-84.

Hoig, Stan. "Old North Tower—Monument to Higher Education." *Outlook in Historic Conservation* (July-August 1979), unpaged.

House, R. Morton. "The Class of 1903 at Oklahoma A. and M. College." *Chronicles of Oklahoma*, vol. 44, no. 4 (Winter 1966-1967), pp. 391-408.

"Invitation Letters." *Oklahoma A. and M. College Magazine*, vol. 9, no. 7 (April 1938), pp. 4, 6, 12, 14, 16.

"Is Old Central Really Oldest?" *Oklahoma A. and M. College Magazine*, vol. 22, no. 9 (May 1951), p. 42.

Jarrell, Alfred E. "My Class." *Oklahoma A. and M. College Magazine*, vol. 27, no. 11 (July 1956), p. 13.

Jarrell, Alfred E. "The Founding of Oklahoma A. and M. College: A Memoir." *Chronicles of Oklahoma*, vol. 34, no. 3 (Autumn 1956), pp. 315-325.

Johnson, Helen. "Old Central Has New Lease on Life." *Oklahoma A. and M. College Magazine*, vol. 1, no. 1 (September 1929), p. 9.

Jones, Olin W. "Aggieland's First Collegiates." *Oklahoma A. and M. College Magazine*, vol. 1, no. 6 (February 1930), pp. 4, 24.

Lindley, Vick. "The Aggie Campus Reminds Me." *Oklahoma A. and M. College Magazine*, vol. 22, no. 3 (November 1950), pp. 8-11.

"Live On, Old Central." *Oklahoma A. and M. College Magazine,* vol. 26, no. 7 (March 1955), p. 23.

"Mark Up Another Vote for Model of Central." *A. and M. Boomer,* vol. 1, no. 4 (1 January 1921), p. 11.

Martin, A. O. "The Secretary's Corner." *Oklahoma A. and M. College Magazine,* vol. 22, no. 7 (March 1951), p. 37.

Maxwell, Amos. "The Sequoyah Convention." *Chronicles of Oklahoma,* vol. 28, no. 2 (Summer 1950), pp. 161-192.

Maxwell, Amos. "The Sequoyah Convention" (part 2). *Chronicles of Oklahoma,* vol. 28, no. 3 (Autumn 1950), pp. 299-344.

Miller, [Freeman E.] "Stillwater and Payne County." *Oklahoma Magazine,* vol. 3, no. 5 (May 1895), pp. 307-308.

Miller, Freeman E. "Exit the Bandit—Enter the College!" *Oklahoma A. and M. College Magazine,* vol. 1, no. 5 (January 1930), pp. 4, 24-25.

[Miller, Freeman E.] "The Oklahoma Agricultural and Mechanical College." *Oklahoma Magazine,* vol. 3, no. 5 (May 1895), pp. 292-306.

"Minutes of the Quarterly Meeting of the Board of Directors of the Oklahoma Historical Society, January 28, 1971." *Chronicles of Oklahoma,* vol. 49, no. 1 (Spring 1971), pp. 132-136.

"Minutes of the Quarterly Meeting of the Board of Directors of the Oklahoma Historical Society, July 22, 1971." *Chronicles of Oklahoma,* vol. 49, no. 3 (Autumn 1971), pp. 394-398.

"Minutes of the Quarterly Meeting of the Board of Directors of the Oklahoma Historical Society, October 28, 1971." *Chronicles of Oklahoma,* vol. 49, no. 4 (Winter 1971-1972), pp. 530-535.

"Minutes of the Quarterly Meeting of the Board of Directors of the Oklahoma Historical Society, February 17, 1972." *Chronicles of Oklahoma,* vol. 50, no. 1 (Spring 1972), pp. 131-134.

"Minutes of the Quarterly Meeting of the Board of Directors of the Oklahoma Historical Society, July 27, 1972." *Chronicles of Oklahoma,* vol. 50, no. 3 (Autumn 1972), pp. 384-389.

"Minutes of the Quarterly Meeting of the Board of Directors of the Oklahoma Historical Society, October 26, 1972." *Chronicles of Oklahoma,* vol. 50, no. 4 (Winter 1972-1973), pp. 515-519.

Nettleton, Kay. "The First Ten Years: An Abundance of Better Minds and Better Hearts." *Oklahoma State University Outreach,* vol. 53, no. 1 (Fall 1981), pp. 16-23.

Oakes, Ruth Randolph. "A. and M. Building Program Progressing." *Oklahoma A. and M. College Magazine,* vol. 9, no. 6 (March 1938), p. 5.

"Oklahoma A. and M. of the Future." *Oklahoma A. and M. College Magazine,* vol. 2, no. 3 (November 1930), pp. 80-81.

"Old Central: Painstaking Job." *Oklahoma State University Outreach,* vol. 14, no. 8 (November 1973), p. 4.

"Old Central Preservation." *Oklahoma State Alumnus Magazine,* vol. 10, no. 9 (December 1969), p. 4.

"Old Central: Safe at Last." *Oklahoma State University Outreach,* vol. 53, no. 4 (Summer 1982), p. 35.

"Old Central to House New Museum of Higher Education." *Oklahoma State University Outreach,* vol. 52, no. 5 (July 1981), p. 9.

Perdue, Phil. "Higher Education for Firemen at the Oklahoma A. and M. College." *Fire Engineering,* vol. 92, no. 12 (December 1939), p. 578.

Power, Bonnie. "Historical Vignettes of A. and M." *Oklahoma A. and M. College Magazine,* vol. 17, no. 5 (February 1945), p. 4.

"President Bennett is Honored in Fourth Annual Founders' Event Celebrating Fortieth Anniversary of the College." *Oklahoma A. and M. College Magazine,* vol. 3, no. 3 (December 1931), pp. 3, 7.

"Reunion at Commencement." *Oklahoma A. and M. College Magazine,* vol. 1, no. 8 (April 1930), p. 10.

Roberts, Clarence. "Three Things to Do." *A. and M. Boomer,* vol. 1, no. 1 (1 October 1920), pp. 10-11.

Showalter, James L. "The Restoration of Old Central." *Outlook in Historic Conservation* (September-October 1982), unpaged.

Shull, Warren E. "Ceremony Launches Renovation of Old Central." *Oklahoma State Alumnus Magazine,* vol. 14, no. 6 (June-July 1973), pp. 10-11.

Thackrey, Russell I. "The Land-Grant Heritage." *Oklahoma A. and M. College Magazine,* vol. 24, no. 4 (December 1952), pp. 8-11.

"That's Geology at A. and M." *Oklahoma A. and M. College Magazine,* vol. 21, no. 12 (August 1950), pp. 4-5.

Thompson, Harry E. "The Territorial Presidents of Oklahoma A. and M. College." *Chronicles of Oklahoma,* vol. 32, no. 4 (Winter 1954-1955), pp. 364-368.

Thompson, Harry E. "1892—A. and M. College—1930." *Oklahoma A. and M. College Magazine,* vol. 1, no. 8 (April 1930), pp. 4, 20. This article was reprinted in the *Oklahoma State University Outreach,* vol. 51, no. 4 (March 1980), pp. 12, 21.

"Touchdown Trophies." *Ethyl News,* no volume, no number (October 1950), pp. 10-11.

Townshend, Major Jesse. "Fire Protection Careers." *Oklahoma A. and M. College Magazine,* vol. 25, no. 5 (January 1954), pp. 10-13.

"A Trip Down Memory Lane." *Oklahoma A. and M. College Magazine,* vol. 24, no. 4 (December 1952), pp. 20-25.

"We Get the College!" *Oklahoma A. and M. College Magazine,* vol. 1, no. 4 (December 1929), pp. 6, 31.

"What About Small, Exact Model of Old Central?" *A. and M. Boomer,* vol. 1, no. 3 (1 December 1920), p. 2.

"What Is Your Idea About Old Central?" *A. and M. Boomer,* vol. 1, no. 2 (1 November 1920), pp. 14-15.

Whitehurst, J. A. "Whitehurst Writes About Old Central." *A. and M. Boomer,* vol. 1, no. 1 (1 October 1920), p. 19.

Wile, Otis. "Sixth Founders' Day Celebration Is Best Yet." *Oklahoma A. and M. College Magazine,* vol. 5, no. 4 (January 1934), pp. 3, 13, 15.

Wile, Otis. "The Bell Clapper Comes Home." *Oklahoma State Alumnus Magazine,* vol. 7, no. 1 (January 1966), pp. 4-8.

Willham, Oliver S. "Looking to the Future." *Oklahoma A. and M. College Magazine,* vol. 26, no. 6 (February 1955), pp. 5-7.

Willham, Oliver S. "OSU Faces a Financial Crossroad." *Oklahoma State Alumnus Magazine,* vol. 4, no. 3 (March 1963), pp. 7-8.

BOOKS

Alley, John. *City Beginnings in Oklahoma Territory.* Norman: University of Oklahoma Press, 1939.

Andreas, A. T. *History of the State of Kansas.* Chicago, IL: A. T. Andreas, 1883.

Arkansas State Gazetteer and Business Directory, 1892-3. Vol. 3. Detroit, MI: R. L. Polk and Company, 1892.

Bicknell, A. J. and Comstock, William T. *Victorian Architecture: Two Pattern Books.* Watkins Glen, NY: American Life Foundation and Study Institute, 1978.

[Chapman, Berlin B.] *Early History of Oklahoma Agricultural and Mechanical College.* [Stillwater: Oklahoma Agricultural and Mechanical College, 1928].

Chapman, Berlin B. *The Founding of Stillwater: A Case Study in Oklahoma History.* Oklahoma City, OK: Times Journal Publishing Company, 1948.

Chapman, Berlin B., editor. *Old Central in the Crisis of 1955.* [Orlando, FL: Golden Rule Publishing Company, 1964].

Crook, J. Mordaunt. *Victorian Architecture: A Visual Anthology.* New York, NY: Johnson Reprint Corporation, 1971.

Cummings, Marcus Fayette and Miller, Charles Crosby. *Victorian Architectural Details: Two Pattern Books.* Watkins Glen, NY: American Life Foundation and Study Institute, 1978.

Cunningham, Robert E., compiler. *Oklahoma Agricultural and Mechanical College: A Book of Photographs.* [Stillwater, OK]: No publisher, 1955.

Cunningham, Robert E. *Stillwater: Where Oklahoma Began.* Stillwater, OK: Arts and Humanities Council of Stillwater, Oklahoma, 1969.

Cunningham, Robert E. *Stillwater: Through the Years.* Stillwater, OK: Arts and Humanities Council of Stillwater, Oklahoma, 1974.

Dusch, Willa Adams. *The Sigma Literary Society, 1893-1897: A Chapter in the History of the Oklahoma A. and M. College.* Edited by Berlin B. Chapman. Stillwater: Oklahoma A. and M. College, 1951.

Encyclopedia of Modern Architecture. New York, NY: Harry N. Abrams, 1964.

Fischer, LeRoy H., editor. *Oklahoma's Governors, 1890-1907: Territorial Years.* Oklahoma City, OK: Oklahoma Historical Society, 1975.

Forbes, Gerald. *Guthrie: Oklahoma's First Capital.* Norman: University of Oklahoma Press, 1938.

Ft. Smith 1894-95 City Directory. No place: Maloney Directory Company, no date.

Gibson, Arrell Morgan. *Oklahoma: A History of Five Centuries,* 2nd edition. Norman: University of Oklahoma Press, 1981.

Gill, Jerry Leon. *The Great Adventure: Oklahoma State University and International Education.* Stillwater: Oklahoma State University Press, 1978.

Gittinger, Roy. *The University of Oklahoma, 1892-1942.* Norman: University of Oklahoma Press, 1942.

Hoig, Stan and Collins, Reba. *In the Shadow of Old North Tower.* Edmond, OK: Central State University, 1972.

Humphreys, Noreen I. K. *Victorian Architects Builders Carpenters Catalog.* Carson City, NV: Noreen I. K. Humphreys, 1976.

Hunt, William Dudley Jr. *Encyclopedia of American Architecture.* New York, NY: McGraw-Hill Book Company, 1980.

Kamm, Robert B. *They're No. One!: A People-Oriented Approach to Higher Education Administration.* Oklahoma City, OK: Western Heritage Books, 1980.

Kansas State Gazetteer, 1888-89. St. Louis, MO: R. L. Polk and Company, 1889.

Kidney, Walter C. *The Architecture of Choice: Eclecticism in America, 1880-1930.* New York, NY: George Braziller, 1974.

Matoy, Ray R. *Thunderbird Tracks: Early History of Will Rogers Council, Boy Scouts of America.* Stillwater, OK: Prairie Imprints, 1988.

Maxwell, Amos DeZell. *The Sequoyah Constitutional Convention.* Boston, MA: Meador Publishing Company, 1953.

Means, R. E., Hall, W. H., and Parcher, James V. *Foundations on Permian Red Clay of Oklahoma and Texas.* Stillwater: Oklahoma Engineering Experiment Station Publication, Oklahoma Agricultural and Mechanical College, 1950.

Mendell, Ronald L. and Phares, Timothy B. *Who's Who in Football.* New Rochelle, NY: Arlington House, 1974.

Miller, Freeman. *The Founding of Oklahoma Agricultural and Mechanical College.* Stillwater, OK: Hinkel and Sons, 1928.

Nashert, Walter. *Teepees to Towers: The Story of Building the Sooner State.* [Oklahoma City, OK: Walter Nashert, 1969].

National Cyclopaedia of American Biography. Vol. 37. New York, NY: James T. White and Company, 1951.

Oklahoma A. and M. College. *Some Graduates of the A. and M. College and What They Are Doing.* Stillwater: Oklahoma A. and M. College, 1905.

Oklahoma A. and M. College. *Equity of Chance.* Stillwater: Oklahoma A. and M. College, 1930.

Oklahoma A. and M. College Catalog and Announcements, 1891-1957.

Oklahoma Agricultural and Mechanical College, Yesterday and Today. Guthrie, OK: Cooperative Publishing Company, [1927].

Oklahoma Historical Society. *Handbook: Historic Sites Preservation in Oklahoma.* Oklahoma City, OK: Oklahoma Historical Society, May 1971.

Oklahoma State University. *Financial Report for the Year Ended June 30, 1963.* Stillwater: Oklahoma State University, 1963.

Oklahoma State University. *Oklahoma State Football 1986.* Stillwater: Oklahoma State University, 1986.

Oklahoma State University Catalogs, 1958-1986.

Peterson, John M. *John G. Haskell: Pioneer Kansas Architect.* Lawrence, KS: Douglas County Historical Society, 1984.

Poppeliers, John C., Chambers, S. Allen Jr., and Schwartz, Nancy B. *What Style Is It? A Guide to American Architecture.* Washington, DC: Preservation Press, 1983.

Portrait and Biographical Record of Oklahoma. Chicago, IL: Chapman Publishing Company, 1901.

Redskin. Oklahoma State University Yearbook, 1910-1987.

Rifkind, Carole. *A Field Guide to American Architecture.* New York, NY: New American Library, 1980.

Rulon, Philip Reed. *Oklahoma State University—Since 1890.* Stillwater: Oklahoma State University Press, 1975.

Savage, Henry Lyttleton Jr., editor. *Nassau Hall, 1756-1956.* Princeton, NJ: Princeton University, 1956.

Scott, Angelo C. *The Story of an Administration of the Oklahoma Agricultural and Mechanical College.* [Stillwater: Oklahoma Agricultural and Mechanical College, 1942].

Shirk, George H. *Oklahoma Place Names,* 2nd edition. Norman: University of Oklahoma Press, 1974.

Short Course Department. *This Is Your Oklahoma A. and M. College.* [Stillwater: Oklahoma A. and M. College, 1952].

Stewart, Dora Ann. *Government and Development of Oklahoma Territory.* Oklahoma City, OK: Harlow Publishing Company, 1933.

Tindall, John H. N., editor. *Makers at Oklahoma.* Guthrie, OK: State Capital Company, 1905.

Who's Who in America. Vol. 28. Chicago, IL: Marquis Who's Who, 1954.

Who's Who in America, 1986-1987. Vols. 1-2. Wilmette, IL: Marquis Who's Who, 1986.

Williams, John and Meredith, Howard L. *Bacone Indian University: A History.* Oklahoma City, OK: Western Heritage Books, 1980.

Yarwood, Doreen. *Encyclopedia of Architecture.* New York, NY: Facts on File Publications, 1986.

Index

Alice's Adventures in Wonderland: comments on Old Central, 194, 259.

Allen, Bess: photograph, 186,

Alpha Society: college literary society, 113.

Alumni Association: board votes in 1920 to retain Old Central, 162; board votes in 1920 to take over Old Central, 163; board votes in 1925 to replace Old Central with campanile, 167-168; office in Old Central, 167, 179; work promoted by 1929 refurbishing of Old Central, 179; in 1940 wants museum in Old Central, 217; and Old Central restoration groundbreaking, 226. *See also* Former Students Association.

Alva: location of Northwestern Normal School, 72, 139; and Old Central, 247.

Alvord, Henry E.: first president housed in Old Central, 51-52; photograph, 56; background, 57; college president, 57-60, 61, 65, 66, 68, 74, 76; resignation, 60-61; president of Association of American Agricultural Colleges and Experiment Stations, 73; develops college land-grant identity, 275.

American College Personnel Association: served by Kamm as president, 219.

Angelo: hotel established by Scott, 83.

Angus, Iowa: source of Stillwater homesteaders, 6.

Animal Husbandry Building: experiences gas explosion, 190.

A. O. Campbell Company: wins Morrill Hall construction contract, 99-100.

Architecture: types found in Old Central, 257-263.

Arkansas City, Kansas: market for early Stillwater area wheat, 8.

Asp, Henry: meets Scott in Washington, 101.

Assembly Building: early name of Old Central, 52.

Assembly Hall: on second floor of Old Central, 39, 40, 55-56, 77, 81, 89-90, 100, 107, 111-113, 115, 119-120, 125-126, 129-130, 137, 139, 149-150, 157, 167, 237; photographs, 243, 247, 251. *See also* Auditorium.

Association of American Agricultural Colleges and Experiment Stations: served by Alvord and Morrow as presidents, 73; 1905 meeting attended by Scott and Fields.

Atchison, Topeka, and Santa Fe Railroad: bridge used by homesteaders in 1889, 4; located west of Stillwater, 6; transports materials for Old Central construction, 38; reaches Stillwater, 86-87; provides

free excursion to college for visiting legislators, 98-99.

Auditorium: on second floor of Old Central, 185, 186, 195, 204, 208-210, 242, 247-248. *See also* Assembly Hall.

Auditorium Building: and Old Central, 101, 140, 188, 230; extensively remodeled, 210, 211.

Automatic Sprinkler System: recommended for Old Central, 192; installed in Old Central, 192-194; photograph of controls, 193; pipes break, 194, 195; new automatic sprinkler system installed, 246.

B

Bacone College. *See* Indian University.

Bank of Deer Creek: employs Hartman as cashier, 128.

Barker, Robert J.: helps market Old Central bonds, 26-27; visits Renfrow concerning Old Central financing, 45; photograph, 47; presides at Old Central dedication, 49-50; resigns presidency under political pressure from Renfrow, 56; annual report completed by Alvord, 57.

Barn of 1902: constructed, 92-93, 101.

Barnes, Cassius M.: becomes Oklahoma governor, 63; photograph, 64; appealed to for college building funds, 76-78; a Republican like Scott, 83; vetoes 1901 college building bill, 91-92.

Barnes, Welden: indicates Old Central is to be preserved, 202.

Bartlett Center for the Studio Arts: part of original campus quadrangle, 101; funded by 1907 legislature, 102; partially burns in 1914, 160; liked by Bennett, 189.

Basement Portico Entrance: 129, 153.

Battle of Round Mountains: and Old Central, 209.

Beaver County: established in Oklahoma Panhandle in 1890, 5.

Belfry: attraction at Old Central, 135-139.

Bell: stored in Old Library, 205; removed from Student Union and reinstalled in belfry, 237.

Bell Clapper Trophy: symbol of OU-OSU football rivalry, 140-149, 269-270.

Bellmon, Henry L.: assists with Old Central restoration, 224.

Bennett, Henry G.: college president, 103, 173-175, 197, 199, 205, 207, 209, 211; photograph, 174; saves and refurbishes Old Central, 175-180, 186, 200, 250; later association with Old Central 185,

187, 195, 196, 217; Twenty-Five Year Plan, 188-192, 217; serves as Assistant Secretary of State, 196; uses Old Central as memorial and spiritual resource, 272-273.

Benton Hall at Oregon State University: compared with Old Central, 274.

Berry, Bruce W., Jr.: plans 1929 refurbishing of Old Central, 176.

Berry, James E.: urged by Hartman to save Old Central, 201.

Beveridge, Albert J.: sponsors Morrill Hall bill in United States Senate, 96.

Bills, Chaplin E.: and 1969 closing of Old Central, 210.

Biological Science Club: college academic discipline club, 113.

Bird, Robert B.: accepts Little Red's headdress for OSU, 146; photograph, 148.

Bivert, Raymond E.: in 1922 found Old Central usable and normal, 165; hit on head by Old Central plaster, 169-170; photograph, 171.

Blackwell Rock-Record: predicts early completion of Old Central, 43.

Blue River Valley: compared with Cimarron River Valley, 24.

Board of Regents: 57, 62, 73; accepts property to locate college, 26; select site for Old Central, 35-36; lets contract for Old Central construction, 37; changed by Renfrow from Republicans to Democrats, 43-46, 56; at Old Central dedication, 50; approves Old Central furnishings and fixtures, 50; unqualified to plan Old Central, 59; accused of patronage activity by Alvord, 60; sued by Willis and Bradford, 64-68; impacted by White House, 68; urges construction funds during Morrow administration, 76-78; establishes engineering and commercial departments, 80-81; during Scott's tenure as president, 85-86, 95.

Boger, Lawrence L.: university president, 242; promotes restoration and museum development of Old Central, 243, 251.

Boggs, James H.: speaks at Old Central restoration dedication, 249.

Bone, John H.: teaching assistant in agriculture, 126-127.

Boomer Creek: bridged to reach Stillwater by rail, 86.

Boren, David L.: impacts Old Central appropriation, 236.

Bost, Armon H.: photographs, 225, 226; transfers Old Central key to Shirk, 227.

Bost, Jessie Thatcher: photograph, 119;

first woman graduate of college, 120; appoints Hartman chairman of Committee to Save Old Central, 201.

Botany Department: and Old Central, 116, 117, 118.

Bowers, George W.: photographs, 119, 138.

Boy Scouts of America: office in Old Central, 207.

Boyd, David R.: meets Scott in Washington, 101.

Boys' Dormitory. See Crutchfield Hall.

Bradford, William R.: sues college board of regents concerning Old Central, 64-68, 268.

Bradley, James W.: photograph, 166.

Bradley, Madeline L.: photograph, 166.

Braught, Gene A.: custodian of Old Central bell clapper at OU, 144; in 1965 presents bell clapper to Henry of OSU, 145; photograph, 146.

Brazil: served by Old Central extension concept, 276.

Brewer, Veldo H.: assists with Old Central restoration, 224.

Brick Sidewalks: and Old Central, 93, 189, 190; photograph, 189.

Brobst, Harry K.: office in Old Central, 204, 210-211; office moved from Old Central, 207.

Broken Arrow: awarded state agricultural secondary school, 275.

Brown, Kenny L.: conducts Old Central restoration research, 239.

Bullen, Clarence K.: watches condition of Old Central closely, 201.

Bullen, Henry B.: photograph of home in Stillwater, 20.

Bull-in-Belfry Prank: an 1894 Halloween stunt at Old Central, 135-136.

Bunsen Burners: used in Old Central chemistry laboratories, 117, 126.

Burford, John H.: photograph, 91; awards writ of mandamus for 1901 college building appropriation, 92.

Burlington Venetian Blind Company: supplies venetian blinds for Old Central, 42.

Burlington, Vermont: and Old Central, 42.

Business. See College of Business Administration.

Byzantine Architecture: in Old Central, 257, 260; photograph, 263.

C

Cade, Cash: superintendent of Old Central construction, 38.

Caldwell, Mable: moves from Old Central,

171; scheduled to prepare college history, 187.

Cameron University: and Old Central, 276.

Campanile: planned to replace Old Central, 167-169; drawing of proposed campanile, 170.

Campbell, Alexander: makes bank loan to construct Old Central, 30.

Campbell, William H.: appointed commissioner to select college site, 22; photograph, 23.

Campus Fire Station: photograph, 191; erected during Bennett administration, 191; quenches Old Central fire, 192, 194-195, 251; damaged by tornado, 238.

Canadian County: established by Oklahoma Organic Act of 1890, 5.

Cantwell, James W.: college president, 135, 140, 141; photograph, 160; retains and refurbishes Old Central, 160; receives petition to save Old Central, 162; ordered to vacate Old Central for class use, 165.

Carillons: in Old Central, 195-196; in Edmon Low Library, 196.

Carnegie Foundation: and Old Central, 207.

Carnegie Music Room: in Old Central, 207.

Caruthers, Frank: represents regents at Old Central dedication, 50.

Cathedral of St. Mark in Venice: influences Old Central design, 260.

Cathedral of the Annunciation in Moscow: influences Old Central design, 260.

Cathedral of the Archangel Michael in Moscow: influences Old Central design, 260.

Caudell, Andrew N.: photograph, 119; marries Penelope Cundiff by telegraph, 128.

Ceiling Collapses: in 1927, 169-170; in 1950, 194, 195.

Centennial Decade (1980-1989): commemorative idea developed by Boger administration, 242.

Centennial Year (1990): commemorative idea developed by Boger administration, 242.

Central Building: early name of Old Central, 52.

Central Food Services: erected, 205.

Central Heating Plant: proposed for campus in 1899, 78; installed in 1902, 93.

Central Normal School. *See* Central State University.

Central Oklahoma State College. *See* Central State University.

Central State University: location established by 1890 legislative assembly, 18, 19; appropriated additional money for first permanent building, 35; additional money held up, 43, 45; construction of first permanent building, 38; served by Murdaugh as president, 72; served by Murdaugh as professor, 72; receives general operating budget funding early, 78; and racial segregation, 79; joins Oklahoma Intercollegiate Athletic Association, 139; and Old Central, 263-267.

Chandler, Emma A.: role in replacing Old Central with campanile, 167-168.

Chantry, Warren: and college site in Perkins, 25-26.

Chapel Meetings: in Old Central assembly hall, 111, 125-126, 129, 137, 139, 149-150.

Chapman, Berlin B.: corrects untrue rumor concerning Old Central cost, 177; assists Bennett in developing Founders' Day, 179; named historian of Half-Century Club, 198; compares Old Central with Harvard Hall, 198-199; disturbed by Willham article concerning Old Central, 200; photograph, 200, 209; plays major role in preservation of Old Central, 202; arranges Oklahoma Historical Society meeting in Old Central, 208-209; arranges graduate examination in Old Central, 209-210; inquires about 1969 closing of Old Central, 210; emphasizes lasting historical significance of Old Central, 251.

Chemistry Association: college academic discipline club, 113; meets in Old Central, 126.

Chemistry Building: 101; funded in 1899, 78; photographs, 79, 97, 158; inadequate for needs, 94.

Chemistry Department: and Old Central, 39, 55, 58-59, 62, 65, 77, 94, 114, 115, 269.

Chemistry Laboratory: in basement of Old Central, 39, 55, 58, 65, 77, 107, 116, 117, 126, 150; photograph, 62.

Chemistry Lecture and Demonstration Classroom: in basement of Old Central, 39, 55, 65, 107, 117, 126-127, 223, 247; photograph, 65.

Cherokee Outlet: photograph, 4; larger leased school land revenues sought by Scott, 96: impact on Old Central, 266.

Chicago, Illinois: home of World's

Columbian Exposition, 84.

Chimes in Old Central. *See* Carillons, in Old Central.

Chronicles of Oklahoma: edited by Wright, 209-210.

Cimarron County: established in Oklahoma Panhandle, 5.

Cimarron River: bridged to reach Stillwater by rail, 86.

Cimarron River Valley: and college location site, 24.

Circus Room: location in Student Union for ringing Old Central bell: 145-146.

City Hotel: houses college site selection commissioners in Stillwater, 22.

City of Stillwater. *See* Stillwater Municipal Government.

Civil War: and college, 22.

Clark, Edward F.: early Stillwater leader, 8; visits Renfrow concerning Old Central financing, 45; photograph, 114, 127; credentials as professor of mathematics, 116.

Clark, John R.: early Stillwater leader and lawyer, 8-9; lobbies for college, 12; locates land for college, 21, 22; accompanies Murdaugh on camping trip, 71.

Clark, John T.: scuffles at joint meeting of Sigmas and Websters, 112-113.

Clark, Samuel W.: elected to territorial house of representatives from Stillwater, 9-10.

Class of 1896: photographs, 108, 118.

Class of 1897: photograph, 119.

Class of 1903: photograph, 94.

Classen, Anton H.: contributes land for Oklahoma Normal School, 19.

Clayton: possible site for Oklahoma A. and M. College, 17.

Cleveland County: established by Oklahoma Organic Act of 1890, 5; and University of Oklahoma, 18, 19.

Cleveland, Grover: 71; impacts Old Central construction, 43; photograph, 44; impacts first faculty occupants of Old Central, 56.

College: an original name of Old Central, 52.

College Addition to Stillwater: purchased for town lots by McNeal near Old Central, 36.

College Athletic Field: scene of class pole fights, 135.

College Auditorium. *See* Auditorium.

College Building: an original name of Old Central, 52.

College Cafeteria Building: office of

O'Collegian and *Aggievator*, 171.

College Glee Club: sings for 1905 visiting legislative delegation, 98.

College Legislature Club: campus literary society, 113.

College Library Room: on first floor of Old Central, 39, 55, 59, 77, 78, 107, 116, 117, 127; photograph, 59.

College of Agriculture: origins in Old Central, 100, 101, 109, 114, 117, 118, 119, 126, 269.

College of Arts and Sciences: origins in Old Central, 269.

College of Business Administration: origins in Old Central, 81, 101, 117, 130, 138, 167, 269.

College of Business Administration Building: erected, 205.

College of Education: origins in Old Central, 117.

College of Engineering: established during Morrow administration, 81.

College of Home Economics: origins in Old Central, 58-59, 269.

College of Veterinary Medicine: origins in Old Central, 117, 269.

College of Veterinary Medicine Building: addition erected, 205.

College Press Bureau: established in Old Central during Murdaugh administration, 72.

Colored Oklahoma Agricultural and Normal University. *See* Langston University.

Columbia University: awards doctorate to Bennett, 173.

Colvin Physical Education Center: constructed in part by student fee money, 205.

Commencement of 1896: in Old Central assembly hall, 119-120.

Commencement of 1897: in Old Central assembly hall, 120.

Congregational Church: site of first college instruction in Stillwater, 26; served by Foster as pastor, 49.

Congress. *See* United States Congress.

Conn, Jack T.: assists with Old Central restoration, 244; speaks at Old Central restoration dedication, 250.

Connell, J. H.: succeeds Scott as president of college, 103.

Connors State College: and Old Central, 276.

Continental Contracting Company: wins Old Central exterior restoration contract, 236-237.

Cooke, Carlos C.: designs Chemistry

Building, 78; plans 1902 barn, 93.
Cooperative Extension Service: established by Smith-Lever Act of 1914, 4.
Cornell University: trains Hadley, 37; provides faculty for college, 75.
Costa Rica: served by Old Central extension concept, 276.
Cotton Bowl: location of football victory in 1944, 144.
Cox, L. Whitley, Sr.: role in Old Central bell clapper trophy, 142-144; photograph, 143.
Cross Farm: source of Old Central sandstone, 38.
Crutchfield Hall: funded by 1907 legislature, 102.
Cundiff, Penelope: marries Andrew N. Caudell by telegraph, 128.
Cunningham, Robert E.: debates comparative age of Old Central, 264-265; finds Old Central monument of courage and fortitude, 272.
Curtin, Gerald T. "Cowboy": rescues Old Central bell clapper from OU, 141-142.

D

Daily O'Collegian: reports visit of Halloween pranksters to Old Central belfry, 138-139; and pilfered Old Central bell clapper, 141; praises ringing of Old Central bell, 142; involvement in return of Old Central bell clapper, 144; role in 1975 Old Central bell clapper incident, 147, 148; no Old Central bell comment about 1976 OU football defeat, 149; Bennett tells plans to save and refurbish Old Central, 175; and Old Central brick sidewalks, 190; promotes Old Central for museum, 217.
Daily Oklahoman: alleges graft in letting Morrill Hall construction contract, 100; and pilfered Old Central bell clapper, 141; Old Central bell comment about 1976 OU football defeat, 149; finds Old Central historic and obsolete, 157; publishes major feature articles concerning demise of Old Central, 171; publishes article on Old North and Old Central, 263.
Dairy Building of 1904: construction, 93, 101; visited by Halloween pranksters, 138.
Dale, Frank: as Willis and Bradford lawsuit trial judge, 66-67.
Daniels, Arthur N.: elected speaker of 1890 Oklahoma House of Representatives, 5.
Davidson, E. Edward: and 1969 closing of Old Central, 210; indicates Old Central will be preserved, 218; serves on Old Central Committee, 220.
Davis, Marcia G.: assistant curator of Oklahoma Museum of Higher Education, 248-249, 250.
Debo, Angie: serves on Maxwell thesis committee, 209.
Democratic Party: in 1890 Oklahoma Legislative Assembly, 5; wants territorial capital moved to Oklahoma City, 11; and location of college, 17; and Old Central, 30-31, 43-47, 50, 56, 62; and college, 71, 95-96, 100, 102, 103.
Department of the Interior: and Old Central, 240; places Old Central on National Register of Historic Places, 250.
DePauw University: awards Miller bachelor's and master's degrees, 56, 115.
Deupree, Harry L.: assists with Old Central restoration, 236.
Dolliver, Jonathan P.: visits Stillwater with college site selection commissioners, 22.
Domestic Science Department: and Old Central, 94, 117.
Donart, Charles: retrieves college site commissioners from Perkins, 25; refuses to increase Stillwater property evaluation, 27.
Donart, Clarence R.: photograph, 112.
Donnell, Philip S.: works with Boy Scouts, 207.
Douglas Cup: won by college, 139; photograph, 140.
Douglas, Raymond J.: role in Old Central automatic sprinkler system, 192-194.
Drake University: employs Kamm as dean, 218.
Draper, Daniel D., Jr.: raises funds for Old Central restoration, 222; photograph, 226; speaks at Old Central restoration dedication, 250.
Drought of 1890: in Stillwater and Payne County, 7-8, 14.
Dryden, Ray E.: advises on Old Central restoration, 228.
DuBois, John D.: assists college with Willis and Bradford lawsuit, 66-68.
Duck, Frank E.: gives land to college, 21-22; sells land for town lots near Old Central site, 22, 29; photographs, 108, 118; class of 1896, 120.
Durant: and Bennett, 173.

E

Eagle-Gazette: deplores holdup of Old Central completion, 45-46; writes optimistically about Old Central completion, 46-47; praises Old Central at time of dedication, 48-49; opposes firing of W. W. Hutto for political reasons, 56; criticizes college Halloween prank, 125.

Early History of Oklahoma Agricultural and Mechanical College: leaflet by Chapman for first Founders' Day, 179.

Easterling, Verlin R.: assists with Old Central restoration, 223, 236; photograph, 226.

Eastern Oklahoma Railroad: reaches Stillwater, 86-87.

Eaton, Maryland: and Murdaugh, 71.

Eclectic Architecture: in Old Central, 259, 261-262, 263.

Edmon Low Library: opens in 1953, 197; addition erected, 205; used for Old Central restoration research, 239; origins in Old Central, 269; contrasted with Old Central, 271.

Edmond: settled in 1889, 5; census of 1890, 6; location of Oklahoma Normal School, 19, 20, 37-38, 43; location of Central State College, 72; location of Central Normal School, 139; association with Old Central, 263.

El Reno: settled in 1889, 5; census of 1890, 6; proposed college relocation site, 62, 63; Morrow gives speech and attends farmers' meeting, 74; home of Layton, designer of Morrill Hall, 100.

Electrical System: in Old Central restoration, 244, 246-247.

Electronics Laboratory. *See* Oklahoma State University Research Foundation Electronics Laboratory.

Engineering Building and Annex of 1898: constructed during Morrow administration, 76; photograph, 79.

Engineering Building of 1902: 101; constructed, 92-93; photographs, 97, 158, 206; and Old Central, 268.

Engineering Building of 1912. *See* Gundersen Hall.

Engineering Department: and Old Central, 55, 117, 118, 128; established during Morrow administration, 80-81.

Engineering North: erected, 205.

Engineering South: erected during Bennett administration, 191; renovated, 205.

England: background for Land-Grant College Act of 1862.

English and History Building: office of *A. and M. Boomer*: 171; ordered vacated of classes, 190.

English Department: and Old Central, 55, 59, 101, 109, 114, 115-116, 117, 118, 167, 207, 269.

Entomology Department: and Old Central, 116-117.

Esau Junction: connected by rail with Stillwater, 86.

Ethiopia: served by university in Point Four program, 197, 199; served by Old Central extension concept, 276.

Ethyl News: features Old Central bell clapper trophy, 144.

Ewing, Amos A.: pressures Renfrow to release Old Central construction money, 45; obtains release of Old Central construction money, 47.

Extension: college concept originated in Old Central, 276.

Extension Courses: first offered during Morrow administration, 74.

Eyler, Orlando M.: early Stillwater merchant, 8.

F

Farm and Ranch Magazine: edited by Connell, Scott's successor as president, 103.

Farnsworth, Darius: introduces bill to establish college, 12.

Faulk, Odie B.: photograph, 221.

Federal Emergency Relief Administration: and Old Central, 189.

Fenimore, Robert D. "Bob": receives Old Central bell clapper in 1944, 144.

Ferguson, Thompson B.: trusted to prevent Morrill Hall graft, 99; appoints Hartman as college regent, 128.

Fieldhouse: erected during Bennett administration, 191.

Fields, John: director of Agricultural Experiment Station, 85, 86, 88, 90, 96, 97.

Finney, W. D. "Jim": assists with Old Central restoration, 250.

Fire: damages Old Central, 160-161, 192, 194-195.

Fischer, LeRoy H.: serves as chairman of Old Central Committee, 220, 221, 222, 226, 227, 236, 238, 249; photograph, 221.

Flagpole: on Old Central roof, 130.

Florida Agricultural Experiment Station: served by Neal as teacher and administrator, 10, 113-114.

Florida State Agricultural College: employs Neal at Agricultural Experiment Station, 10, 113-114.

Flower, Arthur W.: upsets class of 1903 party, 129.

Flynn, Dennis T.: Oklahoma Territory delegate to Congress, 94-95, 99-100; photograph, 95.

Former Students Association: office in Old Central, 185, 186, 187, 188; photograph of office, 186; urged by Hartman to save Old Central, 201; moves to Student Union, 207. *See also* Alumni Association.

Fort Smith, Arkansas: home of Ryan, 37.

Foster, Richard B.: delivers Old Central dedicatory address, 49-50.

Foucart, Joseph P.: designs Library Building, 78; plans addition to Library Building and 1902 Engineering Building, 93.

Founders'. Day: established and emphasized by Bennett, 179, 211; and Old Central, 186-187; value, 188.

Founders' Day of 1929: refurbishing of Old Central speeded, 177, 178.

Founders' Day of 1930: program, 187.

Founders' Day of 1931: program, 187-188.

Frostburg Normal School, Frostburg, Maryland: employs Murdaugh as president, 72.

Frye, E. Moses: serves on Old Central Committee, 220, 222, 224, 236, 251.

G

Galbraith, C. A.: photograph, 66; defends college in Willis and Bradford lawsuit, 66-68.

Gardenhire, George W.: elected president of 1890 Oklahoma Territorial Council, 5; photograph, 9; elected to territorial council from Stillwater, 9; urges college for Stillwater, 10- 14; delivers Old Central bonds to Secretary of State Martin, 21; locates land for college, 21, 22; accompanies college site selection commissioners, 22-23.

Gardiner Hall. *See* Bartlett Center for the Studio Arts.

Geography Department: and Old Central, 109, 116, 117.

Geology Department: and Old Central, 119, 186, 207.

George Washington University: awards Scott law degrees, 83.

Germany: visited by Holter, Magruder, and Waugh for university study, 115.

Gilbert, Norris T.: role in Sigma Literary Society meeting, 112; photograph, 138.

Gindra, Dwain: photograph, 147.

Glass, Bryan P.: serves on Old Central Committee, 240-241, 151.

Glass, Peyton, Jr.: credited with originating Old Central bell clapper

tradition, 142.

Goldenberg, Edward E.: comments on conditions of Old Central, 211.

Goodwell: and Old Central, 196; awarded state agricultural secondary school, 276.

Gothic Architecture: in Old Central, 260.

Graduate School: office in Old Central, 186, 210; office moves to Whitehurst Hall, 207; holds first public examination in Old Central, 209-210.

Great Depression: and Old Central, 189, 190.

"Great Society": furnishes money for campus building expansion, 205.

Guatemala: served by Old Central extension concept, 276.

Gundersen Hall: 101; visited by Halloween pranksters, 138; renovated, 205.

Guthrie: established as Oklahoma capital in 1890, 5; census in 1890, 6; as territorial capital, 11-12, 13, 28, 29, 30, 38, 43, 44, 49, 61, 63, 66, 68; Morrow attends agricultural meetings, 74; home of Foucart, 78; and college, 87, 92, 93, 95, 97, 98-99.

Guthrie National Bank (presently Guthrie First National Bank): involvement with land purchase near Old Central, 22.

Gymnasium Building, 101.

H

Hadley, Herman M.: Old Central architect, 37, 259, 261, 262.

Hale Hall at Yale University: compared with Old Central, 274.

Half-Century Club: organized in 1953 by Thomas J. Hartman, 198; chaired by Jessie Thatcher Bost, 201; members urge Willham to preserve Old Central, 202; pleased with 1963 Old Central repairs, 203-204; in 1955 ensures survival of Old Central, 212.

Halley, Bill D.: serves on Old Central Committee, 222, 251; advises on Old Central restoration, 228.

Halloween Pranks: at Old Central, 125, 135-136, 138-139.

Hamilton, Donald A.: revises Bennett Twenty-Five Year Plan, 188.

Hamilton, Edward L.: sponsors Morrill Hall bill in United States House of Representatives, 96.

Hamilton, Hays: convinces Stillwater leadership to seek Oklahoma A. and M. College, 11-12; photograph, 12; retrieves college site commissioners from Perkins, 25; locates enough additional population to reincorporate Stillwater, 27; meets

McGraw about Old Central bond sale, 30.

Hand, Elsie D.: college librarian, 187.

Hanner Hall: scene of tent campus, 190-191; new office of Tests and Measurements Bureau, 207.

Harmon Construction Company: advises on Old Central restoration, 220.

Harris, Mac R.: assists with Old Central restoration, 250.

Harrison, Benjamin: almost appoints Scott governor of Oklahoma, 84.

Hartman, Mary Jarrell: marries Hartman, who signed her college diploma, 128; hosts party for class of 1903, 129, 150; photograph, 198; says Old Central represents educational struggle.

Hartman, Thomas J.: works on Old Central construction, 38; separates scufflers at joint literary society meeting, 113; serves as college regent, 128; photographs, 138, 198; role in replacing Old Central with campanile, 167-168; advises Bennett on Old Central, 175; pressures Willham to save and refurbish Old Central, 200-202; describes Old Central as monument to education, 271.

Harvard Hall: compared with Old Central, 198-199, 273-274.

Harvard University: awards Wilcox a doctorate, 86; attended by Chapman, 198-199.

Harvey, David A.: elected Oklahoma's first territorial delegate to Congress, 5.

Haston, Hugh "Hudie": rescues Old Central bell clapper from OU, 141-142.

Hatch Act of 1887: establishes agricultural experiment stations, 4; significance emphasized by Neal, 10.

Haug, Leonard H.: custodian of Old Central bell clapper at OU, 144.

Hazell, Thomas A.: conducts Old Central restoration research, 239.

Heating System: in Old Central restoration, 244, 245.

Helena: awarded state agricultural secondary school, 275.

Hennessey: extension courses offered during Morrow administration, 74.

Henry, Hiram H.: role in Old Central bell clapper trophy, 144, 145; photograph, 146.

Hesser, Abe L.: explains removal of Old Central bell from belfry, 145.

Hester Street: connects with semicircular road in from of Old Central, 128, 154; photograph, 161.

Historic Conservation and Recreation

Office: supplies federal matching funds for Old Central restoration, 236, 250.

Historic Preservation Act of 1966: and Old Central, 221.

Historical Significance: distinctive points of Old Central history, 266-274.

History Department: and Old Central, 109, 116, 117, 118, 269.

Hodges, W. E.: meets McGraw about Old Central bond sale, 30.

Holter, George L.: visits Renfrow concerning Old Central financing, 45; photographs, 65, 114; pleased with Old Central, 107; credentials as professor of chemistry and physics, 115; sponsors Chemistry Association, 126; role in mathematics classroom incident, 126-127.

Homesteaders: photograph, 4.

Horticulture Department: and Old Central, 55, 56, 58, 114, 115, 117.

House, R. Morton: reports party upset of class of 1903, 129; hoists 1903 class colors on Old Central, 131, 150.

Hubler, W. L.: role in replacing Old Central with campanile, 167-168.

Hudiburg, Everett S.: comments on 1950 Old Central fire, 195.

Hunt, F. C.: allegedly accepts Old Central financing fee, 30.

Hunter, Ella E.: assistant in preparatory department, 109; photograph, 114.

Hutto, Frank A.: early Stillwater leader, 8; retrieves college site commissioners from Perkins, 25; voices support for northwest Old Central location, 36; Stillwater lawyer and leading Republican, 56; represents Willis and Bradford in college lawsuit, 66-68.

Hutto, W. W.: resigns professorship under political pressure from Renfrow, 56.

I

Indian Territory: location of Indian University, 266.

Indian University Building: compared with Old Central, 266; photograph: 267.

Indiana: boyhood home of Steele and Neal, 10; birth state of Boger, 242.

Industrial Arts Shops: extension erected during Bennett administration, 191.

Ingalls: possible site for Oklahoma A. and M. College, 17.

Iola, Kansas: location of Scott law practice, 83.

Iowa State Agricultural College (present Iowa State University): attended by Lowry, 10; employs Morrow as professor, 73; provides faculty for college, 75; attended by Willham for graduate study, 196.

J

Jacobean Architecture: in Old Central, 260; photograph, 263.

Janeway, George M.: upsets class of 1903 party, 129.

Jardot, Louis J.: supplies brick for Old Central construction, 38; photograph, 39; builds and operates opera house in Stillwater, 88.

Jarrell, Alfred E.: anxious for completion of Old Central, 107: photographs, 108, 118; class of 1896, 120, 128; comments on Old Central bull-in-belfry prank, 136; believes Old Central represents college origins, 271-272.

Jarrell, Alfred N.: gives land to college, 21-22, 128, 270; party at house for class of 1903, 129, 150.

Jarrell, Mary A. *See* Mary Jarrell Hartman.

J. Edwin Thomas Construction Company: wins contracts for Old Central restoration, 240, 244.

Jenkins, William M.: ordered to print 1901 college building appropriation, 92.

Jewell, William E.: 1929 general superintendent of Old Central refurbishing, 176-177.

Johns Hopkins Hospital: supplies college with faculty, 86.

Johnston, Henry S.: chaotic political conditions while governor, 173.

Jordan, H. Glenn: assists with Old Central restoration, 236.

K

Kaiser, William: advises on Old Central restoration, 228.

Kamm, Robert B.: university president, 205-207, 219; promotes restoration and museum development of Old Central, 217-218, 219-222, 224, 226, 231, 239, 250, 251; background, 218-219; photographs, 218, 221, 226.

Kansas: and Old Central, 37, 38, 231; and college, 77, 101; home of Scott family, 83, 85.

Kansas City, Missouri: and college, 88, 128.

Kansas State Agricultural College: attended by Knipe, 24; attended by Waugh, 115.

Kansas State Association of Architects: served as founder and officer by Hadley, 37.

Kansas State Capitol: designed in part by Hadley, 37.

Kay County: and Bennett, 175.

Keeth, Jess R.: photograph, 166.

Kelsey, S. H.: locates Morrow for president of college, 73.

Kerr, Robert S., Sr.: describes Bennett, 173.

Killam, O. W.: legislator who wants Old Central removed, 158.

Kilpatrick, Charles: urges destruction of Old Central and erection of campanile, 168.

King, Sterling P.: early Stillwater leader and lawyer, 9; represents Willis and Bradford in college lawsuit, 66-68.

Kingfisher: settled in 1889, 5; contestant for territorial capital, 6; location of Kingfisher College, 139.

Kingfisher College: joins Oklahoma Intercollegiate Athletic Association, 139.

Knapp, Bradford: college president, 135, 141, 165, 199; proposes removal of Old Central, 167, 169, 180; photograph, 168; hesitates to destroy Old Central, 168-169, 171-173; informally condemns Old Central, 170; speaks at 1936 Founders' Day program, 188.

Knight, Homer L.: serves on Old Central Committee, 220.

Knipe, William A.: debates Payne County seat with Lowry, 7; early Perkins leader, 8-9; photograph, 24; hosts college site selection commission around Perkins area, 24-25; wants Payne County seat in Perkins, 62-63.

Knoblock, Charles J.: signs loan note to construct Old Central, 30.

Knoblock Street: photographs, 102, 161; connects with semicircular road in front of Old Central, 128, 154.

Kreipke, Albert C.: advises removal of classes from Old Central, 165.

Kreipke-Schaefer Construction Company: and Old Central, 165.

L

Lambert Construction Company: wins contract to repair Old Central tornado damage, 239.

Land-Grant College Act of 1862. *See* Morrill Act of 1862.

Land-Grant College Act of 1890. *See* Morrill Act of 1890.

Land-Grant Colleges of Oklahoma: role of Old Central, 274-277.

Landscaping: around Old Central, 189-190.

Central, 209-210.

McElroy, Clarence H.: role in replacing Old Central with campanile, 167-168.

McElwain, John: advises on Old Central restoration, 228.

McGraw, Charles W.: early Stillwater leader, 8; wants Oklahoma A. and M. College in Stillwater, 10; attempts to market Old Central bonds, 26-30; signs loan note to construct Old Central, 30; leads opposition to county seat removal, 63.

McIntosh, Daniel C.: office in Old Central, 186; role in Maxwell thesis examination in Old Central, 209; photograph, 209.

McKinley, William: appoints Barnes Oklahoma governor, 63; a Republican like Scott, 83.

McNeal, Joseph W.: purchases town lots near Old Central construction site, 22; photograph, 29; purchases Old Central bond issue, 29-30.

McReynolds, Arthur B.: photograph, 112.

McReynolds, Samuel A.: calls Old Central Byzantine architecture, 257.

Means, Raymond E.: assists with Old Central restoration, 224, 228.

Meneely and Company: manufacturer of Old Central bell, 136.

Merten, William H.: appointed commissioner to select college site, 22; photograph, 23.

Metcalf, C. Earle: assists with Old Central restoration, 236; speaks at Old Central restoration dedication, 250.

Methodist Church of Perkins: photograph, 25.

Methodist Episcopal Church South, Stillwater: site of 1893 college commencement, 42-43; last housing for college before Old Central, 51.

Metro Construction Company: wins contract for Old Central restoration, 243.

M. F. Fischer and Sons: awarded 1929 Old Central heating and plumbing contract, 176.

Michigan State University: attended by Boger, 242; served as professor by Boger, 242; served by Boger as dean, 242.

Military Science Department: and Old Central, 117-118.

Miller, Freeman E.: voices support for Old Central location nearest Stillwater, 36; appointed professor of English by Democrats, 56, 83, 115-116; directs college press bureau, 72; serves in Oklahoma Council, 88-92; leads attack on

Republicans in college, 96; photograph, 114; speaks at 1930 Founders' Day program, 187; praises Old Central as achievement symbol, 270.

Miller, Louis C.: scuffles at joint meeting of Sigmas and Websters, 112-113.

Miltimore, Cora A.: photograph, 138.

Mississippi Agricultural and Mechanical College: attended by Magruder, 115.

Mississippi River: and college 77, 89. 121, 192.

Morrill Act of 1862: establishes land-grant colleges, 3-4; and endowment land of college, 101.

Morrill Act of 1890: authorizes continuing federal appropriations for land-grant colleges, 4; used by Steele to urge Old Central construction, 10; authorizes separate state black colleges, 80; requires sharing of endowment land of college, 101.

Morrill Hall: need emphasized, 93-94; construction, 96-100, 156, 165; photograph, 100; first occupants, 100-101; burns in 1914, 160; damaged by tornado, 238; and Old Central, 268-269, 275.

Morris, Oscar M.: photographs: 108, 118; class of 1896, 120.

Morrow, George E.: background, 73; college president, 73-81, 84, 86, 89, 117, 120, 131, 153; photograph, 75; resignation and death, 81; followed by Scott as college president, 83; brings stability to college presidency, 268; develops college land-grant identity, 275.

Morse, Oscar M.: sells land to college, 21-22.

Moscow, Russia: and Old Central, 257.

Motor Pool: erected, 205.

Mulhall: 128; serves Stillwater as railroad connection, 6, 86.

Murdaugh, Edmond D.: photographs, 72, 114; college president, 71-73, 74.

Murphy, James B.: wants Oklahoma A. and M. College in Stillwater, 10.

Murphy, Robert M.: raises funds for Old Central restoration, 222, 250; photograph, 226.

Murray Hall: visited by Halloween pranksters, 139; uniquely financed, 191.

Murray, Johnston: attends Maxwell thesis examination in Old Central, 209.

Murray, William H. "Alfalfa Bill": participates in Maxwell examination in Old Central, 209-210; photographs, 209, 275; establishes agricultural education at all levels in Oklahoma, 275-276.

Museum of Higher Education in Old Central: 189, 201, 203, 211, 217, 220, 222, 223, 240, 248, 251-252. *See also* Oklahoma Museum of Higher Education.

Music and Arts Building: ordered vacated of classes, 190.

Music Department: and Old Central, 196.

Muskogee: site of Sequoyah Constitutional Convention, 209; location of Indian University, 266.

Myers, S. Earl: photograph, 138.

N

Nashert, Walter A. "Jack," Jr.: advises on Old Central restoration, 228.

Nashert, Walter A., Sr.: photograph, 226; advises on Old Central restoration, 228.

Nassau Hall at Princeton University: compared with Old Central, 274.

National Association of State Universities and Land-Grant Colleges: served by Kamm as chairman of Council of Presidents, 219.

National Collegiate Athletic Association: Old Central bell sometimes rung for championships, 139.

National Football Foundation Hall of Fame: inducts Waldorf, 142.

National Park Service: appraises Old Central National Register of Historic Places nomination, 221-222; supplies federal matching funds for Old Central restoration, 236, 250; reviews plans for Old Central interior restoration, 240, 244.

National Register of Historic Places: lists Old Central, 221-222, 223, 264; lists Old North, 264; lists Indian University, 266.

Neal, James C.: emphasizes significance of land-grant colleges to Steele, 10; comments on law establishing college, 13; regents meet in his campus home, 36; conducts Old Central tour, 47; comments at Old Central dedication, 50; friend of Alvord, 51-52; reveals college removal plans, 61; urges increase in regents, 62; first director of Agricultural Experiment Station, 113-115; photograph, 114; assembles high quality faculty, 121.

Neal, Kate: photograph, 108.

Neill, Alexander T.: early Stillwater leader and lawyer, 9.

New London, Texas: gas explosion severely impacts Stillwater college, 190.

New Mexico Territory: value of land-grant college buildings compared with Stillwater college, 77.

Night Watchman's Room: on second floor

of Old Central, 40, 55.

Noble Research Center for Agriculture and Renewable Natural Resources: capital campaign arranged by Boger administration, 242.

Norman: settled in 1889, 5; census in 1890, 6; location of University of Oklahoma, 18, 19, 20, 43, 139; and Old Central bell clapper trophy, 141, 142, 143, 144, 145, 147, 148; and Old Central, 263-265, 269.

Northeastern Oklahoma A. and M. College: and Old Central, 276.

Northeastern Oklahoma State University: home of Seminary Hall, 266.

Northup, Frank D.: finds Old Central priceless shrine, 270-271.

Northwestern Oklahoma Normal School. *See* Northwestern Oklahoma State University.

Northwestern Oklahoma State University: served by Murdaugh as president, 72; joins Oklahoma Intercollegiate Athletic Association, 139; provides light fixture pattern for Old Central restoration, 247.

Northwestern University: employs Waldorf as football coach, 142.

O

O'Collegian: photograph of staff, 166; office in Old Central, 167; calls for no delay in removing Old Central, 168; office moves from Old Central, 171; publishes poems lamenting demise of Old Central, 172.

Ohio State University: provides faculty for college, 75.

Oklahoma: and Old Central, 156, 192, 207, 208-209, 240, 243, 249, 252, 263, 264, 268, 272, 274.

Oklahoma A. and M. College: plan to relocate, 61, 62-64; sued by Willis and Bradford, 64-68; and Langston University, 79-80; photograph of student body in 1900, 89; photograph of formal entrance during Scott administration, 102; administered by Oklahoma State Board of Agriculture, 102-103; first Old Central faculty, 113-116; joins Oklahoma Intercollegiate Athletic Association, 139; gains statewide ascendancy in land-grant agricultural education, 275-276.

Oklahoma A. and M. College Athletic Association: organized in Old Central, 139.

Oklahoma A. and M. College Band: and Old Central bell clapper trophy, 144.

Oklahoma A. and M. College Magazine:

office in Old Central, 186; publishes Willham article involving future of Old Central, 199-202; indicates Old Central is to be preserved, 202.

Oklahoma Broadcasters Association: names Kamm "Oklahoman of the Year," 219.

Oklahoma Capital: sought by Stillwater leadership, 9, 11.

Oklahoma Capitol Building: architects same for 1929-1930 Old Central refurbishing, 176.

Oklahoma City: settled in 1889, 5; census of 1890, 6; contestant for territorial capital, 6, 11, 13; and college, 29, 74, 83-84, 88; and Old Central, 143, 144, 176, 192, 220, 224, 225, 240, 244.

Oklahoma City Chamber of Commerce: founded in part by Scott, 84.

Oklahoma City University: served by Scott as professor, 103.

Oklahoma City Young Men's Christian Association: founded in part by Scott, 84.

Oklahoma Council: established, 5; in 1901 approves large building construction bill for college, 88-92.

Oklahoma County: established in 1890, 5; and Oklahoma Normal School, 19.

Oklahoma Daily: role in Old Central bell clapper trophy, 143.

Oklahoma Diamond Jubilee Commission: awards grant for Old Central restoration, 244, 250.

Oklahoma District: opened to settlement in 1889, 5; established as counties in 1890, 5; and Scott, 83.

Oklahoma Hall of Fame: inducts Kamm, 219.

Oklahoma Hawk: lured to Stillwater, 7; staunchly supports Old Central bond issue, 21; criticizes sale of Old Central bonds, 30-31.

Oklahoma Historical Society: 1949 annual meeting in Old Central, 208-209; role in Old Central restoration and museum development, 220-231, 235-253.

Oklahoma House of Representatives: established, 5; in 1901 approves large building construction bill for college, 88-92; in 1905 Morrill Hall bill introduced, 97.

Oklahoma Inspection Bureau: recommends fire safety improvements for Old Central, 192.

Oklahoma Intercollegiate Athletic Association: establishment announced in Old Central assembly hall, 139.

Oklahoma Journal: first newspaper in Oklahoma City, 84.

Oklahoma Legislative Assembly of 1890: establishes Oklahoma A. and M. College, 3, 9-14, 108; photograph, 11; and Payne County legislative delegation, 17, 19.

Oklahoma Legislative Assembly of 1893: legalizes Old Central bonds and their sale, 29, 268; appropriates additional money for Old Central construction, 32, 35, 266, 267; additional funding held up, 43.

Oklahoma Legislative Assembly of 1895: investigates regents, 61-62.

Oklahoma Legislative Assembly of 1897: establishes Colored Oklahoma Agricultural and Normal University (present Langston University), 79.

Oklahoma Legislative Assembly of 1899: appropriates funds for Chemistry Building and Library Building, 78.

Oklahoma Legislative Assembly of 1901: approves large building construction bill for college, 88-92.

Oklahoma Legislative Assembly of 1905: authorized by Congress to finance Morrill Hall, 96, 97; hosted by college for campus visit, 98-99; funds construction of Morrill Hall, 99.

Oklahoma Legislature of 1907: generously increases college appropriation, 102.

Oklahoma Legislature of 1921: fails to appropriate refurbishing money for Old Central reconditioning, 163.

Oklahoma Legislature of 1925: appropriates inadequate funds to refurbish Old Central, 169.

Oklahoma Legislature of 1929: makes appropriation for 1929-1930 Old Central refurbishing, 175-176.

Oklahoma Legislatures, 1971 to 1980: appropriate money to restore Old Central, 222, 223, 224, 225, 235, 236, 239, 243-244, 250.

Oklahoma Museum of Higher Education: in Old Central, 3, 149, 211, 243, 248, 249, 251-252, 274. See also Museum of Higher Education.

Oklahoma Normal School. See Central State University.

Oklahoma Organic Act of 1890: establishes Oklahoma Territory in 1890, 5; designates Stillwater as Payne County seat, 7.

Oklahoma Panhandle A. and M. College. See Oklahoma Panhandle State University.

Oklahoma Panhandle State University: and Old Central carillons, 196; employs Willham, 196; and Old Central, 276.

Oklahoma Penitentiary: considered by Stillwater leadership, 9.

Oklahoma Republican Club: served by Scott as president, 83.

Oklahoma Senate: Scott a member, 83.

Oklahoma State Board of Agriculture: assumes administration of college, 102-103; and Old Central, 161, 162, 163, 165, 168, 175, 178-179, 180, 186; in 1926 votes to remove Old Central, 169; authorizes Bennett to prepare Twenty-Five Year Plan for college development, 188; authorizes Bennett to erect tents at college for instructional purposes, 190; governs state agricultural secondary schools and college, 275-276.

Oklahoma State Board of Public Affairs: lets contracts for Old Central restoration, 224-225, 240.

Oklahoma State Capital: predicts early completion of Old Central, 38; blames Turner for Old Central financing problems, 43-44; praises Old Central upon completion, 49.

Oklahoma State College: name change proposed by Scott for college, 84.

Oklahoma State Department of Vocational-Technical Education: agriculture division in Old Central, 207; vocational rehabilitation division in Old Central, 207-208.

Oklahoma State Historic Preservation Review Commission: approves Old Central nomination, 221; allocates federal matching funds for Old Central restoration, 239-240.

Oklahoma State Regents for Higher Education: establishment urged by Bennett, 174-175; challenges future of Old Central, 197-198, 199.

Oklahoma State Sentinel: comments favorably on Old Central completion, 47; lauds civic spirit of Stillwater, 63.

Oklahoma State University: Old Central lease-contract with Oklahoma Historical Society, 220-221, 222-223.

Oklahoma State University Architectural Services: removes Old Central bell clapper for safekeeping, 149.

Oklahoma State University Board of Regents: and Old Central, 222, 226.

Oklahoma State University Centennial Advisory Commission: promoted by Boger, 243.

Oklahoma State University Foundation: supports Seretean Center construction, 205; traces origins to Old Central, 269.

Oklahoma State University Museum of Natural and Cultural History: and Old Central, 241, 251.

Oklahoma State University Research Foundation Electronics Laboratory: storage location for Old Central artifacts, 241; destroyed by fire, 241-242; photograph of burned items, 241.

Oklahoma State University Security Department: protects Old Central electronically, 247.

Oklahoma State University Student Senate: role in Old Central bell clapper trophy, 145, 146, 148.

Oklahoma State University-University of Oklahoma: Old Central bell clapper trophy, 140-149, 150.

Oklahoma Supreme Court: established, 5; denies college writ of mandamus request, 45; tries Willis and Bradford lawsuit concerning Old Central, 67-68, 268; in 1909 and 1981 sustains Willis and Bradford decision, 68.

Oklahoma Territorial Board of Agriculture: urges 1905 college building and land improvement appropriation, 97-98.

Oklahoma Territory: established by Congress in 1890, 5; and Old Central, 18, 42, 43, 266, 268; and college, 22, 58, 61, 62, 73, 74, 77, 79, 81, 83, 85, 89, 90, 94-95, 96, 103, 109, 110, 120, 128, 139, 268; involvement in Willis and Bradford lawsuit concerning Old Central, 66-68.

Old Botany at Iowa State University: compared with Old Central, 274.

Old Central: construction, 35-52; college library room, 39, 55, 59, 77, 78, 107, 116, 117, 127; chemistry laboratory, 39, 55, 58, 62, 65, 77, 107, 116, 117, 126, 150; first floor, 39, 40, 55, 94, 100, 186, 195, 240, 243, 244-245; basement, 39, 40, 55, 81, 88-89, 94, 100, 101, 128, 153, 155, 178-179, 186, 211, 229, 244, 245; chemistry lecture and demonstration classroom, 39, 55, 65, 107, 117, 126-127, 223, 247; second floor, 39-40, 55-56, 101, 185-186, 204, 224, 240, 243, 247-248; assembly hall, 39, 40, 55-56, 77, 81, 83, 89-90, 100, 107, 111-113, 115, 119-120, 125-126, 129-130, 137, 139, 149-150, 157, 167, 237, 243, 247, 251; president's office, 39, 55, 57, 60, 73, 74, 77, 79, 86, 96, 100, 101, 102, 110-111, 268; night watchman's room, 40, 55; dedication

ceremonies, 48-50; horticulture classroom, 55; mathematics classroom, 55, 126-127; Agricultural Experiment Station administrative office, 56; preparatory department classrooms, 56; Willis and Bradford lawsuit, 64-68; student academic life, 107-121; first faculty, 113-116; Halloween pranks, 125, 135-136, 138-139; flagpole, 130-131, 153-154; tree fights, 131-135, 150; belfry, 135-139; bull-in-belfry prank, 136-137; bell clapper trophy, 140-149; decline and renewal, 153-180; utilities, 154-156, 177, 203, 204, 244, 245, 246-247; Permian red clay problems, 155, 156-157; tie rods installed, 158-159, 167, 178, 179, 217, 230, 258; catches fire, 160-161, 192, 194-195; plans for replacement, 161-162, 163-164, 165, 167-173, 199; condemned in 1921 by Oklahoma State Board of Agriculture, 165; to be replaced by campanile, 167-169; in 1926 Oklahoma State Board of Agriculture votes for removal, 169; ceiling collapses, 169-170, 194, 195; refurbished by Bennett, 175-180, 186, 200, 250; auditorium, 185, 186, 195, 204, 208-210, 242, 247-248; as museum of higher education, 189, 201, 203, 211, 217, 220, 222, 223, 240, 248, 251-252; automatic sprinkler system, 192-194, 195, 246; controversy over possible removal, 199-202; no longer threatened with destruction, 202-203; 1963 repairs, 203-204, 210; 1969 closing of building, 210-211; refurbishing and restoration, 217, 231, 235-253; lease-contract with Oklahoma Historical Society, 220-221, 222-223; restoration groundbreaking ceremonies, 226-227; exterior restoration, 227-231, 236-237, 248; tornado damage, 237-239; interior restoration, 239-248; attic, 243, 245; heating system in restoration, 244, 245; electrical system in restoration, 244, 246-247; air conditioning system in restoration, 245; restoration dedication ceremonies, 249-251; architecture, 257-263; age compared with similar buildings, 263-266; distinctive points of its history, 266-270; sentimental and symbolic values, 270-274; role in Okla-homa land-grant colleges, 274-277.
Old Central Bond: photograph, 31.
Old Central Building: name of Old Central between 1923 and 1929, 52.
Old Central Committee: appointed by Kamm, 220, 222; works on Old Central

restoration and development, 223-231, 235-253.
Old Central In the Crisis of 1955: edited book by Chapman on preservation of Old Central, 202.
Old Central Photographs: exterior, 37, 46, 48, 49, 51, 57, 76, 79, 80, 89, 94, 97, 108, 130, 133, 135, 136, 149, 154, 158, 161, 173, 176, 186, 189, 191, 200, 203, 206, 211, 218, 225, 226, 227, 229, 230, 231, 237, 238, 249, 258, 260, 261, 271; interior, 41, 60, 62, 65, 127, 166, 204, 208, 243, 245, 247, 251, 252, 262, 263.
Old Main at Drake University: compared with Old Central, 274.
Old Main at University of Arkansas: compared with Old Central, 274.
Old North at Central State University: age compared with old Central, 263-266; photograph, 265.
Old Oaken Bucket: similar to Old Central bell clapper trophy, 145.
Omega Literary Society: succeeds Sigma and Webster literary societies, 113.
Orange and Black: reports Old Central tree fights, 132, 133-134, 135; calls for Old Central bell carriage repair, 139; praises ringing of Old Central bell, 140; labels 1917 football victory celebration over OU the greatest, 141; explains need for Old Central tie rods, 158; recommends removal of Old Central, 158-159; recommends refurbishing Old Central for historical museum use, 159-160; likes refurbished appearance of Old Central, 160; comments on causes of 1916 Old Central fire, 161.
Oratorical Association: college literary society, 113.
Oratorical Contests: in Old Central assembly hall, 113.
Orlando: serves Stillwater as railroad connection, 6; and college, 28, 188; and Old Central, 38.
Owen Stadium: and 1927 football victory over OU, 141; and 1933 football victory over OU, 142; and 1945 football victory over OU, 144; and 1965 football victory over OU, 145; and 1976 football victory over OU, 148-149.

P

Paint: exterior Old Central restoration colors, 248.
Pakistan: served by Old Central extension concept, 276.
Parcher, James V.: assists with Old Central restoration, 224.

Paul Miller Journalism Building: early construction, 161.

Pawnee: connected by rail with Stillwater, 86.

Paxton, Illinois: retirement home of Morrow, 81.

Payne Center: competes for Payne County seat, 6-7.

Payne County: established by Oklahoma Organic Act of 1890, 5; and college, 9, 11, 12, 13, 14, 17-18, 19-21, 28, 32, 61, 64; proposed county seat removal, 62-64; legislative delegation, 88; and Old Central, 209, 267.

Payne County Board of Commissioners: authorizes incorporation procedure for Stillwater, 21; rejects Old Central bond offer, 28.

Payne County Courthouse: destroyed by fire, 63.

Payne County District Court: tries Willis and Bradford lawsuit concerning Old Central, 66-67.

Payne County Historical Society: meets in Old Central, 208.

Payne County Populist: writes optimistically about Old Central completion, 46.

Peach, Eugene: calls to verify 1930 removal of Old Central bell clapper, 141.

Pennsylvania State College: provides faculty for college, 75; graduates Fields, 85; attended by Holter, 115.

Pense, J. Ray: comments on 1938 Old Central fire, 192.

People's Party Alliance (Populists): in 1890 Oklahoma Legislative Assembly, 5; and Payne County legislative delegation, 17, 19.

Perdue, Randle: not impressed by Old Central, 157.

Perkins: competes for Payne County seat, 6-7; settled in 1889, 8; struggles to win location of college, 17, 20, 24-26; proposed Payne County seat, 62-63; extension courses offered during Morrow administration, 74.

Perkins Bee: voices frustration about Old Central completion, 46.

Perky, J. B.: office in Old Central, 207.

Permian Red Clay: continuing Old Central foundation problem, 155, 156-157.

Perry: serves Stillwater as railroad connection, 6, 86; and Old Central, 38; extension courses offered during Morrow administration, 74.

Phillips, H. Milt: assists with Old Central restoration and museum development, 221, 236.

Philomathian Society: college literary society, 113.

Philosophy Department: and Old Central, 117, 118, 207.

Photographs of Old Central. *See* Old Central Photographs.

Physics Department: and Old Central, 58-59, 65, 114, 115, 116, 118, 269.

Physiology Department: and Old Central, 109, 116, 117.

Physical Plant Department: uses Old Central basement as repair shop, 167.

Pitzer, John H.: attempts to remove college from Stillwater, 62.

Point Four. *See* Technical Cooperation Administration.

Political Science: and Old Central 118.

Ponca City: source of Old Central limestone steps, 38; and Bennett, 175; and Old Central, 207.

Pond Creek: Morrow gives speech, 74.

Populists. *See* People's Party Alliance.

Prairie Playhouse. *See* Williams Hall.

Preparatory Department: on second floor of Old Central, 56, 101, 114, 116, 127, 129, 131, 132, 159, 167; more students enrolled than on college level, 58; accepts applicants fourteen to thirty years old, 109.

President's Office: on first floor of Old Central, 39, 55, 57, 60, 73, 74, 77, 79, 86, 96, 100, 101, 102, 110-111, 268; photograph, 60.

Press Bureau. *See* College Press Bureau.

Pre-21st Century Decade (1991-2000): commemorative idea developed by Boger administration, 242.

Printing Department: and Old Central, 101, 157, 167.

Printing Services: erected, 205.

Psychology Department: and Old Central, 207, 211.

Public Information Office: origins in Old Central, 269. *See also* College Press Bureau.

Public Works Administration: finances campus buildings, 191.

Publications Department: and Old Central, 167, 170, 171, 186, 207.

Purdue University: attended by Boger, 242.

R

Racial Segregation: and Old Central, 79-80.

Radio Station KVOO: broadcasts 1930 Founders' Day program, 187.

Railroad: comes to Stillwater, 86-87;

construct Old Central, 30.

Shaffer, John J.: allegedly accepts Old Central financing fee, 30.

Sharp, Raymond D.: serves on Old Central Committee, 251.

Shaw, Walter R.: joins college faculty, 86.

Shawnee: extension courses offered during Morrow administration, 74; residence of Cooke, 78, 93.

Shedrick, Bernice: speaks at Old Central restoration dedication, 250.

Sheep Barn: visited by Halloween pranksters, 138-139.

Sherman and Kruger Company: protests Morrill Hall contract, 99-100.

Shirk, George H.: assists with Old Central restoration and museum development, 220, 221, 222, 223, 227, 236, 250; photographs, 225, 226.

Showalter, James L.: curator of Oklahoma Museum of Higher Education, 248-249, 250.

Sigma Literary Society: meets in Old Central, 111-113, 137.

Sigma Literary Society Serenaders: photograph, 138.

Significance of Old Central. See Historical Significance.

Smith, Emma: photograph, 108.

Smith-Lever Act of 1914: establishes Cooperative Extension Service, 4.

Social Club: college literary society, 113.

Southeastern State Teachers College (present Southeastern Oklahoma State University): employs Bennett as president, 173.

Southern Normal School (presently Western Kentucky State University): attended by Thompson, 116.

Southwestern Oklahoma State College: served by Murdaugh as president, 72.

Speed, Horace: speaks at class of 1896 commencement, 120.

Sprinkler System. See Automatic Sprinkler System.

St. Joseph, Missouri, Loan and Trust Company: agrees to purchase Old Central bonds, 28-29, 30.

Stanford University: awards Shaw doctorate, 86.

Steam Boiler Building and Smokestack of 1902: constructed, 92-93.

Steam Boiler Room: in basement of Old Central, 39, 55.

Steele, George W.: vetoes Oklahoma City and Kingfisher for territorial capital, 6; promotes establishment of Oklahoma A. and M. College, 10-13; and location of

college, 17, 19; photograph, 18; appoints commissioners to select college site, 22; announces selection of Stillwater as college location, 26.

Stewart, C. H.: voices support for northwest Old Central location, 36.

Stiles, George W.: class of 1900, 126.

Stillwater: homesteaders, 4; settled in 1889, 5; census of 1890, 6; early fragile existence, 6-8; designated as Payne County seat, 7; photograph of first anniversary, 7; and college, 10, 11-12, 14, 17, 19-20, 61, 63-64, 66, 71-72, 73, 74, 75, 76, 85, 86, 87, 88-91, 97, 98-99, 109, 110, 111, 114, 115, 116, 119, 121, 125, 126, 139, 140, 141, 142, 143, 144, 149, 156, 161, 220, 237, 242; and Old Central, 35, 36, 38, 42, 43, 45, 46, 47, 48, 49, 56, 57, 59, 64, 76, 168, 180, 188, 192, 201, 208, 222, 239, 240, 264, 265, 266, 267, 269, 270, 272; opposes removal of county seat, 63; arrival of railroad, 86-87.

Stillwater Board of Trade: desires the Oklahoma Penitentiary, 9; promotes Old Central construction, 20; holds banquet for Board of Regents, 26; honors Lowry with public reception, 64. See also Stillwater Commercial Club.

Stillwater Board of Trustees: attempts to market Old Central bonds, 26-30.

Stillwater Chamber of Commerce: urged by Hartman to save Old Central, 201.

Stillwater Commercial Club: and Old Central assembly hall, 90; gives smoker for visiting legislators, 90-91. See also Stillwater Board of Trade.

Stillwater Concert Band: serenades visiting legislative delegation to college, 98.

Stillwater Conder: writes optimistically about Old Central completion, 46-47.

Stillwater Creek: scene of Perkins-Stillwater confrontation, 7; source of huge buffalo fish, 8; and Murdaugh incident, 71.

Stillwater Democrat: criticizes Republicans for controlling college, 95.

Stillwater Farmers and Merchants Bank: loans money to construct Old Central, 30.

Stillwater Fire Department: recommends fire safety improvements for Old Central, 192.

Stillwater Gazette: staunchly supports Old Central bond issue, 21; ignores Oklahoma Hawk concerning sale of Old Central bonds, 32; predicts early completion of Old Central, 38; predicts completion of Old Central on time, 43;

comments on 1893 college commencement, 42-43; deplores holdup of Old Central completion, 45; lauds 1891 Oklahoma Legislative Assembly appropriation for college buildings, 90-91; accuses Miller of causing Democratic attack on college, 95-96.

Stillwater Ladies Band: serenades visiting legislative delegation to college, 98.

Stillwater Messenger: wants regents investigated, 61.

Stillwater Municipal Government: efforts to issue and sell Old Central bonds, 21-32.

Stillwater Municipal Water Plant: in 1901 supplies water to college, 93.

Stillwater Orchestra: plays at Old Central dedication, 49.

Stillwater Township: and college, 27.

Stovall, James M.: appointed commissioner to select college site, 22; photograph, 23.

Strand, J. C.: supports 1901 college building appropriations bill, 92.

Stringer, L. E. "Dean": photograph, 226.

Student Association: role in Old Central carillons, 196.

Student Placement Bureau: office in Old Central, 185, 186; office moves to Student Union, 207.

Student Regulations: explained, 110-111.

Student Self-Help Industries: construct model of Old Central, 179; makes clay models of Old Central bell, 187.

Student Senate: office in Old Central, 167; office moves from Old Central, 171.

Student Union: needs once partially met by Old Central, 128-129; Old Central bell placed in tower, 145-146, 147; Little Red's headdress on display, 146-147; and Old Central, 158, 198, 200, 271; addition and parking garage erected, 205; parking lot erected near Old Central, 205; completion begins office departure from Old Central, 207; decreases meeting use of Old Central, 208, 212.

Sugar Bowl: location of football victory in 1945, 144.

Sullivan, Warren E.: assists with Old Central restoration, 220, 224, 228.

Sump Tunnel: under basement hallway floor, 155; discovered in 1929 Old Central refurbishing, 177; rediscovered in Old Central restoration, 248.

Swiler, William A.: settles in Stillwater, 6; wants Oklahoma A. and M. College in Stillwater, 10; signs loan note to construct Old Central, 30.

Swope, Amon W.: lobbies for Oklahoma A. and M. College, 12.

Swope Hall: early Stillwater meeting place, 9.

Swope, Harry: meets McGraw about Old Central bond sale, 30.

T

Taft Stadium Oklahoma City: location of 1944 football victory over OU, 144.

Tahlequah: location of Indian University, 266, 267.

Talbot, Nora A.: presents Bennett with birthday cake, 188.

Taylor, Elizabeth Oursler: photograph, 157; impressed by Old Central, 157; advises Knapp to retain Old Central, 171.

Taylor, Mary Nielsen: finds Old Central interior dilapidated, 217.

Teacher Education Department: and Old Central, 117.

Technical Cooperation Administration (Point Four): headed by Bennett, 196, work in Ethiopia supported by Willham, 197.

Tent Campus: between Hanner and Thatcher halls, 190-191.

Terrill, Ira N.: elected to territorial house of representatives from rural Payne County, 9-10; introduces bills to establish Oklahoma A. and M. College, 12.

Tests and Measurements Bureau: office in Old Central, 204, 207, 210.

Texas: 77, 156; served by Thompson in public schools, 116.

Texas Agricultural and Mechanical University: employs Kamm as dean, 218.

Texas County: established in Oklahoma Panhandle, 5.

Thailand: served by Old Central extension concept, 276.

Thatcher Hall: scene of tent campus, 190-191.

Thatcher, Jessie O. *See* Jessie Thatcher Bost.

Theiss, George: assists with Old Central bond sale, 28.

Theta Pond: early source of Old Central water, 50.

Thompson, Bryan: landscapes college campus, 190.

Thompson, Harry E.: principal of preparatory department, 109, 116, 127-128; photographs, 110, 114; advises Bennett on Old Central, 175; praises Old Central for educational significance.

Thompson, Pauline C.: wants model to replace Old Central, 165.

Thorne, James J.: and 1969 closing of Old Central, 210.

Thurman, Melvena K.: speaks at Old Central restoration dedication, 249.

Tie Rods: installed in Old Central, 158-159, 167, 178, 179, 217, 230; photograph, 258.

Tishomingo: awarded state agricultural secondary school, 275.

Titanic: and Old Central, 211.

Todd, J. F.: opposes 1901 college building bill, 91.

Topeka, Kansas: home of Old Central architect, 37; and Old Central, 41.

Tornado: photographs of damage, 237, 238; strikes Old Central, 237-239.

Tree Fights: immediately west of Old Central, 131-135; photographs, 133, 134.

Triple Alliance: and Old Central tree fight, 134.

Trout, Clement E.: role in Old Central condemnation, 170; office in Old Central, 186.

Truman, Harry S.: names Bennett assistant secretary of state, 196.

Tulsa: and Old Central bell clapper trophy, 142-144; and university, 187, 198.

Turner, Martin L.: option allegedly ignored on Old Central bonds, 30; holds up final Old Central construction funding, 43-46; photograph, 44.

Turnips: save Stillwater and Oklahoma Territory in 1890 drought, 8.

Twenty-Five Year Plan: Bennett program for college development, 188-192; and Old Central, 273.

Tyson, Al: supervising architect of Old Central restoration, 251.

U

Unassigned Lands. *See* Oklahoma District.

United Nations Educational, Scientific, and Cultural Organization: served by Kamm as United States delegate to Executive Board, 219.

United State Congress: establishes land-grant colleges, 3-4; opens Oklahoma District (Unassigned Lands) to settlement, 5; establishes Oklahoma Territory in 1889, 5; authorizes school land leasing in Oklahoma Panhandle, 75-76; passes law prohibiting Morrill Hall construction, 94-95, 96; repeals law prohibiting Morrill Hall construction,

96-97; transfers land section adjacent to college campus, 98; served by Flynn as Oklahoma Territory delegate, 99-100; and Old Central, 221.

United States Department of Agriculture: highly recommends Alvord, 57; statistics used to promote college building construction, 77; employer of Caudell, 128.

United States Department of Housing and Urban Development: grants money to refurbish and restore Old Central, 224, 225, 235, 236, 250.

United States Department of the Interior: and Old Central, 221, 236.

United States House of Representatives: Hamilton sponsors Morrill Hall bill for college, 96.

United States Office of Education: provides funds for modification of Old Central auditorium, 204.

United States Senate: Beveridge sponsors Morrill Hall bill for college, 96.

University Architect's Office: role in refurbishing and restoring Old Central, 220, 239. *See also* University Architectural Services.

University Architectural Services: role in refurbishing and restoring Old Cental, 240, 251. *See also* University Architects Office.

University Auditorium. *See* Auditorium.

University of California: employs Waldorf as football coach, 142.

University of Chicago: supplies college with faculty, 86.

University of Cincinnati: awards Wikoff law degree, 85.

University of Illinois: attended by Wikoff, 10, 85; served by Morrow as professor and administrator, 73; Morrow retires to vicinity, 81.

University of Kansas: alma mater of Scott, 83.

University of Maryland: supplies college with faculty, 86.

University of Massachusetts: served by Waugh as horticulture professor, 115.

University of Michigan: awards Morrow law degree, 73; awards Neal doctor of medicine degree, 113-114.

University of Minnesota: attended by Kamm, 218.

University of Northern Iowa: attended by Kamm, 218.

University of Oklahoma: location established by 1890 legislative assembly, 18, 19; appropriated additional money for first permanent building, 35; additional money held up, 43, 45; early receives general operating budget funding, 78; uses 1850 law for endowment land, 101; served by Scott as professor, 103; joins Oklahoma Intercollegiate Athletic Association, 139; and Old Central bell clapper trophy, 140-149, 150, 269-270.

University of Oklahoma Building: and Old Central, 263-265, 267; photograph, 264.

University of Wisconsin: supplies college with faculty, 86.

Upshaw, Tazwell M.: photograph, 114.

Utilities: installed in Old Central at various times, 154-156, 177, 203, 204, 244, 245, 246-247.

V

Vandergraff: represents firm interested in purchasing Old Central bonds, 27.

Venetian Blinds: original installation in Old Central, 42, 52; installed anew in 1930, 177-178.

Vernacular Architecture: not in Old Central design, 262-263.

Veterans Village Fire Station: quenches Old Central fire, 194-195.

Veterinary Science Department: and Old Central, 117.

Victorian Architecture: in Old Central, 153, 259, 261; photographs, 260, 261, 262, 263.

Victory Bell: student name for Old Central bell, 141, 142.

Virginia: and Murdaugh, 71.

Vreeland, Charles A.: gives land to college, 21-22.

W

Waldorf, Lynn O.: brings championship level football to college, 141-142, 269-270.

Walter A. Nashert and Sons Construction Company: wins Old Central restoration contract, 224-225, 226-231.

Ward, Stephen R.: role in 1975 Old Central bell clapper incident, 147-148.

Warner: awarded state agricultural secondary school, 275.

Washington, D.C.: 57, 92, 128; and Old Central, 68; location of George Washington University, 83; source of federal funds, 88; and college, 96-97, 101.

Washington, George: uses Harvard Hall and Nassau Hall during American Revolution, 199, 274.

Washington House of Reproductions: wins contract for Old Central restoration, 244.

Watkins, Wesley W.: works to revise Old Central bell clapper trophy tradition, 145.

Waugh, Frank A.: photograph, 114; credentials as professor of horticulture, 115.

WAVES. *See* Women Accepted for Volunteer Emergency Service.

Webster Debating Society: meets in Old Central, 111-113.

Wells, John: advises on Old Central restoration, 228.

West Troy, New York: manufacturing location of Old Central bell, 136.

West Virginia Agricultural Experiment Station: served by Magruder as staff member, 115.

Western Farmer: served by Morrow as co-publisher, 73.

Western Rural: served by Morrow as writer, 73.

Wettengel, Jack: assists with Old Central restoration, 236.

White House: impacts board of regents, 68; assists Morrow, 81; and Oklahoma Territory, 96; assists Scott, 103; impacts Old Central, 268.

Whitehurst Hall: visited by Halloween pranksters, 139; construction partially funded, 167; office of publications department, 171; experiences severe gas explosion, 190; new office of Graduate School, 207.

Wichita Eagle: prints Old Central bond issue, 21.

Whitehurst, John A.: president of Oklahoma State Board of Agriculture, 162.

Wichita, Kansas: and college, 28.

Wikoff, Frank J.: early Stillwater leader and lawyer, 8-9; wants Oklahoma A. and M. College in Stillwater, 10, 12; locates land for college, 21, 22; emphasizes urgency of selling Old Central bonds, 30; serves Morrow and Scott as chairman of regents, 74-78, 85, 86, 103; photograph, 75; attends University of Illinois, 85.

Wilber, Philip A.: plans removal of Old Central, 163-164, 165, 167, 169, 180, 199; photograph, 164; becomes chief campus planner, 169; agrees that Old Central could be restored, 175; no active participation in 1929 Old Central refurbishing, 177; revises Bennett Twenty-Five Year Plan, 188; declares old buildings impossible to repair, 190; watches condition of Old Central closely, 201.

Oklahoma State University
Historic Old Central

is a specially designed volume of the Centennial Histories Series.

The text was composed on a personal computer, transmitted by telecommunications to the OSU mainframe computer, and typeset by a computerized typesetting system. Three typefaces were used in the composition. The text is composed in 10 point Melliza with 2 points extra leading added for legibility. Chapter headings are 24 point Omega. All supplemental information contained in the endnotes, charts, picture captions, appendices, bibliography, and index are set in either 8 or 9 point Triumvirate Lite.

The book is printed on a high-quality, coated paper to ensure faithful reproduction of historical photographs and documents. Smyth-sewn and bound with a durable coated nonwoven cover material, the cover has been screen-printed with flat black ink.

The Centennial Histories Committee expresses sincere appreciation to the progressive men and women of the past and present who created and recorded the dynamic, moving history of Oklahoma State University, the story of a land-grant university fulfilling its mission to teach, to research, and to extend itself to the community and the world.